Lecture Notes in Computer Science 8613

Commenced Publication in 1973
Founding and Former Series Editors:
Gerhard Goos, Juris Hartmanis, and Jan van Leeuwen

Elvira Popescu Rynson W.H. Lau
Kai Pata Howard Leung Mart Laanpere (Eds.)

Advances in Web-Based Learning – ICWL 2014

13th International Conference
Tallinn, Estonia, August 14-17, 2014
Proceedings

Springer

Volume Editors

Elvira Popescu
University of Craiova
Computers and Information Technology Department
Craiova, Romania
E-mail: popescu_elvira@software.ucv.ro

Rynson W.H. Lau
Howard Leung
City University of Hong Kong
Department of Computer Science
Hong Kong, Hong Kong SAR
E-mail: rynson@cs.cityu.edu.hk; howard@cityu.edu.hk

Kai Pata
Mart Laanpere
Tallinn University
Center for Educational Technology
Tallinn, Estonia
E-mail: {kpata; martl}@tlu.ee

ISSN 0302-9743 e-ISSN 1611-3349
ISBN 978-3-319-09634-6 e-ISBN 978-3-319-09635-3
DOI 10.1007/978-3-319-09635-3
Springer Cham Heidelberg New York Dordrecht London

Library of Congress Control Number: 2014944565

LNCS Sublibrary: SL 3 – Information Systems and Application,
incl. Internet/Web and HCI

Typesetting: Camera-ready by author, data conversion by Scientific Publishing Services, Chennai, India

Printed on acid-free paper

Springer is part of Springer Science+Business Media (www.springer.com)

Preface

ICWL is an annual international conference on Web-based learning, which started in Hong Kong in 2002 and has so far been held in Asia (China, Malaysia, Hong Kong, Taiwan), Australia and Europe (United Kingdom, Germany, Romania). ICWL 2014, the 13th edition in the series, was organized by Tallinn University (Estonia) and Hong Kong Web Society.

This year's conference was located in the medieval European city Tallinn, the vibrant capital of Estonia, which stands on the ancient trading routes between East and West. This strategic position has made Estonia a hotspot where many cultures have met, battled, traded, and exchanged knowledge. Estonia is a small country situated by the Baltic Sea, with only 1.4 million citizens, but it is one of the ICT flagships in the world, providing its citizens with various innovative services such as e-government, e-elections, and e-learning. We therefore believe the location offered an appropriate cultural and technological context for the ICWL conference.

This year we received 78 submissions from 37 countries worldwide. After a rigorous double-blind review process, 18 papers were selected as full papers, yielding an acceptance rate of 23%. In addition, 9 more short papers were selected. These contributions covered latest findings in various areas, such as: computer-supported collaborative learning; personal learning environments; Web 2.0 and social learning environments; personalized and adaptive learning; game-based learning; intelligent learner modeling and learning analytics; design, model and implementation of e-learning platforms and tools.

Moreover, ICWL 2014 featured 2 distinguished keynote presentations and 8 workshops, which covered a wide range of active and emerging topics in Web-based learning, complementing the main conference areas. The high number of workshops indicated that ICWL is not only a forum for presenting results, but it is the meeting place for an active community, in which new research foci are collectively explored and brought to a new level of maturity.

We would like to thank the entire Organizing Committee and especially the local organization chair, Kairit Tammets, for their efforts and time spent to ensure the success of the conference. We would also like to express our gratitude to the Program Committee members for their timely and helpful reviews. And last but not least, we would like to thank all the authors for their contribution in maintaining a high quality conference - we count on your continual support for playing a significant role in the Web-based learning community in the future.

August 2014

Howard Leung
Mart Laanpere
Elvira Popescu
Rynson W.H. Lau
Kai Pata

Organization

Organizing Committee

Conference Co-chairs

Howard Leung	City University of Hong Kong, Hong Kong
Mart Laanpere	Tallinn University, Estonia

Program Committee Co-chairs

Elvira Popescu	University of Craiova, Romania
Rynson W.H. Lau	City University of Hong Kong, Hong Kong
Kai Pata	Tallinn University, Estonia

Steering Committee Representatives

Qing Li	City University of Hong Kong, Hong Kong
Ralf Klamma	RWTH Aachen University, Germany
Yueh-Min Huang	National Cheng-Kung University, Taiwan

Workshop Co-chairs

Yiwei Cao	IMC Information Multimedia Communication AG, Germany
Terje Väljataga	Tallinn University, Estonia
Jeff Tang	Caritas Institute of Higher Education, Hong Kong

Publicity Chair

Mohammad Smadi	Jordan University of Science and Technology, Jordan

Poster Chair

Vladimir Tomberg	Tallinn University, Estonia

Local Organization Chair

Kairit Tammets	Tallinn University, Estonia

International Program Committee

Marie-Hélène Abel	University of Technology of Compiegne, France
Carlos Alario-Hoyos	Carlos III University of Madrid, Spain

Maria Bielikova	Slovak University of Technology in Bratislava, Slovakia
Yiwei Cao	Information Multimedia Communication AG, Germany
Mihaela Cocea	University of Portsmouth, UK
Stavros Demetriadis	Aristotle University of Thessaloniki, Greece
Yunhua Deng	City University of Hong Kong, Hong Kong
Michael Derntl	RWTH Aachen University, Germany
Giuliana Dettori	Institute for Educational Technology (ITD-CNR), Italy
Darina Dicheva	Winston-Salem State University, USA
Erik Duval	Katholieke Universiteit Leuven, Belgium
Baltasar Fernandez-Manjon	Universidad Complutense de Madrid, Spain
Dragan Gasevic	Athabasca University, Canada
Panagiotis Germanakos	University of Cyprus, Cyprus
Sabine Graf	Athabasca University, Canada
Christian Gütl	Technical University of Graz, Austria
Andreas Harrer	TU Clausthal, Germany
Eelco Herder	L3S Research Center in Hannover, Germany
Martin Homola	Comenius University Bratislava, Slovakia
Pedro Isaías	Universidade Aberta (Portuguese Open University), Portugal
Malinka Ivanova	TU Sofia, Bulgaria
Mirjana Ivanovic	University of Novi Sad, Serbia
Jelena Jovanovic	University of Belgrade, Serbia
Ioannis Kazanidis	Technological Educational Institute of Kavala, Greece
Ralf Klamma	RWTH Aachen University, Germany
Tomaž Klobucar	Institut Josef-Stefan, Slovenia
Milos Kravcik	RWTH Aachen University, Germany
Zuzana Kubincova	Comenius University Bratislava, Slovakia
Vive Kumar	Athabasca University, Canada
Lam ForKwok	City University of Hong Kong, Hong Kong
Jean-Marc Labat	University Pierre et Marie Curie, France
Elise Lavoué	University Jean Moulin Lyon 3, France
Frederick Li	University of Durham, UK
Wei Liu	Shanghai University, China
Xiangfeng Luo	Shanghai University, China
George Magoulas	Birkbeck College & University of London, UK
Katherine Maillet	Telecom SudParis, France
Ivana Marenzi	L3S Research Center in Hannover, Germany
Alke Martens	PH Schwabisch Gmund University of Education, Germany
Harald Mayer	Joanneum Research, Austria

Pablo Moreno-Ger	Universidad Complutense de Madrid, Spain
Kyparisia Papanikolaou	School of Pedagogical & Technological Education, Greece
Alexandros Paramythis	Contexity AG, Switzerland
Philippos Pouyioutas	University of Nicosia, Cyprus
Francesca Pozzi	Institute for Educational Technology (ITD-CNR), Italy
Neil Rubens	University of Electro-Communications, Japan
Demetrios Sampson	University of Piraeus & CERTH, Greece
Olga Santos	Spanish National University for Distance Education, Spain
Ruimin Shen	Shanghai Jiaotong University, China
Marc Spaniol	Max Planck Institute for Computer Science, Germany
Natalia Stash	Eindhoven University of Technology, The Netherlands
Marco Temperini	Sapienza University of Rome, Italy
Stefan Trausan-Matu	Politehnica University of Bucharest, Romania
Lorna Uden	Staffordshire University, UK
Carsten Ullrich	Shanghai Jiaotong University, China
Julita Vassileva	University of Saskatchewan, Canada
Carlos Vaz de Carvalho	Instituto Politecnico do Porto, Portugal
Katrien Verbert	Katholieke Universiteit Leuven, Belgium
Riina Vuorikari	Institute for Prospective Technological Studies, European Commission
Fridolin Wild	The Open University, UK
Zheng Xu	Shanghai University, China
Qinghua Zheng	Xi'an Jiaotong University, China

Additional Reviewers

Jason Bernard	Athabasca University, Canada
Hazra Imran	Athabasca University, Canada
Zoran Putnik	University of Novi Sad, Serbia
Stylianos Sergis	University of Piraeus, Greece
Martin Sillaots	Tallinn University, Estonia
Kairit Tammets	Tallinn University, Estonia
Vladimir Tomberg	Tallinn University, Estonia
Iro Voulgari	University of Patras, Greece
Panagiotis Zervas	ASK, CERTH & University of Piraeus, Greece

Table of Contents

Learner Modeling and Learning Analytics

Personalized and Adaptive Learning

Design, Model and Implementation of E-Learning Platforms and Tools

Pedagogical Issues, Practice and Experience Sharing

Blogging in Obligatory Course: A Bitter Victory

Veronika Bejdová, Martin Homola, and Zuzana Kubincová

Faculty of Mathematics, Physics and Informatics,
Comenius University in Bratislava, Slovakia
{bejdova,homola,kubincova}@fmph.uniba.sk

Abstract. In the course of several years, we employed blogging assignments in an obligatory web design course. The assignment was able to attract interest of few students only, while the majority did not participate, or only very sparsely. It did not help much to make the assignment part of the course evaluation. The course received mixed reviews from the students. The students who were not really interested in the subject, or considered it too much work, complained. In last two years we tried to address this problem by introduction of a tight blogging schedule, and peer-reviews. As we report in this paper, this step radically improved the participation rate, and also learning outcomes were higher, however the student's opinion of these activities was not amended.

Keywords: Blogging, peer-review, engagement, learning outcome, acceptance.

1 Introduction

Incorporating blogging into education has a number of benefits. If the blogging activity is focused on the content of interest, it may help to organize one's own knowledge, and it stimulates reflection [10]. While blogging can be practiced in self-driven informal learning, students in organized curricula may equally benefit from it [15,14,2,11]. Blogging assignments may be used to increase students' involvement with study materials. Skills such as formulating and communicating one's own ideas, presenting and defending one's opinions are stimulated by blogging activities. Within the topic of web design blogging offers in addition an opportunity to practice text formatting for the Web, suitable web writing style, and many other web publishing skills.

In learning groups, an important part of blogging activities is the involvement with outputs of the others, pondering on their understanding of the subject matter, their opinions and viewpoints. In such a way social construction of knowledge [4] is encouraged. While this activity can be facilitated informally via unstructured comments under each blog article, it can be further reinforced via peer-reviews [7,8,16]

However, even if a number of benefits is understood by the lecturers, in reality, application of blogging within the context of organized education faces many challenges. There are open questions concerning how blogging is to be combined with more traditional course activities, and concerning the evaluation methodology [5]. Some studies showed that students may be hesitant to participate in blogging even in an informal setting [1]. Our own experience also confirmed this. We employed blogging assignments

E. Popescu et al. (Eds.): ICWL 2014, LNCS 8613, pp. 1–10, 2014.

in a master's level web design course for several years. We faced the following challenges:

- Only small part of students voluntary participated, and many of them only towards the very end of the semester. However, for social learning to be effective, regular engagement and time for reflection is needed.
- Students wrote and published articles, but they were reluctant to read the output of the others and provide feedback, which again hindered the social learning process.
- The course is mandatory for part of the students, hence not all the students are deeply interested in the topic. Some students objected the blogging exercise.

In the last two years we largely updated the blogging assignment: we organized work into well-defined phases with deadlines and introduced peer-reviews of others' work. We also gave the blogging assignment a larger part in the evaluation. After the first year, we recorded an overwhelming rise in engagement with the blogging assignment, improved learning outcomes, and even the students overall opinions were slightly improved. In the second year we partly relaxed from the requirements, giving the students the option to participate less, still keeping the chance for good grading. To the contrary to our expectations we observed further increase in the engagement with blogging, and the study results were also further improved. This latter result is encouraging, however the students' opinion on the assignment actually went down. We summarize the lessons learned and discuss possible options how the overcome this problem in the future.

2 Our Course and Blogging Assignments

2.1 Course Overview

In this paper we focus on our web design course that is part of the master's curriculum of applied informatics, as a mandatory course. The course is also included in the bachelor curricula, and depending on the student specialization it can be voluntary but also mandatory for some of the bachelor students. All in all there is a number of students who cannot avoid the course even if they are not interested in the topic very much. The main focus of the course is on principles of web site structure, layout, user interface, and content design, giving an emphasis usability and accessibility. Number of enrolled students in 2007–2011 varied from 71 to 158, while in 2012 it was 83 and in 2013 69 students were enrolled.

The all-semester practical assignment (hereafter, "the project") of the course is to design one's own blog. The assignments also feature a blogging activity, where students are supposed to publish meaningful, course related content on their own blogs. We call such an assignment *professional blogging*, as students act like practitioners in the area, building their professional blog. The assignments supplements the project as students thus get some content to organize on their blogs, but it also encourages further engagement with the topic. The course included such an assignment ever since 2006; in this paper we review some of our data collected since 2007.

Before 2012, the blog articles submitted by the students were evaluated shortly after they were published, by a certain amount of evaluation points based on their topicality, originality and estimated usefulness to other students. At the beginning there was no limit on the number of articles one could submit. Blogging was perceived as bonus activity, and students could pass the course even without it, with good grading. While we felt that the activity is useful, only small number of students participated. There were also little comments under the blog posts, as adding comments was not awarded by any points. In addition, most students were active only towards the very end of the semester. As we noted above, blogging activities are meaningful if students engage in them with certain regularity, and there is space for reflection and feedback. Therefore we looked for ways how to engage more students in this activity, and how to encourage recurrent engagement throughout the semester and feedback.

Between 2009 and 2011 we employed several strategies such as limiting the number of articles that can be posted in one week and decreasing number of points with time. These strategies largely failed; they improved regularity a little, but they did not improve engagement and feedback.

2.2 Introducing Peer-Reviews

In 2012 we largely restructured the blogging activity by introducing strict organization of students work and, in addition to article writing, we introduced peer-reviews. The activity was divided into two-week consecutive rounds, the first week of each round reserved for publishing 1 article, and the second week for reviewing 3 randomly assigned articles of the others. Submission deadlines for articles and reviews were strict. There were 5 regular rounds and 2 additional rounds (as some students missed deadlines).

The reviews were structured into five aspects: usefulness, interestingness, comprehensibility, topicality (relevance for the course), and overall impression. Every aspect was rated on the scale 1 (weak)–5 (excellent) together with a verbal justification.

Evaluation points were split into three equal parts: one for article writing, another for reviewing, and yet another for adding additional comments under the peers' articles.

To encourage students engagement, we employed all-or-nothing rule for the first two parts. Students received the full share if they had 5 articles approved by the teachers (or 4 of excellent quality) and if they had 12 reviews approved. Articles were approved or disapproved by the teachers based on similar criteria as students judged in the peer reviews. Reviews were disapproved only if they were inconsistent or if students missed an apparent error in the reviewed article, etc. Evaluation of the third part (comments) was not as strict: in the end of the semester, a certain number of points was assigned based on regularity and quality of each student's comments.

The evaluation points were split among the different course activities as follows: project (25%), blogging (25%), written examination (25%), and oral examination (25%).

2.3 Current Year Changes in the Course Work Evaluation

As we document below in Sect. 3 the boost in students' engagement with the blogging activity was astonishing. The participation rate nearly tripled, marking 92.77%. Also average grading was improved. On the other hand, a number of students expressed the opinion that they only participated in the blogging activity because of the grading, and that they were not really interested in blogging on the topic of the course.

This led us to the conjecture that the rules were now set too strict, and that a desired level of engagement (i.e., smaller but still rather high) together with satisfying learning outcomes could be achieved even in more relaxed settings, thus improving the overall opinions of the students. We reflected this in the 2013 setting as follows:

- The all-or-nothing rule was relaxed, introducing the scheme: full share of score for 5 articles (13 reviews) approved, half of the score for 3 articles (10 reviews) approved, or zero if less were approved.
- The share of points of the blogging activity was decreased to 17.5%. This was counter-balanced by increasing the share for written examination, resulting into the split: project (25%), blogging (17.5%), written examination (32.5%), and oral examination (25%). Students could now earn the C grading without participating in blogging, or still earn A if they collected one half of the blogging activity score.
- The approval requirements for articles were relaxed, focussing more on topicality and correct formatting of the articles for web publication which is more aligned with the actual content of the course.

Otherwise the setting was kept as in 2012. We hypothesized, that these relaxation would have the following effects: (a) the participation in the blogging activity will moderately decrease; (b) the participating students will achieve better learning outcomes than the others, and better learning outcomes than in 2012; (c) the overall students opinion of the course will be improved.

3 Results

We now describe our research results collected during the past seven years in which we employed blogging, and later also peer-reviews, in the course. We first focus on students' engagement in blogging activities; then on their study results; and finally on their perception and opinion on these activities and the course.

3.1 Students' Engagement

Since the beginning we faced low students' engagement in blogging. In Fig. 1 (a) the participation of students in blogging over the year is plotted (i.e., the share of those who posted at least one article). During the first five years participation was fairly low (35.79% on average). After the activity was redesigned, this figure immediately jumped to 92.77% in 2012 and further improved to 94.20% in 2013.

The participation chart in Fig. 1 (a) provides but a gross picture of student's engagement, as students who sent just one article and those who sent many are equally counted here. To get a better insight, we plot the average number of articles sent by the students in Fig. 1 (b). Again the increase in the last two years is rather high, especially considering the average over all students of the course, jumping from 1.23 articles (average of first five years) to 4.34 and 4.52 articles in 2012 and in 2013, respectively. Considering only the students participating in blogging we still see a remarkable improvement, moving from 3.38 articles (average of first five years) to 4.68 in 2012 and to 4.80 in 2013.

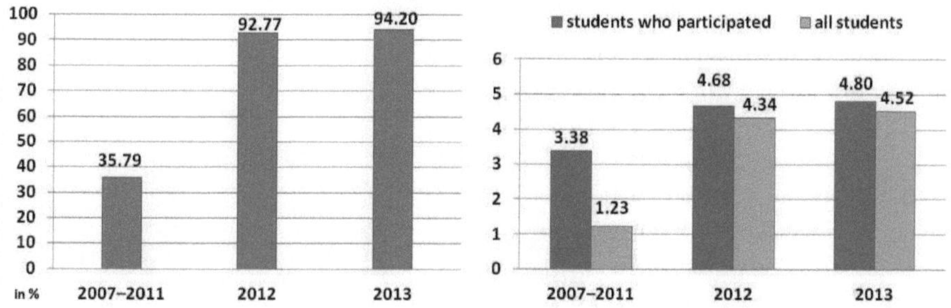

(a) (b)

Fig. 1. (a) Participation in blogging activities (b) Average number of articles posted

So, students' engagement in the blogging activity has significantly improved. We noted above that blogging activities are meaningful if students engage in them with certain regularity, and there is space for reflection and feedback. With more then 4 articles per student per semester we approached this goal very closely. In addition, organization of the activity with deadlines and peer-review rounds ensures that there is enough time and space for feedback and reflection, compared to previous experience when many students became active only in the very end of the semester and posted multiple articles within several days before the final deadline.

To our surprise, even if in 2013 we made the blogging activity less mandatory compared to 2012, the participation actually slightly increased. This further underlines the importance of good organization of the activity, however, we failed our goal to allow those students who are least interested in the course to participate less, and thus to improve their overall opinion (see further discussion below).

3.2 Learning Outcomes

We next compare the study results during the consecutive years. The chart in Fig. 2 (a) shows the average grade in different years. The grades scale is from A (excellent, numerical value 1) to Fx (failure, numerical value 6). We observe that since 2007 the grading was gradually worsening, falling as low as 5.03 in 2011, but as soon as the changes were introduced it jumped to 4.10 in 2012 and then 4.06 in 2013, which is also historically the best average grade achieved through the years.

For better understanding how the grades varied, detailed grading is depicted in Fig. 2 (b). Notice especially the development of the higher grades A–C in the last two years: it is apparent that not only the average grade improved, but also the overall number of excellent grades rose. Another important result is the reduced drop-out rate which fell from the average 42% in 2007–2011 to less than 29% in 2012 and 2013.

From the data in Fig. 2 we see that the grading did indeed improve in the last two runs of the course. However, as the blogging activity also contributed to the overall grading by certain amount of points, this might simply be an effect of increased engagement in this activity. To show that it is indeed not the case, we now take a closer look on the evaluation of projects and the written examination.

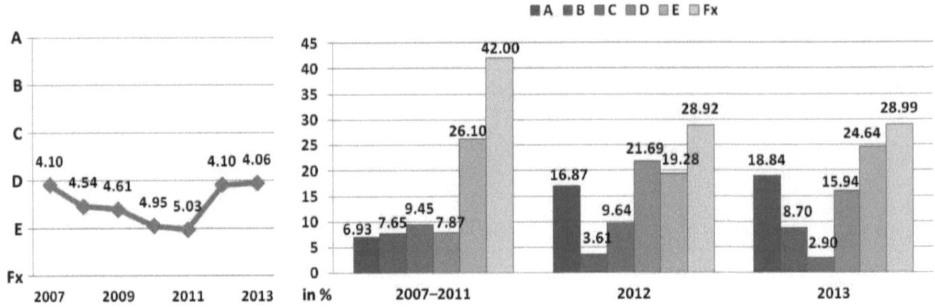

(a) (b)

Fig. 2. (a) Average grade in 2007–2013 (b) Detailed grades in 2007–2013

In Fig. 3 the average percentage achieved in these two activities is plotted. We observe that especially the average project results jumped from 42.09% to 73.76% between 2011 and 2012. This is however also partly due to the changed methodology of this activity, where multiple deadlines were introduced as well. We can however also see a steady improvement the written examination, which used just the same methodology as before: while in 2011 the students achieved on average 43.09% in this exam, this rose to 52.73% in 2012 and then consecutively to 58.03% in 2013.

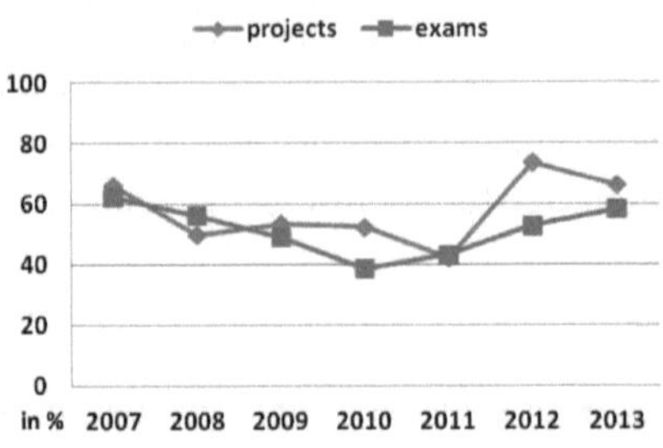

Fig. 3. Percentage in projects and exams in 2007–2013

Furthermore, we compared the achieved exam and project scores with the degree of participation in the blogging activity (the number of articles posted), and in the last two years also with students success in blogging (the number of articles approved).

For the exam results this is showed in Figs. 4 (a) and 4 (b). Note that due to the high participation rate, the number of students who posted less than three articles in the last two years was very low, which produced some degree of randomness in the former result (Fig. 4 (a)). We can observe that while in 2007–2011 the average result improves between 0 and 1 article posted, with more articles it remains fairly static. For the following years we can at least see a clear improvement between 4 and 5 or more.

The latter comparison (Fig. 4 (b)), respective to the number of articles approved by the teachers, provides more insights. We observe that the average exam result clearly

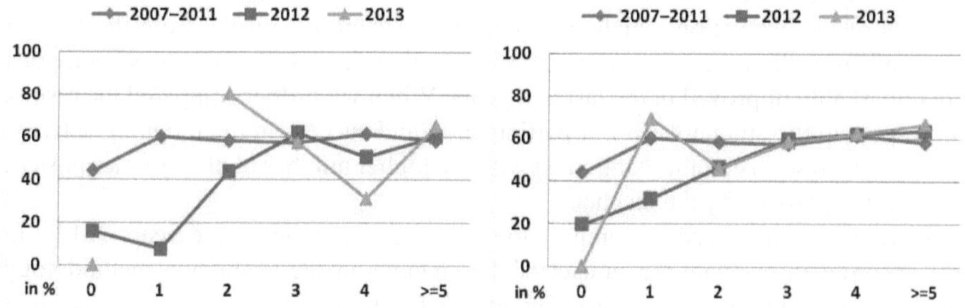

(a) (b)

Fig. 4. (a) Average exam result compared to number of articles posted (b) Average exam result compared to number of articles approved (2012, 2013) and posted (2007–2011)

rises with the higher number of articles approved. Note that the peak for 2012 and one approved article is caused by randomness due to very small number of students with one article approved. Also note that in 2011 and before the articles were evaluated differently (i.e. there was no approval process), we plot here in blue line the values for 2007–2011 from the previous chart just for sake of comparison.

The same comparison but for the project results can be seen in Figs. 5 (a) and 5 (b). Here note an apparent rising trend already in the average result for 2007–2011 (compared to number of articles posted in both charts). This trend is observable also for 2012, for the number of articles posted. Finally, in the comparison with respect to the number of articles approved we note that high average score was achieved already for 3, 4 and 5 or more articles approved, slightly rising for 5 or more. The rising trend in this part of the chart is less apparent, however we see that students with 1 and 2 articles approved performed worse in the project.

In this section we have examined the study evaluation and grading of the students in different runs of the course. We observed that the results were notably improved in the last two years in which better organization of work and peer-reviews were introduced.

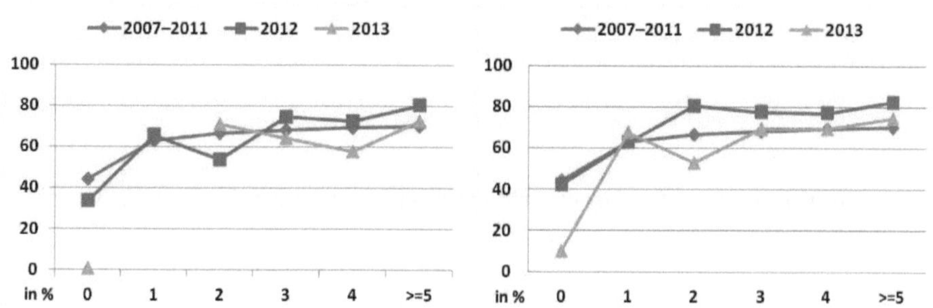

(a) (b)

Fig. 5. (a) Average project result compared to number of articles posted (b) Average project result compared to number of articles approved (2012, 2013) and posted (2007–2011)

As the blogging activity also contributes to the evaluation, we consecutively analyzed two parts of the evaluation which are independent from it – results from the written exam, and from the project assignment. We saw that the results from these activities were remarkably improved in the last two years. When we further compared the results with respect to the students level of participation and success in the blogging activity, we were able to see a certain rising trend with the higher number of blog articles posted, respectively approved by the teachers.

We were also interested to compare the study results between the years 2012 and 2013, in order to evaluate the impact of the changes in the evaluation methodology (the blogging activity was made less obligatory). From Figs. 2 (a) and 2 (b) we see that the change in the average grade was very small, and in fact, it was positive. When we compared the detailed results from the written exam and from the projects (Fig. 3), we saw that the average project result fell while average exam result rose (note that there were also other evaluation categories). This observation is not that significant, compared to the change in overall grading – we can attribute this to the changes between the cohorts each year.

Regarding the interpretation of the results presented in this section it has to be noted, that rather than causality, they indicate a correlation between higher engagement in the blogging activity and improved learning outcomes. That is, based on this research we cannot claim, that blogging directly causes better study results, it may as well be that the students who are more motivated and responsible choose to participate to a higher extent. There are also differences between the abilities and attitudes of each year's cohort, which should be also taken into account. However, what the data clearly shows, is that the changes which we introduced in the last two years had an overwhelming impact on the participation, and that the average grading was improved by one full grade compared to the period of 2011 and before.

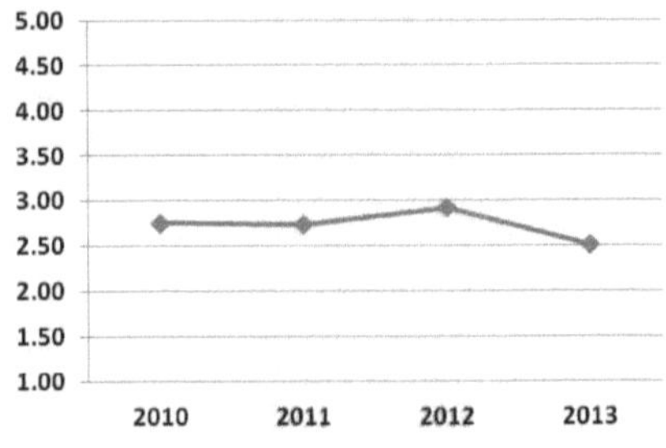

Fig. 6. Evaluation of quality of subject from student questionnaire 2010–2013

3.3 Students' Opinions

Our faculty conducts an anonymous survey of students opinions for each course. The course in question is an advanced course, and especially after it was made obligatory in the curriculum it received mixed reviews for several years. A smaller number of students liked it, while many of them complained that it is too difficult and that blogging is too demanding. Being part of the computer science and applied informatics curriculum, some students frankly admitted that they simply do not like to write.

Apart from written feedback students rate each course with a value between 1 (worse) and 5 (best). As we see in Fig.6, after the changes implemented in 2012, the overall rating sightly improved. Unfortunately in 2013 the rating dropped again, even despite the relaxation in the rules, which we expected to have exactly the contrary effect.

4 Related Work

The benefits of blogging in university courses were discussed in a number of studies [15,14,2,11]. Some studies report the students' willingness and enthusiasm regarding the use of blogs [11], other studies pointing out lower students interest [1] or that some students publish the blog articles solely for the sake of getting the marks what can detract the quality of the experience of the others [15].

Peer-reviews were used to enhance the learning methods in multiple learning contexts [8,7,13,12,3] etc. Several authors studied the relation between the peer-review rating and the teacher's evaluation [6] with the aim to use the peer-reviews in the grading. MacAlpine [9] recommends to split the rating into multiple aspects which helps the students to focus on relevant issues significantly improving the quality of peer-reviews. Other studies explored the use of peer-reviews to reduce teachers' workload [13].

5 Discussion

We presented our seven years experience with blogging as part of a mandatory course in the topic of web design. As we showed, when the blogging activity was not strictly organized, and it provided just bonus evaluation points, the participation was rather low, and students engaged in it just towards the end of the semester. They also did not engage with the others' outputs significantly, thus effectively diminishing the social learning potential. By introducing strict organization of work, a peer-review process, and increasing the share of core evaluation points dedicated to the activity we were able to improve the engagement and feedback to a highly satisfactory level. We also observed an improvement of learning outcomes, and, at least in the first year after the changes, the students opinion measured by an anonymous survey was slightly improved.

The results from the following year were less encouraging: even if we relaxed from a number of rules, aiming to allow a part of the students to participate only partly, while still keeping a chance for good grading, the students did not reflect on this. The engagement peeked even higher (and the learning outcomes further improved), however the students' overall opinion on the course dropped again. While we could explain the difference between the two years by difference in each year's cohort and their general attitude towards study, it is clear, that on average we were not able to achieve a remarkable improvement of the students' acceptance of the blogging activity.

This leads us to the conclusion that while blogging activities and peer-reviews may clearly be beneficial to the students, varying acceptance of these activities in different courses and curricula is an important issue that cannot be overlooked. While we still want to keep content creation and content peer-reviews part of our course, considering the specific needs of our students we plan to take a different approach in the next runs. Specifically, we will consider: (a) emphasizing less on presenting course-related content on one's blog and more on concentrating on practicing the web publishing process, where the actual content is less important; (b) making the activity less demanding and time consuming; (c) introducing some alternative activities for students who do not feel comfortable with blogging; and (d) facilitating social learning by introducing peer-reviews also on more technical aspects of students course work which seems to be much closer to our students, e.g., implementation and functionality of one's blog.

Acknowledgment. This work was supported from the Slovak national VEGA project no. 1/0948/13.

References

1. Andergassen, M., Behringer, R., Finlay, J., Gorra, A., Moore, D.: Weblogs in higher education-why do students (not) blog? Electronic Journal of e-Learning 7(3) (2009)
2. Churchill, D.: Educational applications of web 2.0: Using blogs to support teaching and learning. British Journal of Educational Technology 40(1) (2009)
3. Gehringer, E.F.: Strategies and mechanisms for electronic peer review. In: Proceedings Frontiers in Education (2000)
4. von Glasersfeld, E.: Radical Constructivism. A Way of Knowing and Learning. Falmer Press, London (1995)
5. Homola, M., Kubincová, Z.: Taking advantage of Web 2.0 in organized education (a survey). In: ICL, Villach, Austria (2009)
6. Ken, P.M., Park, K.H., Domazlicky, B.R.: Peer grading of essays in a principles of microeconomics course. Journal of Education for Business 70(6) (1995)
7. Lin, S.S.J., Liu, E.Z.F., Yuan, S.M.: Web-based peer assessment: feedback for students with various thinking-styles. J. Comput. Assist. Lear. 17(4) (2001)
8. Liu, E.Z.F., Lin, S.S.J., Chiu, C.H., Yuan, S.M.: Web-based peer review: the learner as both adapter and reviewer. IEEE Transactions on Education 44(3), 246–251 (2001)
9. MacAlpine, J.M.K.: Improving and encouraging peer assessment of student presentations. Assess. Eval. High. Educ. 24(1) (1999)
10. Mosel, S.: Self directed learning with personal publishing and microcontent. In: Microlearning 2005 Conference (2005)
11. Popescu, E.: Students' acceptance of web 2.0 technologies in higher education: Findings from a survey in a romanian university. In: DEXA 2010 (2010)
12. Popescu, E., Manafu, L.: Repurposing a wiki for collaborative learning-pedagogical and technical view. In: ISTCC (2011)
13. Sterbini, A., Temperini, M.: Dealing with open-answer questions in a peer-assessment environment. In: Popescu, E., Li, Q., Klamma, R., Leung, H., Specht, M. (eds.) ICWL 2012. LNCS, vol. 7558, pp. 240–248. Springer, Heidelberg (2012)
14. Tekinarslan, E.: Blogs: A qualitative investigation into an instructor and undergraduate students' experience. Australasian Journal of Educational Technology 24(4) (2008)
15. Williams, J., Jacobs, J.: Exploring the use of blogs as learning spaces in higher education sector. Australasian Journal of Educational Technology 20(2) (2004)
16. Wu, W.S.: The effect of blog peer review and teacher feedback on the revisions of EFL writers. Journal of Education and Foreign Languages and Literature 3(2) (2006)

Relationships between Blogging Activeness and the Characteristics of Participants and Blogs during Teaching Practice and Induction Year

Piret Luik and Merle Taimalu

University of Tartu, Tartu, Estonia
{piret.luik,merle.taimalu}@ut.ee

Abstract. Blog as the representative of social software has been used in education for several years and its positive effect in the field has been asserted in many studies. This study presents relationships between blog-use activeness and the characteristics of learners and blogs during teaching practice and induction year. 1,137 blog postings of 192 participants from 13 collective blogs and also their self-reports in pre- and post-questionnaires were analysed. Results showed several relationships which accentuated learner's age and perceived benefit of blogging as important factors among participants' characteristics influencing blogging activeness. Among the characteristics of blog most of the correlations emerged between blogging activeness and the strength of social relationships between the participants in the blog and the average number of comments (per new posts). Also mentor's participation in the blog and giving beginning task for learners in the blog seemed to be important factors supporting more active blog-use.

Keywords: blog use, teacher education, characteristics of bloggers, characteristics of blog.

1 Introduction

During the last years several kinds of social software have been applied more frequently in education. One representative of this type of software is blog (weblog) which has ascended as a popular communication tool [1], and is increasingly employed to enhance communication environments in education [2].

Blog can be seen as an Internet-based diary which facilitates interactive computer-mediated communication by text, picture, audio and video [3]. Blogs are like the 21th century's diaries or journals with the possibility to learn from others' and one's own blog [4]. In the blog participants can express their success and unsuccess, hesitances, good and bad experiences in teaching and learning, and also read and comment on other blog users' writings [5, 6]. Blogging is a process including many aspects: writing, reading, reflecting, questioning, and commenting and hence, blog can afford several pedagogical benefits [7], which have important role in active knowledge construction [8], in knowledge sharing with other learners [9].

E. Popescu et al. (Eds.): ICWL 2014, LNCS 8613, pp. 11–21, 2014.

Williams and Jacobs [10] have claimed that students learn as much from each other as from teachers or textbooks. Nowadays, the importance of collective learning, learning from each other, and collaboration have been emphasized more and more, and the significance of professional learning communities is supported because of the positive effect they have on teaching practice and learners' achievement [11]. Blogs are one alternative opportunity for creating and supporting such learning communities. Blogs have the potential to increase reflection, the sense of community and collaboration [9]. On account of this the use of collective blogs has increased in education. The participants of a collective blog are the group of people who share it and write their postings in it. In collective blog the writings support information change and shared knowledge. Additionally, the posts in collective blog offer feedback [12], which is crucial in learning process. However, students collaborating in a collective blog might be less interested in blogging than learners in individual blogs [2], because there are two types of students: individually-oriented, who disliked blogging, and community-oriented, who blogged with enthusiasm [7]. Also, studies have found that while majority of students reported blogging as enhancing learning and giving positive experience, few of them valued peers' comments [9].

Students' engagement in blog is influenced by several factors, both conductive and hindering. Sometimes learners are afraid of using new technologies, but as Cakir [5] affirms blogs as Web 2.0 technologies do not presuppose complex computer technical knowledge from the user and therefore, even technically modestly skilled learners are able to participate in blogging. Several studies underscore the importance of knowing educational purpose and benefit of blogging [5, 13] – why to use the blog (because of requirement or perceived value for communication with other bloggers), what to write about, etc. Also **students' individual characteristics** have found to affect their engagement: motivation and level of challenge offered by blog use [5]; sense of community [9]. Gender or technical skills seem not to have impact on students' engagement [5]. Among **blog characteristics**, also some important factors have been found to influence students' engagement in blogging: attractive content, pleasant atmosphere in the blog, blogging support (including quickly given comments and replies) [14].

It is important to engage learners into blog as active not as passive participants [13]. The hindering factors of using blogs were investigated [13] and divided those into four parts: 1) individual (lack of time, preference for other media, uncertainty what to write about, blog's personal appropriateness or reluctance for certain individuals), 2) social (previous social relationships, the level of participation in the blog – is there enough writers online, other possibilities for face-to-face interaction), 3) pedagogical (purpose of blogging, why and what to write about, voluntary nature or forced writing, lack of assessment on the tasks in blog,) and 4) technological (computer and internet accessibility, perceived difficulty of blogging technology – comfortability with technology) dimensions. According to Andergassen and her colleagues [8] preferring direct (online) communication by students and their privacy concern as inhibiting factors were mentioned.

As previous studies reveal, blogs, including collective ones, are used in educational domain. Individual characteristics of blog writers and how the community in collective blog is formed might have influence on blogging activeness. Therefore, the aim of this study was to find out the relationships between **blogging activeness** and the characteristics of participants and blogs during teaching practice and induction year.

The research questions were as following:

1. Which characteristics of the participants are related to their activeness in the blog?
2. Which characteristics of the blogs are related to the participants' activeness in the blog?

2 Method

2.1 Sample

The sample was formed by 192 participants (103 teacher students and 89 newly qualified teachers who entered the induction year program (i.e. the first-year teachers in schools, who had also some seminars in universities) from the University of Tartu (64%) and Tallinn University (36%). These two universities are the two main institutions in Estonia providing teacher education. Eleven participants (6%) were male. The participants were selected on the way that the sample covered different subjects and school-levels. The average age of the participants was 25.6 (SD=5.88) years.

2.2 Data Collection

1,137 postings (628 new posts and 509 comments) from 13 blogs were used as the first data source. For measuring **participants' activeness in the blog** ten characteristics (e.g. the number of written posts, the average length of posts in words, the average number of different topics per posts etc), were analyzed.

As **blogs' characteristics**, the average number of comments per new posts in the blog, the percentage of the blog postings consisting communication with the other participants, the percentage of the blog postings where participants wrote about success and the percentage of the blog postings where participants wrote about problems were measured. All these postings where participants asked something from the others, replied the others' questions, reacted to some previous issue, added something to somebody's posting from their side etc. were considered postings consisting communication with other participants.

Characteristics of the participants were collected using pre- and post-questionnaires. With the pre-questionnaires individual characteristics (sex, age), evaluation on their computer skills and Internet accessibility, previous blogging experience and Communication Style Scale [15] were measured on 5-point Likert scale. With the post-questionnaire evaluations on blogging experience and perceived support outside the blog from course-mates and supervisors (persons who supervised their lessons in schools) were measured. Perceived support outside the blog from course-mates and supervisors was measured with support items from Teacher Interpersonal Self-Efficacy Scale [16].

2.3 Procedure

The study was carried on during the academic year 2010/11. Before blogging all participants filled in a pre-questionnaire and after blogging a post-questionnaire. Collective blogs were used and all participants were divided between 13 blogs (https://www.blogger.com). Blogs were used during teaching practice in the case of teacher students and during the induction year in the case of newly qualified teachers. One tutor participated in the blog writing, too. Her task was to support participants, answer the questions and solve emerging problems. In all blogs participants were asked to blog voluntarily to write about the topics they wanted to share with others or to ask questions. All the blogs were closed and only the blog authors could read and write in the particular blog. The blogs were differently organized. Those characteristics can be seen also as blog characteristics (see Table 2):

- The number of participants in the blog varied from 5 to 24.
- The number of the participants in the blog, who shared more than two postings varied from 2 to 23.
- Besides the tutor, a mentor of practice participated in 5 blogs. Mentor was the person who coordinated the practice of the students also outside the blog.
- To write about own expectations related to teaching practice/induction year as beginning task was given in 13 blogs.
- The strength of social relationships in blogs was different and was defined on 3-level scale – in 5 blogs they were not familiar with each other and did not meet each other outside the blog (the lowest strength), in 5 blogs participants met in some seminars or in some courses (medium strength) and 3 blogs were staffed with course-mates, who met each other also outside the blog (the highest strength).

2.4 Data Analysis

For analyzing postings quantitative content analysis was used. The content analysis was conducted using elaborated coding manual by three researchers. Summary indices (percentages, means or medians) using quantitative analysis of postings were calculated for each participant as the first step of data analysis. Then the data from questionnaires were matched to the characteristics of the blogs and summary indices of the postings. In order to find relationships Spearman correlations were found. For comparison t-test was used.

3 Results

The average number of new posts per participants was 4.05 (SD=7.59), the average number of comments per participants 3.27 (SD=9.60) and the average of total number of postings 7.33 (SD=15.81). Twenty-six of the participants (13.5%) did not visit the blog during the teaching practice or induction year according to the data from post-questionnaires. Six participants did not post anything in the blogs, but according to their answers in the post-questionnaire they visited the blog, read the others' postings and reflected on these. Eighty-four participants (44%) marked in the post-questionnaire that they did not comment on others' posts in the blog, but they did it in their mind.

The relationships between the characteristics of participants and their activeness in the blog are given in Table 1. Eight statistically significant positive correlations are shown at the evaluation on the statement 'Blogging was helpful during teaching practice/induction year' and seven significant correlations (mostly negative ones) are revealed at the age of the participant. The relationships between the characteristics of blogs and participants' activeness in the blog are given in Table 2. From all measured characteristics of the blog, the strength of social relationships between the participants in the blog and the average number of comments per new posts gave the highest number of positive correlations with the participants' activeness in the blog. Comparison of the participants' activeness in the blog between the blogs with mentors and without mentors and between the blogs with the beginning task and without such a task is given in Table 3.

4 Discussion

To answer the first research question we can say that several relationships have found. The highest number of correlations was found in the case of the age of the participants – this was negatively related to the six characteristics of the participant's activeness in the blog and positively related to one characteristic of the participant's activeness in the blog. Those relationships show that younger learners tend to blog more actively than older participants.

The evaluation on Internet accessibility showed just one positive correlation – those participants who evaluated Internet accessibility higher posted more in the blog. But the evaluations on Internet accessibility were not significantly related to other characteristics of the blog activeness. The evaluation of users' computer skills and previous blogging experience showed no relationships with characteristics of blog-use activeness. Previous studies have shown different findings. For example similarly to our results Cakir [5] found that technical skills have no significant impact on participants' engagement, but Deng and Yuen's [13] have claimed to the contrary that comfortability with technology may have impact on blog-use. Participants' evaluations on blogging experience were also related to the blogging activeness. The participants, who perceived that blogging was helpful during teaching practice or induction year, posted more, their postings were longer and they wrote about more topics in one posting. Also, the other educationalists [13, 14] have pointed out the importance of pleasant atmosphere in the blog, the personal appropriateness of the blog and getting support from the blog, which can be seen as helpful.

The results indicated that the evaluation on supervisors' support outside the blogs was not significantly related to any characteristics of blogging activeness. The average number of topics in comments was negatively related to the evaluation on course-mates' support outside the blog, to the evaluations on the confidence in face-to-face communication and the confidence in computer-mediated communication.

Table 1. Spearman rank-correlation coefficients between the characteristics of the participants and their activeness in the blog

	Number of the new posts	Number of the comments	Number of the all postings	Average length of new posts in words	Average length of comments in words	Average length of the postings in words	Average number of topics in new posts	Average number of topics in comments	Average number of topics in postings	Number of blogging periods
Age	-.37**	-.03	-.21**	-.40**	-.02	-.43**	-.33**	.32*	-.31**	-.11
Evaluation on computer-skills	.16	.13	.12	.14	.07	.11	.16	-.14	.08	.18
Evaluation on Internet access	.06	.14	.17*	.15	.10	.13	.08	-.20	.12	.13
Blogging experience	.13	.10	.06	.07	.14	.09	.16	.20	.13	.00
Evaluations on the confidence in face-to-face communication	-.03	-.01	-.04	.04	-.04	.03	.10	-.27*	-.07	-.12
Evaluations on the confidence in computer-mediated communication	.13	.14	.17*	.24**	.12	.22**	.20*	-.33**	.15	-.04
Blogging was suitable	.23*	.20*	.22*	.15	.15	.12	.07	.19	.04	.23*
Blogging was helpful during teaching practice/ induction year	.28**	.22**	.30**	.25**	.29**	.23*	.19	.25*	.14	.34**
Evaluations on the support from course-mates	.14	.06	.13	.05	-.03	.05	-.13	-,27**	-.15	-.04
Evaluations on the support from supervisors	-.11	-.00	-.08	-.10	-.04	-.10	.00	.02	-.09	-.12

* statistically significant on level .05

** statistically significant on level .01

Table 2. Spearman rank-correlation coefficients between the characteristics of the participants and their activeness in the blog

	Number of the new posts	Number of the comments	Number of the all postings	Average length of new posts in words	Average length of comments in words	Average length of the postings in words	Average number of topics in new posts	Average number of topics in comments	Average number of topics in postings	Number of blogging periods
Average number of comments per new posts	.27*	.02	.15	.44**	-.10	.32**	.31**	-.23*	.18*	.25**
Percentage of the blog postings consisting communication with others	.18	.52**	.35**	-.08	.42**	-.18*	-.02	.29*	-.09	.25
Percentage of the blog postings about success	-.05	-.12	-.07	-.16	-.11	-.21*	-.26*	.12	-.21*	-.10
Percentage of the blog postings about problems	.14	.48**	.30**	-.21*	.40**	-.26*	-.08	.40**	-.13	.23
Number of the participants in the blog	.11	-.21*	-.04	.28**	-.23*	.32**	.22*	-.25*	.22*	.07
Number of the participants in the blog, who shared more than two postings	.17	-.06	.07	.18*	-.12	.18*	.11	-.15	.09	.15
Strength of social relationships between the participants in the blog	.39**	.22*	.32**	.43**	.08	.34**	.33**	.01	.27**	.42**

* statistically significant on level .05
** statistically significant on level .01

Table 3. Comparison of blogging activeness of the participants in blogs in the case of mentor and without mentor, in the case of beginning task and without beginning task

	Blogs with mentor		Blogs without mentor		t-statistic	Blogs with beginning task		Blogs without beginning task		t-statistic
	M	SD	M	SD		M	SD	M	SD	
Number of new posts	8.07	10.96	2.35	2.32	-3.90**	7.48	11.27	3.77	5.68	-2.01
Number of comments	6.45	14.63	1.47	3.67	-2.27*	2.88	6.05	4.67	12.22	.89
Number of all postings	14.52	23.46	4.35	5.13	-3.23**	10.36	16.89	8.46	17.38	-.58
Average length of new posts in words	211.51	117.83	95.12	108.80	-5.72**	198.56	97.18	124.47	133.30	-3.53**
Average length of comments in words	76.18	379.08	117.06	579.27	.46	15.30	26.92	140.26	604.40	1.87
Average length of postings in words	192.51	233.95	115.24	165.81	-2.14*	172.85	89.39	140.39	241.76	-.84
Average number of topics in new posts	1.83	.68	1.37	.51	-4.21**	1.84	.68	1.46	.57	-3.27**
Average number of topics in comments	1.09	.25	1.28	.57	1.69	1.03	.12	1.24	.51	2.54*
Average number of topics in postings	1.62	.57	1.34	.46	-3.09**	1.69	.61	1.35	.44	-3.51**
Number of blogging periods	3.21	2.13	1.86	1.31	-4.15**	2.95	2.12	2.26	1.68	-1.85

The participants, who perceived themselves more confident in computer-mediated communication, wrote more postings, the postings were longer and the average number of topics in the new posts was higher. As we have presented above, that computer skills generally have no impact on blog-use activeness, it seems that self-reported confidence in computer-mediated communication can influence blogging activeness. Andergassen and her colleagues [8] and Deng and Yuen [13] have also studied the impact of learners' communication preferences on blog-use and brought on preferring direct communication or having other possibilities to face-to-face communication as hindering factors.

To answer the second research question we found out that the strength of social relationships between the blog members seems to be a crucial factor. From all measured characteristics of the blog the strength of social relationships between the participants in the blog and the average number of comments per new posts gave the highest number of positive correlations with the participants' activeness in the blog. These results are in concordance with Deng and Yuen's [13] findings who mentioned previous social relationships as important for learners' engagement in the blog. Halic and her colleagues [9] have underscored that the sense of community in the blog affects positively participants' blog-use activeness. If the participants wrote more about their problems during the teaching practice or induction year, the others comment more on their posts and the comments are longer with several topics. Surprisingly, if the participants wrote more about the success, only negative correlations were found with participants' activeness in blogs. Thus, writings about success, sharing positive experiences do not seem to inspire communication in the blog as much as writings about problems or unsuccess.

Also, the number of participants seems to be an important factor which has impact on learners' engagement in the blog. If there is a higher number of participants in the blog, new posts are longer and cover more topics, but the comments are shorter with less topics. Also, the number of the participants in the blog, who wrote more than two postings, influenced positively the length of new posts, but had no impact on the number of postings. Deng and Yuen [13] have emphasized that social factors have impact on learners' engagement in the blog and as one of those they have brought on the level of participation in the blog – if there are enough active writers who write and comment on others' writings and are online frequently.

Finally, having a mentor in the blog and starting the blogging period with the beginning task were found also to be important factors affecting blog-use activeness. We have compared participants' activeness in the blog with mentors and without mentors, and the blogs with the beginning task and without such a task. In the blogs with a tutor and a mentor the participants were more active comparing with the participants in the blogs with a tutor only – eight characteristics out of ten gave statistically significant difference. In the case of blogs with the beginning task the participants wrote longer posts with more topics comparing with the blogs without such a task, but in the blogs without the beginning task the comments were about more topics comparing with the blogs with such a task. One explanation for such results might be that the beginning task taught how to use blog, helped participants better understand the purpose or benefit of blogging, clarified which topics are expected to write there about, and also offered challenge. Such kind of pedagogical factors have been found to be important for successful and motivated blog-use [5, 13]. One possible explanation for the differences in blogging activeness between the blogs with and without a mentor could be the familiarity of the mentor with all blog-members, contrary to the tutor. We think that having the mentor participating in the blog could conduce to higher activeness in blogging because the mentor can offer better support for blog members, which has been found to affect students' engagement in the blog [14]. Mentor could be an important person whose role is to promote the sense of community in the blog, which Halic and her colleagues [9] have found to be an affecting factor for active blog-use.

5 Conclusion and Limitations

The characteristics of the participants and blogs were related to the activeness of the blogging. If the collective blogs are used during teaching practice or induction year, educationalists should pay attention to forming groups of participants and organizing the blogs. Strong social relationships between the participants seem to be one of the crucial aspects for ensuring participants' activeness in the blogs. The important and necessary role of the educator, who is in the blog with the participants, should be taken into consideration. As the social relationships between the members of the blog support blogging activeness, and so are the social relationships between the educator and the other participants. Although all our blogs were used on the voluntary basis, it seems that somewhat forced blogging like giving some compulsory tasks in the blog could be effective.

In this study some essential characteristics of the participants and blogs, which may inform us about how to encourage the use of blogs, were pursued. However, knowing that some characteristics are related to blogging activeness does not give us a full answer to explain the value of these characteristics in improving participants' engagement in blogs and do not indicate what the cause and what the result is. The aim of the blog was also limited, only reflective blogs were used. Further studies should provide more answers concerning the optimal values of the characteristics of the blog for using them in education with different learning goals.

References

1. Sifry, D.: State of the Blogsphere (2006), `http://www.sifry.com/alerts/archives/000436.html`
2. Kim, H.N.: The phenomenon of blogs and theoretical model of blog use in educational context. Computers & Education 51, 1342–1352 (2008)
3. Dearstyne, B.W.: Blogs: The New Information Revolution? Information Management Journal 39(3), 38–44 (2005)
4. Kaplan, A.: Blogs: Finding you voice, finding your audience. The Rosen Publishing Group, New York (2012)
5. Cakir, H.: Use of blogs in pre-service teacher education to improve student engagement. Computers & Education 68, 244–252 (2013)
6. Luik, P., Voltri, O., Taimalu, M., Kalk, K.: On the use of student teacher blogs during teaching practice. Procedia Social and Behavioral Sciences 11, 165–169 (2011)

7. Can, G., Ozdemir, D.: Blogging in Higher Education: Theoretical and Practical Approach. Systemics, Cybernetics and Informatics 4(6), 5–13 (2006)
8. Andergassen, M., Behringer, R., Finlay, J., Gorra, A., Moore, D.: Weblogs in Higher Education – why do Students (not) Blog? Electronic Journal of e-Learning 7(3), 203–215 (2009)
9. Halic, O., Lee, D., Paulus, T., Spence, M.: To blog or not to blog: Student perceptions of blog effectiveness for learning in a college-level course. Internet and Higher Education 13, 206–213 (2010)
10. Williams, J., Jacobs, J.: Exploring the use of blogs as learning spaces in the higher education sector. Australasian Journal of Educational Technology 20, 232–247 (2004)
11. Vescio, V., Ross, D., Adams, A.: A review of research on the impact of professional learning communities on teaching practice and student learning. Teaching and Teacher Education 24, 80–91 (2008)
12. Ndon, U.T.: Hybrid-Context Instructional Model. The Internet and the classrooms: the way teachers experience it. Library of Congress Cataloging in Publication, United States of America (2010)
13. Deng, L., Yuen, A.H.K.: Blogs in pre-service teacher education: exploring the participation issue. Technology, Pedagogy and Education 22(3), 339–356 (2013)
14. Huang, Y.-H., Lo, Y.-F.: What makes blogging attractive to bloggers: a case of college-level constituency users. Journal of Computer Assisted Learning 28, 208–221 (2012)
15. Warschauer, M.: Comparing face-to-face and electronic discussion in the second language classroom. CALICO Journal 13(2&3), 7–26 (1995/1996)
16. Emmer, E.T., Hickman, J.: Teacher efficacy in classroom management and discipline. Educational and Psychological Measurement 51, 755–765 (1991)

Fostering Collaborative Learning with Wikis: Extending MediaWiki with Educational Features

Elvira Popescu, Cristian Maria, and Anca Loredana Udriştoiu

Computers and Information Technology Department, University of Craiova, Romania
popescu_elvira@software.ucv.ro

Abstract. Wikis are increasingly popular Web 2.0 tools in educational settings, being used successfully for collaborative learning. However, since they were not originally conceived as educational tools, they lack some of the functionalities useful in the instructional process (such as learner monitoring, evaluation support, student group management etc.). Therefore in this paper we propose a solution to add these educational support features, as an extension to the popular MediaWiki platform. CoLearn, as it is called, is aimed at increasing the collaboration level between students, investigating also the collaborative versus cooperative learner actions. Its functionalities and pedagogical rationale are presented, together with some technical details. A set of practical guidelines for promoting collaborative learning with wikis is also included.

Keywords: educational wiki, collaborative learning, co-writing, MediaWiki extension, learner tracking.

1 Introduction

Collaborative learning is a widely used approach in education, in which "students are working in groups of two or more, mutually searching for understanding, solutions, or meanings, or creating a product" [17]; the interactions between peers play a highly important role in the process [2]. Co-writing is an effective strategy of collaborative learning, consisting in a joint production of a piece of text by students who clarify, edit and revise each others' contributions [3]; co-writing processes stimulate reflection, knowledge sharing and critical thinking, in a strong social context [19].

During the past several years, wikis have started to be used for such collaborative learning activities, facilitating group work and discussion. Paper [11] offers a comprehensive review on wiki as teaching tool, exploring its contribution to various learning paradigms, as well as actual use cases, as reported in the literature. A more recent review is provided in [9], with the goal to identify factors that influence collaboration in wikis and actions that need to be taken to increase this collaboration.

However, since wikis were not originally conceived as educational tools, many functionalities that could be helpful in the instructional process are not included. More specifically, the need arises for some features to provide support to the instructor in the learner tracking and evaluation process, but also to the student for managing their projects and monitoring their progress. Based on these needs, researchers started to

E. Popescu et al. (Eds.): ICWL 2014, LNCS 8613, pp. 22–31, 2014.

devise dedicated educational wiki platforms, either by extending general-purpose wikis or by building dedicated stand-alone wikis from scratch.

A summary of existing systems is included in the next section. While most of these tools aim for learner assessment support, we decided to propose our own wiki extension solution (starting from the popular MediaWiki platform), called CoLearn, which focuses more on increasing the collaboration level between students and on investigating the collaborative versus cooperative learner actions. An overview of CoLearn, including some technical details, functionalities and pedagogical rationale are presented in section 3. In addition to a good wiki platform, a sound pedagogy is needed to promote collaborative learning; hence some practical guidelines drawn from the literature are included in section 4. The paper ends with some future work directions and conclusions in section 5.

2 Transferring Wikis to Education: Related Work

Based on the growing popularity of wikis in education and the need for specific learner and instructor support, various educational wiki extensions have been proposed, as described next.

Co-Writing Wiki [1] is based on the open source ScrewTurn Wiki[1] and adds several functionalities for the students: i) view group members' actions feed; ii) visualize own contribution charts and compare progress with other peers; iv) view group members currently online; iv) visualize the differences between revisions (color-coded), comment and rate revisions. Similarly, several enhanced features are provided for the teacher: i) the contributions of each group member are marked with a unique color, so that the activity of each student can be easily explored; ii) a revision player is provided, which displays the color-enhanced revisions of a wiki page as a slide show; iii) useful statistical information is shown, both in textual form and as a chart panel; iv) the teacher has the possibility to send feedback to the students and evaluate their contribution.

EdDokuWiki [14] is based on the open source DokuWiki[2] and supports the following set of functionalities: i) peer evaluation support (add comments to wiki pages, rate pages, assess the utility of the comments received); ii) monitor and record all student actions; iii) automatic (quantitative) evaluation of student contributions (number of pages, number of characters on each page, number of internal/external links, amount of time spent on the wiki); iv) instructor evaluation support (visualize a summary of each student contributions, grade student, provide individual feedback).

Tracking Bundle [8] is available as a MediaWiki[3] extension and provides several additional functionalities for the teacher: i) create student groups; ii) configure review criteria and the formula used for computing the students' final score; iii) view all page

[1] `http://stw.codeplex.com`
[2] `http://www.dokuwiki.org`
[3] `http://www.mediawiki.org`

revisions filtered according to various options and add a score and comment for each of the configured criteria; iv) visualize the students' activity and scores in graphical formats.

Apart from the extensions summarized above, another proposed approach was to build a dedicated educational wiki from scratch [6]. **ClassroomWiki**, as it is called, was conceived as a complex Web-based collaborative wiki writing tool, which provides enhanced functionalities both for the students and the teachers: color-coded visualization of revisions, activity tracking, building student model, automatic group formation. Beside the actual wiki module, the platform includes also: i) a communication module (a topic-based forum and an announcement system); ii) a tracking and modeling module (which tracks all students' interactions with the system and with group members and builds a detailed learner model); iii) a group formation module (an agent-based framework in which students' agents negotiate to form heterogeneous groups in terms of student performance) [6]. A comparison between the four wiki platforms presented above is included in [7].

There are also a few commercial hosted wikis designed for educational use, such as: i) **Wikispaces**[4] **- Classroom type** (which includes formative assessment features and tracking learner activity such as reading, writing or saving pages); ii) **PBworks**[5] **– Classroom and Campus editions** (which include some basic learner tracking and assignment management features).

To sum up, the wiki platforms presented above include support for: student group management, communication activities, learner tracking and monitoring, peer and teacher assessment. In this context, we propose an educational wiki extension focused mainly on fostering collaborative learning between students, rooted in pedagogical principles. The starting point is MediaWiki platform, a choice motivated by its popularity, available functionalities, ease of use, good development community support, as well as our own experience with it in educational settings [15].

3 Designing CoLearn

3.1 MediaWiki Extensions

MediaWiki is one of the most active and widely deployed wiki engines, being the platform used by the highly popular Wikipedia. MediaWiki is written in PHP and provides an extension mechanism for customizing its appearance and functionalities. Some of these extensions are maintained by MediaWiki developers, while others are implemented by third-party developers[6]. Extensions can be used for adding reporting and administrative capabilities, changing the look and feel, extending the wiki markup, adding custom authentication mechanisms etc. There are also a few publicly available MediaWiki extensions for educational use (the last two seemingly no longer maintained): i) The Education Program[7] - which provides various interfaces to man-

[4] `http://www.wikispaces.com/`

[5] `http://www.pbworks.com/`

[6] `http://www.mediawiki.org/wiki/Manual:Extensions`

[7] `http://www.mediawiki.org/wiki/Extension:Education_Program`

age courses, students and institutions; ii) eduWIKI[8] – which consists in wiki patches designed for educational usage; iii) TrackingBundle[9] – which was presented in the previous section.

In this context, we designed and implemented an extension specifically aimed at supporting collaborative learning. This extension, called CoLearn, creates various MediaWiki *special pages*, for creating group projects, adding students to projects, visualizing projects and statistics, monitoring student activity etc. CoLearn is based on an MVC architecture and extends the MediaWiki database with information regarding student groups, project pages, revision types, collaborative actions, ratings, comments, grades etc. The new functionalities are added by using the *hooks*[10] provided by MediaWiki, which allow custom code (*event handlers*) to be executed when some defined event occurs (e.g., *onRevisionInsertComplete, onArticleInsertComplete, onOutputPageBeforeHTML*); the front-end uses various *jQuery*[11] plugins, such as *jqPlot, jQuery Raty, DataTables* etc.

3.2 CoLearn Features

CoLearn provides the possibility to set student and instructor roles, offering various functionalities for both of them. Thus, an instructor can:

- Create student accounts
- Manage courses
- Setup student groups (teams)
- Create and assign projects
- Visualize project pages
- Visualize student profiles
- View differences between page revisions by using a custom engine
- Monitor student activity
- View summary information about each project, page, group and student
- View graphical statistics regarding each project, page, group and student
- View student and project activity reports
- View project revision history
- Grade students
- Provide feedback to students.

Similarly, CoLearn offers students the possibility to:

- Create and manage projects for their own group
- Create and edit pages associated to a project
- Annotate each page revision with the type of editing performed and the current group activity
- View project revision history

8 http://www.mediawiki.org/wiki/Extension:EduWIKI
9 http://www.mediawiki.org/wiki/Extension:TrackingBundle
10 http://www.mediawiki.org/wiki/Manual:Hooks
11 http://jquery.com (a fast, small, and feature-rich JavaScript library)

- Add comments and ratings to peers' pages
- View summary information about their project
- View graphical statistics regarding their own activity and comparisons with peers
- Visualize grades and feedback from the instructor.

3.3 Illustrating CoLearn: Some Collaborative Learning Underpinnings

Every time students revise a project page, they are asked to specify the type of revision performed, according to the taxonomy proposed in [12] (see Fig. 1): *Add information, Add link, Clarify information* (i.e., reword existing information in order to clarify the content), *Delete information, Delete link, Fix link, Structure* (originally called *Format* – i.e., change the page structure by moving paragraphs or adding subtitles), *Grammar* (i.e., correct grammatical errors or punctuation), *Mark-up language* (i.e., switch between wiki mark-up language and HTML, but without affecting the appearance of the page or the text), *Reversion* (i.e., restore a previous page version), *Spelling* (i.e., correct spelling mistakes), *Style* (i.e., change the presentation or appearance of the text). The original taxonomy, which referred to public open wikis such as Wikipedia, contained also *Vandalism* actions, but this is not applicable in educational settings, in which only logged-in students are allowed to contribute to the wiki.

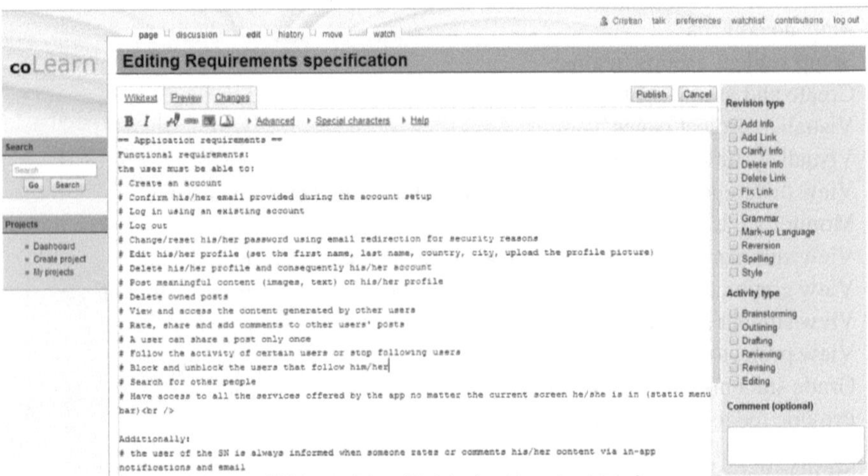

Fig. 1. CoLearn – Revising project page

These revision types describe various levels of collaborative writing between students, as suggested in [3]. Thus, revisions of type *Style*, *Structure* and *Mark-up language* refer mainly to technical issues (presentation and appearance) which indicate a lower level of collaboration. Revisions which directly affect content but without generally changing the meaning of sentences (e.g., *Add information*, *Add link*, *Delete information, Delete link*) can also be considered more as cooperative than collaborative activities. The highest level of collaboration occurs when students revise and alter their peers' contributions and change the meaning of sentences (e.g., through actions of type *Clarify information, Fix link, Grammar, Spelling*).

Furthermore, CoLearn provides students with an interface to specify the activity stage of their collaborative writing, according to the taxonomy in [10]: *Brainstorming, Outlining, Drafting, Reviewing, Revising, Editing* (see Fig. 1).

On one hand, this revision annotation task in CoLearn raises students' awareness regarding their cooperative and collaborative actions, the way they interact with their peers and their contribution toward the group project. On the other hand, the aggregated data obtained from all students provide the teacher with a perspective on the collaboration level inside each group (see Fig. 2). These graphical visualizations provided by CoLearn also help teachers to clearly and easily identify each student contribution, spot free riders and support the grading and evaluation process, replacing the time-consuming manual methods used in [3].

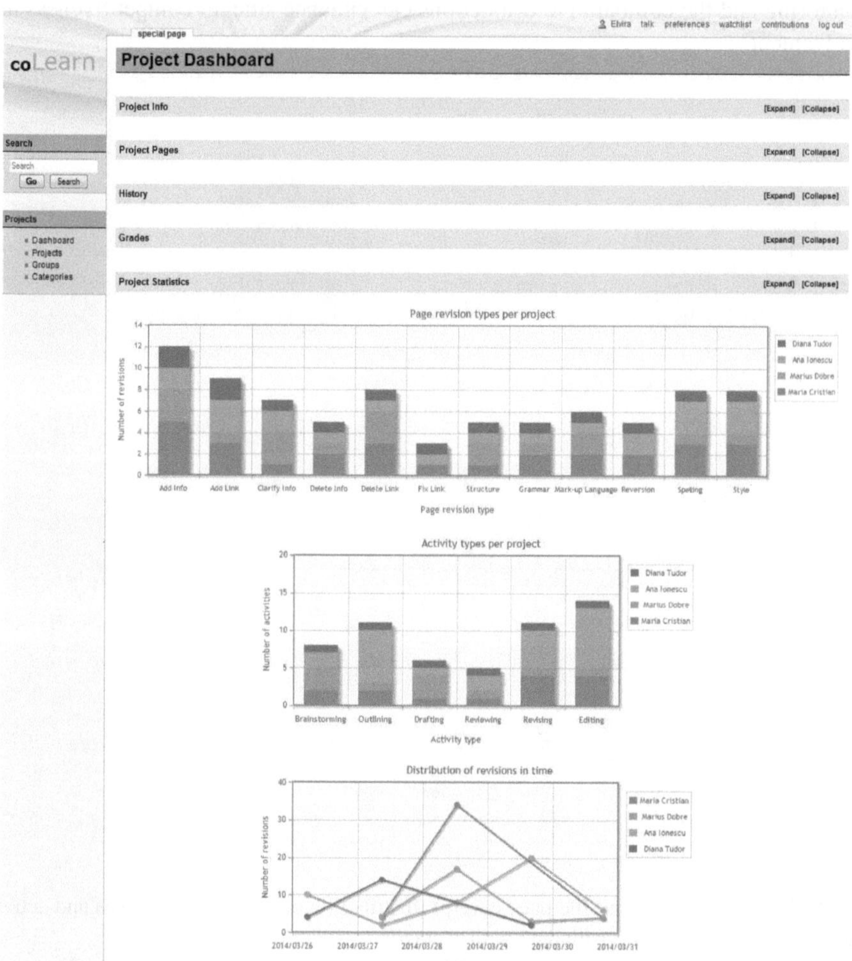

Fig. 2. CoLearn – Project dashboard (graphical statistics of page revisions)

Furthermore, by visualizing the timing of the students' contributions (bottom chart in Fig. 2), the instructor can get a good indicator on the type of work partitioning inside a group: *sequential* (students contribute in successive stages), *parallel* (students work simultaneously on independent subtasks) or *reciprocal* (students work together, mutually adjusting their activities based on peers' contributions) [16].

Another functionality provided by CoLearn is students' access to detailed profile pages, where they can visualize their overall progress, as well as comparative statistics with the group and class average (see Fig. 3); this is a feature which seems to be missing from the other educational wikis [7]. This provides an important self-monitoring and self-evaluation support for students, helping them to take initiative and responsibility for their own learning [4]. Furthermore, the continuous activity monitoring and the comparative evaluations can enhance student competitiveness and involvement.

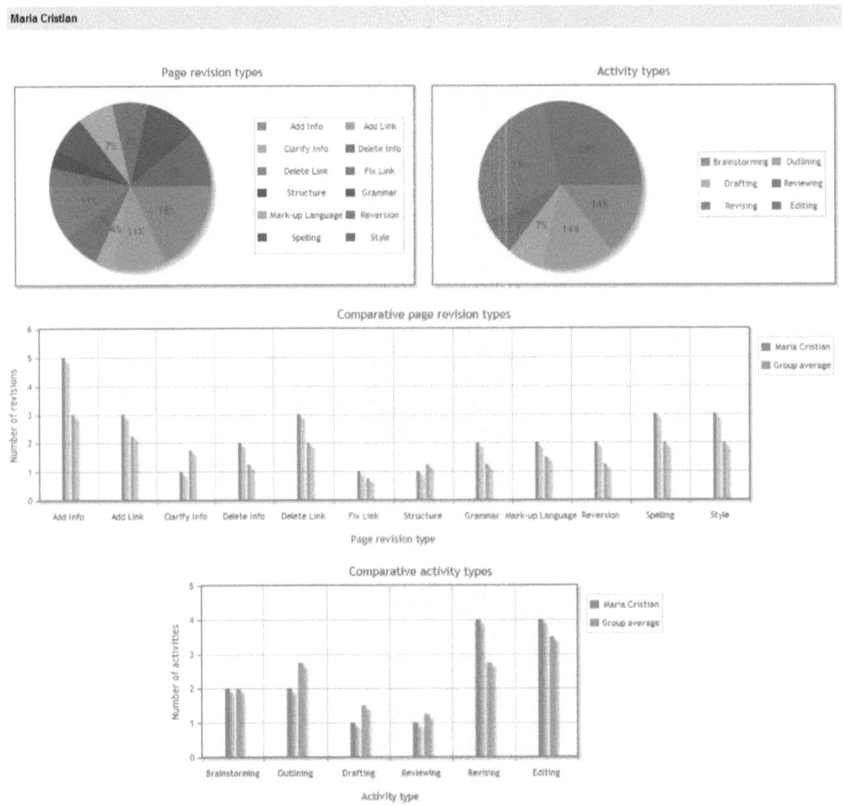

Fig. 3. CoLearn – Student profile page excerpt (distribution of page revision types and activity types, comparative statistics with the group average)

Additionally, students' participation is increased by the possibility to rate and comment on peers' pages, offering help, feedback and constructive criticism (Fig. 4). This peer evaluation enhances students' social motivation for learning, encouraging critical thinking and contributions. Furthermore, peer assessment can be very valuable for the students assessed, as an appropriate substitute for teachers' feedback (since its reliability and validity can be comparable to that of the teacher, given the instructor's time constraints) [18]. Finally, teachers also have the opportunity to provide both private and public feedback to students through CoLearn, which is an essential aspect in order to align collaboration [9].

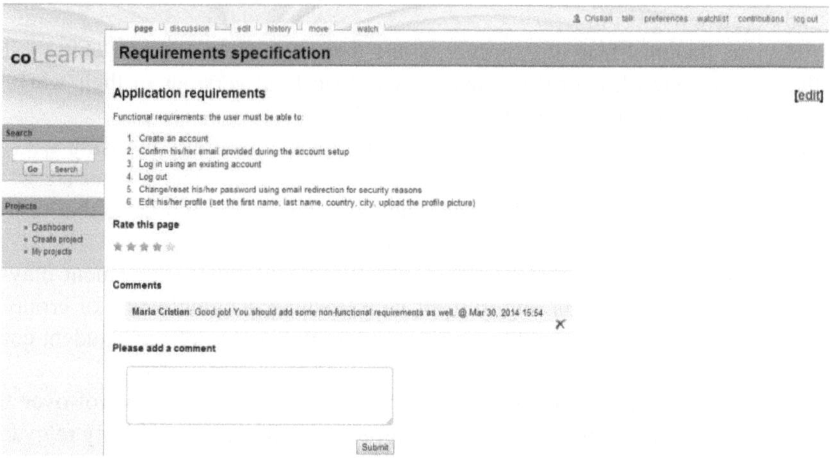

Fig. 4. CoLearn – Peer review functionality

4 Practical Guidelines for Promoting Collaboration in Wikis

In the previous section we focused on the technology-side of the collaborative learning process, providing a short overview of the CoLearn wiki extension. However, a sound pedagogical scenario is needed as well in order to foster collaborative learning in wikis [3], since by itself "a collaborative tool does not necessarily lead to collaborative behavior" [9].

Therefore, in what follows we outline several recommendations for successfully integrating wikis in educational activity and promoting student collaboration; these are drawn from various reports from the literature [3], [5], [9], as well as from our own 5-year experience with using wikis in the instructional process [13], [15].

1. Carefully design the instructional activity, based on a sound pedagogy; the wiki should be integrated with the curriculum, the learning objectives and the assessment.
2. Choose an assignment that inherently requires collaboration.
3. Provide an introductory lecture about collaboration as well as continuous scaffolding, since students may lack collaborative skills, due to the traditional, dominantly individual learning approach.
4. Offer technical training for using wikis in the beginning and continuous technical support.

5. Provide clear guidelines for interaction and educate students to edit peers' contributions (since they are generally uncomfortable to both accept modifications of their own work and alter others' work); creating an atmosphere of trust and confidence encourages students to change peers' contributions and modify content created by others for the benefit of the group.
6. Encourage students to contribute regularly to the wiki, well before the deadline (students' natural tendency to last minute activity hampers interaction, discussions and iterative page edits).
7. Alleviate students' fear of exposure, since they may feel uncomfortable to share their incomplete ideas or drafts and only upload final versions of their work, negating the idea of collaboration.
8. Support discussion and socialization of participants, generally by using wiki discussion pages together with other social media tools (e.g., blog, Twitter etc.).
9. When possible and appropriate, make the wiki open to the public, so that students can be motivated by an authentic audience.
10. Make the wiki task mandatory and explicitly graded, since assessment plays an important part in students' engagement with learning; a combination of group and individual assessment should be used, based on the quality of each student contribution.
11. Ensure also intrinsic motivation, by allowing students to take control over their own learning and by providing a meaningful and authentic task, highly relevant to the student.
12. Ensure positive group climate, team cohesion, discourage individualistic strategies; play the role of facilitator, moderate in case of difficulties, offer support but do not dominate group work.

5 Conclusion

We started this paper with a short overview of adapting wikis for use in the instructional process. The main contribution was our proposal for an educational MediaWiki extension called CoLearn, followed by some practical guidelines for successfully using wikis in collaborative learning.

As future work, we plan to experimentally validate CoLearn. The experimental setup that we envision is a collaborative Project-Based Learning scenario which we have been applying for the past five years in our teaching [13], [15]. The context is an undergraduate course on Web Applications Design, in which MediaWiki is used by the students for collaborative writing of project deliverables (among the members of each team), for gathering and organizing knowledge and resources regarding the project, for clearly documenting each stage of the project as well as the final product. By including the CoLearn extension we hope to increase collaboration between students as well as allow for a more comprehensive investigation of learners' activity.

Acknowledgements. This work was partially supported by the grant number 15C/2014, awarded in the internal grant competition of the University of Craiova.

References

1. AL-Smadi, M., Höfler, M., Gütl, C.: Enhancing Wikis with Visualization Tools to Support Groups' Production Function and to Maintain Task and Social Awareness. In: Proc. ICBL 2011, pp. 16–21 (2011)
2. Dillenbourg, P., Järvelä, S., Fischer, F.: The Evolution of Research on Computer-Supported Collaborative Learning. From Design to Orchestration. In: Balacheff, N., Ludvigsen, S., de Jong, T., Lazonder, A., Barnes, S. (eds.) Technology-Enhanced Learning. Principles and Products, Part I, pp. 3–19. Springer (2009)
3. Hadjerrouit, S.: Wiki as a Collaborative Writing Tool in Teacher Education: Evaluation and Suggestions for Effective Use. Computers in Human Behavior 32, 301–312 (2014)
4. Herder, E., Marenzi, I.: Trends in Connecting Learners. First Research & Technology Scouting Report. STELLAR project deliverable (2010), `http://hdl.handle.net/1820/2824`
5. Judd, T., Kennedy, G., Cropper, S.: Using Wikis for Collaborative Learning: Assessing Collaboration through Contribution. Australasian Journal of Educational Technology 6(3), 341–354 (2010)
6. Khandaker, N., Soh, L.K.: ClassroomWiki: A Collaborative Wiki for Instructional Use with Multiagent Group Formation. IEEE Trans. Learning Technologies 3(3), 190–202 (2010)
7. Kubincová, Z., Homola, M.: How to Get Around with Wikis in Teaching. In: Popescu, E., Li, Q., Klamma, R., Leung, H., Specht, M. (eds.) ICWL 2012. LNCS, vol. 7558, pp. 21–30. Springer, Heidelberg (2012)
8. Kubincova, Z., Homola, M., Janajev, R.: Tool-Supported Assessment of Wiki-Based Assignments. In: Proc. CSEDU 2012, pp. 58–67 (2012)
9. Kummer, C.: Factors Influencing Wiki Collaboration in Higher Education (2013), doi:10.2139/ssrn.2208522
10. Lowry, P.B., Curtis, A., Lowry, M.R.: Building a Taxonomy and Nomenclature of Collaborative Writing to Improve Interdisciplinary Research and Practice. Journal of Business Communication 41(1), 66–99 (2004)
11. Parker, K.R., Chao, J.T.: Wiki as a Teaching Tool. Interdisciplinary Journal of Knowledge and Learning Objects 3, 57–72 (2007)
12. Pfeil, U., Zaphiris, P., Ang, C.S.: Cultural Differences in Collaborative Authoring of Wikipedia. Journal of Computer-Mediated Communication 12, 88–113 (2006)
13. Popescu, E.: Students' Acceptance of Web 2.0 Technologies in Higher Education: Findings from a Survey in a Romanian University. In: Proc. DEXA 2010 Workshops, pp. 92–96 (2010)
14. Popescu, E., Manafu, L.: Repurposing a Wiki for Collaborative Learning - Pedagogical and Technical View. In: Proc. ICSTCC 2011, pp. 452–457 (2011)
15. Popescu, E.: Using Wikis to Support Project-Based Learning: A Case Study. In: Proc. ICALT 2014 (in press, 2014)
16. Sharples, M., Goodlet, J.S., Beck, E.E., Wood, C.C., Easterbrook, S.M., Plowman, L.: Research Issues in the Study of Computer Supported Collaborative Writing. In: Sharples, M. (ed.) Computer Supported Collaborative Writing. Springer (1993)
17. Smith, B.L., MacGregor, J.T.: What Is Collaborative Learning? In: Collaborative Learning: A Sourcebook for Higher Education. National Center on Postsecondary Teaching, Learning, & Assessment, Syracuse University (1992)
18. Topping, K.J.: Peer Assessment. Theory into Practice 48(1), 20–27 (2009)
19. Trentin, G.: Using a Wiki to Evaluate Individual Contribution to a Collaborative Learning Project. Journal of Computer Assisted Learning 25(1), 43–55 (2009)

Multifaceted Open Social Learner Modelling

Lei Shi, Alexandra I. Cristea and Suncica Hadzidedic

Department of Computer Science, University of Warwick,
CV4 7AL, Coventry, United Kingdom
{lei.shi,acristea,s.hadzidedic}@dcs.warwick.ac.uk

Abstract. Open social learner modelling (OSLM) approaches are promoted in order to assist learners in self-directed and self-determined learning in a social context. Still, most approaches only focus on visualising learners' performance, or providing complex tools for social navigation. Our proposal, additionally, emphasises the importance of *visualising both learners' performance and their contribution to a learning community*. We seek also to *seamlessly integrate OSLM with learning contents*, in order for the *multifaceted OSLM*'s prospect for ubiquity and context-awareness to enrich the adaptive potential of social e-learning systems. This paper thus presents the design of *multifaceted OSLM* by introducing novel, personalised social interaction features into Topolor, a social personalised adaptive e-learning environment. The umbrella target is to create and study aspects of open social learner models. An experimental study is conducted to analyse the impact of the newly introduced features. The results are finally concluded to suggest future research and further improvements.

1 Introduction

It is envisaged that learners, especially younger generations familiar with Web 2. 0 (as in social) and Web 3.0 (as in personalised and social [11]) techniques embedded in their daily lives, are expected to have the ability to create and maintain their own personal learning environments, to interact with peers as well as learning resources, and be actively engaged in a social e-learning context. However, the availability of massive open resources and the diversity of connections and interactions have led to many challenges. Successful social e-learning requires tools to assist learners in directing their own learning and having a higher level of presence and engagement in order to participate in meaningful interactions [10], similar to popular social software.

Towards tackling these challenges, *open learner modelling* (OLM) approaches have been adopted in the existing studies. OLM makes it possible for a learner to observe her learning status, so as to promote metacognition (e.g., self-reflection, self-direction and transparency) [21]. It has been suggested that learners studying together may benefit from accessing peers' models and group models [22]. Studies have been conducted to explore the use of OLM [3, 13]. Several of them take into consideration also the social aspect of learning [1, 8]. Yet, much further research needs to be performed to enhance OLM, especially in terms of social personalised visualisation and interaction, which can potentially improve the social e-learning experience.

E. Popescu et al. (Eds.): ICWL 2014, LNCS 8613, pp. 32–42, 2014.

Following from existing studies, the main research goal presented in this paper is to explore the design of *multifaceted* open social learner models (OSLM) in *a social personalised adaptive e-learning environment* [14]. Compared to existing studies, this research aims at enabling interactive visualisation of different OSLM angles, to potentially promote metacognitive activities. Unlike existing approaches that use OSLM visualisation only as a social navigation tool, our approach also seeks to seamlessly and adaptively integrate OSLM with the learning contents, so that its ubiquity and context-awareness can support new adaptation and personalisation methods for social e-learning. It is also noteworthy that, unlike existing studies that focus only on visualising learners' *performance*, we emphasise the possibility and (in our view) necessity of visualising both *performance* and *contribution*, reflecting not only a learner's role as a knowledge consumer, but also that of a knowledge producer, which can better integrate in the Web 2.0 and Web 3.0 era. Importantly, the visualisation is built on a Facebook-like appearance, and on features inspired from popular games, instead of on traditional learning environment visualisations.

In the remainder of the paper, section 2 details related work on OSLM and systems supporting social learner models visualising, explaining the need of a *multifaceted OSLM*. Section 3 shortly describes Topolor, a social e-learning environment and the basis for the new *multifaceted OSLM*. Section 4 elaborates on Topolor's new features. An experimental study is reported in section 5, analysing users' perceived acceptance of these features; and section 6 outlines conclusions and future work suggestions.

2 Related Work

A learner model often refers to a model of knowledge, or other characteristics of a learner, constructed from direct input or observation of learning activities in, e.g., adaptive educational hypermedia systems (AEHS), and updated according to the learner's current understanding of the target learning contents; while an open learner model has specific provisions for the learner to explicitly view the information in her model, so as to support self-reflection of her own and her peer learning processes, and explain the reason of getting a recommendation [9]. OLM have been implemented using a wide range of modelling approaches, and its various educational benefits are thoroughly discussed in the literature, such as raising learners' awareness of their current knowledge levels and encouraging them to reflect on the learning process [6].

In comparison with OLM, social OLM (OSLM) have pushed the research area of AEHS towards fostering diversification of learner modelling, richer visualisation and interaction of learner models [2], and accumulating a great set of theories and techniques to build a variety of e-learning environments with personalised, adaptive and social features. Recent studies, as visited below, mainly focus on visualising the learning progress and providing social navigation support based on learner models.

IntrospectiveViews [8] provides parallel views on models of a learner and her peers. A learner can choose to compare her learning progress (completed, partially completed, pending, following) with either another peer's learning progress or the average progress of the entire learning group. However, the comparisons have limited-level granularity representation of learning contents. QuizMap [1] has a

4-level hierarchical representation of a tree-map, and each level clusters different level of information in detail (from entire class's performance to individual's performance on a single question). A learner can also observe her own performance in comparison with the rest of the class. However, QuizMap cannot fit larger classes that generate too many cells on the TreeMap, causing it to become too crowded (information overload). ProgressiveZoom [12] is built upon the Google-Maps paradigm, seeking to address information overload issues, by enabling learners to zoom in or out in a multi-layer fashion. However, it has limited ability to control comparisons between learners.

To address these limitations, we thus seamlessly integrated *multifaceted OSLM* at all granularity levels of learning contents, i.e., at course level, topic level, resource level, etc. This addresses the limited-level granularity learning content representations in IntrospectiveViews, and the concern of too crowded user interface or information overload in QuizMap. Moreover, a *multifaceted OSLM* allows a learner to compare to individuals and groups, unlike in Progressive Zoom. Additionally, unlike these systems, we build *multifaceted OSLM* with Facebook-like and popular game-like visualisation, which potentially makes features easier to use by now-a-day's learners.

3 Topolor

Topolor is a social personalised adaptive e-learning environment. Its design refers to the connectivist learning theory [7], which argues that learning is process of creating networks of information, contacts and resources [20]. The first version of Topolor [17], launched in Nov 2012, was used as an online learning environment for MSc level students at two universities. It has been evaluated from various perspectives [15, 19]. Based on the evaluation results, the second version Topolor has been developed, as the environment where we added and evaluated the proposed *multifaceted OSLM*. This section only presents those features related to *multifaceted OLSM*. The backbone of Topolor is a hybrid network connecting learning contents and learners. Learning contents are organised in a classic *course-topic-resource* structure: a course consists of a set of tree-structured topics; a topic contains one or more resources, and could be shared by different courses. A learner can, e.g., register to a course, learn a topic, and share a resource. The *multifaceted OLSM* are seamlessly integrated at all granularity levels of learning content pages (Fig. 2) beside learners' profile pages (Fig. 1).

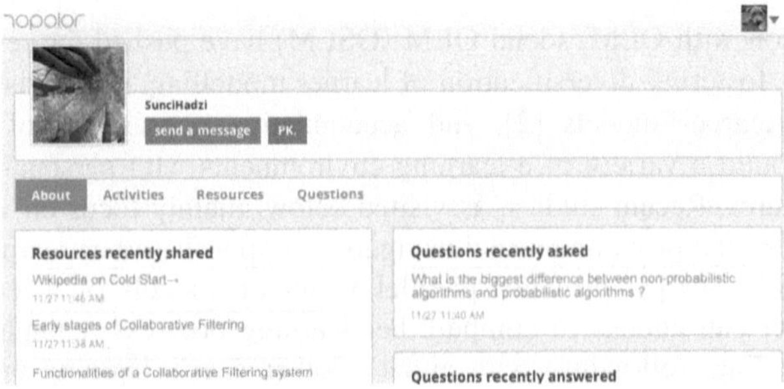

Fig. 1. User interface on tablet: a user profile page

Fig. 1 shows a learner's profile page presenting her model. In the 'about' tab there are lists about her learning status, e.g., topics learnt, questions asked and answered. By clicking on the button 'PK.' she can compare her learner model to the profile owner's learner model. In Fig. 2, (1) and (2) illustrate a course page and a resource page, respectively. Learner models can be visualised in pop-up views by clicking buttons such as "Learning Path" and "My Performance" (see section 4 for details).

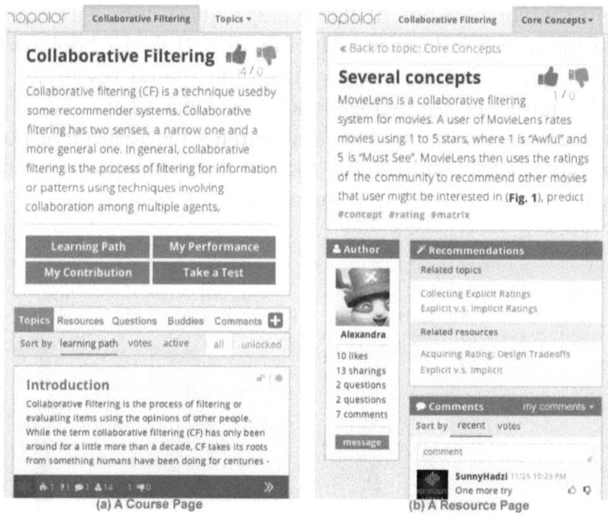

Fig. 2. User interface on smart phone: (a) a course page; (b) a resource page

4 Multifaceted Open Social Learner Modelling

We call the OSLM in Topolor 'multifaceted', because, firstly, a learner can access her model and her peers' models ubiquitously, and Topolor adapts the visualisations to fit *various contexts*, corresponding to the hierarchy course pages, topic pages, resource pages and profile pages. Additionally, it provides various visualisation modes, e.g., comparison between individuals, to all other learners, etc. These modes of *multi-context* and *multi-cohort* comparisons require enhancements of both adaptivity and adaptability, and are expected to further promote metacognitive activities. Unlike existing systems providing a single complex view of OSLM with many criteria to manually select in order to adjust visualisations, We propose to *adapt appropriate views of visualisations automatically*, to potentially improve the system's usability; and to *visualise both learners' performance and contribution*, reflecting learners' roles as both knowledge consumers and producers; specific features are shown below.

4.1 Visualisation of Performance

Visualisation of performance is a common feature in existing OSLM approaches, such as [1], potentially promoting motivation [8]. Topolor emphasises the importance of a *timeline* by presenting, e.g., test score trends, and the importance of *comparisons*, e.g., via the comparison of success rate in test between learners. On a course page (see Fig. 1 (a)) or a topic page, by clicking on the button 'My Performance', a pop-up view shows a learner's performance on the current course or topic. Fig. 3 demonstrates the pop-up view on performance of a course page. The default view contains the test score trends and the comparison of success rates of tests (Fig. 3 left). For brevity not all tabs are shown here, but in short: the tab-view 'Topic / quiz' shows a two column charts presenting the comparisons of the average quiz score between a learner, the whole class and the top 20% learners. The tab-view 'Liked / bookmarked' shows a two column charts presenting how many times the shared resources were 'liked' / bookmarked. The tab-view 'Activities' shows a radar chart and a column chart comparing activities (Fig. 3 right). Fig. 4 illustrates the respective pop-up view of performance in a topic page, showing on the left the comparison of quiz scores, and on the right, the learner's corrected quiz answers.

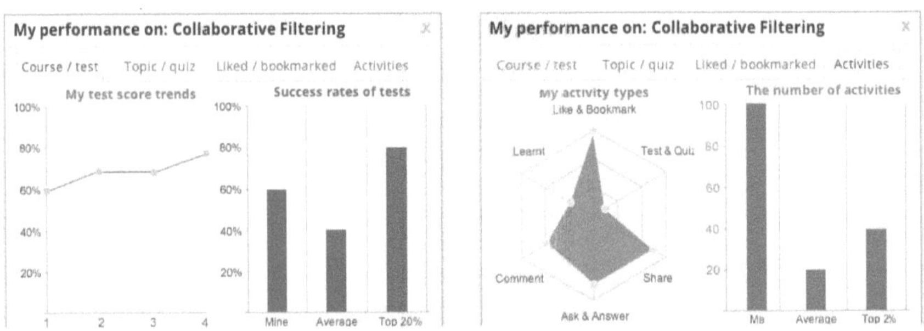

Fig. 3. Pop-up view of performance at a course level

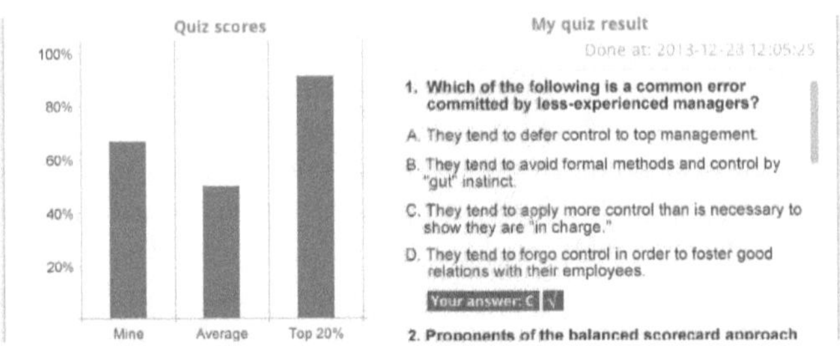

Fig. 4. Pop-up view of performance at a topic level

4.2 Visualisation of Contribution

In a social e-learning environment, learners act not only as learners, but also authors of learning contents. They contribute by, e.g., sharing, commenting, asking, and answering. *Visualisation of ones contribution* potentially encourages contributing more, as seeing each other's contribution may stimulate imitation and competition. By clicking on the button 'My contribution' on a course page or a topic page (Fig. 1 (a)) a pop-up view of the contribution shows, as shown in Fig. 5, presenting comparisons of resources shared, the number of questions asked and answered, and comments.

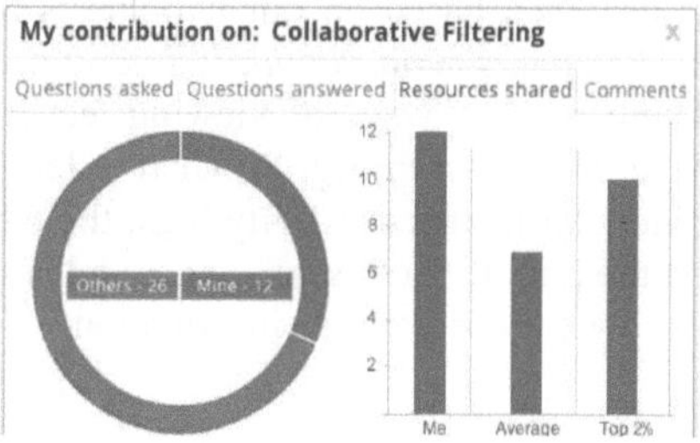

Fig. 5. Pop-up view of contribution, compared to others

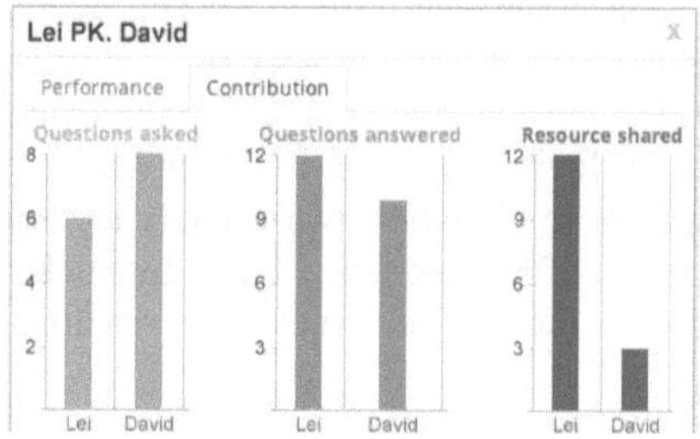

Fig. 6. The PK. mode: one-to-one comparison of contribution of two learners

4.3 The PK. Mode

The PK. mode is designed drawing from educational gamification [18], as an acronym for 'Player Killer'. On a profile page (Fig. 1), by clicking on the button 'PK.', a pop-up view shows, presenting comparisons of *performance* and *contribution* between a learner and the profile page's owner (Fig. 6). Contributions are questions asked and answered, resources, comments shared. Performances include correct tests, topic completion rate, the number of shared ('liked' and bookmarked) resources.

4.4 Visualisation of Learning Path

On a course page or a topic page (see (1) and (2) in Fig. 1), by clicking on the button 'Learning Path', a *learning path visualisation* view pops-up, as shown in Fig. 7. The tree structure graph represents the whole course structure, and the icons represent the learner's progress. For instance, a *hollow circle* means the learner has not learnt this topic yet; a *solid circle* means the learner has already learnt this topic; an *unlocked lock* means the learner is ready to learn this topic; a *locked lock* means the learner should finish learning all the prerequisite topics before start to learn this topic; and the *blue-coloured-background label* with the text 'Up next' recommends the learner that this topic is the most appropriate topic to learn for the next step.

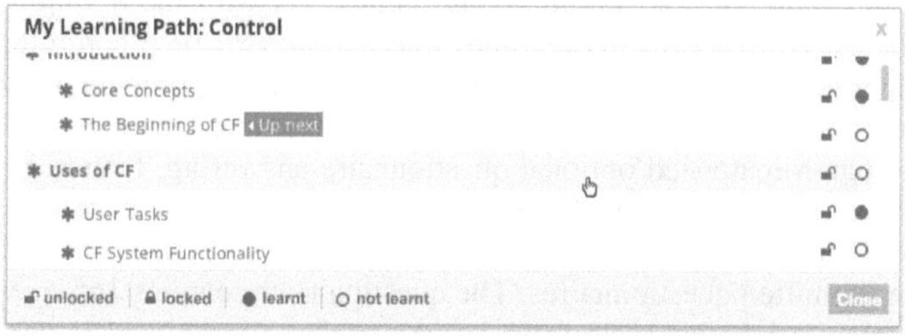

Fig. 7. Pop-up view of learning path

4.5 Visualisation of Activities

Topolor exposes learners' activity logs to learners, and they can 'like' and comment on each other's activity logs. This feature is designed based on our hypothesis that *observation of activity logs of a learner and her peers' can stimulate interactions, hereby improve the system's engagement.* There are two ways of viewing learners' activity logs. One is on the Topolor home page, as shown in Fig. 8, where a learner can filter to view her own activity logs or to view all learners' activity logs; the other is on a profile page (see Fig. 1) by clicking on the button 'Activities', where a learner can view the profile owner's activity logs, to allow various paths to information.

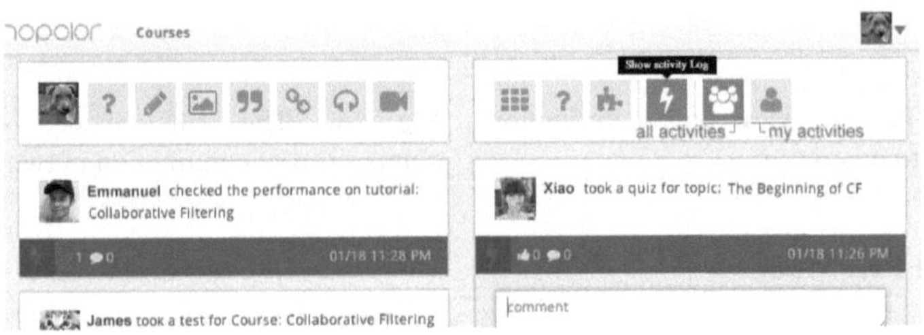

Fig. 8. List of activity logs on the Topolor home page

5 Experimental Study

To investigate students' benefits from Topolor's new features designed based on the multifaceted OSLM, we have started the evaluations from various perspectives such as how and how much these features support and improve learning outcomes by analysing learning behaviour data logged in the database. In this section, to isolate research variables, we focus on students' perceived acceptance of these features. Student perception of technologies is among the determining factors for successful e-learning environments. The technology acceptance model (ATM) [5], incorporating students' perception on the technology's *usefulness* and *ease of use* has the ability to investigate their intention to use a system as a result of a group of perceived qualities, hence interpreting students' desired outcomes. Following ATM, this section reports on the results of perceived *usefulness* and *ease of use* of these new features.

The experiment involved 15 students registered for an MSc module 'Dynamic Web-Based Systems', at University of Warwick, learning a lesson on 'Collaborative Filtering' using Topolor, and familiarizing themselves with the *multifaceted OSLM* features. The experiment was divided into four stages: two time-controlled one-hour learning stages (students sat in the same classroom), one not time-controlled learning stage (students accessed Topolor at their preferred time and location), and finally the survey stage (coordinator-led optional questionnaire answering, feature by feature, to make sure they knew clearly which question referred to which feature). Students were explicitly told that their participation in the survey had no impact on module results. Ten of them submitted questionnaires. The questionnaire contains 165 questions, each of which applies a 5-Likert scale from 1 (*very useless / very hard to use*) to 5 (*very useful / very easy to use*) to evaluate the selected feature's *usefulness* and *ease of use*.

Table 1 compresses these 48 features with the evaluation results including the mean values and standard deviations for their *usefulness* and *ease of use* respectively.

Table 1. The evaluated *multifaceted OSLM*-related features and the evaluation results

	usefulness		ease of use			usefulness		ease of use	
	mean	SD	mean	SD		mean	SD	mean	SD
Home page									
Filter by everyone's activities	4.1	.74	4.2	.63	Filter by my activities	4.3	.48	4.0	.82
Course page									
Learning path - Tree View[@]	4.6	.52	4.5	.71	Performance - Pop-up View[@]	4.3	.67	4.7	.48
Score trends - Line Chart[@]	4.1	.57	4.4	.52	Contribution - Pop-up View[@]	3.8	.79	4.7	.48
Test success rates - Bar Chart[*]	4.2	.63	4.2	.63	Average quiz score - Bar Chart[*]	4.2	.42	4.3	.67
Topic completion - Bar Chart[*]	4.0	.47	4.3	.67	Number of activities - Bar Chart[*]	4.0	.47	4.2	.63
Bookmarked - Bar Chart[*]	3.7	.67	4.4	.52	Questions asked - Bar Chart[*]	3.8	.63	4.6	.52
'Liked' - Bar Chart[*]	4.0	.67	4.4	.70	Questions answered - Bar Chart[*]	3.8	.63	4.4	.70
Activity types - Radar Chart[@]	4.0	.47	4.3	.48	Questions asked - Donut Chart[&]	4.1	.88	4.7	.48
Resources shared - Bar Chart[*]	3.8	.79	4.5	.53	Questions answered - Donut Chart[&]	3.9	.88	4.6	.52
Comments - Bar Chart[*]	3.8	.63	4.5	.53	Resources shared – Donut Chart[&]	3.7	.67	4.4	.70
Comments - Donut Chart[&]	4.1	.74	4.2	.79					
Topic page									
Learning path - Tree View[@]	4.5	.53	4.7	.48	Performance - Pop-up View[@]	4.4	.52	4.7	.48
Contribution - Pop-up View[@]	4.2	.92	4.6	.52	Questions asked - Donut Chart[&]	4.2	.79	4.5	.71
Questions asked - Bar Chart[*]	4.0	.67	4.3	.67	Questions answered- Donut Chart[&]	4.1	.74	4.7	.48
Resources shared - Bar Chart[*]	4.0	.67	4.2	.63	Questions answered -Bar Chart[*]	4.0	.47	4.2	.63
Comments - Bar Chart[*]	4.2	.42	4.6	.52	Resources shared - Donut Chart[&]	3.7	.67	4.3	.48
Comments - Donut Chart[&]	4.2	.63	4.2	.63	My quiz results - Pop-up View[@]	4.3	.48	4.5	.53
View quiz scores - Bar Chart[*]	4.6	.52	4.6	.52					
Resource page									
Author's name and stats	4.0	.67	4.2	.79					
Profile page									
Check my performance	4.6	.52	4.7	.48	Check my contribution	4.3	.67	4.6	.52
PK., compare me with another	4.2	.42	4.3	.67	List of resources shared	4.6	.52	4.4	.52
List of questions asked	4.7	.48	4.4	.52	List of questions answered	4.4	.70	4.3	.48
List of courses learned	4.6	.70	4.4	.52	List of topics learned	4.6	.70	4.2	.63
List of topics learnt	4.5	.71	4.4	.70	Statistics for the profile's owner	4.7	.48	4.3	.48
Waterfall list of activity logs	3.6	.97	4.5	.53	Like an activity log	4.1	.99	4.3	.67
Comment on an activity log	4.2	.92	4.4	.52					

[@]: my data; [&]: comparison between me and the rest of the class;
[*]: comparison between me, the whole class and the top 20% of the class.

As shown in Table 1, the mean values of the perceived *usefulness* of these features rank between 3.6 and 4.7, with standard deviations between 0.42 and 0.99. All the reported mean values are larger than 3 (the neutral response), suggesting students' attitudes to be generally positive. Table 2 also shows that the mean values of the perceived *ease of use* of these features rank between 4.0 and 4.7, and the standard deviations are between 0.48 and 0.82. As all these mean values are greater than 3, we infer most students found these features to be relatively easy to use.

Cronbach's alpha is adopted to measure the reliability of the test. A *Cronbach's Alpha* of 0.8 is considered as highly reliable [4]. The *Cronbach's Alpha* value of *usefulness* is 0.96 and that of *ease of use* is 0.98 (both values are considerably larger than 0.8), suggesting a high level of reliability of the results.

6 Discussion and Conclusion

We introduced a *multifaceted open social learner model (OSLM)*, and populated it with features. The *multifaceted OSLM* visualises not only learners' *performance* but also their *contribution* to a learning community, potentially better catering for social e-learning, where learners are both knowledge consumer and producer. Additionally, the *multifaceted OSLM* provides various comparison modes that allow for visualising the differences between learners' learning history (e.g., in terms of test score trends), between her and another learner, and between her and a group (i.e., the whole class and the top 20% of the class). Moreover, the *multifaceted OSLM* is integrated and adapted to learning contents, so that its ubiquity and context-awareness could enhance any system's adaptivity and adaptability, which potentially improves usability.

We also reported on an experimental study and the evaluation, which illustrates a generally high level of learner acceptance of our proposed *multifaceted OSLM* features. This result may appear possibly counter-intuitive, due to the high number of features introduced, which may seem complex to a learner. In fact, in our previous study [16], we have found that using a Facebook-like appearance, and a game-inspired paradigm, quickly transforms learners into system experts. The main study limitation is the low number of participants, although *Cronbach's Alpha* suggests a high level of reliability of the results. Moreover, Topolor has been opened to public (*www.topolor.com*), with larger learner cohorts expected in the near future, allowing for feedback, use data and suggestions collecting, in further studies. Other evaluation perspectives are on our agenda, e.g., if learners feel in control in interactions with *multifaceted OSLM*; if and how *multifaceted OSLM* leads learners to access recommended learning contents and to communicate with others, if and to what extent it promotes metacognition and makes Topolor more engaging.

It is noteworthy that, apart from the focus of this paper, i.e., the social interaction and visualisation parts, the proposed *multifaceted OSLM* also maintains attributes that record learning status such as "know", "unknown" and "learning", which inherit in traditional user modelling approach in adaptive educational hypermedia area. Besides, though the visualisation of comparisons between a learner and her learning group e.g. top 20% learners of the class hides other learners' personal data, in a "PK." mode it may raise ethic issues in all learners being able to view each other's data. Therefore, further studies are needed to solve this issue, e.g., by introducing privacy management mechanisms to allow learners to expose data to different groups in different ways.

Other suggests on future works include: (1) metacognitive activity visualisation to promote self-reflection, self-direction and transparency; (2) adaptive visualisation-modes to provide personalised visualisation of the same data.

References

1. Brusilovsky, P., Hsiao, I.-H., Folajimi, Y.: QuizMap: Open Social Student Modeling and Adaptive Navigation Support with TreeMaps. In: Kloos, C.D., Gillet, D., Crespo García, R.M., Wild, F., Wolpers, M., et al. (eds.) EC-TEL 2011. LNCS, vol. 6964, pp. 71–82. Springer, Heidelberg (2011)
2. Bull, S., Gardner, P.: Highlighting Learning Across a Degree with an Independent Open Learner Model. In: Proceedings of the 2009 Conference on Artificial Intelligence in Education: Building Learning Systems That Care: From Knowledge Representation to Affective Modelling, pp. 275–282. IOS Press, Amsterdam (2009)
3. Bull, S., Kay, J.: Open Learner Models as Drivers for Metacognitive Processes. In: Azevedo, R., Aleven, V. (eds.) International Handbook of Metacognition and Learning Technologies, pp. 349–365. Springer, New York (2013)
4. Carmines, E.G., Zeller, R.A.: Reliability and validity assessment. Sage (1979)
5. Davis, F.D.: Perceived usefulness, perceived ease of use, and user acceptance of information technology. MIS Q., 319–340 (1989)
6. Dimitrova, V.: STyLE-OLM: Interactive open learner modelling. Int. J. Artif. Intell. Educ. 13(1), 35–78 (2003)
7. Downes, S.: Connectivism and connective knowledge: Essays on meaning and learning networks. National Research Council Canada (2012)
8. Hsiao, I.-H., Bakalov, F., Brusilovsky, P., König-Ries, B.: Open Social Student Modeling: Visualizing Student Models with Parallel Introspective Views. In: Konstan, J.A., Conejo, R., Marzo, J.L., Oliver, N., et al. (eds.) UMAP 2011. LNCS, vol. 6787, pp. 171–182. Springer, Heidelberg (2011)
9. Kay, J.: Stereotypes, Student Models and Scrutability. In: Gauthier, G., VanLehn, K., Frasson, C., et al. (eds.) ITS 2000. LNCS, vol. 1839, pp. 19–30. Springer, Heidelberg (2000)
10. Kop, R.: The challenges to connectivist learning on open online networks: Learning experiences during a massive open online course. Int. Rev. Res. Open Distance Learn. 12(3), 19–38 (2011)
11. Kurilovas, E., et al.: Web 3.0–Based personalisation of learning objects in virtual learning environments. Comput. Hum. Behav. 30, 654–662 (2014)
12. Liang, M., et al.: Collaborative e-learning through open social student modeling and Progressive Zoom navigation. In: 2012 8th International Conference on Collaborative Computing: Networking, Applications and Worksharing, pp. 252–261 (2012)
13. Long, Y., Aleven, V.: Supporting students' self-regulated learning with an open learner model in a linear equation tutor. In: Lane, H.C., Yacef, K., Mostow, J., Pavlik, P. (eds.) AIED 2013. LNCS, vol. 7926, pp. 219–228. Springer, Heidelberg (2013)
14. Shi, L., et al.: A social personalized adaptive e-learning environment: a case study in Topolor. IADIS Int. J. WWWInternet. 11, 2 (2013)
15. Shi, L., Awan, M.S.K., Cristea, A.I.: Evaluating System Functionality in Social Personalized Adaptive E-Learning Systems. In: Hernández-Leo, D., Ley, T., Klamma, R., Harrer, A., et al. (eds.) EC-TEL 2013. LNCS, vol. 8095, pp. 633–634. Springer, Heidelberg (2013)
16. Shi, L., et al.: Social e-learning in topolor: a case study. In: Proceedings of the 7th IADIS Conference e-Learning 2013, pp. 57–64. IADIS Press, Prague (2013)
17. Shi, L., et al.: Social Personalized Adaptive E-Learning Environment: Topolor - Implementation and Evaluation. In: Lane, H.C., et al. (eds.) Artificial Intelligence in Education, pp. 708–711. Springer, Heidelberg (2013)

18. Shi, L., et al.: To build light gamification upon social interactions: requirement analysis for the next version of Topolor. In: Proceedings of the 6th York Doctoral Symposium on Computer Science and Electronics (2013)
19. Shi, L., et al.: Towards Understanding Learning Behavior Patterns in Social Adaptive Personalized E-Learning Systems. In: Proceedings of The 19th Americas Conference on Information Systems, pp. 1–10. Association for Information Systems, Chicago (2013)
20. Siemens, G.: What is the unique idea in Connectivism. Blog - Httpconnectivismcacgi-Binmtmt-Tbcgi 112 (2008)
21. Tschofen, C., Mackness, J.: Connectivism and dimensions of individual experience. Int. Rev. Res. Open Distance Learn. 13(1), 124–143 (2012)
22. Vassileva, J.: Motivating participation in social computing applications: a user modeling perspective. User Model. User-Adapt. Interact. 22(1-2), 177–201 (2012)

What Psychological Factors Enhance a Language Learning Community? Toward Effective CSCL Design for Language Learning Based on a CoI Framework

Masanori Yamada[1], Yoshiko Goda[2], Hideya Matsukawa[3], Kojiro Hata[4], and Seisuke Yasunami[2]

[1] Faculty of Arts and Science, Kyushu University, 744, Motooka, Nishiku, Fukuoka, 8190395 Japan
mark@mark-lab.net
[2] Research Center for Higher Education, Kumamoto University, 2-39-1, Kurokami, Kumamoto, 8608555, Japan
{ygoda,yasunami}@kumamoto-u.ac.jp
[3] Center for Education in Liberal Arts and Sciences, 1-16, Machikaneyamacho, Toyonaka, Osaka, 5600043, Japan
hideya@celas.osaka-u.ac.jp
[4] Faculty of Modern Social Studies, Otemae University, 6-42, Ochayashocho, Nishinomiya, Hyogo, 6620961, Japan
k-hata@otemae.ac.jp

Abstract. The current study investigated the relationship between psychological factors and learning behaviors related to the application of a community of inquiry (CoI) framework for learning English as a foreign language (EFL). An online asynchronous discussion was examined, and data included questionnaires assessing perceived psychological factors and communication logs related to the efficacy of the CoI. Results of a path analysis showed that perceived social presence plays an important role in enhancing perceived cognitive presence, which indirectly increases social interaction and deeper discussions.

Keywords: Collaborative learning, Community of Inquiry, Social Interaction.

1 Introduction

As the importance of practical knowledge and skills, particularly 21st century skills [1] such as way of thinking, citizenship, and communication and collaboration, is addressed by educational organizations worldwide, community-based learning environments are gaining popularity. Computer-Supported Collaborative Learning (CSCL) has been examined for years and is often applied to several educational settings. For instance, several researchers have shown effects of collaboration on language learning through active interaction [12]. Furthermore, the effects of the communication medium on language learning in a CSCL have been revealed, particularly in the context of developing self-awareness during video-mediated communication [15].

E. Popescu et al. (Eds.): ICWL 2014, LNCS 8613, pp. 43–55, 2014.

One key component to designing a CSCL for language learning is to promote active social interaction. Long (1989) indicated that social interaction promotes communication and language acquisition through the active negotiation of meaning and semantics [10]. Practical communication skills are acquired through this negotiation, which is important for learners when faced with communication problems due to a lack of language knowledge. Gass and Torres (2005) suggested the importance of active interaction between learners to obtain effective and comprehensive input to aid performance [5]. In assessing the role of social media on language learning, several studies have revealed the importance of social interaction on learning, especially the relationship between the use of social cues and active interaction [13], as well as the relationship between social interaction and learning performance [16]. Overall, it appears that social interaction has a positive effect on language learning.

However, in addition to language proficiency, a learner's communication style factors into the enhancing role of social interaction in a CSCL for language learning. In order to design effective collaborative language learning in a CSCL, various psychological factors should be investigated.

The goal of the present study was to investigate the elements contributing to the enhancement of collaborative learning in an English learning community. This was accomplished through the design, development, and evaluation of a CSCL system for language learning that used a "Community of Inquiry" (CoI) framework developed by Garrison and Anderson (2003)[3].

2 Community of Inquiry (CoI) Framework

A CoI framework consists of three elements: social presence, cognitive presence, and teaching presence. Social presence is defined as "the ability of participants to identify with the community, communicate purposefully in a trusting environment, and develop interpersonal relationships by way of projecting their individual personalities" [3]. Cognitive presence is enhanced by integrating ideas, exploring relevant information, and so on [3]. Teaching presence is defined as the design, facilitation and direction of cognition and social processes for the purpose of realizing personally meaningful and educationally worthwhile learning outcomes [3]. A CoI is "an environment where participants collaboratively construct knowledge through sustained dialogue, which makes possible personal meaning making through opportunities to negotiate understanding [2]. Finally, a CoI provides viewpoints for evaluating the learning environment and learning community, which leads to assessing the design used for collaborative learning.

Goda and Yamada (2012) investigated the relationship between these three CoI components in a Bulletin Board System (BBS), which is part of Asynchronous Computer-Mediated Communications (ACMC) [6]. Their findings revealed that the teaching and cognitive presence were significantly correlated with discussion satisfaction, and social presence was positively associated with the number of utterances.

However, their findings did not mention the relationship between perceived psychological factors and learning behaviors such as the promotion of social interaction and idea integration during online communication using ACMC. Furthermore, they did not suggest a design direction for an effective CSCL based on a CoI framework. The present study addressed these limitations with the following goals:

1. investigate the relationship between perceived factors and learning behaviors for effective CSCL design
2. consider designing collaborative learning support system based on results of the present study and previous research
3. evaluate the present system based on a CoI framework

In the present study, we focused on a learner-centered learning environment. Therefore, we examined social and cognitive presence in the current study.

3 Experiment 1

Experiment 1 investigated the relationship between perceived CoI factors focused on social and cognitive presence, and expressive social and cognitive presence during an English class using ACMC. This was done to determine an effective CSCL design.

3.1 Subjects and Procedure

Seventy-five freshmen at a University participated in Experiment 1 (Male: 38, Female: 37). These students had minimal computer skills and knowledge (such as keyboard typing) required to participate. The online discussion activities gave students additional opportunities to practice their English communication skills out of class. Online news material, "Voice of America (VoA; www.voiceofamerica.com)" was used to create authentic listening and reading materials for students. Increasing comprehensive input, such as reading or audio materials in the target language, promotes quality interaction through negotiation of meaning [9] during second language acquisition (SLA).

The discussion topic, "Three items to carry during an earthquake," was selected, considering students' interest in enhancing motivation, being engaged, and relating previous knowledge and/or experiences to the topic [8]. The online discussion was conducted in the bulletin board system (BBS) of the learning management system (LMS). All students were required to participate in all activities. Each group consisted of four to six students. Students were randomly assigned to each group. Each discussion lasted two weeks, and after one week, a face-to-face instruction was inserted to provide intervention and facilitation from the instructor.

3.2 Data Collection

The CoI questionnaire was conducted at the end of the semester. Students' CoI level and learning behavior were measured. The CoI survey, according to Swan et al. (2008) displayed in Appendix A, consists of 34 five-point Likert scale items, and internal consistencies, reported with Cronbach's alpha, were 0.91 for Social Presence

(SP: e.g., "Getting to know other course participants gave me a sense of belonging in the course") and 0.95 for Cognitive Presence (CP: e.g., "Combining new information helped me answer questions raised during course activities") [11].

The CoI relationship was evaluated, and students' comments regarding the learner's utterances in discussion activities were encoded with CoI indicators (expressive social and cognitive presences) [2], displayed in Appendix.B in order to determine learning behaviors. The instructor provided most of the feedback and intervention when meeting with students in the classroom. The SP and CP of the CoI provided the focus for asynchronous communication during this study. There were three categories with 12 indicators for SP, and four indicators for CP were adopted for encoding. To increase credibility, they discussed inconsistent encodings and came to agreement for all comments. Garrison et al (2006) highlighted the importance of the unit of analysis for CoI coding [4]. For several years during the 20th century, researchers used the sentence as the unit of analysis [7]. Sentences were employed as a unit of analysis because comments indicated more information. However, the level of detail made encoding procedures more complicated and interpretation much more difficult.

3.3 Results

Perception and Utterances of Social and Cognitive Presence. Fifty-six learners completed the questionnaire and were engaged in the online discussion. Table 1 shows the average CoI questionnaire score for each presence subscale. In order to confirm reliability of each presence in this instrument, Cronbach's alphas were calculated. Table 2 shows the scores related to social and cognitive presence.

Table 1. Average of total scores and Cronbach's alphas for the CoI questionnaire (social and cognitive presence) in Experiment 1

Items	Average Total Score (S.D.)	Cronbach's alpha
Social Presence (9 items)	31.25 (4.85)	0.74
Cognitive Presence (12 items)	41.96 (5.85)	0.86

Path Analysis. We conducted a path analysis using STATA 12 in order to investigate the relationship between perceived sense of, and behaviors concerned with CoI. We used the total SP scores, CP questionnaire items, which consisted of the CoI scale mentioned above, and the total number of SP and CP utterances as observation variables for this analysis. Fig. 1 shows results of the path analysis. Perceived social presence affects both perceived cognitive presence and utterances of social presence. On the other hand, perceived cognitive presence reduces the number of utterances concerned with social presence. These results suggest that through social interaction, participants were engaged in active discussion as part of a cognitive learning process.

Table 2. Average number of utterances for each presence

Presence	Ave.
Social Presence	3.77
Cognitive Presence	1.55

3.4 Discussion for Experiment 1: Effectiveness of the CSCL Design

Results show that perceived social presence plays an important role in active CoI, as previous research suggested that social presence is the fundamental factor in CoI [3]. Social interaction seems to promote a comfortable atmosphere to discuss the CoI, confirming significant relationships between "perceived social presence," "perceived cognitive presence," and "utterance of social presence," as well as the relationship between "utterance of social presence" and "utterance of cognitive presence." Results also indicated that perceived social presence has a positive effect on expressive social and cognitive presence directly and indirectly. In order to design an effective CSCL, the establishment of social presence is one key factor that can include the use of emoticons and reply functions. We confirmed several significant relationships between each presence; however, the number of utterances related to social and cognitive presence seem to be small, especially the utterances for cognitive presence (such as information integration and promotion of deep discussion). Cognitive learning support tools, such as a concept map, might be an important means for enhancing active discussion [14].

4 Experiment 2

One goal of the present study was to evaluate the effects of CSCL functions on the establishment of social and cognitive interaction, which are based on our CoI findings. The purpose of Experiment 2 was to investigate the causal relationship between CSCL functions, perceived social and cognitive presence, and expressive social and cognitive presence. To accomplish this, we used a CSCL system for language learning [17].

4.1 Subjects and Procedure

One hundred and sixty-six freshmen at a University participated in Experiment 2. This experiment was conducted as a class activity. These participants also had the minimal computer skills (e.g., word-processing and email proficiency) required for participation. Subjects were required to participate in an online discussion during the class and discuss a topic provided by an instructor in English for forty minutes. Each group consisted of four or five subjects. Group members were randomly assigned to each group. The discussion topic was, "What do you think about the best ways to select better candidates as future university students?" which considered the subjects' background knowledge.

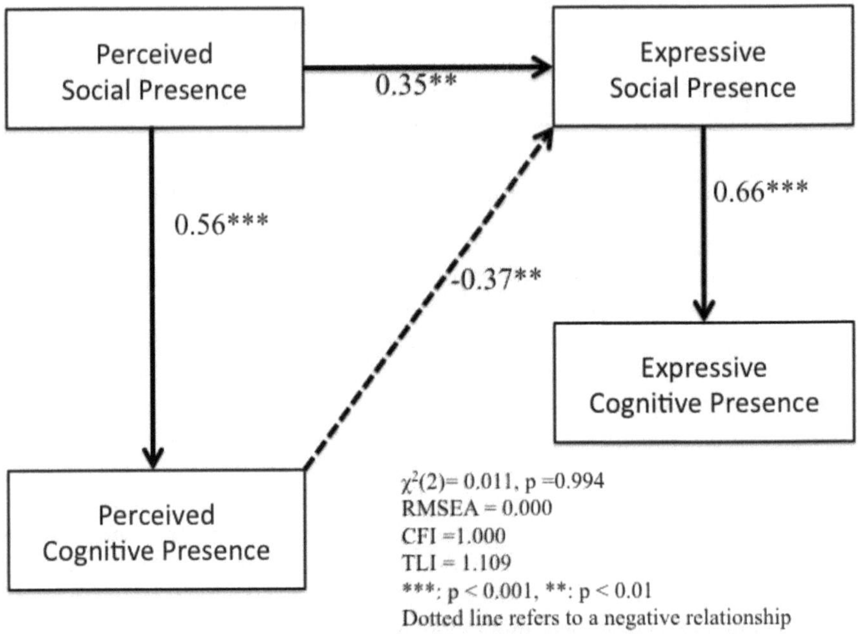

Fig. 1. Path model of the relationship between perceived and expressive presence

The CSCL system, which was used in this study, consisted of a chatbot and a concept map tool "CD-map." The chatbot asks subjects to answer questions regarding the discussion topic, using the Socratic method, before having a discussion with group members. This seems to promote cognitive learning. The "CD-map" allows a subject to chat with group members while creating a concept map. This function consists of two parts: a communication part in the left pane and idea construction concept map in the right pane. This function allows learners to post their ideas and opinions, register postings as "favorites" (similar to the "like" button in Facebook), use emoticons, and create relationships (such as cause-and-result relationships between postings). In order to create relationships, learners click and drag a posting object in the left pane to the right pane, and then learners create relationships between postings using arrow lines in a concept map. Fig. 2 shows the interface of this system.

Subjects were divided into four groups: with or without a chatbot and with or without concept map tool in "CD-map." Subjects in the group, which has the system without a concept map, ware allowed to use chat area for communication with other subjects (a concept map was not displayed). Subjects did not use the other system; in other words, subjects used one system/type. Subject numbers in each group were as follows: 39 subjects who had a chatbot and a concept map, 19 subjects who had a chatbot without a concept map, 37 subjects who had a concept map without a chatbot, and 16 subjects who had neither the chatbot nor the concept map (only chat area was displayed).

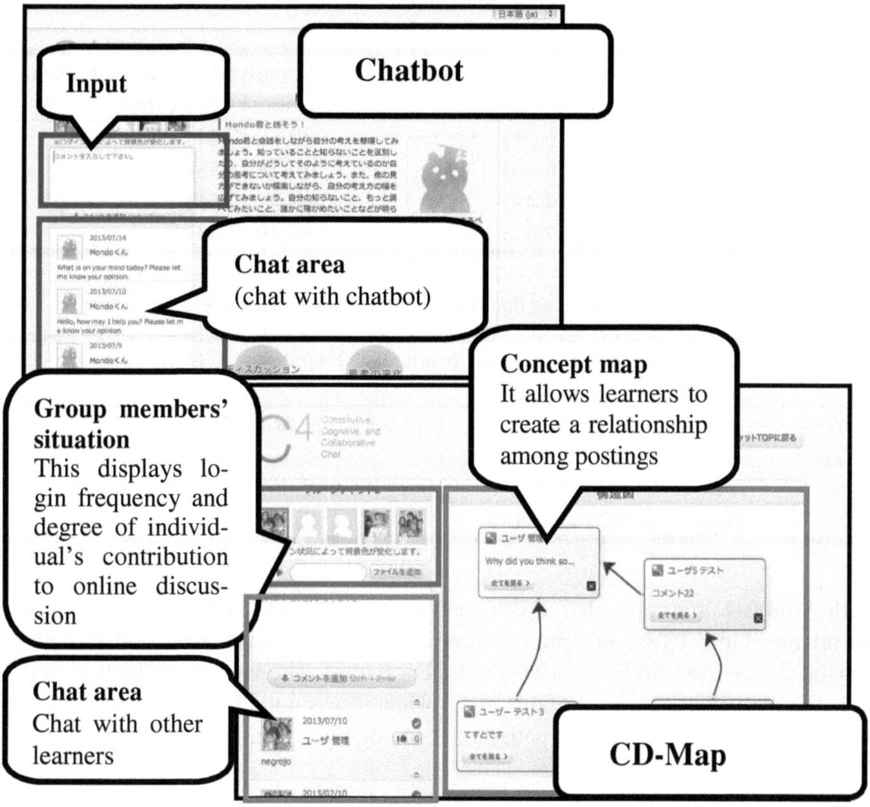

Fig. 2. Interface of the CSCL system used in Experiment 2

4.2 Data Collection

The methods of data collection were the same as Experiment 1. We used the same questionnaire for perceived social and cognitive presence and indicator for the categorization of utterances into expressive social and cognitive presence.

4.3 Results

Perception and Utterances of Social and Cognitive Presence. One hundred eleven subjects completed the questionnaire and took part in the online discussion. Table 1 shows the average total score for each presence (SD) in each group. Reliability for each presence (Cronbach's alpha) are as follows: social presence (9 items): 0.84, cognitive presence (13 items): 0.91. Each reliability value was statistically acceptable, owing to scores over 0.8.

Table 3. Average total scores on the CoI questionnaire (social and cognitive presence) in Experiment 2

Chatbot	Concept map	Perceived social presence (min: 9; max: 45)	Perceived Cognitive presence (min: 13; max: 65)
Yes	Yes	29.00 (6.31)	39.10 (7.44)
Yes	No	30.63 (6.46)	40.26 (8.58)
No	Yes	30.16 (4.49)	40.41 (7.56)
No	No	27.56 (7.47)	36.19 (9.47)

Table 4. Average number of utterances in each presence

Chatbot	Concept map	Expressive social presence	Expressive Cognitive presence
Yes	Yes	6.74 (6.26)	2.66 (2.29)
Yes	No	11.31 (8.02)	2.16 (2.24)
No	Yes	6.18 (5.78)	2.05 (1.88)
No	No	5.75 (3.71)	1.36 (1.74)

Path Analysis. We conducted a path analysis using STATA 12 in order to determine the relationship between functions, perceived factors, and expressive factors. Dummy variables were used to differentiate the function used. The variable "Chatbot" was set to 1 when the chatbot was available and 0 when it was not. "Concept map" was set in the same way. Fig. 3 shows the path model among these relationships.

5 Discussion and Future Work

We conducted practical and comparative research within a University class in order to consider the effective design of a CSCL using a CoI framework. The chatbot and concept maps have slightly significant effects on expressive presence; however, a concept map had a negative effect on the enhancement of expressive social presence. One possible reason for this is that the concept map allows subjects to focus on constructing their own ideas without sharing the concept map function. One of the features of social presence is socio-emotional communication (e.g., using emoticons). Thus, a concept map seems to reduce opportunities to create a social atmosphere during an online discussion. However, the chatbot, which also allows subjects to construct their own ideas during communication, had a positive effect on the enhancement of expressive social presence, but not on expressive cognitive presence. This might be because the chatbot function seems to enhance readiness to communicate with group members. Thus, such cognitive tools might provide important means for enhancing active discussion.

Expressive cognitive presence had a direct positive effect on perceived social presence and an indirect effect on perceived cognitive presence. Several expressions, such as the question and statement of a stance, are concerned with both social and cognitive presence; therefore, expressive cognitive presence can lead to the enhancement of perceived social and cognitive presence.

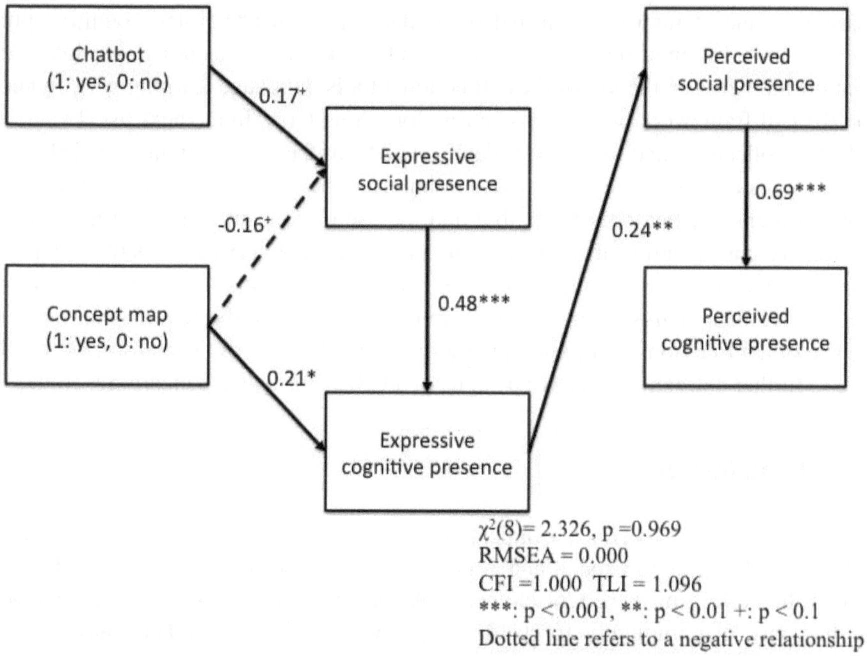

Fig. 3. Path model assessing the relationship between functions, perceived presence and, expressive presence

In Experiment 1, a path from the perceived to the expressive appeared in the model, but in Experiment 2, a path from the expressive to the perceived existed with statistical significance in the model. The differences of two experiments' results might have been caused by presence or absence of the collaborative learning functions, chatbot and concept map. The functions might directly work on learners' behavior (i.e., utterances) since they were designed to support establishing learners' social and cognitive presences. Interactions with the functions help learners express their ideas in the group discussion, and this would be a reason to have the path from the expressive to the perceived in the Experiment 2 model. Then, behavior came first and the behavior might affect their perceived presences. On the other hand, without the functions, students might have to interpret situations and use a cognitive approach first, which might case the path from the perceived to the expressive. Previous research have not come to the agreement about the relationships between the perceived and the expressive in CoI and further investigation should be necessary.

Future research should address the following three points. One involves the influence of sharing the concept map function. Yamada (2010) suggests that sharing a concept map enhances perceived social presence [14]. The relationship between sharing a concept map function and the enhancement of social and cognitive presence should be investigated. Secondly, future research should investigate the relationship between the use of these functional tools, language learning performance, and the CoI framework out-of-class setting for a long term. In the next fiscal year, we will be collecting and analyzing data related to these two points. Third point recommends to investigate the concrete relationship between use of the functions used in experiment 2. Utterances in chatbot and the use of concept map seem to affect on the quality and quantity of utterances in chat with other learners. Chatbot seems to support readiness for online discussion in English. This research focused on quantitative data analysis, but next research should analyze the relationship between the use of the functions by mixing qualitative research methods. Therefore, we will be able to further determine effective designs of a CSCL for language learning.

6 Conclusion

The results in two experiments indicated that the communication tool added several functions, which support social and cognitive learning, promoted expressive elements of CoI directly. Expressive CoI elements played important roles in the enhancement of the sense of community for learning. In CoI model, researchers indicated the relationship between social and cognitive presences [2], [3], [4], however, it was not clear what element(s) supports this relationship. This research suggested the learning system design which is possible to support active collaborative learning based on CoI framework. However, several points, which we should improve, were also found, as mentioned in Discussion. Future research should be required to be conducted, in order to establish effective model for the design of CSCL using CoI framework.

References

1. The Assessment and Teaching of 21st Century Skills, http://atc21s.org/
2. Garrison, D.R.: E-learning in the 21st Century: A Framework for Research and Practice, 2nd edn. Routledge, New York (2011)
3. Garrison, D.R., Anderson, T.: E-learning in the 21st century: a Framework for Research and Practice. Routledge Falmer, London (2003)
4. Garrison, D.R., Cleveland-Innes, M., Koole, M., Kappelman, J.: Revisiting Methodological Issues in the Analysis of Transcripts: Negotiated Coding and reliability. Internet. High. Educ. 9, 1–8 (2006)

5. Gass, S.M., Torre, M.J.A.: Attention when? An Investigation of the Ordering Effect of Input and Interaction. Studies in Second Language Acquisition 27, 1–31 (2005)
6. Goda, Y., Yamada, M.: Application of CoI to Design CSCL for EFL Online Asynchronous Discussion. In: Akyol, Z., Garrison, D.R. (eds.) Educational Community of Inquiry: Theoretical Framework, Research and Practice, pp. 295–316. IGI Global (2012)
7. Harre, R.: The Discursive Turn in Social Psychology. In: Schiffrin, D., Tannen, D., Hamilton, H.E. (eds.) The Hand-book of Discourse Analysis. Blackwell Publishing, Massachusetts (2001)
8. Keller, J.M.: Motivational Design for Learning and Performance: The ARCS Model Approach. Springer, New York (2010)
9. Krashen, S.: The Input Hypothesis: Issues and Implications. Longman, London (1985)
10. Long, M.: Task, Group, and Task-Group Interactions. University of Hawaii's Working Papers in ESL 8, 1–26 (1989)
11. Swan, K., Shea, P., Richardson, J., Ice, P., Garrison, D.R., Cleveland-Innes, M., Arbaugh, J.B.: Validating a Measure-ment Tool of Presence in Online Communities of Inquiry. E-Mentor 2, 1–12 (2008)
12. Warschauer, M.: Comparing Face-to-Face and Electronic Discussion in the Second Language Classroom. CALICO J. 13, 7–26 (1996)
13. Wingham, C.R., Chanier, T.: Study of Verbal and Nonverbal Communication in SecondLife – the ARCHI21 experience. ReCALL 25, 63–84 (2013)
14. Yamada, M.: Development and Evaluation of CSCL Based on Social Presence. In: Sanchez, J., Zhang, K. (eds.) Proceedings of World Conference on E-Learning in Corporate, Government, Healthcare, and Higher Education, pp. 2304–2309. Association for the Advancement of Computing in Education (2010), `http://www.editlib.org/p/35889`
15. Yamada, M., Akahori, K.: Awareness and Performance through Self-and Partner's Image in Videoconferencing. CALICO Journal 27, 1–25 (2009)
16. Yamada, M.: The Role of Social Presence in Learner-Centered Communicative Language Learning using Synchronous Computer-Mediated Communication: Experimental Study. Comp. Educ. 52, 820–833 (2009)
17. Yamada, M., Goda, Y., Matsukawa, H., Hata, K., Yasunami, S.: C4 (C quad): Development of the Application for Language Learning Based on Social and Cognitive presence. In: Bradley, L., Thouësny, S. (eds.) 20 Years of EUROCALL: Learning from the Past, Looking to the Future, Évora, Portugal. Proceedings of the 2013 EUROCALL Conference, pp. 258–264 (2013)

Appendix

Appendix A. Community of Inquiry Instrument (Swan et al, 2008)

#	Category	Item
1	Teaching presence	The instructor clearly communicated important course topics
2		The instructor clearly communicated important course goals
3		The instructor provided clear instructions on how to participate in course learning activities.
4		The instructor clearly communicated important due dates/time frames for learning activities.
5		The instructor was helpful in identifying areas of agreement and disagreement on course topics that helped me to learn.
6		The instructor was helpful in guiding the class towards understanding course topics in a way that helped me clarify my thinking
7		The instructor helped to keep course participants engaged and participating in productive dialogue.
8		The instructor helped keep the course participants on task in a way that helped me to learn.
9		The instructor encouraged course participants to explore new concepts in this course.
10		Instructor actions reinforced the development of a sense of community among course participants.
11		The instructor helped to focus discussion on relevant issues in a way that helped me to learn.
12		The instructor provided feedback that helped me understand my strengths and weaknesses relative to the course's goals and objectives.
13		The instructor provided feedback in a timely fashion.
14	Social presence	Getting to know other course participants gave me a sense of belonging in the course.
15		I was able to form distinct impressions of some course participants.
16		Online or web-based communication is an excellent medium for social interaction.
17		I felt comfortable conversing through the online medium.
18		I felt comfortable participating in the course discussions.
19		I felt comfortable interacting with other course participants.
20		I felt comfortable disagreeing with other course participants while still maintaining a sense of trust.
21		I felt that my point of view was acknowledged by other course participants.
22		Online discussions help me to develop a sense of collaboration.
23	Cognitive presence	Problems posed increased my interest in course issues.
24		Course activities piqued my curiosity.
25		I felt motivated to explore content related questions.
26		I utilized a variety of information sources to explore problems posed in this course
27		Brainstorming and finding relevant information helped me resolve content related questions.
28		Online discussions were valuable in helping me appreciate different perspectives.
29		Combining new information helped me answer questions raised in course activities.
30		Learning activities helped me construct explanations/solutions.
31		Reflection on course content and discussions helped me understand fundamental concepts in this class.
32		I can describe ways to test and apply the knowledge created in this course.
33		I have developed solutions to course problems that can be applied in practice.
34		I can apply the knowledge created in this course to my work or other non-class related activities.

Appendix B. Social and Cognitive presence indicator (Garrison, 2011)

Social presence (pp. 38-39)

Category	Indicator	Definition
Interpersonal communication	Affective expression	Conventional expressions of emotion or unconventional expressions of emotion, including repetitious punctuation, emoticons, etc.
	Self-disclosure	Presents biographies, details of life outside of class, or expressing vulnerability
	Use of humor	Teasing, cajoling, irony, understatement, sarcasm
Open communication	Continuing a thread	Using the reply feature of software, rather than starting a new thread
	Quoting from others' messages	Using software features to quote another's message in its entirety, or cutting and pasting selections from others' messages
	Referring explicitly to others' messages	Direct references to contents of others' posts
	Asking questions	Asking questions of other students or the moderator
	Complimenting, expressing appreciation	Complimenting others or the contents of others' messages
	Expressing agreement	Expressing agreement with others or the content of others' messages
Cohesive	Vocatives	Addressing or referring to participants by name
	Addresses or refers to the group using inclusive pronouns	Addresses the group as "we," "us," "our," etc.
	Phatics, salutations	Communication that serves a purely social function: greetings, closures

Cognitive presence (p. 52)

Phase	Descriptor	Indicator
Triggering event	Evocative(inductive)	Recognize problem Puzzlement
Exploration	Inquisitive(divergent)	Divergence Information exchange Suggestions Brainstorming Intuitive leaps
Integration	Tentative(convergent)	Convergence Synthesis Solutions
Resolution	Committed(deductive)	Apply Test Defend

Open Badges: Challenges and Opportunities

Jelena Jovanovic and Vladan Devedzic

University of Belgrade, Serbia
{jeljov,devedzic}@gmail.com

Abstract. The paper looks at the increasingly popular concept of Open Badges (OBs) and the technology that supports it, and provides several insights that might help researchers and practitioners decide on how to make the best use of OBs in specific educational settings. In spite of the current big hype around OBs among practitioners, academic literature on them is still scarce. There is a number of challenges that developers and the wider educational community face when it comes to developing and enacting an OB system – from pedagogical and motivational ones, to technological, to those related to institutional policies and to validity and credibility of badges. By discussing these challenges, the paper offers a critical overview and a reality check of practical opportunities for using OBs, thus indicating several avenues to inspire further research.

Keywords: Digital Badges, Open Badges (OBs) Initiative, Roles of OBs, OB technology.

1 Introduction

Open Badge (OB) is a digital recognition of someone's achievement or status. It is typically awarded by a learning provider or an employer for completing a certain task (tasks) and/or attaining a certain goal (goals). The issuer creates the criteria that one needs to fulfil in order to 'win' the badge. These criteria are embedded in the badge itself in the form of metadata, along with the information about the issuer, the date when the badge was issued, link(s) to the evidence of the acquired skills/knowledge/competence and the like.

The concept of OBs and the technology that supports it have emerged from a collaborative project of MacArthur Foundation (http://www.macfound.org/), HASTAC (http://www.hastac.org/) and Mozilla Learning team (https://wiki.mozilla.org/Learning), and have continued to progress as a community effort known by the names such as Open Badges, Open Badges initiative, and Open Badges framework (http://openbadges.org/).

An important distinctive feature of the OBs framework is its support for: i) gathering and keeping in one (digital) space badges that originate from different sources, and ii) combining selected badges into custom profiles [1]. Another distinguishing feature is the self-sufficiency of OBs in the sense that they carry all the information one would need to understand and value the achievement/status they refer to. This feature significantly eases the transfer of credentials across different contexts and

E. Popescu et al. (Eds.): ICWL 2014, LNCS 8613, pp. 56–65, 2014.

institutional boundaries, and makes OBs highly suitable as boundary objects in designing and evaluating learning [2].

Even though digital badges are not a new phenomenon, their use prior to the emergence of the OBs initiative was largely associated with isolated efforts of individual organizations, and there was no systematic approach to issuing and using badges. The technology that is in development within the OBs initiative is opening possibilities for making full use of numerous educational opportunities available through different forms of formal and informal education. Furthermore, it is enabling individuals to get recognition for their learning achievements regardless of the chosen form/place of learning. These novel and unique features of OBs are nicely summarized in [3; p.3]: "While similar in format, Open Badges are intended to have wider value outside the community of badge holders, which would differentiate them from the more internally-focused badge systems that have historically characterized other organizations."

Main factors that have led to the emergence of OBs include:

- The rising dissatisfaction with standardized tests that are presently the dominant approach to knowledge assessment and recognition [4].
- The increasing need for proper assessment and recognition of not only subject-specific knowledge and competences, but also of generic competences and soft skills.
- The demand for ever-evolving, tailored training programs that would meet the continuously changing requirements of the workplace, as traditional higher education institutions are slow in adapting the to market needs [5].
- The growing open education movement, including Massive Open Online Courseware, is also contributing to the demand for alternative certification and recognition mechanisms.
- The emergence of decentralized Networked Learning Ecosystems [6] or Personal Learning Environments [7] where OBs could make visible diverse kinds of learning accomplishments achieved in different parts of such environments [8]. An early example of a connected learning ecosystem supported through OBs is Global Kids (http://olpglobalkids.org/).

Some authors see OBs as a disruptive innovation that challenges the credentialing authority of higher education, and its role "as society's primary 'sieve'" [9; p.3]. In particular, the open and networked nature of the OBs framework is perceived as a threat to existing assessment and credentialing systems, controlled by formal educational institutions and accreditation entities [10]. These institutions seem to be exposed to the same kind of disruptive challenges that the recording, publishing, and retail sectors have already experienced [5].

One of the objectives of this paper is to increase the awareness about OBs among researchers in academia, and contribute to the discussion on OBs in academic circles. The body of traditional, peer-reviewed academic work in this area is still scarce, and thus many of the sources cited here are blogs, project websites, and other informal venues. This, in fact, properly reflects the current state of public discourse on OBs and related topics, which is primarily taking place on the open Web, and is led by educational technologists and practitioners who are actively involved in applying OBs in practice.

Another objective is to put the concept of OBs, the current and potential use of OBs in education, and their enabling technologies under a certain scrutiny. Proponents of OBs and early adopters have raised a tremendous interest in certain educational communities, in a number of schools, and among a number of teachers and students. Still, others express a more reserved opinion about OBs and a certain deal of concern and criticism. This paper does not aim or try to take any side; it only presents, from a neutral standpoint, some of the major perspectives and concerns side by side.

2 Roles of OBs in Education: Perspectives and Concerns

By analyzing the available academic literature, as well as numerous case studies, project reports and personal experiences reported by educational researchers and practitioners (typically in the form of blog posts), we have identified main roles that OBs might have in the educational domain. In what follows, we introduce and discuss these roles by indicating both the expected benefits and reasons for concern.

2.1 OBs as a Motivational Mechanism

Acting as rewards for learners' engagement and/or achievements, digital badges have traditionally been used as a motivational mechanism in educational settings [11]. In this role, badges tend to achieve their motivating effect on learners if they are desirable and attainable, yet challenging [1]. In addition, what a badge is awarded for tends to affect motivation. Badges can be awarded for the improvement that learners make or for their performance. Learners who are rewarded for their effort or improvement instead of their performance tend to be more persistent on tasks and more orientated towards learning and improving [12]. Hence, the learners' interpretation of the feedback they receive through digital badges tends to influence their motivation.

Besides the obvious reward mechanism they offer, badges also have the potential to motivate learning through the introduction of novel learning practices, those based on participatory learning approaches and peer-based learning communities [13]. In such a learning environment learners are actively involved in the learning process primarily through peer learning and assessment. Their participation in the assessment process can range from recommending peers for accreditation, to earning the right to be the accreditor [14]. Furthermore, learners do not just receive badges but are requested to comment on them, share evidence around them, and the like; badges become social objects around which interaction takes place. Probably the best example of active enactment of such practices is the Peer2Peer University (https://p2pu.org/).

The motivational effect of OBs also stems from their contribution to building one's reputation within a learning community, as well as the Web community in general. For instance, Santos et al. [15] have developed a dashboard aimed at motivating students to engage in learning activities. The dashboard makes use of OBs to aggregate students' activities and achievements across different communication and collaboration tools that form an open learning environment. Badges are made completely public as to increase the overall awareness of students' achievements and motivate engagement through social comparison. In addition, such a public display of digital badges facilitates the discovery of peers with shared interests and/or skills [16]; this is exemplified by the Makewaves' platform (https://www.makewav.es/) that supports community-building around shared 'badge missions'.

Besides the stated benefits, there are also certain concerns regarding the effect of OBs on students' motivation. One of the most notable is related to motivation displacement [17] which occurs when an extrinsic motivator (in this case, a badge) is introduced in a situation in which people are engaged in some activity for its own sake. Upon being introduced, the external motivator leads to a decline in the interest and task performance, as well as diminished motivation for the given activity on future occasions. This is a realistic concern, but with a properly designed instructional strategy, motivation displacement can be avoided. As suggested in [18], one approach could be to design not only badges that are aimed at recognizing achievements (i.e., status badges), but also badges that award earners certain roles associated with both privileges and responsibilities in the learning community (e.g., becoming moderators, facilitators, editors, etc). While the former kind of OBs serve only as 'goals' in the learning context, the latter become 'means' for further learning.

Another, related concern is that students might focus on accumulating badges rather than on learning activities/materials associated with badges. Carefully designed instructions for obtaining badges could help overcome this challenge, in particular thoughtful design of requirements for earning individual badges as well as chaining of badges in learning trajectories [18].

Finally, it should be mentioned that the motivational role of OBs is sometimes overemphasized and OBs are considered solely as a 'gamification'[1] instrument. However, this is a very restricted view on the potentials of OBs, as the following (sub)sections confirm.

2.2 OBs as a Recognition and Credentialing Mechanism

OBs have introduced a mechanism for recognizing learning in multiple and diverse locations and environments that go beyond traditional classrooms. They also allow for a greater diversity of skills and knowledge to be recognized such as those obtainable by attending different afterschool programs and/or trainings, or by being involved in the work of non-profit organizations. However, it should be noted that OBs are not seen as a replacement, but as a complement of traditional credentials. For instance, Educational Testing Service (http://www.ets.org/), a nonprofit organization that administers and scores more than 50 million tests annually worldwide, has started issuing OBs for some of the tests it administers.

The proponents of OBs emphasize that the digital nature of OBs introduces a new dimension of transparency, and opens opportunities for validity check that have not existed before, at least not to the same extent. With the currently prevailing paper-based certificates, candidates can make any kind of statement about their qualities in a job application letter. Recruiters generally have to accept these statements as trustworthy, as their manual validation could be very time-consuming. With direct links to

[1] Gamification refers to the use of game mechanics in online learning environments with the aim of motivating learners to engage with the contents, activities and tools offered by these environments.

the digital evidence of the knowledge/skill/competence they stand to represent, OBs enable recruiters to immediately check the evidence and make their own judgments about the validity of the badge, i.e., the claims made by the candidate.

However, there are still numerous open questions and concerns related to the use of OBs as a credentialing mechanism [5]. Who should be able to distribute and award badges? Should the system be open, or should entities conferring badges be certified or credentialed? This is related to the employers' concern that OBs could come from issuers the employers have not heard of. In such cases employers would have nothing to support their immediate decision regarding the worthiness of exploring badges further and learning by whom and why they were awarded [19]. This concern is related to the constant need to use the available time in the most efficient way.

A related concern is the one about validity or credibility of an OB. When assessing the value of a badge, prospective badge earners and reviewers of the badge credentials will make their initial judgments on those easily discernible features of badges, such as the image for the badge (how professional/appropriate it is), where the badge is hosted, and what other badges are hosted there. Therefore, when designing an overall OB system, badge issuers have to put a considerable attention to these features that affect people's first-hand experience. Furthermore, since badges are intended to serve as visual identifiers of learners' achievements, it is important that they remain stable and recognizable [2], [19]. This is especially relevant for developing trust as one of the most important functions of any credentialing mechanism. Official endorsements by established companies and educational institutions could be a mean of strengthening the validity of badges: a company could endorse a badge issued by an educational institution and vice versa. Such endorsements would demonstrate that an external party is recognizing and confirming the value of the badge and the rigor of the processes applied in developing, assessing and issuing it [19].

There is also a concern related to the interpretation of the meaning of a badge, i.e., inferring what it actually says about a learner [20]. The challenge becomes greater when many different kinds of badges are integrated into a person's profile: "Formal and informal, long-term or short-term, instructor- or peer-assessed, for skills and experiences in many walks of life – they may be all presented together to create a learner's profile" [18; p.6]. This implies that in order to be meaningful for a reviewer, OBs need to be contextualized. Similarly, Hamilton [19] reports on employers' belief that a badge apathy is likely to develop if they are presented with too many badges they perceive irrelevant in a given context. One approach to resolving this problem is the classification of badges proposed by different badge issuers with the objective to facilitate interpretation of badges by defining their type and relative importance [18]. However, this opens another challenge as different issuers propose different classification schemes that cannot be easily mapped one to another. Another approach to overcoming this problem is to provide learners with tools that would allow them to easily develop custom (i.e., context-specific) learning profiles through curation of their OBs. Initial steps in that direction have been done in the Resume 2.0 project[2].

[2] http://sussesonderby.com/

A related concern is about the definition of what has been recognized with a specific badge and the terminology used express that [19]. This is especially the case with soft skills (e.g., creativity, team work) which could be interpreted in different ways by different individuals/organizations, leading to the issuing of badges based on divergent understandings of what those skills mean and how they should be measured. In other words, there is a need for consistency in the definition of knowledge, skills or competences that a badge stands to represent. Furthermore, the criteria for achieving an OB has to be consistently applied, so that the same badge is issued for comparable levels of effort, achievement or ability.

Considering everything stated above, what could be said about the factors affecting the adoption of OBs as a credentialing system? By referring to the human capital theory, along with screening and signaling theories, Olneck [9] suggests that the success of OBs as a credentialing system depends upon "the information needs of employers, the validity of the information conveyed by badges, the efficiency and practicality of prospective employees acquiring badges, and the efficiency and practicality of prospective employers utilizing them" [9; p.5].

2.3 OBs as Signposts in the Learning Space

OBs also have a cognitive role as 'signposts': they chart learning routes, through their badge-earning criteria and entitlements (i.e., privileges and responsibilities opened up by earning a badge). By making explicit that certain achievements are highly valued, badges might focus students' attention, map a trajectory through the curriculum, and nudge student exploration [21].

Badges can also be used by teachers to direct students through the learning space while still giving them sufficient freedom to choose their own path. This can be done by designing different levels of badges in order to chart out a progression of learning, or by designing learning routes through higher-order badges (known as meta-badges) that are awarded upon the completion of a specified set of lower badges [22]. For instance, in the Planet Stewards project (http://planetstewards.wordpress.com/), badges are used to constrain learners as they perform quest-based learning, as well as to indicate to them what are the available options and to suggest where to go first.

OBs might be particularly useful in supporting self-directed learning, as they allow for continuous tracking of what has been learned and give insights into what the next step might be. Thus badges provide a framework for learners to reflect on their learning experiences and plan future learning activities. These meta-cognitive activities facilitate the development of self-regulated learning skills [23] - highly desirable skills for life-long learners.

Mozilla's Open Badges Discovery[3] project aims at showcasing how OBs can be leveraged to assist learners in the discovery of new learning opportunities, as well as in finding one's way through the learning space. At the time of writing, the project is still in its early phase, but it promises to demonstrate how a directory of OBs might be used to provide learners with recommended (personalized) learning paths. The idea is not just to indicate to learners the skills to be obtained but also to offer them narratives that make the learning process more interesting and appealing. For learners with

[3] `https://github.com/mozilla/openbadges-discovery`

well-developed self-regulatory skills, the project aims to offer dashboard with different ways of browsing through and reviewing one's own badges as well as exploring where those badges could lead them further. This way the project intends to support self-reflection and planning activities of self-regulated learners.

3 The State of Supporting Technology

Mozilla's Open Badge Infrastructure (OBI) , is an open infrastructure technology that supports independent badge issuers and badge display sites. It consists of an open source platform, free software and an open technical standard that includes badge metadata specifications, badge backpack(s), badge authentication/verification framework, and a comprehensive API for developers. OBI enables any organization, group, or community, to develop websites to issue badges with standardized metadata. It also enables any learner to earn digital badges from multiple sources, collect them in her badge backpack and display them across the Web on her resume, personal website, social network profile, employment sites, or just about anywhere she chooses. Thus OBI addresses a number of concerns regarding the implementation of the OBs concept, such as moving badges earned at one location to another, and sharing, organizing, and displaying badges in different ways and in diverse settings and situations [5].

Several organizations have built badge issuing platforms on top of OBI. Examples include WordPress' BadgeOS (http://badgeos.org/), Purdue Passport (http://www.itap.purdue.edu/studio/passport/), and Mozilla BadgeKit (http://badgekit.openbadges.org/). They all allow users to easily define achievements that badges are issued for (i.e., badge earning requirements), as well as to issue sharable badges. The requirements and assessment options can be customized to the user's goals and community, and can include the right mix of social and self-directed activities. The badges can be designed to support a desired visual identity, and can be shared on any Web site or community.

At the time of writing, badge issuing platforms are generally at various stages of completion, levels of ease-of-use, and reliability. There are a lot of betas, not-so-reliable pluggins, platform-hosting issues (spam, security, maintenance costs, administration), and even unexpected and not-so-clear public-hosting policies [24]. As a result, badging experiences vary a lot. As Klein [25] has aptly put it, "Many people who try to implement a badge system or even something as basic as attempt to issue a badge to a single person... realize that it is really difficult to accomplish [with current technology]". Worse still, in spite of the core idea for OBs to be open, it turns out that it is easier to build a closed badging system (relying on a single selected platform/technology), even if it is OBI-compliant [26]. Users' privacy or secured longevity of the contents can be compelling reasons for deciding to use a proprietary badging platform, but can easily result in a system that is "too closed, too expensive, or too big" [27]. Likewise, knowing about all idiosyncrasies of a specific platform is difficult before it is deployed and run, which conflicts with the need for easy decision-making when it comes to selecting a badging platform.

To address these issues, Mozilla, as the developer of OBI, has ventured in developing BadgeKit [26]. Expected to be launched in March 2014, BadgeKit is announced as a lightweight, simple, easily extensible, open badge building and issuing platform, fully aligned with OBI. It integrates a suite of existing Mozilla Open Badges tools, such as Badge Studio (for visually designing badges), Open Badger (for defining badges, issuing them, tracking whether someone has accepted an issued badge, and the like), Aesthimia (checking learners-submitted evidence and criteria in learners' applications for badges), Mozilla Backpack (sharing, collecting and managing badges), and so on. A specific novelty in the BadgeKit is its badge discovery feature that enables learners, issuers and employers to discover new badges and badge owners.

4 Conclusion

The overall concept of OBs is tightly related to the emerging forms of assessment that *i*) put an increasing focus on one's ability to apply knowledge in real-world settings, and *ii*) 'democratize' the assessment process by involving learners and community members in the assessment activities [5]. OBs are also closely connected to the need for alternative forms of knowledge/skill recognition and credentialing that are not necessarily issued by traditional educational institutions, and are portable across different life, learning and working contexts. Therefore, one could expect that the adoption of OBs paradigm will be largely influenced by the social acceptance of and support for these novel assessment, recognition and credentialing forms.

The key milestone in the adoption of OBs is expected to occur when large and authoritative organizations start accepting them [28] [29]. The adoption trend has already started. The OB standard is already implemented by over 2000 organizations[4], including well-known education-technology providers such as Moodle and Blackboard. The latest group to join the OBs initiative include names such as Pearson, edX and Workforce.io. who have made formal commitments, during the Open Badges Summit to Reconnect Learning[5], to incorporate OBs into their existing operations, and help in further spreading of the OBs ecosystem. At the time of writing this article, the Badge Alliance (http://badgealliance.org/) is announced as a network of organizations committed to the further development of the OBs ecosystem, and the promotion of values such as openness, learners' agency, and innovation [30].

Obviously OBs are rapidly gaining traction among educational practitioners as well as education-oriented companies and non-profit organizations. It is left to be seen whether OBs will manage to get through the current hype and establish themselves in the roles outlined in Section 2. This will largely depend on their ability to fulfill the expectations, i.e., the perceived benefits associated with each of those roles. It will also depend on the ability of the technology to provide the required support.

So far, there have been only a few research studies aimed at validating the propositions of either proponents or opponents of OBs. Thus, there is an apparent need for applying research rigor in this field in order to get a better understanding of not only OBs and their potential roles, but also the larger educational ecosystem within which they operate and evolve.

---

[4] `http://goo.gl/qH5BZW`

[5] `http://www.reconnectlearning.org/pledge/`

Acknowledgements. This publication was partially supported by the European Commission under the Lifelong Learning Program (LLP), the GRASS project (no.543029-LLP-1-2013-1-RS-KA3-KA3MP). The publication reflects the views only of the authors, and the Commission cannot be held responsible for any use which may be made of the information contained therein.

References

1. Glover, I.: Open Badges: A Visual Method of Recognising Achievement and Increasing Learner Motivation. Student Engagement and Experience Journal 2(1) (2013)
2. Halavais, A.M.C.: A Genealogy of Badges. Information Communication Society 15, 1–20 (2011)
3. Goligoski, E.: Motivating the learner: Mozillas open badges program. Access to Knowledge: A Course Journal 4(1) (2012), `http://ojs.stanford.edu/ojs/index.php/a2k/article/view/381/207` (retrieved January 10, 2014)
4. Baker, E.L.: 2007 Presidential address the end(s) of testing. Educational Researcher 36(6), 309–317 (2007)
5. Sullivan, F.M.: New and Alternative Assessments, Digital Badges, and Civics: An Overview of Emerging Themes and Promising Directions. CIRCLE Working Paper #77 (March 2013), `http://goo.gl/zXzyUY` (retrieved December 15, 2013)
6. Ito, M., Gutiérrez, K., Livingstone, S., Penuel, B., Rhodes, J., et al.: Connected Learning: An Agenda for Research and Design. Digital Media and Learning Research Hub., Irvine (2013), `http://goo.gl/o76iI0` (retrieved January 25, 2014)
7. Attwell, G.: The Personal Learning Environments - the future of eLearning? eLearning Papers 2(1) (2007)
8. Ash, K.: 'Digital Badges' Would Represent Students' Skill Acquisition. Education Week: Digital Directions (June 13, 2012), `http://www.edweek.org/dd/articles/2012/06/13/03badges.h05.html` (retrieved on January 24, 2014)
9. Olneck, M.: Insurgent Credentials: A Challenge to Established Institutions of Higher Education. Presented at: Education in a New Society: The Growing Interpenetration of Education in Modern Life, Cambridge, Massachusetts, April 26-27 (2012), `http://goo.gl/vF03Hz` (retrieved on January 18, 2014)
10. Maney, D.: 'Badges' Fill Credential Gaps where Higher Education Fails. Denverpost.com (April 1, 2012), `http://goo.gl/xSksaI` (retrieved on January 19, 2014)
11. Dominguez, A., Saenz-de Navarrete, J., de Marcos, L., Fernandez-Sanz, L., Pages, C., Martınez-Herraiz, J.J.: Gamifying learning experiences: Practical implications and outcomes. Computers & Education 63, 380–392 (2013)
12. Henderson, V.L., Dweck, C.S.: Motivation and achievement. In: Feldman, S.S., Elliott, G.R. (eds.) At the Threshold: The Developing Adolescent, pp. 308–329. Harvard University Press, Cambridge (1990)
13. Williams, R., et al.: Emergent learning and learning ecologies in Web 2.0. The International Review of Open and Distance Learning 12(3) (2011), `http://www.irrodl.org/index.php/irrodl/article/view/883` (retrieved on January 26, 2014)
14. Joseph, B., et al.: Six Ways to Look at Badging Systems Designed for Learning (2012), `http://goo.gl/qfDPn6` (retrieved on January 5, 2014)

15. Santos, J.L., Charleer, S., Parra, G., Klerkx, J., Duval, E., Verbert, K.: Evaluating the use of open badges in an open learning environment. In: Hernández-Leo, D., Ley, T., Klamma, R., Harrer, A. (eds.) EC-TEL 2013. LNCS, vol. 8095, pp. 314–327. Springer, Heidelberg (2013)
16. Gibson, D., Ostashewski, N., Flintoff, K., Grant, S., Knight, E.: Digital badges in education. Education and Information Technologies (November 2013)
17. Deterding, S.: Situated Motivational Affordances of Game Elements: A Conceptual Model. In: CHI Conference on Human Factors in Computing Systems, CHI 2011, pp. 1–4 (2013)
18. Rughinis, R.: Talkative objects in need of interpretation. re-thinking digital badges in education. In: CHI 2013 Extended Abstracts on Human Factors in Computing Systems (CHI EA 2013), pp. 2099–2108. ACM, New York (2013)
19. Hamilton, G.: Evidencing Employability Skills with Open Badges (2014), http://goo.gl/eiBlim (retrieved January 28, 2014)
20. Nelson, S.: Comment to: Unpacking Badges for Lifelong Learning, by Grant, S. HASTAC (September 24, 2011), http://goo.gl/hz3ep5 (retrieved December 21, 2014)
21. Rughinis, R.: Badge Architectures in Engineering Education. Blueprints and Challenges. In: The 5th International Conference on Computer Supported Education (CSEDU 2013), Aachen, Germany, pp. 548–554 (2013)
22. Hickey, D., Itow, R., Schenke, K., Tran, C., Otto, N., Chow, C.: Badges Design Principles Documentation Project. Interim Report (January 20, 2014), http://iudpd.indiana.edu/JanuaryReport (retrieved from)
23. Greene, J.A., Azevedo, R.: A Theoretical Review of Winne and Hadwin's Model of Self-Regulated Learning. Review of Educational Research 77(3), 334–372 (2007)
24. O'Byrne, W.I.: Challenges in Launching and Hosting an Open, Digital Badge Initiative (July 31, 2013), http://goo.gl/kZ2Icj (retrieved on February 11, 2014)
25. Klein, J.: BadgeKit: An Invitation to Innovation (October 21, 2013), http://goo.gl/v1UeIA (retrieved on February 11, 2014)
26. Knight, E.: BadgeKit, the Why (October 29, 2013), http://erinknight.com/post/65443778764/badgekit-the-why (retrieved on February 11, 2014)
27. Cole-Karagory, M.: Introducing BadgeKit (November 19, 2013), http://www.slideshare.net/megan_cole/mozilla-badge-kitfinal (retrieved on February 10, 2014)
28. Carey, K.: The Higher Education Monopoly is Crumbling as We Speak. The New Republic (March 13, 2012), http://goo.gl/uHZZcu (retrieved on January 25, 2013)
29. Young, J.R.: 'Badges' Earned Online Pose Challenge to Traditional College Diplomas. Chronicle of Higher Education (January 8, 2012), http://chronicle.com/article/Badges-Earned-Online-Pose/130241/ (retrieved on January 25, 2013)
30. Surman, M.: How We're Making Education More Like the Web (February 12, 2014), http://goo.gl/58aqVd (retrieved on February 15, 2014)

Developing Language Learning Strategies in a Personal Learning Environment: Pilot Study

Katrin Saks* and Äli Leijen

University of Tartu, Tartu, Estonia

Abstract. English is indisputably the *lingua franca* of today's globalizing world. Despite Estonians' high proficiency in English, methods used in the teaching process have not supported the active use of language and have probably hindered communication. Advanced language learning strategies (LLS) have been found to be connected with higher language proficiency. The aim of the current study is to develop assignments within personal learning environments (PLE) for an English course promoting advanced LLS. The developed assignments were carried out by 28 first-year students studying Tourism English. Data was collected through pre- and post-testing. Additional data about the students' learning experiences was collected with focus group interviews. The results of the study showed a significant improvement in compensation and social strategies. A significant relationship was found between compensation strategies and content knowledge. Further research should focus on reinforcing the assignments, especially regarding advancing the cognitive and metacognitive strategies.

Keywords: language learning strategies, personal learning environment, language proficiency.

1 Introduction

English is indisputably the lingua franca of today's globalizing, delocalizing, and decentralizing world. It is the bridging tool when communication is no longer tied to geographical borders. In Estonia considerable attention is paid to teaching foreign languages, especially English, which is the first foreign language taught. The study of English starts at 8–9 years of age. The relatively strong results in the state English examination for 18-to-19-year-old students demonstrates the importance of English in Estonia (in 2012, M=68.6 points out of 100, SD=16.1) [19]. According to the reports of the EF English Proficiency Index, Estonia ranks fourth out of 60 countries studied, placing it in the category of very high proficiency countries [3]. Despite relatively good indicators and rankings, Estonians often face difficulties when communicating in English. The prevalent approach to teaching foreign languages since the Soviet period is a grammar-translation method, which emphasizes accuracy over fluency. Insufficient attention to a communicative approach has caused many people to be

* Corresponding author.

E. Popescu et al. (Eds.): ICWL 2014, LNCS 8613, pp. 66–76, 2014.

afraid to use it actively because of insufficient practice and fear of making mistakes, even after many years of studying the language. Thus the main problem in the current language learning system is insufficient teaching of communicative skills and readiness.

Active use of language presumes conscious implementation of certain language learning strategies (LLS). The acquisition of these strategies is supported with a communicative approach. Strategies are the learner's toolkit for active, conscious, purposeful, and attentive learning, and they pave the way towards greater proficiency, learner autonomy, and self-regulation [6]. Several researchers have produced different classifications of strategies [20,23,16], giving their input to the six-strategy taxonomy that Rebecca Oxford designed in 1990 [17], from which the present study also proceeds. Four out of six groups of strategies (cognitive, compensatory, metacognitive, and social) are considered to be the ones that support language learning at the advanced level, which is necessary at all levels of education. However, the students who are used to employing the lower-level strategies, such as memory and affective strategies, may find it difficult to change their learning habits to apply higher-level strategies, especially metacognitive strategies. Metacognitive skills are important in all learning situations. More specifically, self-regulation and reflection are two often-targeted metacognitive activities in educational settings [regarding self-regulation, see, e.g., 7,14; regarding reflection, e.g., 9,11]. Two self-reflective processes, self-judgment and self-reactions [1], help learners to observe their behavior in the learning process and regulate it. The four distinctive types of criteria—mastery, previous performance, normative, and collaborative—that learners use to evaluate themselves all contribute to the process of self-reflection and regulation [26]. The other factors influencing the learner's performance are a combination of internal and external factors. The internal factors are represented by affect and motivation, metacognition and cognition factors. The external factors consist of traditional learning tasks and human interaction [22]. Using a variety of advanced language learning and metacognitive strategies has been found to be connected with higher language proficiency. Therefore, it is vital to contribute to the advancement of these strategies if we aim to support students' language studies and language proficiency.

One way of making language learning more effective is by employing personal learning environments (PLE). PLE is a dynamic digital environment with a structure and tools that depend on the user's needs at the moment [8]. PLEs are becoming more and more widely used environments, thanks to the advancements of Web 2.0 technologies that are flexible, correspond to learners' needs, and can be easily integrated into various digital environments. PLE, created by the user him- or herself, depends on his/her preferences, expectations, needs, and personal development. Designing and using a PLE presumes that the learner is aware of his/her learning styles and habits and at the same time supports the development of self-regulated learning skills. It is accompanied by the learners' control over their learning environment and process, thus empowering responsibility for one's learning activities [25]. It also enables support for active communicative language learning by including different communication tools and conducting activities that implement language learning strategies within the four advanced strategy groups.

Aiming to make use of the affordances and benefits of PLE, the focus of the current study is to develop learning assignments that would help students apply the strategies of active language use, as well as cognitive and metacognitive strategies. To assess the possible change in the usage of language learning strategies, a pilot study was conducted in the first-year English for Specific Purposes (ESP) course, which was a blended course combining traditional face-to-face instruction with independent learning in students' personalized blog-based learning environments. More specifically, we aimed to answer the following research questions: (1) How do students perceive their learning outcomes following the four assignments developed to support their use of advanced language learning strategies? (2) How effective are the developed learning assignments for enhancing students' advanced LLS when teaching ESP with the support of the personal learning environment? (3) Is there a relationship between using advanced LLS and the development of students' content knowledge?

2 Methods

2.1 Participants

Data was collected from 28 students who took the first-year English for Specific Purposes, Tourism English course during a four-month period (40 academic lessons). There were four men (14.3%) and 24 women (85.75%) in the group. The average age of the students was 19.5 (SD=1.1). They had studied English for approximately 10 years (M=10.04, SD=2.3). The average score of the national English examination (B2) that they had taken four months earlier was 73.6 points out of 100 (SD=17.4).

2.2 Learning Environment

The traditional face-to-face instruction in the classroom was supported with PLE, which combined the feed aggregator, course blog, and the students' personal blogs. The aggregator, EduFeedr, is programmed at Tallinn University [18] and has been successfully used in many open education courses. EduFeedr was used to bring together all posts and comments with a specific tag from the course blog and students' blogs (Figure 1). The course blog, which was written and managed by the teacher, served as a model for students when building up their own PLEs based on blogs.

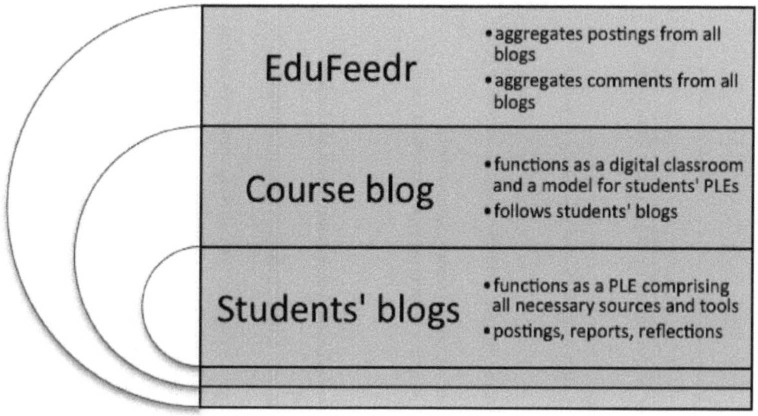

Fig. 1. The functions of feed aggregator and blogs in the ESP course

In the first class the environment and its tools and affordances were demonstrated. The students were shown how to start the blog, how to add in-built widgets and external Web 2.0 tools, and how categorizing and tagging works. Students were also told which tools had been aggregated to the course blog and why. They learned about the affordances of Dropbox, bookmarking, embedding, and so on. In addition to technical affordances, they discussed the didactic affordances proceeding from students' needs and expectations. The environment was used to co-ordinate work in the classroom and students' independent work at home, uploading assignments, commenting and giving feedback, and storing necessary learning materials. Students used their blogs to reflect their learning process, upload their coursework, communicate within pair work, comment and give feedback to peers, add widgets that supported their learning activities and link the learning materials. Unlike students in other similar studies [24], our learners had no difficulties when choosing and applying Web 2.0 tools in their PLEs. Most of them have previous e-learning experience, as using ICT is common in secondary schools in Estonia.

2.3 Assignments

Within the course, four specific learning assignments were created to support the development of students' language learning strategies (Table 1). The assignments were specially designed to take maximum advantage of the affordances of Web 2.0 tools that the students were encouraged to include in their PLEs. Special attention was paid to students' active use of language when solving real-life situations (Tasks 3 and 4). Students' interaction and communication were encouraged throughout all tasks, as well as in preparatory and follow-up phases. Throughout the course, students were encouraged to apply different cognitive strategies when working on new material or reporting the results. The whole learning activity was reflected orally in the classroom as well as in written form in students' blogs.

Table 1. Assignment descriptions

Assignment	Description	Strategies
Learning plan	Discussing students' expectations from the course: needs, learning styles and habits, expectations from the teacher, etc. Formulating learning plans on the blog (online). The learning plan is presented and explained at the beginning of the course.	Metacognitive—analyzing needs, setting goals for the course, identifying prior knowledge, planning appropriate strategies. Cognitive—activating prior learning strategies. Compensation—freedom to express one's own ideas using their own vocabulary in written form.
Essay	Selecting attractions in one's home place, gathering information, writing an essay, and illustrating the post with appropriate photos and/or videos. Before posting on the blog, the student must read the rubrics of the assessment. Other students' posts are read and feedback is given to them.	Metacognitive—setting goals for the task, planning the task, time management, activating prior knowledge, self-evaluation. Cognitive—working with source material, scanning, critical reading, summarizing. Compensation—guessing the meaning when working with new material, expressing ideas in written form using one's own vocabulary. Social—peer assessment.
Evaluating a destination (in pairs)	Collecting information about a new destination with the aim of analyzing its suitability as a tourism destination (geographical location, access, natural features, social and political features, general price range, etc.). The work process is described on the blog. An oral presentation is given with the results described and demonstrated. A self-assessment and peer assessment is made on the basis of the rubrics provided.	Metacognitive—setting goals for the task, planning the task, time management, division of work, activating prior knowledge, self-evaluation. Cognitive—working with source material, scanning, critical reading, comparing/contrasting, summarizing. Compensation—creative thinking when guessing the meaning from working with new material, expressing ideas in both written and oral forms using one's own vocabulary. Social—negotiating, compromising, decision-making, peer assessment.
Comparing tourism enterprises (in pairs)	Compiling a comparison of three tourism enterprises (hotel, restaurants, adventure parks, etc.) and presenting the findings orally. The process is described on the blogs, where students also self-assess their work individually and as a pair.	Metacognitive—setting goals for the task, planning the task, time planning, division of work, activating prior knowledge, self-evaluation. Cognitive—working with source material, scanning, critical reading, comparing/contrasting, summarizing, presenting. Compensation—guessing the meaning when working with new material, expressing ideas in written form using one's own vocabulary. Social—negotiating, compromising, decision-making, peer assessment, public presentation.

2.4 Data Collection and Analysis

In order to detect possible changes regarding students' language learning strategies and outcomes, the study employed pre- and post-test design. Both tests included measures of language learning strategies and content knowledge of the English language. Students' use of language learning strategies was assessed with Strategy Inventory for Language Learning (SILL), which was designed by Rebecca Oxford [17]. The SILL consists of 50 items divided into two main scales—direct and indirect strategies—and six subscales: memory (9 items), cognitive (14), compensation (6), metacognitive (9), affective (5), and social strategies (6). Four of them—cognitive, compensation, metacognitive, and social—are considered the strategies of advanced learners, while memory and affective strategies are considered the strategies of beginners. The respondents rated the items on a five-point Likert scale. In the adaptation process of the SILL for Estonian learners, the translation-backtranslation method was used, followed by semantic and linguistic editing. The coefficients of the subscales remain between 0.59 for memory strategies and 0.84 for the metacognitive strategies' group.

Students' language skills were assessed with a test on content knowledge focusing on Tourism English, since the students' main subject is tourism. Their thematic vocabulary and general language skills were tested. The test was developed by the first author of the paper.

To compare the data collected from pre- and post-tests, t-tests and correlation analyses were conducted. In order to collect additional information about the students' learning process, three group interviews were conducted with a total of 16 people after the four-assignment exercise. Five or six students participated in one group interview. The interviews lasted approximately one hour; they were fully transcribed and analyzed based on the rules of a thematic analysis [21] by one researcher.

3 Results

3.1 Students' Perception of the Assignments

Group interviews were conducted to collect data about students' perceptions of language learning following the four assignments given. Most students admitted that it had been difficult for them to set the goals for the entire course as well as for certain assignments, partly because they had no experience in this area. However, students who had some experience with setting learning goals considered it a natural activity (*"Having done it before, you already know what you want and what you need"*). The same can be said about working in pairs. Students who had experience working with others were better at planning and regulating their tasks when working in pairs. Earlier experience enabled them to discuss and negotiate the process with their partner and to plan their work more efficiently (*"I enjoyed pair work because, thanks to my secondary school experience, I knew how to do it*"). These results seem to indicate that students' prior experience related to the assignments had an influence on their learning activities. Students without relevant experience might have had difficulties carrying out the required tasks in this current research study and may have required more support.

Pair work was considered the most motivating and useful type of assignment, mostly because of the real-life aspects of the task engaging with authentic materials relevant to their field of study in tourism. They were able to practice and experience the potential role of a future tourism service specialist. These tasks were also approved because of the learning skills they facilitated—pair work, negotiating, compromising, responsibility, and so on. However, a couple of students admitted that occasionally they would have preferred to do the tasks individually ("*If your partner wasn't really motivated and interested in it, it was very difficult to work with her*"). This shows that although students considered collaborative learning assignments very valuable, some students also experienced problems that have been widely reported in previous studies [10,12].

The students were asked about the cognitive strategies they used throughout different assignments; the variety of strategies they use daily turned out to be quite limited. There are certain strategies they use for learning vocabulary or working with a new text. At the same time, the students do not feel the necessity to expand the variety of strategies, believing that they can manage with the existing ones ("*My learning habits are mostly already shaped, but I think I still developed a little bit more as a learner*"). However, students seem to be aware of their learning styles, and they use the strategies suitable for these consciously. When students were asked how they assessed their own work in the context of the course, they admitted that such assessment was very difficult for them, as they tended to be more tolerant of their own mistakes. Their peers' mistakes were easier for them to notice. On the other hand, it was difficult for students to point to their peers' mistakes and criticize their performance ("*You don't want to hurt your friend, but there is no point in beautifying the situation*"). Students also appreciated a fuller development of their language skills, which was assessed throughout the course, and not simply individual language mistakes they happened to make in their utterances. The assessment criteria added to each assignment helped to clarify what was expected of them, along with the result they were expected to achieve ("*It is easier to plan your work if you know what is assessed*"). Students considered the course successful if they received a good grade, but they also valued a good inner feeling about it. A month after the end of the course, many of the students admitted that they could have worked harder ("*It wasn't actually a difficult course; I could have learned much more there*"). These findings illustrate that students are not used to monitoring their learning process. Promoting these methods could also take longer and require further support. Evidence suggests that through specially designed learning assignments, it is possible to lead students through the process step-by-step and help them to notice and realize the importance of certain strategies to enhance their learning process.

3.2 Change in Language Learning Strategies

In order to answer the second research question, we compared the pre- and post-test mean scores of six language learning strategy scales. To estimate the frequency of students' use of LLS, we conducted a t-test to compare the means of all six strategy groups of the pre- and post-test. The results are reported in Table 2. The table shows a significant difference in the scores for compensation strategies pre-test (M=3.49, SD=0.69) and post-test (M=3.7, SD=0.69); t (27)= -2.142, p=0.042. Another strategy group that revealed statistical significance was social strategies in the pre-test (M=3.62, SD=0.65) and post-test (M=3.85, SD=0.63); t (27)= -2.325, p=0.028.

Table 2. Differences between students' (N=28) language learning strategies in pre- and post-tests

	Pre-test M(SD)	Post-test M(SD)	t	df	p
Memory	2.79(0.36)	2.96(0.56)	-1.894	27	.070
Cognitive	3.19(0.53)	3.35(0.49)	-1.979	27	.059
Compensation	3.50(0.69)	3.70(0.69)	-2.142	27	**.042**
Metacognitive	3.72(0.51)	3.79(0.52)	-.773	27	.446
Affective	3.05(0.49)	2.92(0.56)	1.151	27	.261
Social	3.62(0.65)	3.85(0.63)	-2.325	27	**.028**

These results indicate that the developed assignments seem to promote usage of some of the more advanced LLS. Moreover, they suggest that it is easier to promote compensatory and social strategies. In order to advance the use of metacognitive strategies, it appears that students need additional support.

3.3 Relationship between LLS and Content Knowledge

In order to answer the third research question, we conducted a Pearson correlation analysis between the scores of the LLS scales and results of the students' content knowledge test (both measures were collected in a post-test). The only significant correlation was found between compensation strategies and content knowledge: r=.42, p<.05, indicating an average correlation between the two measures. This is expected, as the content of the ESP course enables learners to rely significantly on deduction based on preliminary knowledge and experience. The students had a large amount of course material to work on, which led them to apply several compensatory strategies (*"For pair work we had to work through a lot of material. At first it took time, but after a while you already know how to read it and how to find the necessary information faster"*). The other strategy groups did not significantly correlate with the content knowledge, which could have been influenced by the relatively small sample. However, we also expected the cognitive and metacognitive strategies to correlate with the content knowledge, as these connections have been found in previous studies

[15,4,5], and the development of current assignments also considered these factors. In the interview several students admitted that the strategies applied in secondary school were not helpful in the ESP course, as the tasks and expectations were rather different (*"We needed to analyze the texts and discuss them in our course; we never did that in secondary school"*). However, students admitted that they enjoyed the different approach to language learning and felt that learning a language this way gave them a more adequate feeling of authentic language use. These findings indicate again that although students might value advanced LLS and assignments that promote their development, promoting such activities might take longer and require further support.

4 Discussion

Students' perceptions of the developed learning assignments were varied and depended upon their previous learning experiences. Planning the learning activities for the course and evaluating them based on expectations outlined in the learning plan (Task 1) was a new approach for most of the students. It caused difficulties, as they could not yet think ahead or plan their learning. However, self-assessment within the course became a familiar activity, as this had to be done regularly following all tasks. Writing an essay (Task 2) caused neither difficulties nor excitement, as students were used to receiving such assignments from their secondary school. The pair work (Task 3, 4) was the most time-consuming and assumed a lot of individual work as well as teamwork. The students who had practiced and worked in pairs before were better at managing their time, negotiating, and collaboration strategies. There were students who, despite being able to motivate their less interested partners, would have preferred to do the tasks individually. However, the majority of the students still enjoyed doing the tasks.

The study showed some evidence concerning the effectiveness of enhancing students' advanced LLS with the support of learning assignments within a personal learning environment. The results of the t-test revealed statistically significant changes in both compensatory and social strategies. These two are considered an inseparable part of language learning in a communicative language class. The assignments were developed with the aim of supporting students' active and natural use of language by working with authentic materials and solving real-life problems. Although the development of metacognitive strategies was also supported throughout the course, it appears, based on the results of the focus group interviews, that these skills need deeper enhancement through planning, monitoring, and evaluating phases. One reason why the differences did not appear significantly in the other strategy groups may also be that the number of respondents was relatively small ($N = 28$). It has been emphasized that LLS can be taught and that it should be applied consistently and consciously [13]. The teacher's role in guiding and supporting the process cannot be underestimated. Students who consciously use a wide variety of strategies by combining them more skillfully with some awareness of their own strategy will develop their metacognitive skills and autonomy.

In the relationship between the language learning strategies and content knowledge, compensation strategies stand out as the best predictor of proficiency. Similar results have also been reported in an earlier study [2]. Compensation strategies are needed to overcome gaps in the knowledge of language [17], and they seem to be more relevant for experienced language students. The limited use of cognitive and metacognitive strategies may indicate the inadequate awareness of learners' own strategy use [2], which also became evident with the interview answers in the current study. The relationships between language learning strategies and content knowledge need complementary studies.

5 Limitations of the Study and Recommendations for Further Research

There are some potential limitations in the current study. The first limitation is the relatively small sample of 28 people. This also entails the need to repeat the experiment next year, expanding the sample and enhancing the intervention, especially the cognitive and metacognitive aspects. Another limitation is having only one experimental group, which was also necessitated by the small number of people participating in the experiment. If the experiment is repeated, the inclusion of a control group must be considered. Despite the obvious shortcomings, the results of the study can be considered valuable, since we have reported some positive results regarding changing LLS in the context of PLE. Showing a relationship between compensation strategies and language proficiency among tertiary-level students is a significant contribution. The findings of the current study need to be scrutinized and investigated further in subsequent studies.

Acknowledgements. The present research was supported by the European Social Fund.

References

1. Bandura, A.: Social Foundations of Thought and Action: a Social Cognitive Theory. Prentice-Hall, Englewood Cliffs (1986)
2. Chamot, A.U.: The Role of Learning Strategies in Second Language Acquisition. In: Breen, M.P. (ed.) Learner Contributions to Language Learning. New Directions in Research, Pearson Education Ltd. (1998)
3. EF English Proficiency Index. EF Education First Ltd., `http://www.ef.com/epi/downloads/`
4. Ehrman, M., Oxford, R.: Cognition Plus: Correlates of Language Learning Success. Modern Language Journal 79(1), 67–89 (1995)
5. Green, J.M., Oxford, R.: A Closer Look at Learning Strategies, L2 Proficiency and Sex. TESOL Quarterly 29(2), 261–297 (1995)
6. Hsiao, T., Oxford, R.: Comparing Theories of Language Learning Strategies: a Confirmatory Factor Analysis. Modern Language Journal 86(3), 368–383 (2002)

7. Kondo, M., Ishikawa, Y., Smith, C., Sakamoto, K., Shimomura, H., Wada, N.: Mobile Assisted Language Learning in University EFL Courses in Japan: Developing Attitudes and Skills for Self-Regulated Learning. ReCALL 24, 169–187 (2012)
8. Kop, R.: Moving towards a Personal Learning Environment (2012), `http://nrc-ca.academia.edu/RKop/Papers/684316/Moving_towards_a_Personal_Learning_Environment`
9. Kori, K., Pedaste, M., Leijen, Ä., Mäeots, M.: Supporting Reflection in Technology-Enhanced Learning. Educational Research Review 11, 45–55 (2014)
10. Leijen, Ä., Admiraal, W., Wildschut, L., Simons, P.R.J.: Students' Perspectives on E-Learning and the Use of a Virtual Learning Environment in Dance Education. Research in Dance Education 9(2), 147–162 (2008)
11. Leijen, Ä., Valtna, K., Leijen, D.A., Pedaste, M.: How to Determine the Quality of Students' Reflections? Studies in Higher Education 37(2), 203–217 (2012)
12. Lockhorst, D.: Design Principles for a CSCL Environment in Teacher Training. Doctoral dissertation, IVLOS Institute of Education of Utrecht University (2004)
13. Magno, C.: Korean Students' Language Learning Strategies and Years of Studying English as Predictors of Proficiency in English. TESOL Journal 2, 39–61 (2010)
14. Michalsky, T.: Shaping Self-Regulation in Science Teachers' Professional Growth: Inquiry Skills. Science Education 96(6), 1106–1133 (2012)
15. O'Malley, J.M., Chamot, A.U., Stewner-Manzanares, G., Kupper, L., Russo, R.P.: Learning Strategies Used by Beginning and Intermediate ESL Students. Language Learning 35(1), 21–46 (1985)
16. O'Malley, J.M., Chamot, A.U.: Learning Strategies in Second Language Acquisition. Cambridge University Press, Cambridge (1990)
17. Oxford, R.L.: Language Learning Strategies: What Every Teacher Should Know. Newbury House/Harper and Row, New York (1990)
18. Põldoja, H.: EduFeedr: Redesigning the Feed Reader for an Open Education. In: Proceedings of the Open 2009 Symposium, Finland (2009)
19. Riigieksamite statistika 2012 (Statistics of State Exams 2012), `http://www.innove.ee/UserFiles/Riigieksamid/2012/Riigieksamid%202012%20%C3%BCldstatistika.pdf`
20. Rubin, J.: What the "Good Language Learner" Can Teach Us. TESOL Quarterly 9, 41–51 (1975)
21. Ryan, G.W., Bernard, H.R.: Techniques to Identify Themes. Field Methods 15(1), 85–109 (2003)
22. Saks, K., Leijen, Ä.: Distinguishing Self-Directed and Self-Regulated Learning and Measuring Them in the E-Learning Context. Procedia, Social and Behavioral Sciences 112, 190–198 (2014)
23. Stern, H.H.: What Can We Learn from the Good Language Learner? Canadian Modern Language Review 31, 304–318 (1975)
24. Ullrich, C., Shen, R., Gillet, D.: Not Yet Ready for Everyone: An Experience Report about a Personal Learning Environment for Language Learning. In: Luo, X., Spaniol, M., Wang, L., Li, Q., Nejdl, W., Zhang, W. (eds.) ICWL 2010. LNCS, vol. 6483, pp. 269–278. Springer, Heidelberg (2010)
25. Väljataga, T., Fieldler, S.: Supporting Students to Self-Direct Intentional Learning Projects with Social Media. Educational Technology and Society 12(3), 58–69 (2009)
26. Zimmerman, B.J.: Attaining Self-Regulation: a Social Cognitive Perspective. In: Boekaerts, M., Pintrich, P.R., Zeidner, M. (eds.) Handbook of Self-Regulation, pp. 13–39. Academic Press, San Diego (2005)

The Potential of e-portfolio in Transition from Estonian Higher Education to Working Life

Kairit Tammets and Mart Laanpere

Tallinn University, Institute of Informatics, Narva road 25,
10120, Tallinn, Estonia
Kairit.Tammets@tlu.ee

Abstract. The paper explores the potential of using the e-portfolio as a transition tool from academic institutions to professional institutions. The main aim is to investigate what are current practices and attitudes of using e-portfolios and investigate if the employers are ready to use the e-portfolio as an alternative to the traditional recruitment approaches like resumes. Study was the first phase of the larger design research, which aims to develop the competence-based portfolio for ICT sector. The survey was distributed among teachers, HR managers and students in ICT field for evaluating their knowledge and experiences of the e-portfolios and their perception about using the e-portfolio in recruitment process. Additionally semi-structured interviews were conducted with the teachers and HR managers for exploring the current practices with the e-portfolio and recruitment processes. Study revealed that in Estonian settings mainly teachers are using e-portfolios with the professional purposes. Also under certain circumstances the e-portfolio could be potential tool in recruitment.

Keywords: e-portfolio, recruitment, professional learning, transition to working life.

1 Introduction

Estonia has faced a continuing growth in the use of technology to support many aspects of teaching and learning in higher education. Among other technologies like learning management systems, virtual learning environments and social media, e-portfolio has also gained quite a lot of attention. Stroheimer [1] claims that for some time, electronic portfolios have constituted a prominent educational innovation, which aims at the systematic self-controlled development of qualifications. It has been reported that the process of preparing a portfolio of prior learning experiences appears to enhance learning transfer between the classroom and the real world as well as to alter learners' perspectives about themselves [2]. Still, less has the practice focused on how to integrate the educational activities to working life in order to smoothen the theory and practice and movement from one organization into another.

Specific research focus in the current paper is on the field of ICT. Paper aims to investigate the possibilities to use the e-portfolio as a transition tool from higher and

E. Popescu et al. (Eds.): ICWL 2014, LNCS 8613, pp. 77–86, 2014.

vocational education to apprenticeship or working life in Estonian settings. More over, the research paper aims to find answers to two research questions:

- Which are the current attitudes and habits of using e-portfolios in the context of Estonian laboring and educational system?
- What is the potential of implementing e-portfolio as a transition tool from higher education to working life in Estonia?

2 Theoretical Overview

Strohmeier [1] argues that several e-portfolios identified in the literature can be categorized by the objective: a) development oriented e-Portfolios (e.g. learning and process portfolio); b) assessment oriented e-Portfolios (e.g. accountability or assessment portfolio); c) documentation oriented e-Portfolios (e.g. showcase or presentation portfolio). In this study we look at the concept of e-portfolio in the light of the professional education and as a connection tool between the academic and workplace learning. In that sense, based on the categorization distinguished above [1], the e-portfolio is seen mainly as the development-oriented e-portfolio. Several authors [3, 4] have pointed the encouragement of competencies and standard orientation in teacher education and how it helps new teachers convey their personality and professionalism. Competence is considered as personal characteristic (e.g. skills, knowledge, attitudes) that an individual possesses or needs to acquire, in order to perform an activity within a specific context, whereas performance may range from the basic level of proficiency to the highest levels of excellence [5]. The importance of the competence-based education and standard orientation could be transferred to other contexts beside the teacher education, where the e-portfolio implementations are studied nearly the most. Competence-based evaluation is important to enterprises as well as an explicit and successful management and development of competences within a company, where expert knowhow is essential, can have a significant positive effect on value creation [6]. Based on that assumption, we claim in our paper that competence-based e-portfolio, which has been developed since the initial studies through entire academic practice, is valuable piece of information to the employer and could be used as a tool for moving from one organization to another.

Curyer, Leeson, Mason & Williams [7] have proposed several transition scenarios for the e-portfolios in vocational educational (VET) context. They see the e-portfolio as tool to transit out of the VET system to further education or work, to manage the a VET workforce and to transit into the self employment. In these scenarios the central idea is based on the competencies and validation of the competencies with the evidences like artefacts during the studies and in the process of the recognition of the prior learning. The potential for competence-based e-portfolio for the employers is in the possibility to gather information about employees' competencies or to assemble project teams based on this information [7].

The idea of the e-portfolio as a transition tool between academic and professional learning can be expanded with idea to use the e-portfolio as recruitment or job application tool. Strohmeier [1] conducted the conceptual analysis of the e-portfolio as a potential recruitment tool and although he admitted the potential of the e-portfolio in job application process, he also revealed some of the challenges (e.g. demanding task to set up the portfolio-based recruitment process). Additionally Okoro, Washington and Cardon [8] have said that although the e-portfolio has high a potential to replace the traditional resume format in job application process, still in most cases the authors do not invest enough effort in the quality and consistency of e-portfolios. Other studies have still indicated the process of preparing and developing ones digital application portfolio for job application process gave the participants a better understanding of their skills and characteristics and made them more self-confident [9] and had a remarkable positive effect on improving job application skills [10].

Based on the overview present above, it can be concluded that several attempts have been done to implement competence-based e-portfolios as a transition tools from academic institution to working life. Still there is need to investigate what prerequisites should be filled for preparing the implementation of the e-portfolios in larger scale.

3 Research Design and Methods

Research of the study was carried out in the context of the EC funded project "E-portfolio for Human Resource" (2012-2013) in collaboration with German, French, Estonian and Russian researchers. Project focused on investigation of the usage and perception of e-portfolio as part of online applications during transition processes from higher education institutions to the working life.

The current study used mixed methods as a baseline of the research design. In mixed methods research design quantitative and qualitative research methods, approaches, and concepts are combined into a one study [11] or in a multiphase series of studies [12]. In the current study the web-based questionnaire and focus group interviews were used for finding answers to the research questions for the first study phase, which aimed to map the current practices and identify the attitudes of the e-portfolio users.

3.1 Participants

In the current research study the web-based questionnaire was responded by 104 Estonian teachers, 41 students from the higher and vocational educational institutions in the ICT field and only 10 HR managers. Additionally three HR managers from ICT sector and ten teachers participated in semi-structured interviews.

3.2 Data Collection and Analysis

Web-based survey was developed in collaboration in EhR project. The separate questionnaire was developed for each target group. In general the questionnaires were similar, some specific context-related differences were included. Questionnaires had following blocks of the questions: background information; experiences with e-portfolios; e-portfolios in the future; components of e-portfolio; implementing e-portfolio. Roughly each block of the questions involved five questions. Multiple-choice questions were on Likert-scale. Specific research interest was related with the trust within the e-portfolio and therefore some questions related with investigating the trust issues, were added. Questionnaires were developed with the web-based LimeSurvey tool and distributed via e-mails and mailing lists to the participants.

Questions for semi-structured focus group interviews were also developed in collaboration with the EhR project. For the current research paper the additional questions were added to the questionnaire with the specific focus on recruitment practices and perceptions and experiences of using e-portfolio in the recruitment process.

Questionnaire was analyzed with the descriptive statistical methods. Qualitative analysis of the focus-group interviews was carried out based on the framework of Miles and Huberman [13]. Their framework suggests first reducing the data, displaying it and drawing and verifying the conclusions.

4 Results

4.1 Experiences with the e-portfolio

93% of the students who participated in the study had never used e-portfolio. Students pointed that they haven't used e-portfolio, because they have never heard about it (55%), they have not been asked to use it (42%) and because they don't have the need to do it (3%). Only 5 students out of 41 pointed that they have used e-portfolio in their educational projects.

Three HR managers admitted that they have heard about e-portfolio and two of them have previous experience with using it.

Among participated teachers, the concept of e-portfolio is familiar. 89% of the teachers have heard about the e-portfolio and 64% of them have used it. 36 teachers out of 104 said that they have used the e-portfolio because it was the course/university requirement, 16 teachers used it on their own initiative and two of them had used the e-portfolios in a job application process. Those teachers, who don't have the experiences with the e-portfolio, said that they don't have the need to develop own e-portfolio (7 teachers); the current e-portfolio structures don't fit to them (8 teachers) and in their institution they have their own assessment system (3 teachers).

4.2 E-portfolio Technologies

Most of the study participants, who mentioned what kind of technologies do they know for developing e-portfolio and what they have used themselves, were teachers. Figure 1 illustrates that participants know mainly open technologies like Google Sites and weblogs. Only teachers marked that they know also special open technologies for creating the e-portfolios. Additionally teachers mentioned that they know non-network instruments. HR managers and students know as well mainly open technologies, but also Europass and LinkedIn were mentioned. One participant also has used Skydrive as an e-portfolio, although in the focus of the current research the Skydrive is more like a repository of the created and collected materials.

The results also indicate that in Estonia special e-portfolio technologies are not known and used, even if the teachers' awareness of the concept is quite high. It means that social media or specific professional networks are mainly used with the purpose to create e-portfolios. It also indicates that if 2/3 teachers have received their e-portfolio experience through formal education, the open technologies are probably taught there as well.

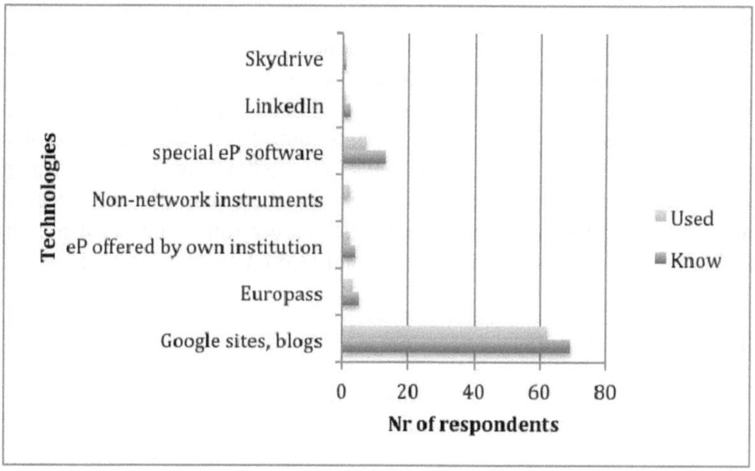

Fig. 1. Known and used technologies of e-portfolio

4.3 E-portfolio Components

Selection of the possible e-portfolio components was provided for the research participants. As there were too small amount of respondents of the HR managers for that question, then the Figure 2 illustrates only the research results of the students and teachers.

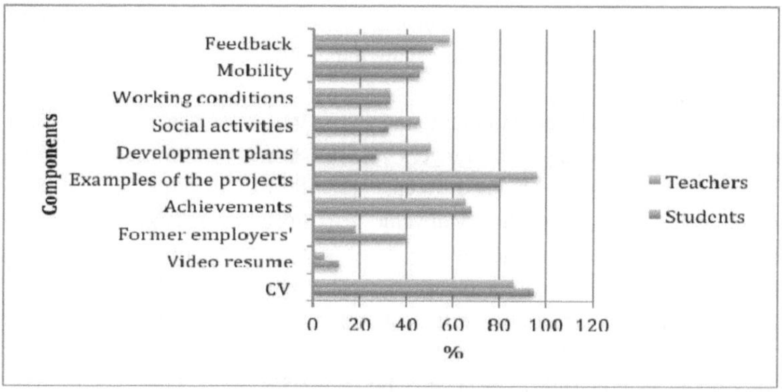

Fig. 2. e-portfolio components

As it is seen, then in general teachers, who are more experienced and students with more theoretical understanding of the e-portfolio concept, perceive the components in a quite similar way – CV, achievements and example of the projects are perceived as one of the important components. That is in line with the theoretical baseline with the e-portfolio concept as well.

Students and teachers evaluate the video resume and also working conditions less important component of the e-portfolio. Teachers tend to consider the development plans and feedback more important than the students do. Results indicate that firstly, students perceive the e-portfolio as a tool that demonstrates the achievements – what and how well the owner of the e-portfolio done in his/her professional journey. Additionally the results indicate that teachers, who are experienced and aware of the e-portfolio concept, perceive that e-portfolio should not only be product tool for demonstrating the results of ones achievements, but also as the process tool with the professional development plans. Additionally the feedback is important for teachers, which may refer to the need for the evidencing of the content in the e-portfolio, but surprisingly the former employees' references was not important. That may hint that informal feedback is more valuable than official references from formal institution.

4.4 Trust in e-portfolio

One of the research aims was to investigate the participants' general attitudes related with the trust in e-portfolio, because the development of the e-portfolio may face several trust related issues. The questions were divided into several blocks of questions: a) general trust of people; b) sharing in Internet; c) e-portfolio as professional development tool; d) trusting the content in e-portfolio.

Table 1. Trust in e-portfolio

	Teachers	Students	HR managers
People should be trusted	88%	68%	80%
Noone should be trusted	25%	17%	20%
Should be careful when trusting the strangers	3%	10%	20%
Like to select with whom I share the information	95%	95%	90%
Like to have the control over the people I share the information	99%	93%	90%
Like to share with those who are familiar to me	91%	76%	90%
If needed, I share the materials with strangers	80%	76%	70%
E-portfolio is useful for me (for being different)	89%	76%	70%
E-portfolio increases owners' professional value	86%	61%	50%
E-portfolio shows openness to criticism	80%	48%	30%
E-portfolio shows creditability of the owner	79%	51%	30%
E-portfolio guarantees successful image of the owner from the ICT perspective	87%	66%	60%
Materials created in e-portfolio are created by its owner	95%	73%	70%
Reflections in e-portfolio are written by its owner	85%	66%	60%
E-portfolio in application process is more creditable than CV	71%	39%	30%
E-portfolio presents the courage of the owner to be public in Internet	83%	66%	50%
Materials in e-portfolio should be verified by third parties	46%	59%	40%

Table 1 describes that the results of the students and HR managers, who don't have the practical experience with the e-portfolio, are not sharply contrasting. There seems to be no evidence that if a person doesn't trust people in general, then they are rather skeptic with the development of e-portfolios as well. The results of the teachers are rather more interesting. Experienced users of e-portfolios, as the teachers seem to be, have more hindrances with trusting people and sharing the information in public compared with students and HR managers. But they believe more that e-portfolio is useful for visualizing the professional profile of the owner and could be more reliable compared with the traditional CV.

4.5 E-portfolio in the Recruitment Process

The following block focuses on the questions from questionnaire and focus group interviews that investigate HR managers' and students' current experiences and attitudes of using the e-portfolio in the recruitment process.

8 HR managers out of 10 admitted that an applicant with e-portfolio has not approached them and two of the HR managers have been approached with some of the components of e-portfolio. 4 HR managers admitted that have not used an e-portfolio for selecting and employee, because they have never heard about the concept, one have not had a need before and the rest of the five respondents did not answered the questions.

Still, nearly all HR managers (8 out of 10) claim to collect information on prospective employees from social networks and one of them from Internet. Such result indicates that HR managers need some additional information instead of the traditional CV and e-portfolio could be the option.

None of the responded HR managers agree that e-portfolio could replace the interview. In the case when candidate present e-portfolio, four HR managers said that they would invite the candidate for an interview; 2 would admit the applicant in the second round of the selection process and two of them would look at the e-portfolio, but wouldn't prefer the candidate because of the e-portfolio format.

The same question was discussed in focus group interviews. The results were analyzed and categorized into following larger concepts: current practices (of recruitment); potential of e-portfolio (in recruitment) and aspects of e-portfolio (in recruitment).

Current Recruitment Practices - Current dominant practices of recruiting new staff for ICT companies is mainly based on internship, company-provided workshops/courses in colleges/universities or summer schools organized by companies. These three long-term (6-12 weeks) apprenticeship formats allow senior ICT staff and recruitment specialists to evaluate candidates in the authentic context, reducing the need for e-portfolios and competence assessment based on professional qualification standards or formal competence models.

However, all three aforementioned forms of apprenticeship are highly competitive, requiring significant pre-filtering of candidates in two rounds. The first round filters out 40-80% of applications based on CV-s, while in most of the cases, no specific CV format is enforced – except in Microsoft/Skype, which expects the candidates to submit a LinkedIn-based CV/portfolio. The second round involves practical assignment, e.g. programming task to be completed within a fixed period of time (ranging from 4 hours to one week).

Potential of e-portfolio - e-portfolios have been regularly used in recruiting designers and graphic artists – mainly as an initiative of candidates themselves. Yet, the HR specialists see the great potential in using competence-based e-portfolios in the recruitment process in the future, but under some circumstances (discussed below).

Aspects of e-portfolio - HR managers pointed that firstly, e-portfolios should be introduced already during the ICT studies in vocational schools, colleges and universities. Secondly, e-portfolios should follow the similar structure and competence models, in order to be easily comparable by HR specialists. Thirdly, users should be able to select their own platform for building e-portfolio and design it creatively. And lastly, the threats to digital privacy and IPR (e.g. revealing previous, copyrighted works made for other companies) should be minimized.

4.6 Interviews with the Teachers

Focus group interviews were conducted with the teachers who had previous experience to develop own e-portfolio. For the current study we categorized the results of the discussions in two larger categories: possibilities of the e-portfolio and perceived barriers of the e-portfolio.

Possibilities of the e-portfolio. The main value that respondents perceived about e-portfolio was related with the possibility to store electronically the materials in one place, which can be systemized and easily accessed from different places. Respondents believed that one of the values of e-portfolio is its free format and the possibility to personalize it with different medias. It was also pointed that with the e-portfolio the owner can evaluate his/her appropriateness to certain job positions and use it in different appraisal situations.

Barriers of the e-portfolio. Respondents divided the barriers related with the usage of e-portfolio to technical, organizational and personal.

Technical barriers mean that people don't have enough competencies to build their e-portfolio. Currently used technologies for creating the e-portfolio don't support different templates and there is lack of standards to rely on when developing own portfolio. Therefore everyone prepares something that s/he thinks could be named as e-portfolio and therefore the level is quite different. Participants pointed that they would like to have the possibility to publish only selected materials; especially they don't like to publish all the reflections in their weblogs. There should be possibility to publish materials to at least selected groups of people.

Personal barriers are for instance the lack of self-confidence to present yourself in the public, internal resistance to reflect, analyze, plan, report and so on. Lack of time was also mentioned as a barrier that inhibits the development of e-portfolio. Systemic update of the e-portfolio requires lot of extra work and teachers claimed that they don't have time for that. However all the respondents pointed that e-portfolio becomes powerful only when it is updated systemically and also the content should be reflected. It was also believed that such systemic update will motivate user to update it more and more as it is inspiring to see what has been done. Respondents mentioned that not updated e-portfolio decreases the trust towards the owner of the e-portfolio. Systemic update of e-portfolio was considered important from the teaching perspective as well. When using e-portfolio as an assessment tool it is not enough to evaluate students' competences based on the results of the one course, but based on longer period of learning and practicing.

Lack of supportive *organizational culture was* also mentioned as a barrier. Employers, commissions, boards do not accept the e-portfolio as an application tool and therefore users are less motivated to create the e-portfolio.

5 Discussion and Conclusions

The study aimed to find out what are the current practices and attitudes of using e-portfolio in the Estonian academic settings and what might be the potential of implementing e-portfolio as a transition tool from school to workplace. Most of the ongoing research in the field of connecting the academic and professional learning with the e-portfolio is in the health field and also to some extent in the field of (teacher) education. Hughes, Linsay and Purnell [14] have said that it could be that education and health related subjects in vocational areas place heavy emphasis upon reflective practice. This is the reason why we involved teachers to the study – to get more practical insight to the e-portfolio experiences. Based on the collected data with the web-based questionnaire we identified two groups of respondents: those who have experiences with e-portfolio and those who don't know what e-portfolio exactly is. Experienced group of respondents are teachers as expected, whereas students and HR managers are the less experienced group.

Qualitative results collected in focus-group interviews indicated that although teachers perceive the e-portfolio to be useful and probably potential tool in future employment, then there are several issues to be considered – mainly the technical issues - there is no software in Estonia, which is meant for the development of competence-based portfolio. But additionally the supportive elements from the boards like employment, accreditation and evaluation of the prior learning should be provided in order to assure the motivation to develop and systematically update the e-portfolio – the audience should be persuaded. HR managers pointed they see the future potential for the e-portfolio, but e-portfolios should then present lifelong competence-based learning from the beginning of academic studies.

In order to address these issues, the next step in the larger design phase would be to work out the general conceptual design of the competence-based e-portfolio and investigate the possibilities to integrate it to the academic studies as early as possible. It would be worth to consider adding the open badges to the competence-portfolio design. Open Badges are images, with embedded validation information, which are awarded after demonstrating specific learning achievements, such as understanding a particular topic or acquiring a specific skill [15]. There is a link between the e-portfolio concept and open badges approach. As indicated by Glover and Latif [15, there are two significant features of Open Badges that would allow their use as a rudimentary portfolio; a badge must contain a link to the requirements for obtaining it, and badges can be linked to evidence in meeting those requirements. Based on that assumption, the open badges could be used in e-portfolio design as an additional achievement recognition mechanism.

References

1. Strohmeier, S.: Electronic Portfolios In Recruiting? A Conceptual Analysis of Usage. Journal of Electronic Commerce Research 11(4), 268–281 (2010)
2. Stevens, K., Gerber, D., Hendra, R.: Transformational learning through prior learning assessment. Adult Education Quarterly 60(4), 377–404 (2010)
3. Campbell, D.M., Cignetti, P.B., Melenyzer, B.J., Nettles, D.H., Wyman, R.M.: How to develop a professional portfolio. A manual for teachers. Pearson, New York (2004)
4. Imhof, M., Picard, C.: Views on using e-portfolios in teacher education. Teaching and Teacher Education 25, 149–154 (2009)
5. Sampson, D., Fytros, D.: Competence Models in Technology-enhanced Competence-based Learning. In: Adelsberger, H.H., Kinshuk, Pawlowski, J.M., Sampson, D. (eds.) International Handbook on Information Technologies for Education and Training, 2nd edn. Springer (2008)
6. Rindlisbacher, B.: Conceptual Specification of an E-Portfolio System for Enterprise Trainee Programs. Master thesis. Fachhochschule Nordwestschweiz FHNW (2013)
7. Curyer, S., Leeson, J., Mason, J., Williams, A.: Developing e-portfolios for VET: Policy issues and interoperability. Australian Flexible Learning Framework (2007), `http://hdl.voced.edu.au/10707/69149`
8. Okoro, E.A., Washington, M.C., Cardon, P.W.: Eportfolios in Business Communication Courses as Tools for Employment. Business Communication Quarterly 74(3), 347–351 (2011)
9. Stevens, H.: The impact of e-portfolio development on the employability of adults aged 45 and over. Campus-Wide Information Systems 25(4), 209–218 (2008)
10. Temple, V., Allan, G., Temple, B.: Employers' and students' perceptions of electronic employment portfolios. In: Jeffery, P.L. (ed.) Proceedings of the International Conference of the Australian Association for Research in Education 2003, Auckland (2003)
11. Johnson, R.B., Onwuegbuzie, A.J.: Mixed Methods Research: A Research Paradigm Whose Time Has Come. Educational Researcher 33(7), 14–26 (2004)
12. Creswell, J.W.: Educational Research. Planning, Conducting and Evaluating Quantitative and Qualitative Research. Pearson Education, Inc., New Jersey (2002)
13. Miles, M.B., Huberman, M.A.: Qualitative Data Analysis, 2nd edn. Sage Publications, Inc., Thousand Oaks (1994)
14. Hughes, J., Linsey, D.P., Purnell, E.: Developing Professional Reflective Practice in Vocational Subjects using an Eportfolio System. Connections 3(3) (2008)
15. Glover, I., Latif, F.: Investigating perceptions and potential of open badges in formal higher education. In: Proceedings of World Conference on Educational Multimedia, Hypermedia and Telecommunications 2013, pp. 1398–1402. AACE, Chesapeake (2013)

A Multi-server Approach for Large Scale Collaborative Game-Based Learning

Yunhua Deng and Zhe Huang

City University of Hong Kong, Kowloon, Hong Kong, China

Abstract. E-learning through online games, where users play collaboratively to gain knowledge, has great potential to significantly change the way we learn. As the number of participants is no longer limited by the classroom, the learning process could potentially involve tens of thousands of learners. However, hosting massive users playing in a shared game world is nontrivial, as the underlying servers may get overloaded by the constantly changing workload due to user activity. In this work, we adapt a multi-server approach with dynamic load balancing to enable large scale collaborative game-based learning. Through simulation, we thoroughly evaluate its performance and identify the optimal settings of the key load balancing parameters under different scenarios. Results imply that the multi-server approach can support tens of thousands of users learning together, through combining the power of multiple servers each of which only can handle hundreds of users.

1 Introduction

The increasing availability of broadband Internet access as well as the rising popularity of mobile devices have revolutionized many industries, including music, movie, gaming, news and retail. Education, which has been developing relatively slowly, is expected to be the next target. As a result, e-learning research is booming in recent years. For example, Second Life and Minecraft have been used for educational purposes (Fig. 1), and currently massive open online courses (MOOCs) have already hit the market, attracting millions of users to conduct learning online (e.g., Cousera has over 7 million users as of 2014).

One attractive possibility of e-learning is that a large number of users may participate in learning activities in the same online learning environment. To achieve

Fig. 1. Examples of using online games for collaborative learning: (left) a class held in Second Life [1]; (right) a roller coaster being built collaboratively by students [2]

E. Popescu et al. (Eds.): ICWL 2014, LNCS 8613, pp. 87–97, 2014.

this, the scalability of e-learning technology is vital. As discussed in [11,12,10], due to the enormous amount of computational resources demanded in large scale e-learning applications like knowledge retrieval, simulations, electronic whiteboard and educational 3D games, the simple client-server architecture where one server handles the requests of all users does not suffice, and multi-server architectures must be used. Collaborative game-based learning (CGBL) is an attractive application of e-learning, as it engages the students much better than traditional lecturing. In particular, the social aspect of gaming can incentivize students to participate and improve their skills.

As the concept of CGBL is still experimental, the number of users in educational online games is small compared to the popular massively multiplayer online games (MMOGs). However, we envision that the scale of CGBL systems will match that of contemporary popular MMOGs someday, and it will then face the scalability challenge. In the future, online courses might be gamified, and massive users might interact in a game. For example, they might be collaboratively managing international affairs in a simulation game like PeaceMaker, or completing education-oriented quests in Quest Atlantis. At this large scale, the underlying server architecture will face serious scalability problems. The common approach taken by most popular MMOGs today is *sharding*, which is to separate users into multiple isolated copies (or shards) of the game where users can only play together with others in the same copy. This in fact undermines the original intention of CGBL, and motivates us to improve the scalability of CGBL systems without the need of sharding. In particular, we propose to adapt a multi-server approach [7] which is originally developed for distributed virtual environments (DVEs) to enable large scale CGBL. A DVE allows users from different geographical locations play and interact in a shared computer-generated environment through the Internet.

Deng and Lau [7] study the generic scenario where users have purely random movement behavior, and this is surely different from the recent practices of CGBL [1,2,15] where users tend to form groups and have their own territories. The difference of user behavior will affect the performance of the underlying dynamic load balancing algorithm of the multi-server approach [7]. We use an abstract CGBL model inspired by recent practices [1,2,15] to evaluate the multi-server approach [7], and identify the optimal settings of its parameters under various CGBL scenarios. Through simulation, we show that, after being adapted, the multi-server approach [7] can handle the computational demand imposed by large scale CGBL with tens of thousands of users involved.

The rest of this paper is organized as follows. Section 2 summarizes existing relevant methods. Section 3 describes the abstract model of collaborative game-based learning we concern here. Section 4 elaborates the multi-server approach and the underlying dynamic load balancing method. Section 5 presents and discusses the simulation results. Section 6 finally concludes this work.

2 Related Work

Our work is related to computer-supported collaborative learning (CSCL), which is a pedagogical approach that learning takes place via social interaction through the Internet. Since the earliest practice of computer-supported intentional learning environments [20], various systems have been built, such as Cool Modes [4] and the face-to-face educational environment coFFEE [5]. The effect of CSCL on learners have long been a subject of study with various theories having been established. For a survey of recent development of CSCL, we refer readers to [13]. Our work is in line with CSCL research in that we focus on the server technology to support large scale CGBL which is the most attractive form of CSCL.

As mentioned in Section 1, the sharding approach currently taken by most MMOGs for achieving scalability does not suit CGBL. In recent DVE research, a number of multi-server techniques have been developed to improve the scalability of DVE systems while maintaining user experiences. These techniques do not separate users in different copies of the game world, but allow them play in the same virtual space. Here, distributing users to servers has to take special caution, as a high cost will be induced if users on different servers interact (which is in fact inevitable) and servers are distributed remotely [17]. Suppose that we can ignore the inter-server communication delay problem [6] by assuming servers are all physically co-located, we still need to consider another problem, that is, how to prevent server overloading at runtime. This problem is nontrivial, as users can freely change servers as they move into different parts of the virtual world that are handled by different servers, causing some servers becoming highly-loaded while others remaining idle. To this end, many methods have been proposed to address this consequent *dynamic load balancing* problem, and they can be classified into two groups: global and local methods.

Global methods have a central load balancer to evenly distribute the workload among servers and utilize the time-varying load information of all servers to derive workload transfer solutions for rebalancing. For instance, [14] formulated the problem as an optimization problem with the objective of minimizing the amount of workload transfers while resolving the workload imbalance among servers which is finally solved using linear programming. A similar global method based on optimization is proposed in [25]. Both methods are slow due to the complexity of the optimization process.

Local methods address this performance problem. For instance, some works [9,16,8] resolve the server overloading by transferring workload from the heavily loaded servers to the less stressed neighboring servers based on some local information only. However, these local methods tend to produce short-term solutions, and the servers may quickly become overloaded again after a short while. Most recently, a method proposed in [7] overcomes this problem by adopting the heat diffusion model and is proved to be computationally efficient and yet effective. Hence, we adapt this method to address our scalability problem faced by large scale game-based learning. In a broader context, our work is part of the efforts to build infrastructure to support synchronous CGBL [11], so that CGBL applications [24,21] can one day support millions of users playing together.

3 Model of Collaborative Game-Based Learning

We describe an abstract model of CGBL, which is motivated by [15] where children form groups to build 3D structures in a virtual world. Although the study is small scale (only several children in a group), we envision that large scale collaboration may take place in the future, in a form like WesterosCraft project, which creates a virtual world for large scale collaboration. For example, students may recreate Yellowstone National Park to learn its geographical features.

Collaborative learning usually takes the form of group work, where users in the same group tightly cooperate with each other to achieve a common goal. Meanwhile, intergroup competition [19] or collaboration [18] may be adopted by instructors to enhance student performance. As such, we assume the following behavior patterns: 1) users form groups, those in the same group spend much time together in a local region; 2) users sometimes move to regions belonging to other groups and interact with other groups.

Similar to the work [7], we model users as points in the game world. Each user can move freely in the game world and has a field of view (FOV) represented as a circle, where he can interact with other users if they are within this area. For simplicity, we assume that the user is *always* interacting with other users in his FOV, as even seeing each other leads to interaction.

4 A Scalable Multi-server Approach

Given a set of servers all with the same capacity, and a number of users playing together in a contiguous map, in the following we investigate the problem of assigning the total workload (in terms of users) to servers such that none of them will be overloaded during the game's runtime.

4.1 Service Architecture

Since a single server cannot afford the huge computing and bandwidth demand by massively multi-user gameplay, a viable solution is to use a multi-server approach that is scalable. Our proposed multi-server architecture consists of components shown in Fig. 2. Each game server is in charge of maintaining the

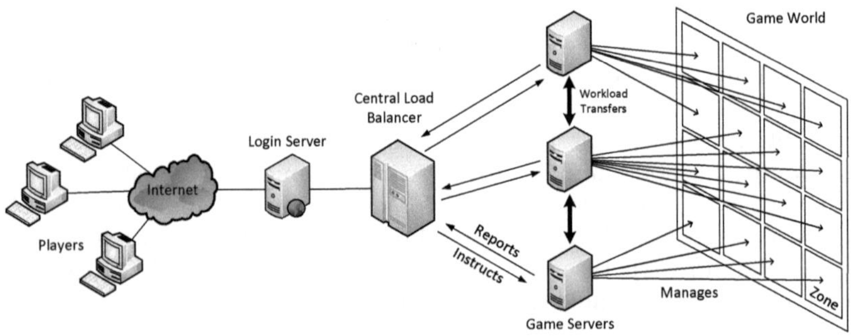

Fig. 2. The service architecture of the multiplayer game. The game world is divided into a set fixed boundary zones, and each game server handles a subset of them. The zones assigned to a server may change during the game based on the workload dynamics (i.e., varying number of players) in those zones. If necessary, servers transfer workload to neighbor servers, that is, change the zone-to-server assignment, based on the instructions issued by a central load balancer that keeps monitoring workload information of all game servers and computing workload transfer plans.

responsiveness and consistency perceived by the users within the zones under its management in terms of continuously sending state updates of other users and the environment near to those users in question. In addition, if a user is moving into a zone that is handled by another serves, the original server has to handle such inter-server handover seamlessly by communicating with the destinate server. Fortunately, users likely stay in zones with others that belong to the same group or have the same interest (refer to Section 3), such that handover events do not happen so frequently. Below we present the dynamic load balancing problem and algorithm by revisiting the solution [7].

4.2 Dynamic Load Balancing

Due to the uncertainty and randomness of user mobility, workload on zones can dynamically changes, such that the current zone-to-server assignment may become invalid (or imbalanced) as time goes by. This motivates us to adapt the algorithm proposed in [7] which is simple yet efficient and suitable for large scale gaming systems that usually contain hundreds of servers and tens of thousands of users. Basically this algorithm is derived from the heat diffusion model by considering server workload as heat that will naturally diffuse from hotter regions (heavily loaded servers) to cooler regions (lightly loaded servers) smoothly (preserving zone adjacency) and eventually a global heat equilibrium state (load balance) will be achieved. We give a brief technical review of this algorithm based on the model illustrated in Fig. 2.

The central load balancer periodically monitors the workload on each server; if a load balancing process is needed after detecting that some servers are too busy while others are idle, it computes the a plan of workload transfers using the heat diffusion model (presented below) and instructs game servers to carry out plan by exchanging zones with neighbor servers. The amount of workload needed to be transferred between each pair of neighbor servers (namely, s_i and s_j) is referred to as *balancing flow* and denoted by $\lambda_{i,j}$. The load balance can be achieved if all those balancing flows are found out: $\bar{l} = l_i - \sum_{s_j \in N_i} \lambda_{i,j}$, where l_i is the workload of s_i, $\bar{l}$ is the average workload over all servers, and N_i is the set of neighbor servers of s_i. Let us denote $L = (l_1, l_2, ..., l_n)^T$ as the workload vector of n servers, and $L^{(k)} = (l_1^{(k)}, l_2^{(k)}, ..., l_n^{(k)})^T$ as the intermediate workload vector at k^{th} iteration step ($k \geq 0$). Here, "intermediate" means that $L^{(k)}$ does not represent an actual workload vector; it is just some intermediate load values during the computation of balancing flows. Given the initial workload vector, $L^{(0)}$, we compute the intermediate workload vector at k^{th} iteration by: $L^{(k)} = DL^{(k-1)}$, where $D = (d_{i,j})_{n \times n}$ is called *diffusion matrix* and given by:

$$d_{i,j} = \begin{cases} c_{i,j} & \text{if } i \neq j \text{, and } s_j \in N_i \\ 1 - \sum_m c_{i,m} & \text{if } i = j \\ 0 & \text{otherwise,} \end{cases} \quad (1)$$

where $c_{i,j}$ is the diffusion coefficient proposed by Boillat [3] that chooses the portion of the load difference between s_i and s_j to be exchanged between them and is computed by: $c_{i,j} = 1/(\max\{|N_i|, |N_j|\} + 1)$, where $|N_i|$ is the number of neighbor servers of s_i. As proved by [3], the diffusion matrix will guarantee the iterative balancing flow computation to converge after N iterations ($N \geq 0$) such that each server may have roughly the same workload:

$$\max\{l_i^{(N)} \in L^{(N)}\} \leq \bar{l}(1 + \theta_{imb}), \tag{2}$$

where θ_{imb} is *imbalance tolerance* defined by the percentage deviation from the average server load value $\bar{l}$. In general, smaller θ_{imb} can prevent the mostly loaded servers from being overloaded even if the global utilization is high. However, sometimes tolerating more load imbalance by setting larger θ_{imb} is beneficial as this can potentially reduce total amount of workload transfers. Finally we accumulate all intermediate load values to obtain balancing flows: $\lambda_{i,j} = \sum_{k=1}^{N} c_{i,j}(l_i^{(k)} - l_j^{(k)})$. After determining the balancing flows, the central load balancer instructs game servers to conduct proper workload transfer by exchanging boundary zones between neighbor servers. To accelerate the workload transfer process in practical implementation, we can duplicate all user information such as user profiles and geometry data of their avatars in each game server. Hence, we only need to send lightweight information such as IDs and positions of all users within each transferred zone to the target server. We refer readers to [7] for the detailed implementation of workload transfer. The dynamic load balancing eliminates the chance of server overloading through performing inter-server zone exchanging, which inevitably introduces affect user experiences. This leads to the following discussion of imbalance tolerance parameter setting.

5 Adaptation and Experimental Evaluation

In the following, we discuss the adaptation of the dynamic load balancing method presented in Section 4 to CGBL setting through extensive experiments.

5.1 Adaptation

The algorithm presented in Section 4 has an important parameter: the imbalance tolerance θ_{imb} as defined in Equation (2), which determines how aggressive the algorithm is in rebalancing servers' workload. A small imbalance tolerance encourages the algorithm to eliminate even a small workload imbalance, thus triggering a lot of migrations, that is, user being transferred from one server to another during exchanging zones between servers. Such a migration event can potentially cause service interruption, particularly when the servers involved are not physically co-located. On the other hand, a large imbalance tolerance puts some of the servers at the risk of being overloaded, and the crowded servers will have to frequently prevent new users from joining in. Either way, some users will be affected, and such a negative experience induces a cost. A good setting of θ_{imb} should strike to minimize this cost. As mentioned before, Deng and Lau [7] examine the proposed dynamic load balancing algorithm through a generic scenario where users are constantly moving towards random locations, which is different from the CGBL setting as described in Section 3. Thus, we need to examine the good settings of θ_{imb} by considering the characteristics of CGBL.

We investigate the following three scenarios, corresponding to three different user behavior patterns exhibited in different kinds of learning game setting: *low activeness*, representing that users tend to spend more time with their group members, rather than visiting other groups; *medium activeness*, representing that users tend to spend equal amount of time with their group members and visiting other groups; *high activeness*, representing that users tend to spend more time visiting other groups, rather than with their group members.

Games that mainly focus on internal collaboration, such as Minecraft, have low activeness; games that mainly focus on exploration, such as Quest Atlantis, feature high activeness. Games that do not have a clear focus, like Second Life, may have medium activeness characteristic.

5.2 Simulation Setup

Game World and User Population. The game world used in simulation contains 10000 zones, where each zone is assigned to a user group. Each group has 5 users, so there are 50000 users in total.

Zone Attractiveness Specification. In practice, groups are diverse, and they do not receive the same amount of attention from others, hence the zones they occupy have different attractiveness. Groups that are working on more interesting projects, or more competent, or simply more friendly to others, naturally attract more visits from others. There are 3 levels of attractiveness: low, medium, and high (detailed settings are listed in Table 1). As the game progresses, the attractiveness of zones will change. Every 30 minutes, attractiveness levels are shuffled among all zones except half of the highly attractive ones.

Table 1. For each attractiveness level, *individual probability* is the probability of a zone being visited, *count* is the approximate number of zones at this attractiveness level per 100 zones in total, and *accumulated probability* is the probability of the zones at this attractiveness level as a whole being visited, which is equal to the multiplication of *individual probability* and *count*

	individual probability	count	accumulated probability
low attractiveness	0.00875	80	0.7
medium attractiveness	0.0111	18	0.2
high attractiveness	0.05	2	0.1

User Behavior Modeling. In each scenario, the user alternatively spends time with his group members and visiting other groups. He first spends α minutes with their group members, then β minutes visiting other groups, and then start over again. α a random number between m_α and M_α, and β is sampled similarly. m_α,M_α,m_β,M_β are 10,30,1,5 for lowly active users, and 1,5,10,30 for highly active users. The three scenarios discussed in Section 5.1 have different population structure: the low, medium and high activeness scenarios have 20%, 50% and 80% of highly active users respectively. When a user is going to visit other zones, he first decides whether to explore a zone nearby (probability is 0.8), or teleport to a remote zone (probability is 0.2). In the first case, he picks a neighboring location among the 4 neighbors; in the second case, the zone is selected among all zones except his home zone (i.e., the zone belonging to his group) and the previously visited zone. Either way, the probability of a zone being selected is proportional to its attractiveness level. When the user moves to a new zone, he stays there for 1 to 3 minutes randomly. The physical size of each zone is 256 by 256, and a user has a field of view of 128.

Server Capacity and Utilization. The capacity of a server is the maximum number of users that can be handled by the server, and it is set to 500, similar to the capacity of most Minecraft servers (`http://minecraft-server-list.com`). The utilization is equal to the total number of users divided by the number of users supported by all the servers collectively. In the simulation, the utilization values tested are 0.75, 0.8 and 0.85.

Performance Measurement. There are two sources of negative user experience: user migration and non-servicing. User migration happens when the load balancing algorithm decides to transfer a user from one server to another, and non-servicing happens when the user is entering a zone whose servicing server is too busy (working at full workload). There is cost in both cases, and generally non-servicing is worse than migration. As such, we give non-servicing cost more weight, and compute the total cost as $c = 0.2m + 0.8n$, where m and n are the average number of migrated users and non-serviced users per minute. The simulation is set to run for 240 minutes for each setting.

5.3 Results and Discussion

We first show the effects of θ_{imb} under different user activeness settings, and discuss the optimal settings. Then we demonstrate the effectiveness of dynamic load balancing approach (presented in Section 4) in handling large numbers of users, compared to *static load balancing* approach which assigns zones to servers at the beginning (each server roughly handling the same number of zones) and maintains this assignment regardless of the workload dynamics during runtime.

Examining Impact of θ_{imb}. In Fig. 3 we can see how θ_{imb} affects the cost under different server utilization settings. As expected, load balancing is generally more useful when the servers are crowded, as the cost difference of using lower θ_{imb} (which corresponding to more aggressive load balancing) and higher θ_{imb} is larger when the utilization is higher. We can also see that, using a very aggressive load balancing is not always optimal, because to achieve a more balanced load, more users have to be migrated, which may offset the benefit of reducing the number of non-serviced users. In addition, higher server utilization requires more aggressive load balancing setting (smaller imbalance tolerance). One interesting observation is that the activeness level generally has little effect on the optimal choice of θ_{imb}, unless when there are neither non-serviced nor migrated users (see the rightmost subfigure of Fig. 3), where dynamic load balancing has no effect. This is counter-intuitive and worth further investigation in the future.

Examining Load Balancing. We examine the effectiveness of dynamic load balancing over static load balancing. Here we show the case where server utilization is 0.8 and θ_{imb} is 0.4 (obtained according to Fig. 3 middle). In Fig. 4,

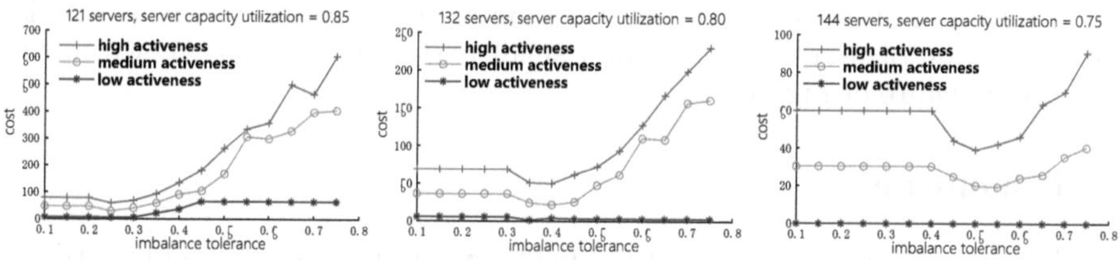

Fig. 3. Cost of each activeness level under different server utilization. θ_{imb} is set to 0.25, 0.4 and 0.5 in each case from left to right, respectively.

one can see that dynamic load balancing clearly outperforms the static one, in that it generally achieves better workload balance and leads to less overloaded servers and cost. This means that the scalability of the game is surely enhanced by dynamic load balancing. Furthermore, the average workload imbalance and average number of overloaded servers almost do not change with user activeness using dynamic load balancing, showing that it adapts to the users' behaviors very well. The difference between the two methods gets larger as more active users are into the game, as expected. We shown the workload distribution among servers as well as population density at the 210*th* minute in-game time in Fig. 5, where static load balancing has multiple overloaded servers which are eliminated using dynamic load balancing. We choose this moment for illustration because

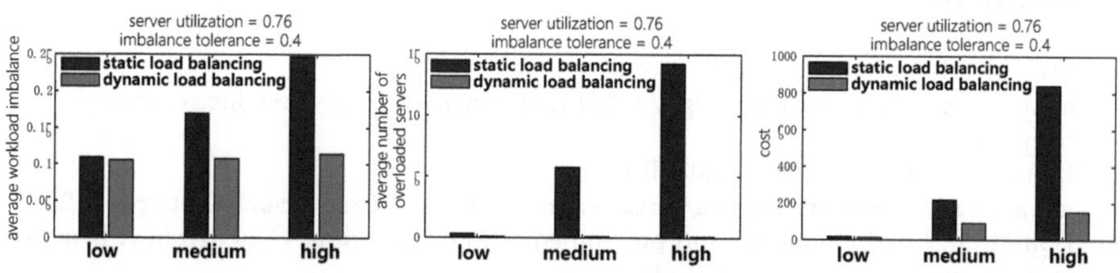

Fig. 4. Comparing static and dynamic load balancing on average workload imbalance (left), average number of overloaded servers (middle), and cost (right), with low, medium, and high user attractivness levels

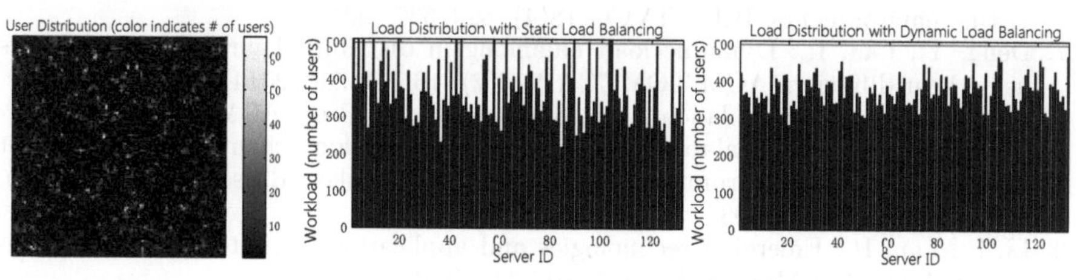

Fig. 5. User and load distribution at 210*th* minute (in-game time). On the left each pixel in the heat map represents a zone, and the color corresponds to the number of users in that zone. In the middle and on the right, the red line indicates the server capacity, and a server is overloaded if its workload is above the line.

the distribution of users is most skewed (non-uniform) in this moment, that is, a large portion of users gathering in a small portion of zones as shown in the leftmost subfigure of Fig. 5.

6 Conclusion

In this paper, we propose to adapt the multi-server approach and its underlying dynamic load balancing algorithm originally developed for DVEs to facilitate the scalability of CGBL systems which are attracting increasingly larger numbers of users playing and learning together. In particular, we investigate the effects of the imbalance tolerance parameter setting under various game-based learning scenarios with different user activeness levels. Through extensive experiments based on our proposed user mobility model which is capable of simulating user activities in an abstract level, we examine the optimal imbalance tolerance setting for different scenarios. After adaptation by choosing appropriate imbalance tolerance parameters according to the unique characteristics of CGBL, the proposed multi-server approach is shown to be able to help a CGBL system accommodate tens of thousands concurrent users without compromising system performance and user experience. In the future work, we plan to establish a more sophisticated CGBL model, and examine more user activities related to CGBL. (This work was partly supported by a multi-resolution project [22,23].)

References

1. Second Life in educational purposes, `http://anulik.edublogs.org/2010/11/06/second-life-in-educational-purposes`
2. Using Minecraft to teach Math literacy, `http://www.itslearning.eu/using-minecraft-to-teach-math-literacy123`
3. Boillat, J.: Load balancing and poisson equation in a graph. Concurrency: Practice and Experience 2(4), 289–313 (1990)
4. Bollen, L., Hoppe, H., Milrad, M., Pinkwart, N.: Collaborative modelling in group learning environments. In: Proc. System Dynamics Conference (2002)
5. De Chiara, R., Di Matteo, A., Manno, I., Scarano, V.: CoFFEE: Cooperative Face2Face educational environment. In: Proc. CollaborateCom (2007)
6. Deng, Y., Lau, R.: On delay adjustment for dynamic load balancing in distributed virtual environments. IEEE TVCG 18(4), 529–537 (2012)
7. Deng, Y., Lau, R.: Dynamic load balancing in distributed virtual environments using heat diffusion. ACM TOMCCAP 10(2), 16:1–16:19 (2014)
8. Lau, R.: Hybrid load balancing for online games. In: Proc. ACM MM (2010)
9. Lee, K., Lee, D.: A scalable dynamic load distribution scheme for multi-server distributed virtual environment systems with highly-skewed user distribution. In: Proc. ACM VRST (2003)
10. Li, F., Lau, R.: Emerging technologies and applications on interactive entertainments. Journal of Multimedia 6(2), 107–114 (2011)
11. Li, Q., Lau, R., Shih, T., Li, F.: Technology supports for distributed and collaborative learning over the internet. ACM TOIT 8(2), 5:1–5:24 (2008)
12. Li, Q., Lau, R., Wah, B., Ashman, H., Leung, E., Li, F., Lee, V.: Guest editors' introduction: Emerging internet technologies for e-learning. IEEE Internet Computing 13(4), 11–17 (2009)

13. Ludvigsen, S., Mørch, A.: Computer-supported collaborative learning: Basic concepts, multiple perspectives, and emerging trends. The International Encyclopedia of Education 5, 290–296 (2010)
14. Lui, J., Chan, M.: An efficient partitioning algorithm for distributed virtual environment systems. IEEE TPDS 13(3), 193–211 (2002)
15. Berg Marklund, B., Backlund, P., Johannesson, M.: Children's collaboration in emergent game environments. In: Proc. FDG (2013)
16. Ng, B., Lau, R., Si, A., Li, F.: Multi-server support for large scale distributed virtual environments. IEEE TMM 7(6), 1054–1065 (2005)
17. Ng, B., Li, F., Lau, R., Si, A., Siu, A.: A performance study of multi-server systems for distributed virtual environments. Information Sciences 154(1) (2003)
18. Puntambekar, S., et al.: Intra-group and intergroup: An exploration of learning with complementary collaboration tools. In: Proc. CSCL (1997)
19. Sancho, P., Gómez-Martín, P., Fernández-Manjón, B.: Multiplayer role games applied to problem based learning. In: Proc. DIMEA (2008)
20. Scardamalia, M., Bereiter, C.: Computer support for knowledge-building communities. Journal of the Learning Sciences 3(3), 265–283 (1994)
21. Short, D.: Teaching scientific concepts using a virtual world - minecraft. Teaching Science: The Journal of the ASTA 58(3), 55–58 (2012)
22. To, D., Lau, R., Green, M.: A method for progressive and selective transmission of multi-resolution models. In: Proc. ACM VRST (1999)
23. To, D., Lau, R., Green, M.: An adaptive multi-resolution method for progressive model transmission. Presence 10(1), 62–74 (2001)
24. Toro-Troconis, M., et al.: Design and delivery of game-based learning for virtual patients in second life. In: Researching Learning in Virtual Worlds (2010)
25. Van Den Bossche, B., et al.: Autonomic microcell assignment in massively distributed online virtual environments. JNCA 32(6), 1242–1256 (2009)

The Effects of Prior Knowledge for Incidental Vocabulary Acquisition on Multiplayer Online Role-Playing Game

Ben-Gao Huang and Jie Chi Yang

Graduate Institute of Network Learning Technology, National Central University,
Jhongli, Taiwan
{hbg,yang}@cl.ncu.edu.tw

Abstract. The affordances of MMORPGs provide authentic contexts for vocabulary acquisition. This study conducted incidental vocabulary learning on an MMORPG and investigated the effects of prior knowledge. The prior knowledge in the study was including English proficiency and gaming experience. To evaluate the learning effectiveness, 12 target words were appeared in task dialogues and flashcards on the MMORPG. An experiment was conducted for 52 fifth-grade students. The results show that the learners with medium gaming experience level had significant learning effectiveness for the vocabulary positioned in task dialogues. On the contrary, except high gaming experience learners, the learning effects of flashcard were more influenced by English academic level. In other words, the vocabulary in gaming requirement condition were more noticed by medium gaming experience learners, and the vocabulary in non-requirement condition were more perceived by higher English proficiency learners.

Keywords: incidental vocabulary acquisition, MMORPGs, prior knowledge.

1 Introduction

The popularity of computer games has attracted many educators being aware the potential of Digital Game-Based Learning (DGBL). It is a new territory for computer assistant language learning (CALL) during the last decade. A number of studies have investigated the effects of computer games on second language acquisition. In these games, Massive Multi-player Online Role-Playing Games (MMORPGs) had gained the attention of language educators for their amazing features. Some studies indicated that the characters of MMORPGs could provide an authentic context for vocabulary acquisition, such as simulation scenarios, communication affordances, and meaningful game tasks. More interestingly, the findings from these studies of MMORPGs are confirmed to be beneficial for vocabulary acquisition [1,2,3].

Recently, researchers further indicated that MMORPGs have the potential for incidental vocabulary acquisition [4]. In the past decades, books reading was the main source for incidental vocabulary acquisition [5,6,7]. Due to technology advance, some

E. Popescu et al. (Eds.): ICWL 2014, LNCS 8613, pp. 98–105, 2014.

researchers tried to use other media to conduct incidental vocabulary acquisition lately [8,9]. More specifically, the many affordances of MMORPGs provide rich reading context, such as task dialogue, advertisements or message banners, and chat room. Though MMORPGs offer reading contexts for vocabulary acquisition, there were few studies investigated incidental vocabulary acquisition in MMORPGs. Regarding DGBL, the prior knowledge is a main factor for learning effectiveness [10]. Prior knowledge includes domain knowledge and playing knowledge, the former is concerned with learning content and the latter is related with gaming skill [11]. In order to investigate the effects of prior knowledge for incidental vocabulary acquisition on MMORPG, a study was conducted to answer the following questions: 1. How does the students' English proficiency influence incidental vocabulary acquisition on MMORPGs? 2. How does the students' gaming experience influence incidental vocabulary acquisition on MMORPGs?

2 Related Works

2.1 Incidental Vocabulary Acquisition

Incidental vocabulary acquisition occurs in reading contexts that does not ask learners to pay attention on the meaning of unknown words and has no significant learning purposes [12]. These contexts providing some clues which surrounding unknown words could help learners to infer unknown words meanings. Many studies demonstrated that incidental vocabulary learning is an effective method for vocabulary acquisition [7], [9], [12].

Though most previous incidental vocabulary acquisition studies were reading-oriented, the learning strategies were diverse, such as glossing method, material presentation, or learning tasks. Accordingly, there were many studies to conduct incidental vocabulary learning in different ways. In addition to above methods, some studies considered using technology to assist learners acquiring vocabulary. For example, based on duel-code theory, researchers utilized Web allowing learners to read English text and pictures online. They found that these Web learning materials could help learners acquiring vocabulary [13]. Beside Web materials, video in a CALL program could support L2 learners to comprehend vocabulary, and both low and high proficiency learners showed significant progress [14]. Watching second language TV programs and playing related computer games also had positive effects on incidental vocabulary acquisition [15]. Among these media, especially computer games, which provided learners with fruitful forms of activities in highly motivating contexts [16]. Some researchers based on game-based learning approach to design computer games for incidental vocabulary acquisition. McGraw, Yoshimoto, and Seneff (2009) utilized speech recognition technology to implement a card-game to help EFL learners to acquire vocabulary incidentally [17]. Recently, many researchers noticed the amazing MMORPGs, which characteristics could provide abounding resources for learners' interaction and construct authentic contexts for learners to acquire vocabulary [1,2], [18]. Regarding MMORPGs could provide L2 learners with a linguistically rich virtual environment, playing MMORPGs could be another approach for incidental vocabulary acquisition [4].

2.2 MMORPGs for Vocabulary Acquisition

Considering the game-based learning approach, there were many studies utilized MMORPGs for vocabulary acquisition. MMORPGs offer beneficial environments for vocabulary acquisition that facilitate learning motivation of learners and have positive learning effectiveness. The impressive 3D scenarios, interaction and communication within players, and interesting game tasks can provide a vigorous learning mechanism and embed learning content into edutainment [2]. When players immerse in the game, they would be assigned many interesting game tasks to reach higher level or take newer adventures. In order to complete these game tasks, players should read many text messages, accord situational conditions to make decisions, and via communication to cooperate with other players. These processes evolve plentiful reading context, which were beneficial for learning vocabulary [2,3]. Thus, some vocabulary might be appeared along with game tasks frequently or occurred in scenarios meaningfully. The motivation of learners, occurrence times of vocabulary, and meaningful clues of context are important factors for incidental vocabulary acquisition [19]. Hence, MMORPGs have the potential to make valuable contexts for incidental vocabulary acquisition.

Regarding DGBL, many researchers indicated that learners' prior knowledge would influence the learning effectiveness. The prior knowledge is divided two main types, one is domain knowledge and the other is gaming experience [11], [20]. The prior knowledge might have positive or negative effects for learning effectiveness. For example, the higher vocabulary ability learners might acquire unknown vocabulary easily [19], but the high gaming experience learners might have more cognitive resource to learning or pay too much attentions on playing to ignore learning [11]. To investigate the effects of different prior knowledge for incidental learning on MMORPGs is an interesting issue. For incidental vocabulary acquisition on MMORPGs, task dialogues and advertisement banners afford read contexts. It is another interesting topic to investigate the learning effectiveness within different prior knowledge learners in different reading conditions. To this end, the study embedded learning content in MMORPG task dialogue boxes and evaluated the learning effectiveness of different prior knowledge learners for incidental vocabulary learning.

3 Methods

3.1 Participants

This study was conducted at an elementary school. A total of 52 fifth-grade EFL students participated in this study. All the participants had at least 2.5 years English lessons, and had the basic computer skills to operate a digital game.

3.2 The MMORPG Environment

In the study, the participants were exposed on a virtual environment of MMORPG. The background story and game tasks in the game were adapted the textbooks of their English lessons and a Chinese legend. When playing the MMORPG, players would be assigned game tasks in the vivid 3D environment one by one. To finish these game tasks, they should read a series texts dialogues. These text dialogues were important for players to interact with NPC and conquer the monsters. Generally, a small advertisement banner is attached to the dialogue box, and players sometimes might notice the advertisement incidentally. The texts of dialogues were related with game playing. In contrast, the player can ignore the banner. To measure the learning effects, there were six target words were positioned in dialogue texts, and another six target words were designed as flashcards and replaced advertisement banners. When moved to next dialogue, another vocabulary was showed on the flashcard randomly (Fig. 1).

Fig. 1. Screenshot from the MMORPG

3.3 Instruments

Gaming Experience Questionnaire. To count learners' average playing hours of per week, an open questionnaire was used to survey learners' gaming experiences in past two years. They should fill out what game they had played and the playing duration.

Vocabulary Knowledge Test. To measure the effectiveness of incidental vocabulary learning, the tests used in this study were vocabulary knowledge tests including pre-test and post-test. These tests consisted of 30 vocabulary in pre-test and 12 vocabulary in post-test. The 12 target words were selected from a new word list. These new words were selected and confirmed by three English teachers. A non-experiment fifth-grade class was measured the prior knowledge of those words, and served 12 words unknown to most students as the target words. To reduce the pre-test effect, some non-target words were added to the pre-tests [12], [22]. The vocabulary knowledge test used Paribakht and Bingham's Vocabulary Knowledge Scale (VKS) five scales to measure participants' incidental vocabulary acquisition [23]. It can be utilized evaluate the depth of vocabulary knowledge [24].

3.4 Procedure

The procedure of this study consisted of five steps. In the first step, participants completed the gaming experience questionnaire and vocabulary knowledge pre-test in approximately 30 minutes. To reduce the effect of the pre-test, the pre-test was carried out one week before playing the MMORPG [12], [22]. The second step was demonstrating how to complete a game task and practice about 20 minutes. The third step was the participants playing the MMORPG designed by the study for 80 minutes. Students were not asked to learn any vocabulary, but they were encouraged to finish each task at their best. In the fourth step, participants completed the immediate post-test in approximately 20 minutes. Finally, to investigate learners' perception with the MMORPG, an interview was conducted.

3.5 Data Analysis

The study was a quasi-experimental design which used a single experimental group. The data were collected from students' academic score in English course of the first semester of fifth grade, gaming experience questionnaire, the vocabulary knowledge pre-test, the vocabulary knowledge post-test and interview. According students' English academic score the participants were divided into two groups with different prior knowledge: low English academic score group and high English academic score group. As for learners' per week play hours distributed widely, the study based on the gaming experience survey to divide low, medium, and high three levels. The independent variables of the study were two English academic levels and three gaming experience levels. The dependent variable of the study was VKS score. In addition to descriptive statistics analysis, the study utilized two-way ANOVA to evaluate the differences of the learning effectiveness between the different prior knowledge learners. With respect to qualitative evaluation, the study employed interview data as a complementary approach for more detailed analysis of diverse gaming behaviors and perceptions due to different levels of prior knowledge.

4 Results

4.1 Target Words Related with Game Playing

A two-way ANOVA for gain scores of task dialogue showed a significant effect for gaming experience ($F=4.711$, $p=.014$), and no significant main effects or interactions were observed for English academic level.

Post-hoc analysis revealed that the gain score of the participants with medium gaming experience were significantly better than those with low ($p=.007$) or high ($p=.015$) gaming experience. That is to say the medium gaming experience learners have better learning effectiveness for the target words in related game condition (Fig. 2). The reason might be low gaming experience participants required more attention on how to deal with and how to play in gaming situations, which cause them to spend less time on learning content. On the other hand, the high gaming experience learners might use their playing skill to complete game tasks, and to skip learning content [11]. One high gaming experience participants of interviews said that he seldom noticed the task dialog, but guess these questions randomly. He also did not pay any attention on flashcard and had no impression on it. Further study should consider what mechanisms could assistant low gaming experience players playing on the game and attract high gaming experience players to pay more attention on learning content.

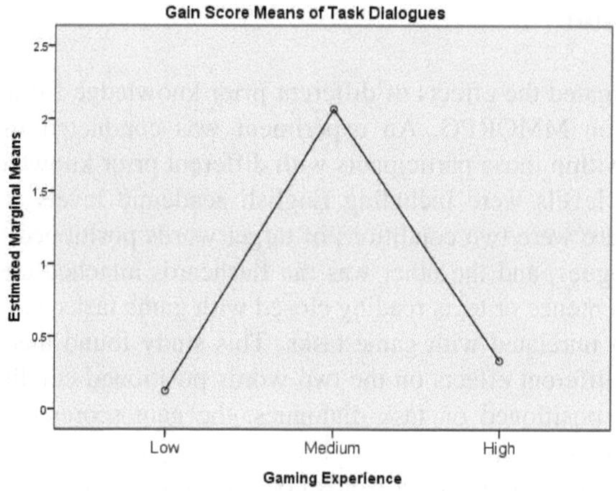

Fig. 2. The gain score of different gaming experience learners in task dialogues

4.2 Target Words Unrelated with Game Playing

The flashcards were appeared on the position of advertisement banner that were unrelated with game tasks, and it is not a necessary condition for game playing. The results revealed a significant interaction between English academic score and gaming experience (F=3.775, p=.030). Regarding the English prior knowledge of participants within different gaming experience levels, the gain score of low achievers did not reveal significant differences within three gaming experience levels. Regarding high English academic achievers, the gaming experience had significant simple main effects (F=6.61, p=.003). The gain score of medium gaming experience participants was higher than high gaming experience learners significantly (t=3.664, p<.001). This might be due to the fact that high gaming experience participants felt that to pay attentions in task dialogue is a time waste, so they might not notice the flashcards too [11].

Comparing the different English achievers with same gaming experience, the gain score of high English achievers was significant better than the low English achievers both within the low (t=-3.360, p=.002) and medium (t=-3.618, p=.001) gaming experience participants, and the high gaming experience did not. In this study, the flashcards were located on original advertisement banners. These high achievers showed better improvements might be because they have better implicit memory of advertisements in online game [25]. Due to the fact that the main goals of the MMORPGs were not learning vocabulary, these target vocabulary on flashcard might be paid attention implicitly or acquired incidentally. Incidental vocabulary might involve some peripheral attentions [19]. The gain score of high achievers with high gaming experience was not better than low achievers. According the interview, the possible cause was that the high gaming experience participants found some other ways to finish tasks quickly, so they might not pay attention on flashcard.

5 Conclusion

The study investigated the effects of different prior knowledge for incidental vocabulary acquisition on MMORPG. An experiment was conducted for comparing the learning effects within those participants with different prior knowledge levels. These prior knowledge levels were including English academic levels and gaming experience levels. There were two conditions of target words positioned in this study, one was in task dialogues, and the other was the flashcards attached under the dialogue. The former is a sentence or texts reading closed with game tasks and the latter is similar advertisement unrelated with game tasks. This study found that two prior knowledge types had different effects on the two words positioned conditions. Concerning the target words positioned on task dialogues, the gain scores of medium gaming experience participants were higher than low and high gaming experience participants significantly. With regard the target words positioned on flashcards, the result showed except high gaming experience learners that the high English academic level participants had better improvements. The gain scores of three gaming experience level were no significant difference within low English academic level participants.

However, the findings are subject to some limitations, for instance, the 52 participants were seems not enough, the gaming experience levels divided by per week play hours was roughly, and only focus on the effect of flashcard. Future research should involve more participants and concentrate on more affordance on MMORPG for incidental vocabulary acquisition.

References

1. Rankin, Y., Gold, R., Gooch, B.: 3D role-playing games as language learning tools. Proceedings of EuroGraphics 25(3), 211–225 (2006)
2. Peterson, M.: Massively multiplayer online role-playing games as arenas for second language learning. Computer Assisted Language Learning 23, 429–439 (2011)
3. Thorne, S.L., Black, R., Sykes, J.M.: Second language use, socialization, and learning in Internet communities and online gaming. The Modern Language Journal 93, Focus Issue, 802–821 (2009)
4. Sylvén, L.K., Sundqvist, P.: Gaming as extramural English L2 learning and L2 proficiency among young learners. ReCALL 24(3), 302–321 (2012)
5. Day, R.R., Omura, C., Hiramatsu, M.: Incidental EFL vocabulary learning and reading. Reading in a Foreign Language 7, 541–551 (1991)
6. Krashen, S.D.: We acquire vocabulary and spelling by reading: Additional evidence for the input hypothesis. Modern Language Journal 73, 440–464 (1989)
7. Nagy, W.E., Herman, P.A., Anderson, R.C.: Learning words from context. Reading Research Quarterly 20, 233–253 (1985)
8. Kuppens, A.H.: Incidental foreign language acquisition from media exposure. Learning, Media and Technology 35(1), 65–85 (2010)
9. Dalton, B., Grisham, D.L.: eVoc Strategies: 10 Ways to Use Technology to Build Vocabulary. The Reading Teacher 64(5), 306–317 (2011)

10. Jenkins, C., Corritore, C.L., Wiedenbeck, S.: Patterns of information seeking on the Web: A qualitative study of domain expertise and Web expertise. IT & Society 1(3), 64–89 (2003)
11. Tsai, F.H., Yu, K.C., Hsiao, H.S.: Exploring the Factors Influencing Learning Effectiveness in Digital Game-based Learning. Educational Technology & Society 15(3), 240–250 (2012)
12. Swanborn, M.S.L., De Glopper, K.: Impact of reading purpose on incidental word learning from context. Language Learning 52(1), 95–117 (2002)
13. Yoshii, M., Flaitz, J.: Second Language Incidental Vocabulary Retention: The Effect of Picture and Annotation Types. CALICO Journal 20(1), 33–58 (2002)
14. Lu-Fang, L.: A video-based CALL program for proficient and less-proficient L2 learners' comprehension ability, incidental vocabulary acquisition. Educational Media International 47(3), 199–216 (2010)
15. Kuppens, A.H.: Incidental foreign language acquisition from media exposure. Learning Media and Technology 35(1), 65–85 (2010)
16. Gee, J.P.: Good Video Games Plus Good Learning. Peter Lang, New York (2007)
17. McGraw, I., Yoshimoto, B., Seneff, S.: Speech-enabled card games for incidental vocabulary acquisition in a foreign language. Speech Communication 51(10), 1006–1023 (2009)
18. Suh, S., Kim, S.W., Kim, N.J.: Effectiveness of MMORPG-based instruction in elementary English education in Korea. Journal of Computer Assisted Learning 26(5), 370–378 (2010)
19. Ellis, R.: Factors in the Incidental Acquisition of Second Language Vocabulary from Oral Input: A Review Essay. Applied Language Learning 5(1), 1–32 (1994)
20. Orvis, K.A., Horn, D.B., Belanich, J.: The roles of task difficulty and prior videogame experience on performance and motivation in instructional videogames. Computers in Human Behavior 24(5), 2415–2433 (2008)
21. Ko, M.H.: Glossing and second language vocabulary learning. Tesol Quarterly 46(1), 56–79 (2012)
22. Kost, C.R., Foss, P., Lenzini, J.J.: Textual and pictorial glosses: Effectiveness on incidental vocabulary growth when reading in a foreign language. Foreign Language Annals 32(1), 89–97 (1999)
23. Paribakht, T.S., Wesche, M.B.: 'Reading comprehension and second language development in a comprehension-based ESL program. TESL Canada Journal 11(1), 09–29 (1993)
24. Read, J.: Assessing vocabulary. Cambridge University Press, Edited work, Cambridge (2000)
25. Yeu, M., Yoon, H.S., Taylor, C.R., Lee, D.H.: Are Banner Advertisements in Online Games Effective? Journal of Advertising 42(2-3), 241–250 (2013)

Gamification of Higher Education by the Example of Course of Research Methods

Martin Sillaots

Tallinn University
martins@tlu.ee

Abstract. The course of Research Methods is one of the most important subjects in the university curriculum. It provides essential guidelines for conducting the surveys needed for finishing the school. Unfortunately the subject is perceived as dry and boring by most of the students. Can gamification of the course make it more engaging and enjoyable? To find out how the students accept game elements in the non-gaming context a course of Research Methods was designed as a game and feedback information was collected. In general students found the gamified course engaging but some of them was worried because the focus shifted too much from course content to gameplay.

Keywords: Gamification, Game elements, Research Methods.

1 Introduction

What are students doing in the classroom? The preferred answer should be, they are learning. Unfortunately in many cases this is not so. Sometimes they do anything else but focus on the topic of the class. Usually it's because the traditional learning methods (e.g. presentation) are not very engaging. Teachers and instructional designers are looking for new methods in order to increase the engagement among students [1][2][3]. One method among others how to increase the students' engagement is to use game elements for making the learning activities more appealing. This approach is called gamification [4]. The method is not new. It is already frequently used in marketing and business conditions [5]. Education is a field where game elements have started to use lately [6]. The assumption is that game elements like challenges, competition, awards etc. make students to learn and achieve more. What are such elements and how can they be integrated with the course design? How will students receive game mechanics in a non-game environment? To answer to those questions, a course of Research Methods was designed as a game. Later, a survey was conducted among students to find out how they perceived different game elements. The goal of this paper is to describe how game elements contribute to the education, to provide ideas how to integrate them with the course, and to find out what students thought about it?

2 Game Elements

To find out what game elements can be used for gamification it is important to make clear what game is? Ernest Adams [7] provides a definition that covers most aspects

E. Popescu et al. (Eds.): ICWL 2014, LNCS 8613, pp. 106–115, 2014.

of a game: "**Game** is a activity of play in the pretended reality where participants try to achieve challenging goal by acting in accordance with rules." This definition does not assume a game to involve competition, or that it would need to be purely entertaining. For example, educational games have a serious goal.

Gamification is the use of game elements in non-gaming environment. Lee Sheldon [8] demonstrates how a whole course can be organized as a multiplayer game. Karl M. Kapp has analysed several examples of gamified educational activities [6]. He points out that gamification is not only about experience points and scoreboards, although most of the gamification examples in his book focus on the use of scoreboard as an external motivator. Game elements that can be used in gamification are:

Goals - course coals can be defined as a game goals [7].

Interactive activities are necessary for achieving the goals and for completing the challenges. Course activities can be designed as game activities. E.g. easiest way to implement interactive activity is to use quiz instead of test [8].

Characters are avatars and non-player characters (NPC). When it's time consuming to integrate NPC's with course content and learning activities, the avatar design is sometimes the first assignment for students in game like course [8]. Avatars can help immersion to the course and is useful in scoreboards. Students don't have to feel embarrassment because their personal name is not on desired level in scoreboard.

Rules are game resources, objects and relationships. They declare how players and game environment interact with each other. One part of the rules is the conditions for progression. How the player can earn points and what are the pass or fail conditions? This part can be easily implemented in education. E.g. grades are **experience points** (XP), XP's form the **score** and players are listed in the **scoreboard** [7].

Levels can be implemented in various ways. Usually they are parts of the game world. Levels equal to learning units in the course context. They can also indicate the rating of the player based on her score. In this case, the level can be applied as the final grade for the course. They also can refer to the difficulty of the game. In this case, levels can describe different versions of similar assignment. The easiest way to integrate levels in educational context is to bind them with scores and grades [8].

Balance. For providing an enjoyable playing experience, different game elements must be in balance [7]. For example balancing the scoring system means how many points one can get for certain activity, and how can the student progress on the scoreboard. A balanced scoring system alone does not guarantee the balanced user experience. The playing activities and the learning content should be also in balance. In the gamified course there is a risk that too much effort is put on the play and some important information is missed. Also the **difficulty** of the learning activities should be increasing during the course, in order to keep the assignments in balance with increased skills. Assignments should be balanced on the level where the learner is kept away from the boredom on one hand and anxiousness on the other, in terms of Csikszentmihalyi [9].

Luck or randomness is a factor of game mechanics. Some games are heavily based on risk and luck (e.g. gambling). Usually players don't want to be affected by randomness. They prefer to believe that their achievements are based on their skills. Luck can be integrated to the course by rolling the dice for selecting the student who has to make presentation [8].

Collaboration is one form of interactivity. When the majority of games are based on competition, the collaboration mode is used in party-based interaction, as well as in role-playing games. In both cases, collaboration is associated with teamwork [7].

Competition – Not all games involve competition (e.g. simulators), and not all players want to compete. But often it is seen as one of the key fun factors in games. Competition is not commonly used in education [7]. The easiest way to implement competition in the classroom is to introduce the scoreboard [8]. Also learning activities can be designed as competition or fight. E.g. test in the format of quiz. Debate between two students or teams can be seen as fight.

Game Aesthetics – Modern computer games are heavily graphical [7]. It is complicated to design an educational course on the level of details commercial videogames have. But it is realistic to design virtual learning environment (VLE) as a game world, or to use game-like icons for illustrating the course materials.

Story – Games do not have to be based on story. E.g. for buzzle, only the rules are important. Some genres (e.g. adventure games) are based on a story. Stories are also used in education as stand-alone assignments. To build the entire course as a story is a challenging task, although possible. One way to design a course as a story based game is to implement a journey of the hero [10]. It can be integrated with avatar design in the beginning of the course, and associated with character growth during the course.

Feedback in games is instant and rich [6]. Unfortunately, this is not always the case in the education. Teachers do not always have enough time to provide qualitative and fast feedback to students. Easy ways to provide fast feedback during the course are to organise interactive activities in the classroom, or to design game-like virtual learning environments that provide feedback to typical activities (e.g. "Upload of your home assignment was successful").

Risk – Games are entertaining because they provide safe environments for taking risks. Often players fail with missions several times before they achieve the goal. Unfortunately, this is not acceptable behaviour in educational assignments. Failures are often punished with negative grades. In many educational contexts taking the final exam more than twice is not accepted. On the other hand, in computer games it is normal to have several attempts before defeating the big boss. [8]

Game World is an imaginary place within a magic circle where players go during the game play. Usually it is created with the help of a story and a set of graphical elements, but not always. Sometimes a virtual space in players' head suffices [7]. One possibility to design game worlds to the course is to design VLE as a game world.

Immersion – When the goals are clear and activities are organised in an engaging way the participants may loose the sense of time and stop worrying about themselves. This kind of immersion is typical for computer games [7][9]. This state is achieved, thanks to engaging missions, appealing graphics and an interesting story.

3 Case: Research Methods Course

To find out how game elements can be used in education the course of Research Methods was created as a game. The course was designed for the second year master students taking the curriculum of IT Management or Educational Technology. 31 students enrolled to the course and 28 of them completed it. Classes took place from

Sept to Dec 2013 in Tallinn University. All learning sessions (7 sessions, 4 hours per session) took place in a physical classroom. Classroom activities were supported with the Elgg based VLE. It was used for delivering learning materials as well as for uploading individual or group assignments. The content of the course was traditional, covering the process of the research work, research plan, work with literature, research questions, research designs, methods for data collection and data analysis. The course was organised as a game with following elements: goals, avatars, XP's, scoreboard, levels, luck, collaboration, competition and feedback. The goal was to achieve a deep immersion among students. Game aesthetics and story were left out because it is too time consuming to integrate them with the learning activities.

Course started with introducing the course **goals**. First assignment was the design of personal **avatar**. Students were encouraged to use nicknames that are related with the course content. They were also asked to design an icon for the avatar and write character background story. The main objective for avatar design was to generate safe names that can be used in the scoreboard (protecting the personal data).

For every class students had an individual home assignment about **reading** one scientific research paper. In the beginning of the class students were divided in groups and they discussed about the content of the paper from the research methods point of view (what was the goal, what methods were used, etc.). In the end of the discussion one group was selected with the help of online **random** number generator (RNG). Selected group introduced the paper from the positive perspective (like author or supervisor). Later on another group was randomly selected and asked to introduce the same paper from the constructively negative perspective (like reviewer). After that groups were encouraged to start the debate around presented paper.

Some course topics (methods for dada collection, formatting and presenting research results) were introduced in the format of **quiz**. Traditional presentations were mixed with questions. Before explaining the theory the questions were presented and students were asked to answer to them. Theoretical explanations were provided between the questions.

Students were asked to investigate **research designs** in groups. Later on they introduced their findings to the rest of the class. They also had to design **personal research plans**. Students introduced their plans inside their groups. They select the best plan and the winner had a chance to introduce her work to the rest of the class. Course ended with the online assignment of writing essay about student's personal research plan.

Most of the activities involved **cooperation** inside the groups and **competition** between groups and provided immediate oral **feedback** to the students. Every activity generated certain amount of **experience points** (XP). Based on XP's students were listed by their avatar names in descending order in the **scoreboard**. The scoreboard was renewed before every contact lesson. **Levels** (grades) were based on scores. Course included several bonus activities and possibilities to earn extra XP's like participation in online surveys and providing links to additional learning materials.

4 Methodology

An online questionnaire was applied for data collection. 25 students (89%) out of the 28 course participants answered. It had 29 questions with single choice answers and with additional text field for comments. An interval scale with values: Yes = 4, Rather yes = 3, Rather no = 2, No = 1 was applied. The neutral answer was left out intentionally to motivate students to take clearer standpoints. Arithmetical averages were calculated per every question and the group of questions (corresponding to a game element). The total score for the case is arithmetical average from the question results and not from the game element summary results. Later average results were tied with text-based explanations. Average scores within the range between 4 and 3,26 are to be interpreted that this game element was successfully integrated and accepted by the students. If the aggregated result falls in the range from 3,25 to 2,51 then the interpretation is that the game element was partly successful. If the result is between 2,5 and 1,76 then the game element was not successfully integrated (Rather No). No evaluations fell in the range from 1,75 to 1. All quantitative estimations are combined with qualitative feedback to find out are the numbers valid and reliable.

5 Results

In general the implementation of selected game elements in the course context was partly successful. The weighted average score for the course is 2.99 (rather yes), indicating the degree to which the students agreed that learning methods requiring active participation are better than passive ones.

Table 1. Average ratings for the game elements

Game Elements	Average	Success
Clear goals	3.48	Yes
Avatar	2.04	Rather no
Scoreboard	2.87	Rather yes
Luck	2.51	Rather yes
Collaboration	3.34	Yes
Reading activities	3.15	Rather yes
Competition	3.06	Rather yes
Feedback	3.37	Yes
Immersion	2.76	Rather yes
Average	**2.99**	**Rather yes**

Some appreciated that this kind of course design did not let them to deal with issues not related with the course. The course generated also some humorous situations and students enjoyed them a lot. Some of the participants suggested implementing even more active learning activities (e.g. playing drama-based role playing game). Some students mentioned that they are not sure did they get the holistic picture of the research methodology because too much effort was spent on gaming activities. One commented that she don't like playing because learning must be serious.

5.1 Learning Goals

Majority of the students agreed that goals were clear enough (average 3.48 - yes). On the side of negative comments they stated that scoring was sometimes not clear enough but this is more question about grading, not goals.

5.2 Avatar

The main idea for the avatar design was to use artificial names in the scoreboard and to not violate the law of protection of personal data. It was also assumed that the use of avatar will lead to better immersion [6]. Unfortunately this did not happen. In the positive comments the students mentioned that the creation of new identity was an interesting experience and it created a relaxing atmosphere during the course. It caused more positive attitude to the course activities and created a safe environment. However, most of the students did not understand why the avatar was needed. Some of them thought that it would be fine to act under the real name. In general, the creation of the avatar was justified from the scoreboard point of view. Unfortunately, the rest of the potential of the avatar was not used during this course. To increase the avatar's effect on the deeper immersion, character design should be integrated with other learning activities during the entire course e.g. setting personal learning goals, collecting artefacts for showing the achievements and self-evaluation in the end of the course.

Table 2. Average ratings for the avatar

Avatar	**2.04**	**Rather no**
Design of a personal avatar was good for the immersion to the course	2.29	Rather no
Avatar influenced my behaviour on that course	1.79	Rather no

5.3 Experience Points, Scoreboard and Levels

Students found that the amount of XPs provided by the assignments was in balance with the effort needed to complete them. The use of scoreboard created the feeling of competition for a part of the students. Half of the students mentioned that this was highly engaging to them. They wanted to earn more points and progress on the scoreboard. Some students mentioned that they did not care about their points and the position in the scoreboard. They were interested in what they can learn during this course. One student suggested providing some additional reward for the winner. Currently it was missing. The only reward was a good final grade. Some students pointed out that this kind of competition was really annoying. They got frustrated because of the lower position in the scoreboard.

Table 3. Average ratings for scoreboard and XP's

Scoreboard and XP	**2.87**	**Rather yes**
Scoreboard generated the sense of competition	2.64	Rather yes
Scoreboard motivated me to achieve more	2.72	Rather yes
Provided XP's were in balance with the effort needed	3.24	Yes

The scoreboard partly motivated students to contribute more. “Nobody wants to be the last”, they said. Some mentioned that their motivation decreased when the sufficient amount of points was achieved. Also a lower position in the scoreboard affected motivation in a negative way. The scoring system should be more carefully balanced. The amount of points required for reaching to positive (grade) level should be higher. And the mechanics for helping laggards is needed.

5.4 Luck

The element of luck was integrated with the course design because of the relatively big amount of participants. Groups were selected randomly for making presentations. There was not enough time to let them make presentations in equal level. Another reason was to keep students alert all the time and to make them feel that there is always a chance to be selected even if they just finished the presentation. Unfortunately this leaded to the situation where students felt that XP’s are earned randomly and the points reflected only partly their actual knowledge. Students were not happy because the RNG did not give all of them equal chance to answer. Instead of real RNG some pseudo RNG should be used. In this case, the student who just finished their presentation has a lower chance (but not zero) to be selected for the next assignment.

Table 4. Average ratings of using the element of luck

Luck	2.51	Rather yes
Points that I earned depended on luck	*2.33	Rather yes
Points that I earned depended on my knowledge and contribution	2.68	Rather yes

* Inversed scale (yes is bad)

5.5 Collaboration

To enforce collaboration, students were divided in to groups. This was well accepted by the students. They enjoyed discussions in groups because they were able to gather some extra knowledge through these settings. The only negative effect of this was the fact that work in groups provides opportunities to cheat. It was possible to earn points without active contribution to the group work. Studying research designs in groups was engaging. Students mentioned to learn more by preparing the presentation and introducing the specific design to fellow students. As negative comments they mention that they did not pay a lot of attention to presentations done by others’.

Table 5. Average ratings for using group work for collaboration

Group work	3.34	Yes
Forming groups was justified	3.44	Yes
The way how the groups were formed, was suitable	3.68	Yes
Investigation and introduction of research designs in groups was engaging	3.48	Yes
Thanks to the group work it was possible to earn points without real contribution	*2.77	Rather no

* Inversed scale (no is good)

5.6 Competition

Reading Assignments involved small part of competition. In general, the students were rather satisfied with the reading activities. The only problem was related with the fact that some students did not read articles. Discussion in the classroom provided a good overview about the articles, but the debate between two groups took place only partly.

Table 6. Average ratings for using competition in reading assignments

Reading articles	3.15	Rather yes
I read articles during this course	2.72	Rather yes
Reading assignments were justified	3.20	Rather yes
Discussion in groups provided good overview about the article	3.60	Yes
Analyse of read articles in the format of debate was engaging	3.08	Rather yes

Another element for achieving the competition between groups was the **quiz.** Quizzes forced students to think more actively and helped them to concentrate on the topic. Unfortunately, the backgrounds of the groups were quite different, so they had not equal opportunities.

Table 7. Average ratings for other competition elements (quizzes, research plans)

Competition	3.06	Rather Yes
Using quiz instead of presentation was justified	3.24	Rather yes
Competition during the quiz increased the active participation	2.92	Rather yes
It's fair that group selected the best research plan ...	2.80	Rather yes
I had a feeling that something important was left out because of competition	*3.28	No

* Inversed scale (no is good)

Some level of competition was included through the assignment of making personal **research plans**. Students had to create such plans as a home assignment and to introduce the first version of it to their groups. Then the group was asked to select the best research plan, and the owner of that plan had a chance to introduce it to the rest of the class. Students found this approach only partly justified. It was also investigated did the play and competition caused the situation where some important aspects were not learned? Luckily, majority of the students did not have this feeling.

5.7 Feedback

A lot of effort was put in the course feedback to make it feel instant and rich like in games. All students were satisfied with the speed and the nature of the feedback. They had the feeling that the teacher really cared about what was going on in this course. However, the students had some difficulties with using course VLE. They mentioned that the structure of the VLE starting page should be clearer. A clear overview of the students' progress was achieved thanks to the frequently updated scoreboard.

Table 8. Average ratings for feedback

Feedback	3.37	Yes
Feedback to the learning activities was fast enough	3.64	Yes
Feedback was rich enough	3.57	Yes
The virtual learning environment was easy to use	2.83	Rather yes
I had clear overview about my progress during the entire course	3.42	Yes

5.8 Immersion

In this case, immersion was partly achieved. Students felt stronger engagement and connection with fellow students. From time to time, there was a feeling of the flow – time flied faster then expected. But it did not always lead to the immersion. Not many students would forget their everyday troubles and concern about self.

Table 9. Average ratings for immersion

Immersion	2,76	Rather yes
Learning activities were engaging	3,28	Yes
During the learning activities I forgot my everyday troubles	2,29	Rather no
During the learning activities I felt that time is passing faster than usually	2,60	Rather yes
During the learning activities the concern about self disappeared	2,32	Rather no
During the learning activities I felt emotional connection with the other students	3,32	Yes

6 Discussion and Conclusion

The goal of this paper was to find out how different game elements can be used in educational circumstances and how students accept them. Several game elements were chosen and integrated with learning activities in order to increase the student's engagement. Some of them like goals, feedback and collaboration based learning activities were successfully integrated through the course design. Students enjoyed the discussions in groups the most although it provided some possibilities to cheat. It was possible to earn points without actual contribution to the group work. One method to avoid this is to provide certain amount of XP's to the group and they can decide how to share them between group members.

Some game elements like quizzes and scoreboard were partly successfully implemented. They created controversial opinions among students. Some enjoyed the competition and some of them did not. The scoreboard motivated some students and some of them became frustrated. One solution to avoid this is to design game based course that focus on collaboration or cooperation among students and the competition will be only against personal goals, not between students.

Some game elements like luck and avatar were not so successfully integrated with the course. The use of random number generator should be decreased or replaced with other selection methods. E.g. students with lower score can have bigger chance for being selected. This again can lead to the situation where more active students get bored.

For conclusion we can say that gamification of the course with the help of selected game elements leaded to some level of immersion. Course design provided possibilities for active involvement. It also added the fun factor to the otherwise serious environment. Unfortunately, some students don't want to play even if the goal of the game is to learn. But for the majority of students, a gamified course is a nice exception in the row of traditional courses. "This was the most exiting course with the most boring content," one of them said.

References

[1] Lee, J.J., Hammer, J.: Gamification in Education: What, How, Why Bother? Academic Exchange Quarterly 15(2), 5 (2011)

[2] Fitz-Walter, Z., Tjondronegoro, D., Wyeth, P.: Orientation Passport. In: Proceedings of the 23rd Australian Computer-Human Interaction Conference on, OzCHI 2011, pp. 122–125 (2011)

[3] Muntean, C.I.: Raising engagement in e-learning through gamification, p. 7

[4] Domínguez, A., Saenz-de-Navarrete, J., de-Marcos, L., Fernández-Sanz, L., Pagés, C., Martínez-Herráiz, J.-J.: Gamifying learning experiences: Practical implications and outcomes. Comput. Educ. 63, 380–392 (2013)

[5] Huotari, K., Hamari, J.: Gamification' from the perspective of service marketing. In: CHI 2011 (2011)

[6] Kapp, K.M.: The Gamification of Learning and Instruction: Game-based Methods and Strategies for Training and Education [Hardcover], 1st edn., p. 336. Pfeiffer (2012)

[7] Adams, E.: Fundamentals of Game Design, 2nd edn., p. 700. New Riders (2009)

[8] Sheldon, L.: The Multiplayer Classroom: Designing Coursework as a Game [Hardcover], 1st edn., p. 304. Cengage Learning PTR (2011)

[9] Csikszentmihalyi, M.: Flow: The Psychology of Optimal Experience. Harper & Row (1990)

[10] Campbell, J.: The Hero's Journey. New World Library, Novato (2007)

Contextual Gamification of Social Interaction – Towards Increasing Motivation in Social E-learning

Lei Shi[1], Alexandra I. Cristea[1], Suncica Hadzidedic[1], and Naida Dervishalidovic[2]

[1] Department of Computer Science, University of Warwick, CV4 7AL, Coventry, United Kingdom
[2] Department of Information Systems, University Sarajevo School of Science and Technology Hrasnička cesta 3a Sarajevo, 71 000, Bosnia and Herzegovina
{lei.shi,acristea,s.hadzidedic}@dcs.warwick.ac.uk, naida.dervishalidovic@ssst.edu.ba

Abstract. In current e-learning studies, one of the main challenges is to keep learners motivated in performing desirable learning behaviours and achieving learning goals. Towards tackling this challenge, social e-learning contributes favourably, but it requires solutions that can reduce side effects, such as abusing social interaction tools for 'chitchat', and further enhance learner motivation. In this paper, we propose a set of *contextual gamification strategies*, which apply *flow* and *self-determination theory* for *increasing intrinsic motivation in social e-learning environments*. This paper also presents a social e-learning environment that applies these strategies, followed by a user case study, which indicates increased learners' perceived intrinsic motivation.

1 Introduction

Social e-learning is a process in which learners achieve learning goals via social interaction within learning communities [15]. In such an environment, connectedness and interactivity try to satisfy learners' basic innate needs such as autonomy, competence and relatedness [12], and thus lead to an increase of motivation [1]. However, the flourish of social features may also result in, e.g., abusing them for 'chitchat' purposes [17]. *Gamification* is "the use of gameplay mechanics for non-game applications" [11], and presents a solution to engage users and motivate their activities thus promoting learning [8]. It has been incorporated into numerous domains, as a way of creating strong connections between users and environments.

Recently, theories and practices of gamification in social e-learning have been explored, showing positive emotional and social impacts [18]. However, evidence also shows that many systems are not motivating students enough, and in some cases they are even discouraging [4]. To alleviate these issues, we believe that the social gamification approach to e-learning needs to be firmly rooted in motivation theories. Thus, in this paper, following-up our prior study [17] that proposed *light gamification mechanisms* to symbiotically build upon social interaction features without replacing the existent social learning communities, we present *specific contextual gamification*

E. Popescu et al. (Eds.): ICWL 2014, LNCS 8613, pp. 116–122, 2014.

strategies that apply motivation theories for reducing the side effects and further increasing learner motivation.

2 Motivation Theories

Motivation is an inner drive. It corresponds to physiological processes that influence directions and persistence of behaviours [9]. Among motivation theories applied in learning, *self-determination theory* (SDT) is an empirical one that focuses on the degree to which individual behaviours are self-determined and self-motivated [12]. Social e-learning that applies SDT is expected to sustainably increase learners' intrinsic motivation, leading to an efficient self-determined learning experience [5, 19]. Hence, in this study, SDT guides the design of the contextual gamification strategies.

Studies show that motivation levels need to be strengthened, so as to keep learners inside an area of optimal performance or *flow* [3]. Flow is a consciousness state experienced by individuals when their activities are fully immersed in a feeling of energized focus and deep involvement and enjoyment [2]. Studies [4, 18] also show that flow has positive influences on learning behaviours and performances. For these reasons, our contextual gamification strategies are informed by the flow theory.

Gamification has been criticised for its overjustification effect, which occurs when an expected external incentive de-motivates learners with already existing high intrinsic motivation [7]. It is believed that people pay more attention to external rewards than internal enjoyment and pleasure obtained from the activity itself [10]. Evidence has shown increased extrinsic motivation reduces learning performance [6]. Therefore, we adopt a *contextual* gamification approach that applies motivation theories to promote intrinsic motivation in existing social e-learning environments, rather than a full-fledged gamification approach that may "over-gamify" the existing mechanics.

3 Contextual Gamification Strategies for Social E-learning

Self-determination theory (SDT) proposes three basic needs [12] to be satisfied:

1. *Autonomy*: a sense of internal assent of one's own behaviours;
2. *Competence*: a sense of controlling the outcome and experience mastery;
3. *Relatedness*: a sense of connection and interaction with others within a community.

Flow theory postulates three conditions to meet for achieving a flow state [2]:

- Being involved in activities with clear and structured goals and progress;
- Performing tasks with articulate and immediate feedbacks;
- Having a good balance between the perceived challenge level and skill level.

SDT and flow theory have some overlaps, but there are also differences: SDT is a "larger" theory, alike to intrinsic motivation in general, that associates with all the three innate needs, but flow is "smaller" and often related to only two of the innate needs, i.e., autonomy and competence. Our proposed strategies address each innate need defined by SDT, whilst flow is referred when appropriate.

Towards Satisfying the Need of Autonomy. To satisfy the need of autonomy, we suggest to provide learners with meaningful and flexible choices to continuously balance their curiosity, skills and goals against a finite pool of resources, so that learners feel their behaviours are based on their own intentions. To reduce overjustification effects and maintain intrinsic motivation, we suggest to provide intrinsic choices of voluntary behaviours [7]. To achieve a flow state [2], we suggest to provide goals and progress markers with clear description, tasks at hand with clear and immediate feedback, and customisable learning context. The suggestions on satisfying the autonomy need are summarised as below:

A1. *A set of learning goals with clear description and multiple paths to achieve;*
A2. *Various interaction tools to complete a task;*
A3. *Clear and immediate feedback for learning activities;*
A4. *Meaningful options with consequences;*
A5. *Customisable learning context that can be adjusted by learners themselves.*

Towards Satisfying the Need of Competence. To satisfy the need of competence, we suggest to support the perceived extend of learners' own behaviours as the cause of desired consequences, multiple choices of learning paths, and customised interaction tools, so that learners can build their own competence. To enhance competence feelings, it is essential to provide unexpected, direct and positive feedback, optimal challenges and freedom of demeaning evaluations [12]. Furthermore, when experiencing enjoyment and fun, learners can become intrinsically motivated [14]. Hence, it is important to offer interesting challenges, by combining well-defined rules and goals [7]. To achieve a flow state [2], we suggest to break a learning goal into small and achievable pieces and increase the difficulties during the learning process. The suggestions are summarised as below:

C1. *Reasonable small chunks of learning goals with increasing difficulties;*
C2. *Tasks with unexpected positive feedback;*
C3. *Multiple choices to go along and retrace the learning paths;*
C4. *Learner in control of the learning process moving forward;*
C5. *Enjoyable and fun learning activities.*

Towards Satisfying the Need of Relatedness. Experiencing relatedness means feeling connected to peers, belonging to communities, and contributing to things "bigger" than oneself. Relatedness can be supported by various social interactions such as tagging, rating, commenting, and the visualisation of social status and reputation, such as levels, badges and leaderboard that connect learners to a community with the same interests [13]. Therefore, the suggestions on satisfying the relatedness need are to provide:

R1. *Opportunities to discover and join learning communities;*
R2. *Connections of interest and goals between learners and communities;*
R3. *Various tools for interaction, collaboration, discussion and mutual assistance;*
R4. *Visualisations of social status, reputation and contribution;*
R5. *Promotions to show appreciation to others (such as "like").*

4 Applying the Contextual Gamification Strategies

This section presents the new gamification features introduced into the second version of Topolor [16], a social e-learning environment, guided by the proposed strategies.

Structured and Chunked Goals with Increasing Challenges. In Topolor, a *course* is composed of structured *topics*. Learners have various "layers" of goals: a *long-term goal* to complete the *course*, a *medium-term goal* to finish each *topic*, and a *short-term goal* to achieve each *objective*. They cannot jump goal "layers", but they can decide which unlocked topic to learn next (Fig. 1). A higher-level goal is usually more difficult and complicated, so that learners incrementally master new skills, and thus enhance the experience of a flow state. These features were designed based on the suggestion A1, A5, C1 and C3 from the strategies.

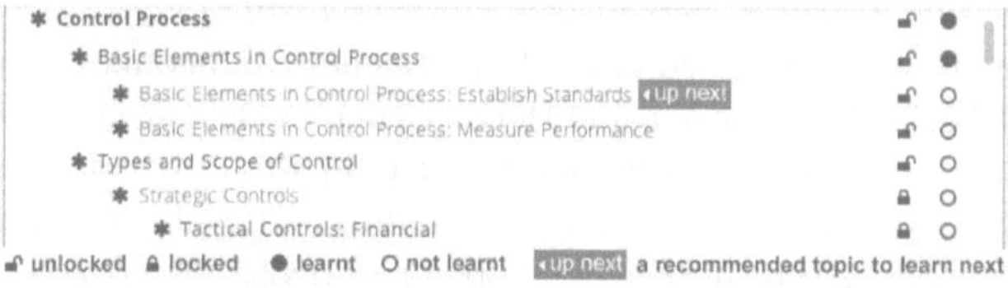

Fig. 1. Visualised course structure (learning path for a course)

Immediate and Positive Feedback with Guidance on the Next Step. Topolor provides immediate and positive feedback for learning activities to satisfy learners' needs of autonomy and competence. For instance, after finishing the pre-test of a course, Topolor shows "congratulations" and encourages learners to start the course. After submitting a test, Topolor immediately shows the result and recommends which topics the learner may need to review (in Fig. 2, 'Control Process' is recommended). These features were designed based on suggestion A3, A4, C2, C4 and R1.

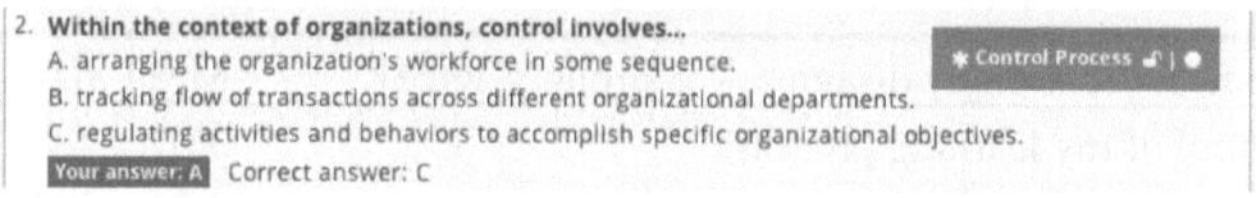

Fig. 2. Immediate feedback when taking a quiz

Visualisation of Social Status, Comparisons and Learning Progress. Topolor's support for the sense of competence and relatedness include the comparison of learner performance and contribution, based on suggestion A3, C5, R2, R3 and R4 (Fig. 3).

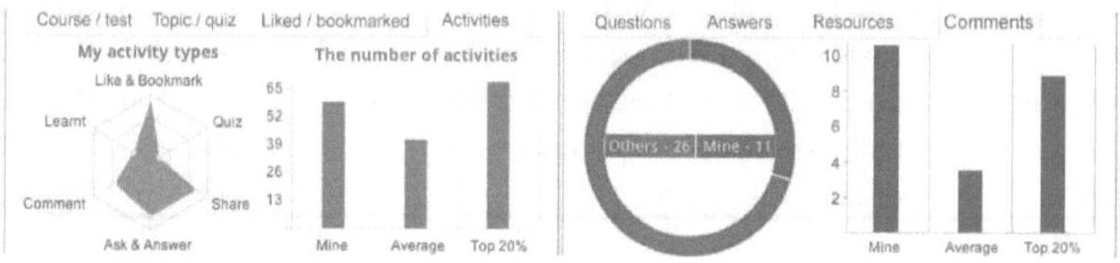

Fig. 3. Pop-up view – comparison: performance (left), contribution (right)

Other gamification features of Topolor are as follows: **storytelling**: tours for guiding 'newbie' learners to use various features (A3, A4 and C4); **profile** pages: publishing learning activities, learning status statistics, visualisations of performance and contribution (C5, R3 and R4); **leaderboard** (R4); **team building**: discussing and commenting on learning contents (R3); **peer reviewing**: rating peers' posts and comments (R5).

5 Case Study

A case study was conducted to evaluate the SDT and flow-motivated gamification features. Both qualitative and quantitative data were collected and analysed. The main research question of the case study is: *can Topolor's newly introduced gamification features increase the learners' perceived intrinsic motivation?*

The experiment was conducted at the Department of Economics, Sarajevo School of Science and Technology, Bosnia and Herzegovina, in December 2013. 20 students, 2 observers and 1 course instructor participated in the 1.5 hours online learning session - using Topolor to learn a course on 'Control'. After the initial online session, students were encouraged to further use Topolor to revise the covered materials, for two weeks. After that, students were asked to complete an optional online survey. Meanwhile, a logging mechanism in Topolor kept track of each student action. Out of the 20 students who participated in the online course, 15 completed the online survey. The survey responses (see Table 1) show three main results, including perceived satisfaction of *autonomy needs* (questions 1-4), *competence needs* (questions 5-8) and *relatedness needs* (questions 9-12). The means rank between 3.60 and 4.33, and their standard deviations range between 0.49 and 0.70. All the means are greater than 3 (the neutral response), suggesting the students were intrinsically motivated.

Table 1. Survey Results of SDT-based Contextual Gamification Features

	Likert statement (1: strongly disagree – 5: strongly agree)	Mean	SD	SDT need
1	I felt in control of my learning process.	3.67	.488	Autonomy
2	I was interested in using Topolor.	3.73	.594	Autonomy
3	I felt confident to use Topolor.	3.93	.704	Autonomy
4	I felt my learning experience was personalised.	3.80	.676	Autonomy
5	I enjoyed and had fun using Topolor.	3.73	.704	Competence
6	I felt I only needed a few steps to complete tasks.	3.60	.632	Competence
7	I felt it was easy to understand why I received recommendations.	4.33	.488	Competence
8	I felt it was easy to find the content I need.	4.13	.516	Competence
9	I felt it was easy to share content with peers.	3.60	.507	Relatedness
10	I felt it was easy to access the shared resources from peers.	3.73	.594	Relatedness
11	I felt it was easy to tell peers what I like/dislike.	3.60	.632	Relatedness
12	I felt it was easy to discuss with peers.	3.80	.561	Relatedness

6 Discussion and Conclusion

Qualitative feedback was also received from the course instructor, the observers and the students. The general feedback was consistent with the questionnaire results, and a number of participants expressed interest in using Topolor in the future. Besides, the activity records show that the students performed a wide variety of action types, indicating the students were motivated in trying interaction features in Topolor.

The main limitation of this study is the low number of participants. However, the new Topolor with gamification features has been opened to public (topolor.com), thus a larger cohort of users is expected in the near future. Another limitation is that more detailed evaluations are needed to examine each gamification features' influence. For future work, we will conduct deeper evaluations based on a larger data collection.

To conclude, motivation plays a crucial role in the success of the learning process, and gamification has the potential to increase learners' intrinsic motivation. To keep learners motivated in performing desirable learning behaviours and achieving learning goals, we proposed *contextual gamification strategies* rooted in self-determination and flow theories. The case study results indicated that our approach was promising.

References

1. Chen, K.-C., Jang, S.-J.: Motivation in online learning: Testing a model of self-determination theory. Comput. Hum. Behav. 26(4), 741–752 (2010)
2. Csikszentmihalyi, M., et al.: Flow: The psychology of optimal experience. Aust. Occup. Ther. J. 51(1), 3–12 (2004)
3. Csikszentmihalyi, M.: Beyond boredom and anxiety. Jossey-Bass (2000)
4. Domínguez, A., et al.: Gamifying learning experiences: Practical implications and outcomes. Comput. Educ. 63, 380–392 (2013)
5. Giesbers, B., et al.: Investigating the relations between motivation, tool use, participation, and performance in an e-learning course using web-videoconferencing. Comput. Hum. Behav. 29(1), 285–292 (2013)
6. Gillet, N., et al.: Intrinsic and extrinsic school motivation as a function of age: the mediating role of autonomy support. Soc. Psychol. Educ. 15(1), 77–95 (2012)
7. Groh, F.: Gamification: State of the art definition and utilization. In: Proceedings of the 4th Seminar on Research Trends in Media Informatics, pp. 39–46 (2012)
8. Kapp, K.M.: The gamification of learning and instruction: game-based methods and strategies for training and education. John Wiley & Sons (2012)
9. Moos, D.C., Marroquin, E.: Multimedia, hypermedia, and hypertext: Motivation considered and reconsidered. Comput. Hum. Behav. 26(3), 265–276 (2010)
10. Neil, R., et al.: Psychology: The Sci. of Behavior. Pearson Education, Incorporated (2007)
11. Raymer, R., Design, E.-L.: Gamification: Using Game Mechanics to Enhance eLearning. Elearn Mag. 2011(9), 3 (2011)
12. Ryan, R.M., Deci, E.L.: Overview of self-determination theory: An organismic dialectical perspective. In: Ryan, R.M., Deci, E.L. (eds.) Handbook of Self-Determination Research, pp. 3–33. University of Rochester Press, Rochester (2002)
13. Ryan, R.M., Deci, E.L.: Self-determination theory and the facilitation of intrinsic motivation, social development, and well-being. Am. Psychol. 55(1), 68 (2000)

14. Sackett, A.M., et al.: You're having fun when time flies the hedonic consequences of subjective time progression. Psychol. Sci. 21(1), 111–117 (2010)
15. Shi, L., et al.: Social e-learning in topolor: a case study. In: Proceedings of the 7th IADIS Conference e-Learning 2013, pp. 57–64. IADIS Press, Prague (2013)
16. Shi, L., Gkotsis, G., Stepanyan, K., Al Qudah, D., Cristea, A.I.: Social Personalized Adaptive E-Learning Environment: Topolor - Implementation and Evaluation. In: Lane, H.C., Yacef, K., Mostow, J., Pavlik, P. (eds.) AIED 2013. LNCS, vol. 7926, pp. 708–711. Springer, Heidelberg (2013)
17. Shi, L., et al.: To build light gamification upon social interactions: requirement analysis for the next version of Topolor. In: Proceedings of the 6th York Doctoral Symposium on Computer Science and Electronics (2013)
18. Simões, J., et al.: A social gamification framework for a K-6 learning platform. Comput. Hum. Behav. 29(2), 345–353 (2013)
19. Street, H.D.: Factors influencing a learner's decision to drop-out or persist in higher education distance learning. Online J. Distance Learn. Adm. 13(4) (2010)

A Flexible and Extendable Learning Analytics Infrastructure

Tobias Hecking[1], Sven Manske[1], Lars Bollen[2], Sten Govaerts[3], Andrii Vozniuk[3], and H. Ulrich Hoppe[1]

[1] University of Duisburg-Essen, Germany
{hecking,manske,hoppe}@collide.info
[2] Universtiy of Twente, The Netherlands
l.bollen@utwente.nl
[3] École polytechnique fédérale de Lausanne, Switzerland
{sten.govaerts,andrii.vozniuk}@epfl.ch

Abstract. Currently architectures for learning analytics infrastructures are being developed in different contexts. While some approaches are designed for specific types of learning environments like learning management systems (LMS) or are restricted to specific analysis tasks, general solutions for learning analytics infrastructures are still underrepresented in current research. This paper describes the design of a flexible and extendable architecture for a learning analytics infrastructure which incorporates different analytics aspects such as data storage, feedback mechanisms, and analysis algorithms. The described infrastructure relies on loosely coupled software agents that can perform different analytics task independently. Hence, it is possible to extend the analytic functionality by just adding new agent components. Furthermore, it is possible for existing analytics systems to access data and use infrastructure components as a service. As a case study, this paper describes the application of the proposed infrastructure as part of the learning analytics services in a large scale web-based platform for inquiry-based learning with online laboratories.

1 Introduction

The analysis of the increasing amount of educational data at large scale in order to improve learning processes has become a growing research topic in the recent years [1]. The emerging field of learning analytics brings together different fields i.e. business intelligence, web analytics, educational data mining and recommender systems [2]. Apart from that, there has also been research focused on the pedagogical and epistemological aspects of learning analytics [3]. However, solutions to support web-based learning environments as a whole with analytics services on the technical level are still underrepresented in the field. There exist learning analytics systems tailored for special use cases. Especially in web-based learning environments with flexible authoring facilities, that are not bound to a single domain, the set of different learning scenarios that can be supported by analytics features is unpredictable. Hence, instead of presenting a closed software system for a limited set of analytics tasks, the aim of this paper is to design an analytics infrastructure for web-based learning

E. Popescu et al. (Eds.): ICWL 2014, LNCS 8613, pp. 123–132, 2014.

environments, which functions as a general framework for several aspects of learning analytics. This comprises logging mechanisms for student actions, data storage and retrieval as well as intelligent user feedback. Algorithms for data analysis are implemented as independent software agents which makes the infrastructure flexible and extendable. The work is based on current achievements in the ongoing EU project Go-Lab on personalised online experiments with virtual- and remote labs for usage in school. To achieve this, Go-Lab offers a web-based platform [4], which allows teachers to set up reusable inquiry learning scenarios for students in an easy way. Consequently the descriptions in this paper concentrate on analytics for this platform.

2 Functional Characteristics of a General Analytics Infrastructure

There are various opportunities to use the Go-Lab environment to create inquiry scenarios with virtual and remote labs. This requires the possibility to create custom analytics solutions as well as the offering of general services by integrating existing systems. While many systems meet the demand of modularity, they dismiss the chance to tailor learning analytics to multiple stakeholders. Analytics services can be used for ex-post analysis by researchers to get insights into learning processes or to design new guidance mechanisms. In contrast to the perspective of ex-post analyses, the learners can also immediately benefit from such systems, typically through interventions.

Action Logging. Before an analysis can be performed, the user activities need to be captured through the system, which can be achieved through action logging. Action logs must consistently reflect the users' actions in the system. This comprises user access to resources as well as specific actions when using web apps. The logs have to be in an agreed format so that analysis methods can be developed independently.

User Feedback. Learning analytics can be conceived as a cyclic process in which analysis and feedback steps are interleaved with learning. Referring to the learning analytics cycle, Clow [5] describes the key to the successful application of learning analytics as "Closing the loop' by feeding back this product to learners through one or more interventions". Therefore, appropriate channels need to be established. To produce immediate results to intervene, analysis components should be triggered in such way, that notifications can be generated on time to be fed back to the learners. Scaffolding tools have to be able to handle different kinds of notifications ranging from prompts to reconfiguration of tools to provide tailored guidance mechanisms.

Ex-post Analysis. For many analytics task it is important to collect data over a certain period of time. In order to improve a learning environment as a whole, retrospective analysis of large datasets can be used for providing decision support to teachers and educational designers, and they are also very important as research and validation instruments. Learning analytics and educational data mining can be used in such cases to acquire knowledge about the learners in a larger scale. The intervention does not immediately affect the same learners that produce the data, but following generations of learners. Another reason for long time storage of data is to use real datasets for the data driven development of new analytics and guidance components and the comparison of algorithms on different datasets [6]. These tasks require an adequate data management where data from different sources can be aggregated for analysis purposes. In order to be open, the gathered data must be accessible by various analytics technologies that might already exist outside the infrastructure.

3 Background

3.1 The Go-Lab Inquiry Learning Spaces Platform

The Go-Lab portal is an inquiry learning portal that allows teachers to discover, use and enhance online labs as part of their courses. Based on these labs, students can acquire skills in applying scientific methods while doing experiments using online labs. The pedagogical background is based on inquiry learning, where students are supposed to acquire knowledge in a scientific process by going through a cycle of orientation, conceptualisation, experimentation and conclusion. In Go-Lab, the experimentation phase is supported by online labs that can either be pure virtual labs or real physical labs that can be controlled remotely over the web.

The learning activities take place on a platform that provides a variety of inquiry learning spaces (ILS) connected to remote labs [4]. The platform is based on the Graasp environment [7], available at *http://graasp.epfl.ch*. Teachers themselves can author specific inquiry learning spaces for students. Apart from online labs, such an ILS can include learning material, scaffolding apps in form of OpenSocial widgets[1] for particular phases of the inquiry cycle, like a concept mapping tool for conceptualisation.

3.2 Existing Learning Analytics Infrastructures

Currently architectures for learning analytics software systems are being developed in different contexts. This incorporates also business analytics and data mining tools [8]. The most tools are designed for specific types of learning systems like learning management systems (LMS). LMS platforms like Blackboard[2] and Desire to Learn[3] offer their own analytics services packages which are dedicated to the end-user exclusively and hence not extendable. Fortenbacher et al. [9] developed the LEMO tool which is capable of descriptive analysis of resource usage and student activity as well as more complex analysis like the identification of frequent learning traces. This tool offers several connectors to learning management systems from different vendors.

PSLC datashop [10] is a more research oriented platform that enables sharing of large learning datasets. Even if the focus is on effective data management it also offers some analysis and visualisation tools. Another platform dedicated to analysts is the CRUNCH infrastructure[4]. It offers an analytics workspace to create analyses and

---

1 `http://opensocial.org`
2 `http://www.blackboard.com`
3 `http://www.desire2learn.com`
4 `http://crunch.kmi.open.ac.uk/`

reports based on R scripts. Scripts can be released as public web services and hence reused by others. Tools like PSLC datashop and CRUNCH are more focused on the development and reuse of analytics services and data. They can be used to develop and test analytics services very well, but do not provide direct feedback mechanisms for teachers or students on their own. More emphasis on analytics systems for intelligent user feedback comes naturally from intelligent tutoring systems research (ITS). In the MiGen project [11] a layered architecture for intelligent feedback is presented. Feedback is produced when activity data flows through an analysis layer where several components analyse different aspects of the learner behaviour. An aggregation layer aggregates the analysis results to a learner model and a feedback layer presents personalised scaffolds to the learner.

All the mentioned systems serve different aspects of learning analytics. The challenge is to integrate different approaches into one open and extendable infrastructure in order to prevent fragmentation.

The Open Learning Analytics project [12] advocates for modular systems that allow openness of process, algorithms, and technologies which is an important feature in a heterogeneous field as learning analytics. This should also be the line followed by the analytics architecture in Go-Lab presented in this paper.

Two existing learning analytics infrastructures that also go into this direction are the analytics services of the Metafora platform [13] and the ROLE sandbox [14]. The Metafora platform is a web-based multi-tool environment for complex learning activities in small groups. It uses heterogeneous and decentralised components for action logging, analysis of group behaviour across the usage of multiple tools and user feedback. The ROLE sandbox is a platform for Personalised Learning Environments (PLEs). Its analytics system of uses widely accepted protocols and standards for action log data and web services in order to achieve interoperability of datasets and services. This system implements a pipeline based processing of action logs in which it is also possible to enrich action logs with context information and metadata.

4 Architectural Proposal

4.1 Overview

Our Learning Analytics Backend Services provide four interface components for different aspects of data acquisition, analysis and feedback mechanisms that are connected to the other components of the Go-Lab portal. These are the Action Logging Service, the Notification Broker, the Analytics Service, and the Artefact Retrieval Service (see figure 1). Logs of learner activities are a major data source for learning analytics as stated in section 2. The Activity Logging Service establishes an endpoint for clients to push event logs of user activities to the server. In the Go-Lab portal, user tracking is handled by the ILS Tracking Agent. This agent collects logs that are generated when a learner interacts with apps or learning resources and sends it to the mentioned Activity Logging Service. Action logs are encoded in the well-defined ActivityStreams format[5]. In order to keep the client server communication transparent the Action Logging Client API encapsulates the complexity of sending logs to the

[5] `http://activitystrea.ms`

server in the right format and can be used by every client component as a Javascript library.

Another component for the acquisition of data is the Artefact Retrieval Service. This service can be considered as an adapter to different external data sources which allows the internal analytics components to gather artefacts from databases e.g. metadata repositories. A typical application of this service is to retrieve a list of keywords for a subject domain from the Go-Lab lab repository [4] to adapt a concept mapping app with a predefined selection of concepts in order to assist the learner in concept map creation. The second requirement described in section 2 is the ability to fed back analysis results to the client side for intervention. For this purpose the Notification Broker is a dedicated endpoint to establish a backchannel to the Go-Lab portal. Clients (i.e. guidance apps in the portal) can register for certain messages by establishing a socket connection via Socket.io[6] with the Notification Broker by using the Notification Client API. Displaying a message that has been created by the backend is completely handled on the client then. In order to enable the ex-post analysis of data gathered over a certain period of time as described in section 2, there will be data gathered over a certain period of time that reflects longer term information. Hence, the learning analytics infrastructure provides the Analytics Services interface, which allows access to these data from other services and analysis tools.

4.2 Agent Based Analytics Infrastructure

The internal components of the learning analytics infrastructure are depicted in figure 2. The architecture is based on a multi-agent system with a distributed shared memory in the form of a Tuple Spaces, which is implemented using SQLSpaces [16]. This component provides a shared memory for agent coordination and communication and also a workspace for analysis. Basically it can be seen as a blackboard through which agents exchange messages in the form of tuples as flat ordered collections of data. Software agents, for example an agent that analyses artefacts produced in inquiry learning spaces, can register listeners by specifying certain tuple templates. Whenever a tuple that matches such a template is added to the space the SQLSpace will notify the subscriber agent. This enables a loose coupling of components because data exchange and communication is completely mediated by the shared memory, manifesting an implicit protocol for agent communication. Agents can be designed to perform analyses and data acquisition autonomously or on-demand. This approach has been used successfully in other inquiry learning environments [17]. For Go-Lab the shared memory is intended for temporary storage of tuples. For persistent data storage we rely on a data warehouse approach [18]. This is a common way to aggregate heterogeneous data from different sources for analytics purposes. The Action Logging Broker (figure 2) writes incoming activity logs to the shared memory for direct analysis but also into the data warehouse for long term storage. In the data warehouse these activity logs can be enriched by resource content gathered by the Artefact Retrieval Service. The data in the data warehouse can then be used for long term ex-post learning analytics and is available for specialised analysis tools and apps.

[6] http://socket.io

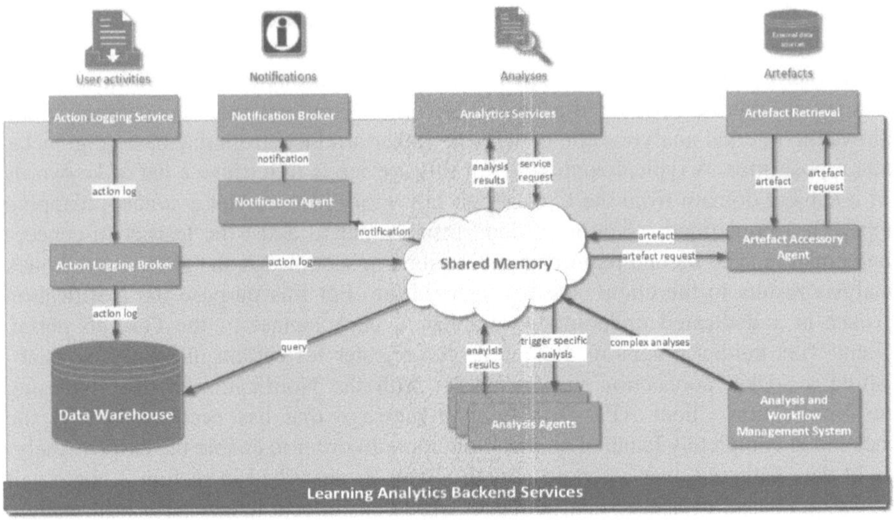

Fig. 1. The Learning Analytics Backend Agent System

4.3 Feedback Mechanisms and Example Case

In order to implement and provide an effective feedback loop for immediate intervention as described in section 2 this section outlines the typical information flow when feedback should be given to a student directly by scaffolding apps. Figure 3 depicts the complete data flow cycle when activity logging in the portal and backend analysis is involved. Given a scenario where a student uses a concept mapping tool and receives guidance in form of a concept recommendation. The concept mapping app uses the notification API to subscribe to the Notification Broker as a listener for messages from the analytics backend services on start-up (1.1) by providing a unique client id. Whenever the student modifies the concept map the action is logged by the corresponding app. The user tracking agent AngeLA takes these logs (1.2) and sends them to the Action Logging Service (2) which itself delegates the log to the Action Logging Broker (3). This broker stores the received logs in the data warehouse for long-term storage (4.1) but also in the form of tuples in the shared memory (SQL spaces) (4.2). The action logs contain a unique id for the app that sends the logs. A dedicated concept mapping analysis agent listens for tuples that have been send by corresponding apps, and hence it is triggered whenever action logs from these apps are written into the SQL spaces (5). When the agent detects that the student constructs a concept map in an unappropriated way, e.g. adds only a few sparsely connected concepts, it sends a concept recommendation message back to the app by inserting a notification tuple into the SQL spaces (6). Therefore it uses the unique client id which can be extracted from the action logs. Then the Notification Agent becomes actively notified by the SQL spaces that there is a new notification (7). This agent then uses the Notification Broker to send the message to the right client (8). Because the client app is registered with its unique id as a listener, the Notification Broker can choose the right socket connection to emit the message (9). The final handling/displaying of the concept recommendation is under the responsibility of each particular app.

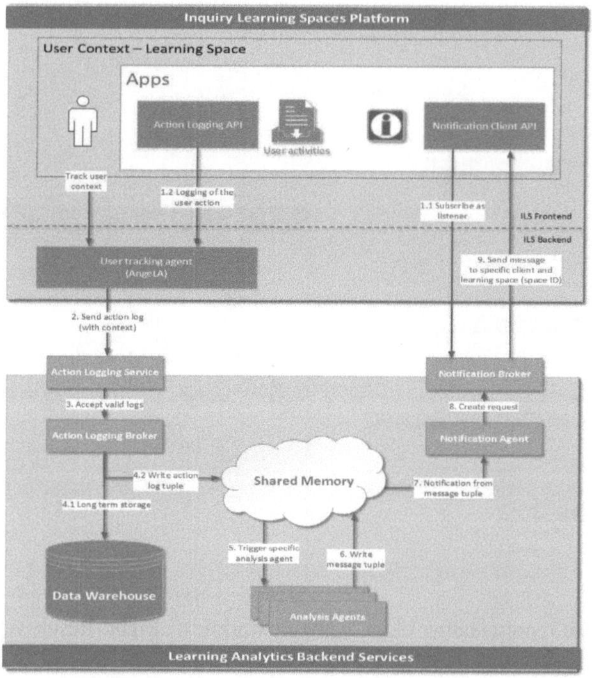

Fig. 2. The feedback loop of the Go-Lab analytics infrastructure

4.4 Integration of an Existing Analytics Workbench

To allow for a visual specification of complex analysis workflows, our analytics infrastructure is integrated with an analytics workbench that has been developed in the recently finished EU project SiSOB[7]. The SiSOB project was devoted to using network models and techniques from social network analysis (SNA) to enhance the monitoring and prediction of social impact of science beyond classical bibliometric methods. A technical outcome of the project was a web-based visual environment for the composition and execution of analysis workflows, including a variety of visualization techniques [19]. The left side of figure 3 shows an example workflow, where the different concept maps created by students in a single session are used to build an aggregated graph, which is displayed in the end as analytics app for the teacher at the right side of figure 3. The node sizes correspond to the number of connections of the concept to other concepts, which may help the teacher to get a better picture of the common understanding of the topic of the students.

The main benefit for Go-Lab from integrating this workbench is to enforce a multi-stakeholder perspective on learning analytics which goes along with the requirements. A separation of analysis (authoring of workflows) and target platform (displaying the results) helps to address different target groups as students, teachers, researchers and lab owners. The outcome of the integration is a system that creates portable widgets

7 `http://sisob.lcc.uma.es/`

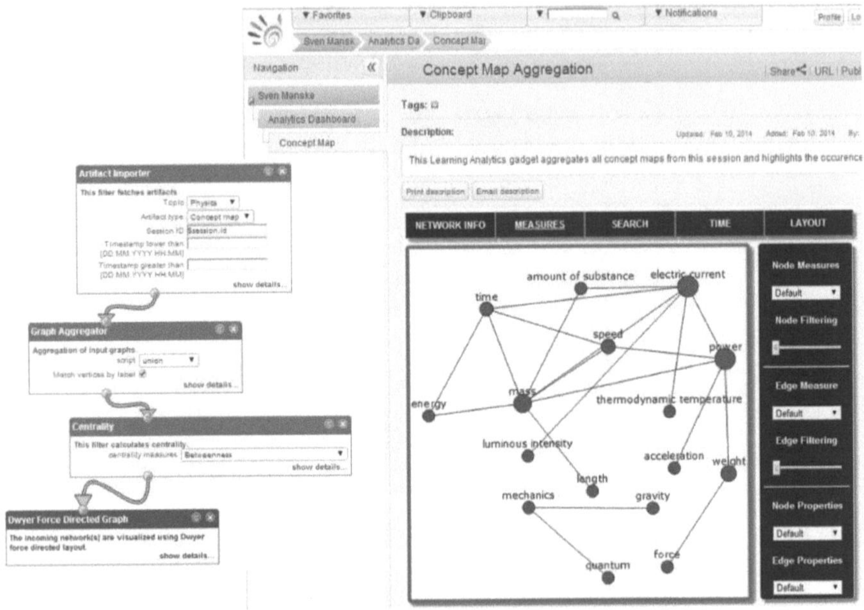

Fig. 3. Left: visual representation of an analytics workflow. Right: Result visualisation in the Graasp platform.

automatically out of workflows. These small applications can be embedded in widget platforms, particularly the Go-Lab ILS Platform as can be seen in figure 4. While the widget is authored through a graphical programming language, the created widget can be used by a teacher to foster collaborative work in the classroom supported through the analytics system. Besides the graphical approach, the workbench offers in its integrated version the possibility to create analytics services through an externally triggered execution of a workflow. From an architectural perspective, the workbench is integrated into the backend services, sharing the same infrastructure, namely the shared memory for agent coordination and data transportation. By using the Analytics Service interface it can also access data from the data warehouse, see section 3.2.

5 Conclusion and Outlook

The paper is one of the first attempts to describe a general learning analytics infrastructure that can be adapted to a wide range of scenarios. In other analytics fields such as business analytics those infrastructures are already quite elaborated. In the case of learning analytics there is still some work to do. With this paper we aimed to draw attention to the problematic of general approaches for analytics infrastructures in web-based learning environments and proposed our solution for this as part of the Go-Lab environment. The backend components of the infrastructure are implemented as an agent system which agents communicating over a shared workspace. This allows for the flexible integration of new functionality for example analysis algorithms. Well defined data formats and interfaces enable communication channels for action logging, feedback mechanisms and data access from analytics tools that use the learning analytics backend. In further work will focus on the integration of more analytics algorithms and the creation of specific guidance mechanisms for students.

Acknowledgements. This research was partially funded by the European Union in the context of the Go-Lab (grant no. 317601) project under the ICT theme of the 7th Framework Programme for R&D (FP7).

References

1. Drachsler, H., Greller, W.: The pulse of learning analytics understandings and expectations from the stakeholders. In: Proceedings of the Second International Conference on Learning Analytics and Knowledge, pp. 120–129. ACM (2012)
2. Ferguson, R.: Learning analytics: drivers, developments and challenges. International Journal of Technology Enhanced Learning 4, 304–317 (2012)
3. Knight, S., Buckingham Shum, S., Littleton, K.: Epistemology, pedagogy, assessment and learning analytics. In: Proceedings of the Third International Conference on Learning Analytics and Knowledge, pp. 75–84. ACM Leuven (2013)
4. Govaerts, S., et al.: Towards an online lab portal for inquiry-based STEM learning at school. In: Wang, J.-F., Lau, R. (eds.) ICWL 2013. LNCS, vol. 8167, pp. 244–253. Springer, Heidelberg (2013)
5. Clow, D.: The learning analytics cycle: Closing the loop effectively. In: Proceedings of the Second International Conference on Learning Analytics and Knowledge, pp. 134–138. ACM, Vancouver (2012)
6. Verbert, K., Manouselis, N., Drachsler, H., Duval, E.: Dataset-Driven Research to Support Learning and Knowledge Analytics. Journal of Educational Technology & Society 15 (2012)
7. Bogdanov, E., Limpens, F., Li, N., El Helou, S., Salzmann, C., Gillet, D.: A social media platform in higher education. In: Global Engineering Education Conference (EDUCON), pp. 1–8. IEEE (2012)
8. Kraan, W., Sherlock, D.: Analytics Tools and Infrastructure. Technical Report, CETIS Analytics Series, vol. 11 (2013)
9. Fortenbacher, A., Beuster, L., Elkina, M., Kappe, L., Merceron, A., Pursian, A., Schwarzrock, S., Wenzlaff, B.: LeMo: A learning analytics application focussing on user path analysis and interactive visualization. In: 7th International Conference on Intelligent Data Acquisition and Advanced Computing Systems, pp. 748–753. IEEE (2013)
10. Koedinger, K.R., Baker, R.S.J., Cunningham, K., Skogsholm, A., Leber, B., Stamper, J.: A data repository for the EDM community: The PSLC DataShop. In: Handbook of Educational Data Mining, pp. 43–55. CRC Press (2010)
11. Gutierrez-Santos, S., Mavrikis, M., Magoulas, G.: Layered Development and Evaluation for Intelligent Support in Exploratory Environments: The Case of Microworlds. In: Aleven, V., Kay, J., Mostow, J. (eds.) ITS 2010, Part I. LNCS, vol. 6094, pp. 105–114. Springer, Heidelberg (2010)
12. Siemens, G., Gasevic, D., Haythornthwaite, D., Dawson, S., Shum, S.B., Ferguson, R., Duval, E., Verbert, K., Baker, R.: Open Learning Analytics: an integrated & modularized platform. Proposal to Design, Implement and Evaluate an Open Platform to Integrate Heterogeneous Learning Analytics Techniques (2011)

13. Harrer, A.: Analytics of collaborative planning in metafora: Architecture, data, and analytic methods. In: Proceedings of the Third International Conference on Learning Analytics and Knowledge, pp. 255–259. ACM (2013)
14. Renzel, D., Klamma, R.: From micro to macro: Analyzing activity in the ROLE sandbox. In: Proceedings of the Third International Conference on Learning Analytics and Knowledge, pp. 250–254. ACM (2013)
15. Gelernter, D.: Generative communication in Linda. ACM Trans. Program. Lang. Syst. 7, 80–112 (1985)
16. Weinbrenner, S.: SQLSpaces: A Platform for Flexible Language Heterogeneous Multi-Agent Systems. PhD Thesis, Universtiy of Duisburg Essen, Hut, Munic (2012)
17. Giemza, A., Weinbrenner, S., Engler, J., Hoppe, H.U.: Tuple spaces as a flexible integration platform for distributed learning environments. In: Proceedings of the 2007 Conference on Supporting Learning Flow through Integrative Technologies, pp. 313–320 (2007)
18. Inmon, W.H.: Building the Data Warehouse, New York. John Wiley & Sons NY, USA (1992)
19. Göhnert, T., Harrer, A., Hecking, T., Hoppe, H.U.: A workbench to construct and re-use network analysis workflows - concept, implementation, and example case. In: Proceedings of the 2013 IEEE/ACM International Conference on Advances in Social Networks Analysis and Mining. IEEE (2013)

A Learning Analytics Approach to Career Readiness Development in Higher Education

Eman Abu Khousa and Yacine Atif

Faculty of Information Technology. UAEU
P.O. Box 15551, Al-Ain, UAE
{emanak,yacine.atif}@uaeu.ac.ae

Abstract. There are increasing demands to improve the quality of higher education to facilitate the development of 21st Century professional competencies such as lifelong learning, critical thinking and creativity. Learning analytics is an emerging approach that can provide educators with the necessary information to understand learners then assist them to develop such skills. In this paper, we introduce career dispositions as a 6-dimesional model comprises core skills that engender professional actions, and influence the ability to manage career growth. We then present the process to develop and validate a new scale to evaluate career readiness along these dimensions. The developed scale is a self-report instrument that consists of 22 items and six subscales was validated using exploratory factor analysis (EFA). EFA results demonstrated discreet item loadings into the six factors ranging from 0.3 to 0.8 representing an acceptable level of convergent validity. The developed instrument can be integrated into a career readiness platform and used as analytical tool to identify and analyze the complexity and diversity of student's learning behaviors and skills that may impact their future career readiness and professional performance.

Keywords: learning analytics, career readiness, career dispositions, portal.

1 Introduction

The world of work is changing at an ever-faster pace so few graduates are expected to have a fixed, single career path. Instead, they are likely to follow a route that encompasses multiple careers [1]. Individuals have to manage their own careers in order to realize their professional growth and meet their occupational goals [2,3]. This situation calls for personal ownership and autonomy of career readiness for future graduates to successfully impact their career aspirations and meet appealing opportunities [4,5]. They are now expected to develop a set of qualities or dispositions necessary for building up their professional competencies while enrolled in formal academic programs to be able to make an informed career development progression from the onset of their student life and proceed along a predestined career path. We refer to this set of soft skills that are related to career readiness as "career dispositions." [6,7].

The produced practices are the strategy-generating principles which enable individuals to cope with unforeseen and ever-changing situations [6,7,8] which are inherent to career related domains. Career dispositions allow individuals to build mental abilities to make choices as they encounter new professional environments or fields [9,10].

E. Popescu et al. (Eds.): ICWL 2014, LNCS 8613, pp. 133–141, 2014.

This proactive career behaviors refer to the anticipatory and planning actions that individuals take to enable a future career outcome by embracing habits, which affect themselves and/or their environments [11, 12]. Career dispositions are dominated by the earliest experiences acquired in the family, school and college, but further refined by subsequent career-specific traits [8]. In doing so, this paper claims that career success is a gradual process that unfolds over higher-education time. The remaining sections of this paper are organized as follows. Section 2 provides some background and explores some related works. Section 3 reveals our proposed career disposition dimensions and Section 4 suggests a related instrument to evaluate career readiness alongside these dimensions. The proposed instrument is validated using a well-known methodology. Finally, Section 5 concludes the paper with our future work, which employs the proposed instrument into an enterprise-wide career readiness portal.

2 Background and Related Work

2.1 Career Success Personal Traits

The literature on career success identifies five categories of personal traits (termed Big Five personality factors) that influence the general mental ability of career success [13]. The Big Five dimensions are openness, conscientiousness, extraversion, agreeableness, and Neuroticism. Openness refers to the degree to which an individual is deemed intellectual, creative, curious and open to new ideas and experiences. Individuals with high openness degree seem to thrive in situations that require flexibility and learning new skills, which make them highly adoptable to change. Conscientiousness is the extent to which an individual is dependable, organized, systematic, punctual and achievement-oriented. It is related to an individual's degree of self-control as well as the need for order, persistence and achievement. It emerged as the most personality trait that is consistently related to performance across jobs, i.e. predict how high the individual can perform across a variety of career prospects. Extraversion refers to the degree to which an individual is socially oriented (outgoing and expressive), ambitious, adventuresome and assertive. Extraverts tend to build social networks (with great numbers of close friends) then use them effectively to collect information and feedback to adjust to a new job. They are also more likely to take leadership roles. Agreeableness refers to the degree to which an individual is likeable (good natured, caring and gentle), cooperative and sensitive.

Moreover, researchers on proactive behaviors pertaining to career readiness have stated that proactive personality dimensions constitute a significant predictor of career success [11]. Proactive career behaviors consist of a cognitive component that indicates the insights that individuals develop towards their career aspirations; and a behavioral component that refers to the actions they need to perform to manage their developmental progress. The cognitive component, which allows individuals to make meaningful choices about their careers, is deemed to be an antecedent of career success [11]. Several studies which investigate the relationship between the behavioral component and career outcomes reveal a set of different behaviors such as seeking feedback on performance and competencies; and networking to collect information about existing or possible career opportunities as actual determinants of career success [5].

Proactive personality refers to the individual's tendency to change things, fix what is wrong and solve problems. It is also related to the individual's ability to plan and manage future actions that instill a meaningful change [12]. This capacity enables those individuals to establish effective relationships, and develop greater understanding of the political environment within the workplace, which helps them to adjust quickly to new jobs. Proactive personality manifests itself in three related traits that are self-efficacy, self-direction and self-evaluation [12]. Self-efficacy is the belief of the individual's ability to perform a specific task successfully. Self-direction refers to personal independency; while self-evaluation refers to the ability to assess and improve personal performance toward achieving pre-set goals.

2.2 Lifelong Learning Dispositions

Effective lifelong learners are able to: (1) set goals; (2) apply appropriate knowledge and skills; (3) engage in self-direction and self-evaluation; (4) locate required information; and (5) adapt their learning strategies to different conditions. Deakin Crick [14] modeled learning dispositions as a 7-dimensional construct known as Learning Power which comprises: 1) changing and learning "a sense of myself as someone who learns and changes over time"; 2) critical curiosity "an orientation to want to 'get beneath the surface"; 3) meaning making "making connections and seeing that learning 'matters to me'"; 4) creativity "risk-taking, playfulness, imagination and intuition"; 5) learning relationships "learning with and from others and also able to manage without them" ; 6) strategic awareness" being aware of my thoughts, feelings and actions as a learner and able to use that awareness to manage learning processes"; and 7) resilience "the readiness to persevere in the development of my own learning power."

3 Career Dispositions Dimensions

As a concept, career dispositions are underpinned by the constructs originally presented in the Big Five model and lifelong learning dispositions. The Big Five model identifies five categories of personal traits that influence career success; while lifelong learning dispositions make up the individuals' capacity for developing lifelong learning attributes. Career dispositions emerge as the joint set of attitudes and generic skills that dispose individuals to engage profitably with learning in order to be able to adapt to career changes and to manage their own career growth. They produce the behaviors and practices, which enable individuals to cope with unforeseen and ever-changing situations, and respond effectively to professional growth needs. In this essence, career dispositions can be defined as a scheme of attitudes, assumptions and skills that engenders professional actions; and influences the ability to adapt and respond to changing work situations and environments. It can be modeled as a 6-dimensional construct that comprises: Openness to challenge (OC), Critical Thinking (CT), Resilience (R), Learning Relationships (LR), Responsibility for Learning (RL), and Creativity (C) (See Fig 1). The six dimensions of the career dispositions describe the natural tendencies, mind state and preparations of each individual towards a professional practice. These tendencies generate and organize practices, which enable individuals to cope with unforeseen and ever-changing situations. Thus, the practical efficiency of career dispositions is what allows individuals to act intellectually and to make choices encountered through new job-related environments or fields. A brief definition of each career dispositions dimension is discussed next, while Table 1 summarizes the individual characteristics of high and low scores along each dimension.

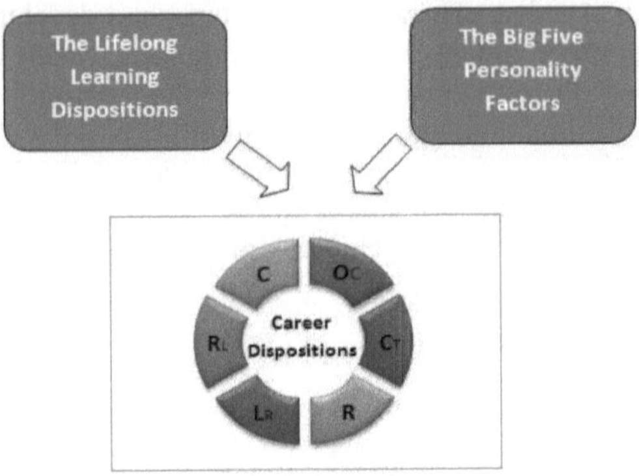

Fig. 1. Career Dispositions

Openness to Challenge (OC) refers to the degree to which an individual is intellectual, creative, curious and open to new ideas and experiences. Individuals with high openness degree thrive in situations that require flexibility and learning new skills, which make them highly adaptable to change. They also tend to seek feedback on their performances; and to build new relationships [13]. Critical Thinking (CT) refers to the degree to which an individual is investigative, attentive reader/listener, inquisitive, analytical and an evidence-based decision-maker. Critical thinkers strive for understanding, keep curiosity alive, remain patient with complexity, and are ready to invest time to overcome confusion. They tend to develop their own ideas about any topic, however, they show interest in other people ideas even if they disagree on the principle, in order to practice fair-mindedness and avoid extreme views.

Resilience (R) refers to the degree to which an individual is conscientious, determined, assertive and achievement-oriented. Individuals with high resilience degree have good communication and social skills, thrive in social contexts and generally make a positive impression of themselves.

Responsibility for Learning (RL) refers to the degree to which an individual is dependable, autonomous, motivated, organized and punctual. Responsible learners tend to take part on deciding what will be learned and how

Creativity (C) refers to the degree, to which an individual is intellectual, imaginative, adventuresome, curious and original. Creative individuals tend to regard problems and controversial issues as exciting challenges. Further details of these attributes and their achievement levels are shown in Table 1.

4 Instrument Development and Evaluation

In order to measure career dispositions, we developed a scale that is conceptually underpinned by constructs from career success and lifelong learning literature. Data is routinely generated from the proposed instrument to elicit quantitative reflection of career disposition and qualitative feedback from the supervising coach via an enterprise-wide electronic platform, which is the scope of a separate contribution. In this paper, we focus on the social and pedagogical theoretical foundations to formulate career dispositions, and on the induced analytics to validate and use the produced data out of the developed instrument. This will ensure that the instrument is measuring what it is intended for and is administrated in a standardized way to infer a career profile for higher education students.

Table 1. Career Dispositions scores

Dimension	High Scores are	Low scores are
Openness to Challenge (OC)	Intellectual, creative, curious ,open to new ideas and experiences	Skeptical, conventional, practical
Critical Thinking (CT)	Investigative, attentive reader/listeners, inquisitive, analytical, experimenting, evidence-based decision makers	Inpatient with complexity, confused, impression-based decision makers , impulsive
Resilience (R)	Determined, assertive, energetic, social, competitive, achievement oriented	Passive, inconsistent, droopy
Learning Relationships (LR)	Cooperative, expressive, agreeably, social oriented	Quite, uncooperative, distant, introvert
Responsibility for Learning (RL)	Dependable, autonomous, motivated, organized, dedicate, punctual	Dependent, unreliable, carless, feeble
Creativity (C)	Intellectual, imaginative, adventuresome, curious and original	Mechanical, unoriginal, spontaneous

4.1 Development of the Instrument

Self-Reflective Career Dispositions Scale (SRCDS) metric is a self report instrument that asks respondents to describe their attitudes and behaviors in terms of the identified six dimensions ($D = Dn \ldots Dp$) of career dispositions. The scale is presented as 35 items of a questionnaire against which respondents are asked to rate each items, as it relates to them using a five point Likert scale from 1 (Not at all lime me) to 5 (very like me). Some items were negatively worded - marked as "reversed"- in order to help prevent response biased responses. Those items have to be reversed before an individual's score can be computed. If an item has to be reversed, a respondent who has circled 1 for that item now receives a score of 5 for the positively worded version of that item and so on). A higher total dimension score SDn indicates a higher level of readiness for a professional career along the given dimension. In developing the questionnaire items for our instrument, we considered research results from educational psychology domains to derive the most widely used and validated scales based on which we drew relevant items that measure the psychological traits encompassing the six proposed dimensions.

4.2 Instrument Validation

The SRCDS was validated using Exploratory Factor Analysis (EFA) in Matlab to identify the underlying relationships between the measured items of the instrument.

EFA is a well-known multivariate statistical technique used to identify common clusters (called factors) of inter-correlated items. This is to confirm that the questionnaire items do measure the intended dimensions of the survey. This validation methodology is commonly used in psychometrics instrument development, in order to simplify the structure used for data collection by exploring and summarizing underlying correlations between factors. This approach has three basic decision points: (1) decide the number of factors, (2) choose an extraction method, and (3) choose a rotation method (to check whether items relate to more than one factor). Next, we elaborate further on each step of this validation methodology and show how these basic decisions were used to validate our proposed instrument.

Sample Adequacy
This step checks whether our data set is suitable for EFA through examining:

- Sample size: the literature suggests that sample sizes should be 100 or greater. Our survey was administrated in hard copy to groups of University students (individually and during class time). The participants were senior students in an Information Technology undergraduate program (58 female and 42 male). The completed survey responses (N= 100) were then used to demonstrate the factorial validity of SRCRS.
- Outliers: few outliers were identified (3 values). However, EFA is sensitive for outlying cases and so the mean was substituted for the extreme value.
- Factorability of the correlation matrix: the correlation matrix that is used in the EFA process displays the relationships between individual variables. Factorability of the correlation matrix is checked by inspecting the matrix for correlation coefficients over 0.3. If no correlations exceed 0.3 then factor analysis is most properly not the appropriate statistical method to utilize. In other words, if the factors account for approximately 30% relationship within the data sample, it would indicate that a third of the variables have too much common variance, and hence it is not practical to determine the level of correlation between variables.

Factors Extraction
The most common used method to extract factors is the Principal Components Analysis (PCA). This method produces loading matrix (L) and Eigen Values (EVs). Loading matrix is a matrix of coefficients or weights (Factor loadings FLs) for a set of linear equations relating v observed variables (or items) to m factors (or dimensions). The rows of the matrix correspond to the observed variables and the columns correspond to the factors while FLs indicate relative importance of each item to each factor. EVs represent the variance accounted for by each underlying factor. EVs are represented by percentages which cumulated value is the number of items. Each factor has EV that indicates the amount of variance each other factor accounts for. A good factor solution is the one that explains the most variance with fewest factors.

A common approach to decide the number of factors is the Kaiser-Guttman rule which simplies states that the number of factors are equal to the number of factors with EVs *>1.0*. Table 2 demonstrates the results obtained by applying PCA on SRCDS data. As shown, a cumulative percentage of variance of *82.2%* is explained by a total of *6* components (factors) which have an $EV > 1$. The first factor explains the most variance and the last factor explains the least variance. The first six factors account for most of the variance, while the remaining factors all have small EVs ranging from 0.9 to 0.0. However, until FLs are rotated (in Step 3 of the validation process), it is difficult to interpret and extract factors. A rotation of the *L* matrix helps to find more interpretable FLs as well as the factors they represent.

Table 2. Total variance explained by identified factors

Eigen Values	% of Variance	Cumulative %
20.71	54.5	54.5
2.86	7.5	62.0
2.67	7.2	69.0
1.72	5.7	74.8
1.119	4.5	82.2

Rotation Method

Rotation produces a simple data structure by maximizing the high item loadings and minimizing low item loadings. This consideration decides how many factors to analyze based on whether a variable might relate to more than one factor, to simplify the data structure used by the instrument. A simple data structure is defined as "a condition in which variables load at near 1 (in absolute value) or at near 0 on an eigenvector (factor). Variables that load near 1 are clearly important in the interpretation of the factor, and variables that load near 0 are clearly unimportant. EFA results for our proposed SRCDS data sample were rotated using two orthogonal methods and one oblique method. The best fit was produced by the Promax, which is a common oblique method; which indicates that the underlined factors are highly correlated.

Interpretation and Labeling

After rotation, lines of best fit (vectors) were re-arranged as seen in Table 3 to optimally go through clusters of variables in order to make it easier to interpret LFs and factors they represent. However, due to the low communalities, some items or variables didn't load highly on any factor. Low communality of a variable indicates that a considerable proportion of this variable' variance is unexplained by the extracted factor. In the case of low communalities, more factors have to be extracted in order to explain the variance or these variables should be removed from the EFA. We removed unexplained items and ended up with 6 factors that explain the variance of 22 items/variables. Each of the extracted factors shows 3 or more strong loadings. The analysis also indicates 8 complex variables. This result is expected as the underlying factors are theoretically correlated. Factor 1 was labeled OC as it reflects elements of openness to new learning experiences. Factor 2 relates more to practices that reflect questioning things and developing new ideas. Consequently, we have labeled it CT. Factor 3 highlights elements that define determination, flexibility, resource management and attitude to hard working and so it was labeled R. Factor 4 consists of items related to the ability of establishing learning relationships and work with other learners and so it was labeled LR. Factor 5 reflects all core components of developing decision-making ability, responsibility of learning and autonomous learning. Thus, Factor 5 was labeled RL. Finally, Factor 6 relates to creativity reflecting practices of accepting new ideas, focusing on details, and asking questions. Consequently, Factor 6 was labeled C. Table 3 demonstrates the factors after labeling and the items selection.

Table 3. Factors Labeling and Item selection

Items	Factor 1	Factor 2	Factor 3	Factor 4	Factor 5	Factor 6
	OC	CT	R	LR	RL	C
I try to understand contents as thoroughly as possible	-0.0287	-0.0633	0.0063	-0.0004	**0.4935**	0.2726
I know what I want to learn even if cannot guarantee a good grade	0.2329	0.0267	0.2191	-0.0097	**0.3056**	0.0066
I take responsibility for my learning experiences	0.2524	0.0349	0.006	0.0355	**0.3495**	-0.0161
I am good at meeting deadlines	-0.2238	**-0.5657**	-0.8785	0.1396	**0.408**	-0.2864
In a learning experience, I prefer to take part in deciding what will be learned and how	0.2948	0.0018	-0.0543	-0.0577	**-0.5631**	0.1181
I rarely think about my own learning and how to improve it. (REVERSED)	-0.0114	**0.3497**	0.1099	0.3271	0.153	0.1318
I like new learning experiences	**-0.4238**	-0.0656	0.126	0.054	0.1466	0.1262
I prefer course material that stimulates my curiosity, even if it is difficult to learn.	**0.7799**	**-0.7906**	**-0.6012**	0.2143	-0.2219	0.1061
I often find myself questioning things I hear or read to decide if I find them convincing	**-0.4528**	**0.3824**	-0.019	-0.017	0.0221	0.0089
I try to play around with ideas of my own related to what I am learning in the class	0.0558	**0.3306**	0.146	-0.0631	0.0429	-0.1028
I try to relate academic learning to practical issues	-0.0189	**-0.3984**	-0.1411	0.1926	0.0151	-0.0694
When I approach new material, I try to relate it to what I already know	-0.1194	0.1214	0.1944	0.0863	-0.0793	-0.122
I write brief summaries of the main ideas in a course from the readings and the concepts presented in the lectures	0.2419	-0.0333	**-0.3181**	0.0826	-0.2841	-0.0252
I do not mind making mistakes so I can learn from them	-0.0039	-0.1896	**-0.352**	-0.2776	0.1023	0.2293
Even when course materials are dull and uninteresting, I manage to keep working until I finish	0.0291	0.2399	**0.316**	**-0.3634**	0.0271	-0.1103
I think of other students as partners in my learning process (providing information, support, and collaborative work)	**-0.3907**	-0.0776	-0.1901	**-0.3143**	0.1396	-0.0375
I try to identify students in this class whom I can ask for help if necessary.	0.0094	-0.1471	**-0.4711**	**-0.6803**	-0.1227	-0.1092
Even if I have trouble learning the material in this class, I try to do the work on my own, without help from anyone. (REVERSED)	**0.3572**	-0.0929	0.0579	**-0.3842**	0.0891	-0.2581
I plan the time and required resources for any learning task effectively	**0.3939**	0.2352	**0.4319**	-0.0738	-0.1289	-0.0293
In a classroom situation, I expect the instructor to tell all class members exactly what to do at all time. (REVERSED)	-0.0921	-0.2488	**-0.384**	0.1171	-0.0712	**0.8387**
When I learn something new, I focus on the details and ask questions rather than only accepting what I am told.	-0.0962	0.1623	0.1276	-0.1098	0.0373	**0.3708**
When solving assignments or doing projects, I tend to add an extra dimension beyond what it is established in the area of this assignment or project	-0.0565	0.1946	0.2454	0.0047	0.1165	**0.4075**

5 Conclusion

This paper introduces and presents the conceptual basis of career dispositions as a six-dimensional model that describes attitudes, skills and preparations of each individual towards a professional practice. We suggest that this model can be used to diagnose and improve career success related skills and behaviors of current learners in higher education institutions. We also developed a quick, reliable and valid scale (Self-Reflective Career Dispositions Scale (SRCDS)) to measure career dispositions. The developed scale could be useful in such tasks such as obtaining early indictors of learner's future professional behaviors, evaluating the effectiveness of coaching process and educational interventions to enhance these behaviors, and helping individual learners to take greater responsibility of their learning by becoming aware of their learning profile of strengths and weakness

References

1. Brown, J.S., Adler, R.P.: Open education, the long tail, and learning 2.0. Educause Review 43(1), 16–20 (2008)
2. Arthur, M.B., Khapova, S.N., Wilderom, C.P.M.: Career success in a boundaryless career world. Journal of Organizational Behavior 26, 177–202 (2005)
3. Briscoe, J.P., Hall, D.T.: The interplay of boundaryless and protean careers: Combinations and implications. Journal of Vocational Behavior 69, 4–18 (2006)
4. Mackenzie Davey, K., Arnold, J.: A multi-method study of accounts of personal change by graduates starting work: Self-ratings, categories and women's discouses. Journal of Occupational and Organizational Psychology 73, 461–486 (2000)
5. Sturges, J., Guest, D., Mackenzie Davey, K.: Who's in charge? Graduates' attitudes to and experiences of career management and their relationship with organizational commitment. European Journal of Work and Organizational Psychology 9, 351–371 (2000)
6. Bourdieu, P.: Intellectual Field and Creative Project. Social Science Information 8, 89–119 (1968)
7. Bourdieu, P.: The Logic of Practice. Polity Press, Cambridge (1990)
8. Bourdieu, P.: Outline of a Theory of Practice. Translated by Richard Nice. Cambridge University Press, New York (1977)
9. Brubaker, R.: Social theory as habitus, pp. 212–234 (1993)
10. Lizardo, O.: The cognitive origins of Bourdieu 's habitus. Journal for the Theory of Social Behaviour 34(4), 375–401 (2004)
11. Parker, S.K., Williams, H.M., Turner, N.: Modeling the Antecedents of Proactive Behavior at Work. Journal of Applied Psychology 91(3), 636–652 (2006)
12. Grant, A.M., Ashford, S.J.: The dynamics of proactivity at work. Research in Organizational Behavior 28, 3–34 (2008)
13. Costa, P.T., McCrae, R.R.: Revised NEO personality inventory and NEO five-factor inventory professional manual. Psychological Assessment Resources, Odessa (1992)
14. Deakin Crick, R.: Learning how to learn: The dynamic assessment of learning power. The Curriculum Journal 18(2), 135–153 (2007)

Prediction of Students' Grades Based on Free-Style Comments Data

Shaymaa E. Sorour[1,2], Tsunenori Mine[2], Kazumasa Goda[3], and Sachio Hirokawa[4]

[1] Kafr Elsheik University, Kafr Elsheikh 33516, Egypt
[2] Kyushu University, Motooka, Fukuoka 819-0395, Japan
[3] Kyushu Institute of Information Science, Dazaifu, Fukuoka 818-0117, Japan
[4] Kyushu University, Hakozaki, Fukuoka 812-8581, Japan
shaymaasorour@gmail.com, gouda@kiis.ac.jp, mine@ait.kyushu-u.ac.jp, hirokawa@cc.kyushu-u.ac.jp

Abstract. In this paper we propose a new approach based on text mining technique to predict student's performance using LSA (latent semantic analysis) and K-means clustering method. The present study uses free style comments written by students after each lesson. Since the potentials of these comments can reflect students' learning attitudes, understanding and difficulties to the lessons, they enable teachers to grasp the tendencies of students' learning activities. To improve this basic approach, overlap method and similarity measuring technique are proposed. We conducted experiments to validate our proposed methods. The experimental results illustrated that prediction accuracy was 73.6% after applying the overlap method and that was 78.5% by adding the similarity measuring.

Keywords: Comments Data, Overlap method, Similarity measuring.

1 Introduction

Effective learning depends on formative assessment to discover and monitor students' understanding and their attitudes towards learning. By revealing what students already know and what they need to learn, it enables teachers to build on existing knowledge and provide appropriate scaffolding [12]. If such information is timely and specific, it can serve as valuable feedback to both teachers and students so that it will improve students' performance. Yet interpreting assessment in the learning environment remains a challenge for many reasons. Most teachers lack training in the assessment of understanding beyond the established testing culture. Externally designed tests offer limited information due to less varied and frequent assessment, as well as delayed and coarse-grained feedback [13]. The solution to these problems is to grasp all the class members' learning attitudes and tendencies of learning activities. Goda et al. proposed the PCN method to estimate students' performance from comments freely written by students. The PCN method classifies students' comments in three items:

E. Popescu et al. (Eds.): ICWL 2014, LNCS 8613, pp. 142–151, 2014.

P (Previous), C (Current), and N (Next). Item P indicates the learning activity before the class time. Item C shows the understanding and achievements of class subjects during the class time, and item N tells the learning activity plan until the next class [5]. These comments have vital roles in educational environment. For example, helping students to communicate with their teacher indirectly, and providing a lot of clues or hints to the teacher for improving his/her lessons.

To reveal the high potential of comments data for predicting students' performance, this paper proposes a new method for predicting students' grades using comments of C item (C-comments in short) from the PCN method [5]. The basic method uses LSA technique to extract semantic information from students' comments by using statistically derived conceptual indices instead of individual words, then classifies the obtained results into 5 groups according to students' grades by using K-means clustering method. The proposed method averagely achieves 66.4% of prediction accuracy of students' grades. To improve the prediction accuracy, we propose additional overlap and similarity measuring techniques. Experiments were conducted for validating our newly proposed methods; the results illustrated that, the proposed methods achieve 73.6% and 78.5%, respectively prediction accuracy of students' grades by overlap and similarity measuring techniques. The contributions of our work are the following:

- We adopt LSA to analyze patterns and relationships between the extracted words and latent concepts contained in unstructured collection of texts (students' comments), then classify LSA results into 5 groups according to students' grades by using K-means clustering method.
- We propose a similarity measuring method that calculates similarity between a new comment and comments in the nearest cluster, which is created in the training phase.
- We introduce for stable evaluation, an overlap method that allows to accept the adjacent grade of its original grade corresponding to 5-grade categories. To this end, we classify students' marks into 9 grades.
- We conduct experimens to validate our proposed methods by calculating F-measure and accuracy for estimating the final grades in each method. The experimental results illustrate the validity of the proposed methods by comparing between basic method, overlap method and similarity measuring method.

This paper is organized as follows. Section 2 discusses related work. Section 3 describes the proposed methods to predict the students' final grades. Section 4 discusses some of highlighted experimental results. Finally Section 5 concludes the paper and describes our future work.

2 Related Work

The ability to predict students' performance is very important in educational environments. Increasing students' success in their learning environment is a long-term goal in all academic institutions. Students' academic performance is based upon diverse factors like students' marks, personal, social, psychological and other environmental variables. Various experiments have been carried out in this area to predict students' academic performance by using data mining methods and recently text miming techniques.

2.1 Educational Data Mining and Students' Grade Prediction

The implementation of data mining methods and tools for analyzing data available at educational institutions is defined as Educational Data Mining (EDM). Extensive literature reviews of the EDM research field are focused mainly on retention of students, improving institutional effectiveness, enrollment management and alumni management [9]. The implementation of predictive modeling for maximizing student recruitment and retention is presented by several studies in recent years. For example, Nandeshwar and Chaudhari developed the enrollment prediction models based on students' admission data by applying different data mining methods [11]. Some researchers indicated that external data are very important sources beside university performance to predict students' performance. For example, Kotsiantis et al. used data mining techniques to explore the socio-demographic variables and study environment that may influence persistence or dropout of students, identifying the most important factors for students' success and developing a profile of the typical successful and unsuccessful students [8]. According to previous studies, students' external data are important to predict their performance. On the other hand, understanding individual students' more deeply, careful observation, recognition of their learning status and attitudes have vital roles to give feedback to each of them. To this end, we use their free-style comments written during class time and apply text mining techniques to the comments.

2.2 Text Mining and Students' Grade Prediction

Currently, there are only several studies about how to use text mining techniques to analyze learning related data. For example, Tane et al. used text mining (text clustering techniques) to group e-learning resources and documents according to their topics and similarities [14]. Hung used clustering analysis as an exploratory technique to examine e-learning literature and visualized patterns by grouping sources that share similar words and attribute values [6]. In addition, Goda et al. proposed a student's grade prediction model based on comments data using the PCN method. Their experimental results illustrated that as comments of students get higher PCN scores, the prediction performance of the students' grades becomes higher [5].

3 Prediction of Students' Grade

Fig.1 displays the overall procedures of the proposed method to predict students' grades. The procedures are based on five phases: 1- Comments data collection, 2- Data preparation, 3- Training phase, 4- Noisy data detection, 5- Test phase. The details of these phases will be described later.

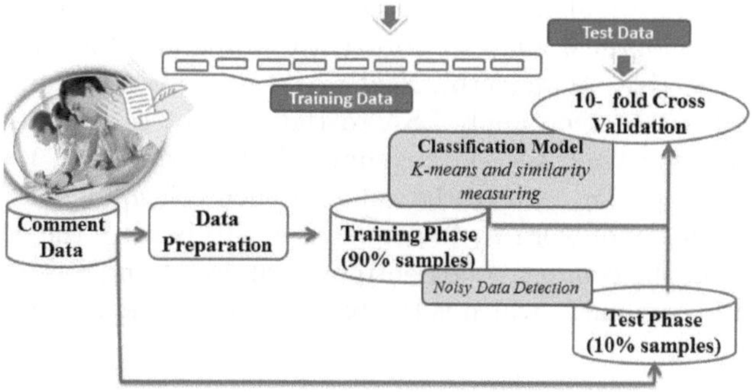

Fig. 1. Procedures of the Proposed Method

3.1 Comments Data Collection

In the first phase, C-comments were collected to predict student's grade. C-comment indicates the understanding and achievements of class subjects during the class time. In addition, it has a strong correlation with prediction accuracy than P- and N-comments [5]. We illustrate examples of C-comments written by students' as follows.

- I was completely able to understand the subject of this lesson and have confidence to make other functions similar to ones I learned in this lesson.
- I didn't finish all exercise, because I can't understand the last two methods and the time is up.

Comments data collected from 123 students in two classes. They took Goda's courses that consisted of 15 lessons. In this research, we use the students' comments collected for the last half, from the 7th to 15th lessons. Main subjects in those lessons are introductory C programming. Although, we have 123 students in all lessons, some students didn't submit their comments because they did not write any comments or were absent. Table 1 displays the number of comments in each lesson. The number of words appeared in the comments is about 1400 in each lesson. In addition, the number of distinct words is over 430 in each lesson.

3.2 Data Preparation

The data preparation phase covers all the activities required to construct the final data set from the initial raw data. In our method, we preprocess the

Table 1. Number of Comments

Lesson	7	8	9	10	11	12	13	14	15
Number	104	103	107	111	107	109	107	111	121

C-comments. First, we analyze the comments with Mecab program[1], which is a Japanese morphological analyzer to extract words and their part of speech (verb, noun, adjective, and adverb). Next we create a word-by-comment matrix with extracted words, then apply LSA to the word-by-comment matrix. This word-by-comment matrix, say A, is comprised of m words w_1, w_2,. . , w_m in n comments c_1, c_2, ...,c_n, where the value of each cell a_{ij} indicates the total occurrence frequency of word w_i in comment c_j. To balance the effect of word frequencies in all the comments, log entropy term weighting was applied to the original word-by-comment, which is the basis for all subsequent analyses [2].

3.2.1 Latent Semantic Analysis (LSA)

Latent Semantic Analysis (LSA) is a theory and method for extracting and representing the contextual-usage meaning of words by statistical computations applied to a large corpus of text. The underlying idea is that the aggregate of all the word contexts in which a given word does and does not appear provides a set of mutual constraints that largely determines the similarity of meaning of words and sets of words to each other [2]. The mathematical foundation for LSA lies in singular value decomposition (SVD), which is a matrix approximation method for reducing the dimensions of a matrix to the most significant vectors [1]. SVD yields a simple strategy to obtain an optimal approximation for matrix A using smaller matrices. The number of singular dimensions to retain is an open issue in the latent semantic analysis literature. Based on the research [2, 4] retaining dimensions 2 to 100 resulted in satisfactory performance. In this research, we apply LSA to matrix A and retain only the first four ranks by keeping the first four columns of U, S, and V.

3.2.2 Prediction Methods of Students' Grades

To predict students' grades from their comments, 5-grade categories are used to classify students' marks. The method considers prediction is correct only if one estimated grade with 5-grade category is the actual grade of a student. We call this method **5-grade prediction method**. The assessment to a student was done by considering average mark of the student's reports assigned three times, and attendance rate. In this paper, in addition to 5-grade category, we use 9-grade categories so that we allow to accept the adjacent different grade of its original grade in 5-grade categories of a mark range, i.e., make one mark range correspond to two grades in 5-grade categories. We call this method **overlap method or 9-grade prediction method** for the contrast of 5-grade prediction method. Tables 2 and 3 show the correspondence relation between the 5- and 9-grade categories and the range of students' marks. For example, we assume a student's mark is 87; the grade of the mark of 5-grade categories is A, and that of 9-grade category is AS; AS corresponds to two grades: A and S, in 5-grade categories. The reasons why we adopt the overlap method are the following: some students' learning status with the upper mark in a grade and others with

[1] `http://sourceforge.net/projects/mecab/`

Table 2. 5-Grades

Grade	S	A	B	C	D
Mark	90-100	80-89	70-79	60-69	0-59
#Student	21	41	23	17	21

Table 3. 9-Grades

Grade	S	AS	AB	BA	BC	CB	CD	DC	D
Mark	90-100	85-89	80-84	75-79	70-74	65-69	60-64	55-59	0-54
#Student	21	35	6	10	13	9	8	2	19

the lower mark in its one upper grade are not so different from the points of view of teachers' observation. Therefore it is worth noting that handling the two adjacent grades as one grade sometimes helps teachers to grasp students' real learning situations, and to give stable evaluations to students. For example, the mark range of grade AS is from 85 to 89, and that is closer to the lowest mark 90 of grade S than the lowest mark 80 of grade A.

3.3 Training Phase

In this phase, we classify LSA results into 5 clusters by using K-means clustering method [7]. Fig.2(a) displays the results of training phase for lesson 7 after classifying student's comments into 5 clusters. Here we call the grade that most frequently appears in a cluster, **dominant grade** in the cluster; dominant grades in Cluster 1, 2, 3, 4, and 5 are S, A, B, C, and D, respectively. We analyzed each lesson from 8th to 15th as well.

3.4 Prediction of Students' Grade in Test Phase: Basic Method

Discovering useful knowledge from unstructured or semi-structured text is a hard process, especially if we need to estimate students' grades, and distinguish between them. To predict students' grade based on their comments, we established the following steps:

1. Extract words from a new comment.
2. Transform the comment to a K-dimensional vector (KDV) using LSA [1].

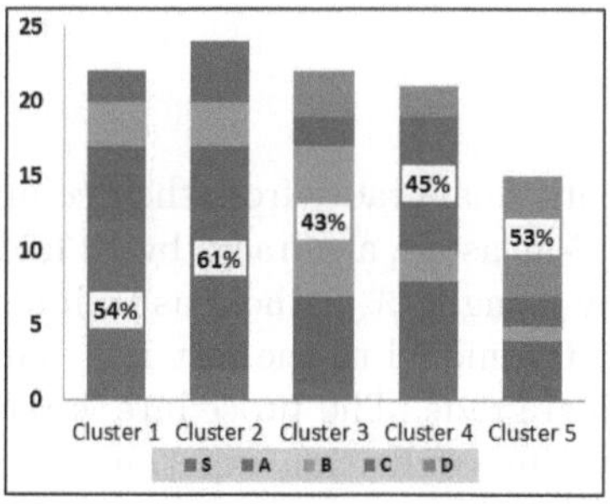

(a) Training Phase

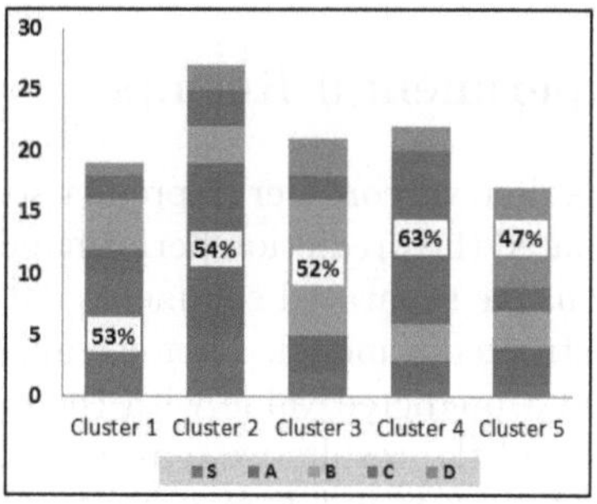

(b) Test Phase

Fig. 2. Students' Grade Prediction based on their Comment Data for Lesson 7

3. Identify which cluster center is the nearest to the comment, by measuring the distance between the comment and cluster centers.
4. Return the dominant grade in the cluster to which the identified cluster center belongs to, where the dominant grade in a cluster means the grade that most frequently appears in the cluster. After performing the above steps, we evaluated the prediction performance by 10-fold cross validation. Fig.2(b) presents the results of students' grade prediction: (Cluster 1, S=53%), (Cluster 2, A= 54%), (Cluster 3, B=52%), (Cluster4, C=63%), (Cluster 5, D=47%).

3.4.1 Similarity Measuring in the Cluster

After identifying the nearest cluster center to the new comment, we measure the similarity by calculating cosine values between the new comment, say s_{new}, and each member, say s_k, in the identified cluster, and then return, as an estimated grade of s_{new}, the grade of s_k that gets the maximum cosine value among all members in the cluster. We call this method **similarity measuring method**.

3.5 Noisy Date Detection

Outlier detection discovers data points that are significantly different from the rest of the data. In text mining, outlier analysis can be used to detect data that adversely affect the results [10]. In this paper, we detect outliers in two phases: training phase and test phase. We call such outliers **noisy data** from the points of view of grade prediction. In the training phase, we calculated standard deviation (Sd) to each cluster. As the higher the Sd is, the lower the semantic coherence is [3]. Thus, we define such a data as noisy data that the difference between a new comment and its cluster center goes over Sd. In the test phase, we measure the average distance between a new comment and cluster center. Here let c_i be the center of the i-th cluster, and $s_{k,i}$ be the k-th member of the cluster. Let $d_{i,ave}$ be the average distance between members in the cluster and c_i. if $|s_{k,i} - c_i| > d_{i,ave}$, then $s_{k,i}$ is a noisy data for the cluster, otherwise $s_{k,i}$ is not a noisy data for the cluster. We separated off about 10% to 15% of comments data as noisy data.

4 Experimental Results

In this section, we consider to predict students' final grades from their comments. We evaluated the prediction performance (F-measure, accuracy) by 10-fold cross validation. We separated comments data by using 90% of them as training data and constructed a model. Then we applied the model to the rest 10% data and compared a predicted value with the original grade. The procedure is repeated 10 times and the results were averaged. We run evaluation experiments by calculating Accuracy and F-measure by the following:

Let G be 5-grade categories (S, A, B, C and D) or 9-grade categories (S, AS, AB, BA, BC, CB, CD, DC and D), X be a subset of G; let *obs* (s_i, X) be a function that returns 1 if the grade of student s_i is included in X, 0 otherwise, where $1 \leq i \leq n$, and n is the number of students; pred(s_i) be a function that returns a set of grade categories only including a predicted grade for student s_i; !pred (s_i) returns a complement of pred(s_i). TP, FP, FN and TN are defined as follows:

$$TP = \{s_i | obs(s_i, pred(s_i)) = 1\} \qquad \text{Precision} = \frac{TP}{TP+FP}$$
$$FP = \{s_i | obs(s_i, pred(s_i)) = 0\} \qquad \text{Recall} = \frac{TP}{TP+FN}$$
$$FN = \{s_i | obs(s_i, !pred(s_i)) = 1\} \qquad F\text{-measure} = 2 * \frac{(Precision * Recall)}{(Precision + Recall)}$$
$$TN = \{s_i | obs(s_i, !pred(s_i)) = 0\} \qquad \text{Accuracy} = \frac{TP+TN}{TP+TN+FP+FN}$$

First, we checked the effect of K-means clustering method without LSA from lesson 7th to 15th. As shown in Fig.3(a), the average overall prediction accuracy results between (19.0%) and (26.4%). It is much lower than those with LSA. In addition the prediction results between (59.0%) and (71.02%) for 5-grade categories, (71.0%) and (76.0%) by the overlap method through the analysis of all comments data. To examine the effect of similarity measuring method, Fig.3(b) displays the comparison results of prediction accuracy for students' grades with and without the similarity measuring method. We can see the effect of the similarity measuring method, especially when checking the fact that the accuracy results of 5-grade prediction with the similarity measuring method is better than those of overlap method without the similarity measuring method.

In addition, Table 4 shows the effect of noisy data detection by evaluating the average overall prediction results across all lessons between our methods, before and after detecting noisy data. Finally, Fig.3(c) shows the relation between C-comments data from lesson 7th to 15th and the accuracy of predicting students'

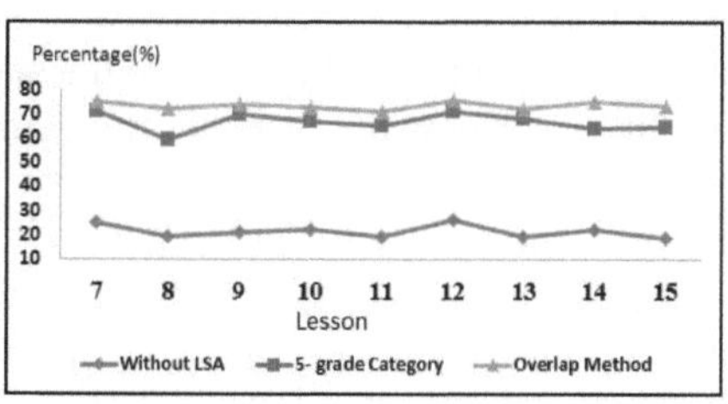

(a) The Effect of LSA

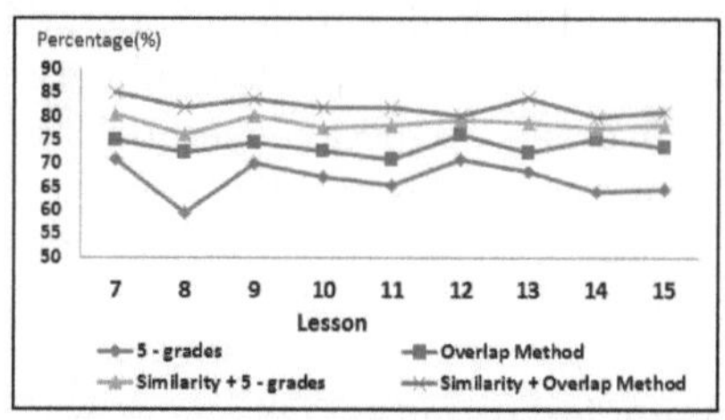

(b) Similarity Measuring Method

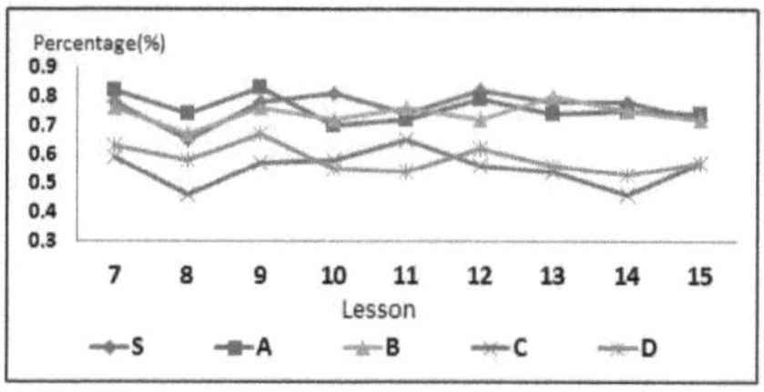

(c) Prediction by Grade

Fig. 3. The Average Overall Prediction Accuracy Results

in each grade after detecting noisy data . The results display that we can clearly distinguish higher grade groups (S, A and B) from lower ones (C, D). The reason why prediction accuracy of grade C and D became lower came from the smaller number of comments in those grades.

Table 4. Overall Prediction Results

	Precision	Recall	F-measure	Accuracy
Method	After(Before)	After(Before)	After(Before)	After(Before)
5-grade category	0.530(0.452)	0.589(0.536)	0.554(0.480)	0.696(0.664)
Overlap Method	0.682(0.662)	0.642(0.545)	0.622(0.596)	0.771(0.736)
Similarity +5 grade	0.645(0.631)	0.697(0.695)	0.680(0.661)	0.822(0.785)
Similarity +9 grade	0.787(0.765)	0.735(0.721)	0.762(0.743)	0.864(0.842)

5 Conclusion and Future Work

The free-style comment data is a quantitative method to interpret student's behavior during a class. The present study discussed students' grade prediction methods based on their free-style comments. In this paper, we discussed the basic method that adopted LSA technique and K-means clustering method. Furthermore, we proposed two new methods: overlap and similarity measuring methods to improve the basic method and conducted experiments to validate the two methods. Through experiments, we made confirmation that overlap method with 9-grade category enables more stable evaluation than 5-grade category. The average overall prediction accuracy results became better than those of classifying students' marks to 5-grade category. Next, we calculated similarity between a new comment and comments in the nearest cluster. The results of two methods (5- and 9- grade prediction methods) were better than before. Moreover, the results of the 9-grade prediction method (the overlap method) are distinguished from 5 grade prediction method. In near future, we will try other machine learning techniques to improve prediction accuracy, and also investigate such words that are clues for improving students' performance, or for judging learning problems.

Acknowledgments. This work was supported in part by PEARL, enPiT of Project for Establishing a Nationwide Practical Education Network for IT Human Resources Development under the MEXT, Japan, and JSPS KAKENHI Grant Number 24500176, 25350311, 26350357 and 26540183.

References

1. Berry, W., Dumais, S., O'Brien, G.: Using linear algebra for intelligent information retrieval. SIAM Review 37(4), 573–595 (1995)
2. Botana, G.J., Leo'n, J.A., Olmos, R., Escudero, I.: Latent semantic analysis parameters for essay evaluation using small-scale corpora. Journal of Quantitative Linguistics 17(1), 1–29 (2010)

3. Dhillon, I.S., Modha, D.S.: Concept decompositions for large sparse text data using clustering. Machine Learning 42(1-2), 143–175 (2001)
4. Drineas, P., Kannan, R., Mahoney, M.W.: Fast monte carlo algorithms for matrices iii: Computing a compressed approximate matrix decomposition. SIAM J. Computing 36(1), 184–206 (2006)
5. Goda, K., Hirokawa, S., Mine, T.: Correlation of grade prediction performance and validity of-self-evaluation comments. In: SIGITE 2013 Proceedings of the 14th Annual ACM SIGITE Conference on Information Technology Education, Florida, USA, pp. 35–42 (2013)
6. Hung, J.: Trends of e-learning research from 2000 to 2008: Use of text mining and bibliometrics. British Journal of Educational Technology 43(1), 5–15 (2012)
7. Kanungo, T., Mount, D.M., Netanyahu, N.S., Piatko, C.D., Silverman, R., Wu, Y.A.: An efficient k-means clustering algorithm: Analysis and implementation. IEEE Transactions on Pattern Analysis and Machine Intelligence 24(7), 881–892 (2002)
8. Kotsiantis, S., Pierrakeas, C., Pintelas, P.: Prediction of student's performance in distance learning using machine learning techniques. Applied Artificial Intelligence 5, 411–426 (2004)
9. Landauer, T.K., Foltz, P.W., Laham, D.: An introduction to latent semantic analysis. Discourse Processes 25, 259–284 (1998)
10. Mansur, M.O., Md. Sap, M.N.: Outlier detection technique in data mining: A research perspective. In: Proceedings of the Postgraduate Annual Research Seminar (2005)
11. Nandeshwar, A., Chaudhari, S.: Enrollment prediction models using data mining. information reuse and integration, `http://nandeshwar.info/wp-content/uploads/2008/11/DMWVU_Project.pdf` (retrieved January 10, 2009)
12. Pellegrino, W., Chudowsky, N., Glaser, R.: Knowing What Students Know: The Science and Design of Educational Assessment. National Academy Press, Washington (2001)
13. Shepard, L.A.: The Role of Classroom Assessment in Teaching and Learning (CSE Technical Report 517). Center for the Study of Evaluation, Los Angeles CA (2000)
14. Tane, J., Schmitz, C., Stumme, G.: Semantic resource management for the web: An e-learning application. In: Proceedings of the WWW Conference, New York, USA, pp. 1–10 (2004)

Integration of Theory, ICT Tooling and Practical Wisdom of Teacher: A Case of Adaptive Learning

Anna Mavroudi[1], Thanasis Hadzilacos[1], Panagiota Panteli[2], and Anna Aristodemou[2]

[1] Open University of Cyprus, Cyprus
{anna.mavroudi,thh}@ouc.ac.cy
[2] Ministry of Education, Cyprus
{panagiotapanteli,mmsarist}@gmail.com

Abstract. Teachers adapt their lessons with or without the use of technology – but in a traditional class setting they target the imaginary "average student". This paper discusses how the teacher's "wisdom of practice" can intervene and inform the Technology Enhanced Learning process. Our methodology is developed and enacted upon two theories: a domain-specific learning design theory in mathematics and a generic model derived from curriculum studies. The products of the intervention are: an adaptive learning strategy and an adaptive e-course in the domain of mathematics. Also, a roadmap is proposed concerning the stakeholders' involvement, especially the active role of the teacher in the design process. It is based on conceptual mappings between the design-based research steps and the theories used to orientate the research.

Keywords: adaptive learning, pedagogical content knowledge, learning analytics, design-based research.

1 Shulman's Model of Pedagogical Reasoning and Action and Simon's Mathematical Teaching Cycle

Many educational researchers have been influenced by Shulman's view about Pedagogical Content Knowledge (PCK) which is captured in his writings [11] as follows:

"Within the category of pedagogical content knowledge I include [...] in a word, the ways of representing and formulating the subject that make it comprehensible to others. Since there are no single most powerful forms of representation [emphasis added], the teacher must have at hand a veritable armamentarium of alternative forms of representation, some of which derive from research whereas others originate in the wisdom of practice. Pedagogical content knowledge also includes an understanding of what makes the learning of specific topics easy or difficult: the conceptions and preconceptions that students of different ages and backgrounds bring with them to the learning of those most frequently taught topics and lessons."

The key observation of Shulman that links his PCK theory with adaptive instruction is that "there are no single most powerful forms of representation", which implies the need for tailored instructional approaches. Additionally, although "there is no best instructional practice and the teacher is equipped with alternative forms of representation", she is in practice restricted to a single one at a time, at best addressed to an

E. Popescu et al. (Eds.): ICWL 2014, LNCS 8613, pp. 152–158, 2014.

idealized average student. The question then becomes: how can we feed the teacher's PCK and her personal student understanding to a technology-enhanced environment that would be capable to distinguish specific student learning characteristics and provide to each a personalized learning path?

Shulman's model of Pedagogical Reasoning and Action consists of:

1. Comprehension, which relates to teachers' critical views and understandings about the subject matter structures and the educational purposes of teaching it
2. Transformation, which contains the following sub-phases:
   (a) Preparation and critical interpretation of the given learning materials
   (b) Representations in the forms of analogies, images, stories, examples etc
   (c) Selections of teaching methods and instructional strategies
   (d) Adaptation and tailoring to student characteristics, like preconceptions, alternative conceptions, motivations, difficulties etc. It is here that ICT can provide a substantial addition at the level of the individual student.
3. Instruction, including questioning, interactions and grouping, learner control etc.
4. Evaluation of performance, in the level of the individual student as well as in the class level. Again technology-enhanced adaptive instruction allows for personalized performance evaluation, for example through e-portfolios.
5. Reflection through critical analysis of the teacher's and the students' performance
6. New comprehensions, that is, consolidation of new understandings from the teaching experience

Simon [14] in his Mathematical Teaching Cycle describes the process by which a "teacher can make decisions in conjunction with the content, design, and sequence of mathematical tasks". In short, this cycle consists of the following broad parts [14]:

1. Assessment of student's prior knowledge and aptitudes.
2. Identification of learning goals, of mathematical concepts and skills to be learnt as well as hypotheses about a path on which students might move in order to achieve these goals (Hypothetical Learning Trajectory).
3. Planning and design of appropriate learning activities and enactment
4. Iteration of the process after reassessing students' understanding, if needed.

2 Our Adaptive Learning Strategy

According to studies in the didactics of mathematics, the concepts of ratio and proportion present difficulties for the students [15]. It has been argued that in their attempts to solve problems related to these two concepts, the students use low level cognitive strategies based upon additive reasoning, as opposed to higher cognitive strategies that utilize multiplicative reasoning [5, 9]. Also, students have the tendency to treat pseudo-proportionality problems as if they were actual proportionality problems and, consequently, they apply linear models to them [7]. A classic example of a pseudo-proportionality problem -created by Markovitz et al. (1984) mentioned in [17]- is the following : "If the height of a ten-years-old boy is 1 meter and 40 centimeters, then how tall will he be when he will reach the age of 20 years?" Our e-learning strategy takes into account:

- That students faced with authentic problems [1] are more likely to abandon the stereotypical, "mechanical" way to solve the problem and engage in a meaningful problem-solving behavior.

- The affordances of adaptive and personalized learning that correspond to the student's characteristics. The adaptation parameters that intervene in the design are: student prior knowledge, inherent learning difficulties of the subject matter and learning style. In particular, with regards to the latter, the VARK taxonomy which distinguishes among the visual, aural, read-write, kinaesthetic, multimodal type of learner [2, 8] is used.

Based on these factors, the learning activities and their sequencing are differentiated, that is, each student traverses a potentially different learning path. Also, based on the learning style preference the presentation of the content is differentiated, that is the same content will be presented through an image or a diagram to the visual type, through a narration to the aural type, the "read-write" type will read it through a text format etc. A more detailed description of this specific e-learning strategy can be found in [6].

Other elements incorporated in this course are: the provision of adaptive feedback and the opportunity of learning from errors. When a student makes an error in a question that examines her prior knowledge in the diagnostic phase or in the problems she encounters later, our adaptive system detects the error and takes remedial actions aiming at provoking the destabilization of the student's alternative conception.

Concerning the learning analytics issue, the student's trajectory and his choices are monitored and online textual information is presented to the teacher. This enables her to know where exactly the students are facing difficulties and whether they have overcome them. Consequently, the teacher can know how student learning is progressing at the individual student level, as well as, at the classroom level.

3 Application of the Methodology Proposed in the Setting of the Intervention

<u>Orientation/First steps</u>: In order to orientate the adaptive learning strategy close to the teachers' views from the beginning of the design, the researcher conducted an online survey and subsequent semi-structured interviews with ten teachers internationally active in primary and secondary education (from various disciplines), who have some background in learning design and educational technology. The results of this survey confirmed that [6]: the learning style, the learning objectives and the prior student's knowledge were deemed as important parameters by the teachers.

The next step was to select the specific learning style taxonomy that was to be utilized in our adaptive learning strategy [6, 10] and matched our needs.

<u>Problem statement and consultation with practitioners</u>: Next, the researcher discussed with the specific teacher who participated in the intervention on the analogies course the possibilities about creating an adaptive e-course for this topic. The researcher explained the adaptive learning strategy and discussed with the teacher about the learning style aspect and how it might be related to the content transformation- see [6]. After the discussion, the teacher informed the principal of the school in order to obtain an initial approval, since all stakeholders' involvement is crucial in the DBR process [16].

<u>Development of solutions informed by existing design principles and technological innovations</u>: It was decided to exploit the teacher's PCK and "wisdom of practice" more extensively in the adaptive learning strategy, since the educational problem at stake could be even more meaningful pedagogically if the learning objectives (as an

adaptation parameter) focused on the inherent difficulties of the subject matter. Following, a literature review conducted by the researcher led to the selection of the specific mathematics topic (i.e. analogies and proportions) as a subject matter for which clear and plenty evidence exist in the literature that converge on specific difficulties. Also, Shulman's model of Pedagogical Reasoning and Action and Simon's mathematical teaching cycle were selected as components of a theoretical framework that shed light on how to cope with the adaptation issue. At that point of the methodology, the researcher consulted teacher's comprehension on the core concepts, the structures and the learning difficulties of the subject matter. With regards to the learning difficulties, they were confirmed by the teacher.

Next, the prerequisite knowledge, the identification of the learning goals, the hypothetical Learning Trajectory and the transformations of the content were discussed with the teacher. The initial prototype adaptive e-course was created and uploaded online. Two consecutive cycles of design and enactment in classroom settings took place, resulting at the refinement of the final solution.

<u>Iterative cycles of testing & refinement of solutions in practice</u>
Between the iterative cycles (80 minutes in each iteration) , an elapsed time of a month was devoted to make the needed refinements on the initial design. The main refinement after the first cycle was related to the use of media elements in accordance with the learning style. From the participants' observation it became evident that, in some cases where students were diagnosed as having a single-preference, alternative media were needed in addition to those supposedly preferred.

The refinements made after the second cycle involved aspects of adaptive feedback and remedial actions. Based on classroom observations, the need for more elaborative, topic-related and immediate feedback emerged [12]. Another refinement made after the second cycle involves the incorporation a teacher façade (literally, a dedicated digital space in the form of a webpage) in the adaptive e-course in which some basic learning analytics are available. The rationale is to inform the teacher about: the diagnosed learning style preference of each student, the student performance and their learning trajectory. The analytics are created in a real-time mode and presented to the teacher in the form of textual representation. The dialogue between researchers and practitioners in order to guide the development of new techniques for analytics is critical [13] and this refinement is in line with this approach. Learning analytics can be defined as: "the measurement, collection, analysis and reporting of data about learners and their contexts, for purposes of understanding and optimizing learning and the environments in which it occurs", as mentioned in [13]. In this research endeavor, the analytics are expected to play an important role in providing useful insights concerning: 1) the curriculum design through the assessment of the effectiveness of the remedial actions, as well as, 2) the teacher support in the student profiling process.

4 Implications: The Design Methodology

Table 1 generalizes the methodology described above and illustrates the conceptual mappings between the phases of: DBR enactment as mentioned in [3], the Simon's mathematical teaching cycle and Shulman's model of pedagogical reasoning and action. Understandably, the two theories have common elements and overlapping phases, like: discuss teaching/discuss instruction, discuss about the assessment of students' understandings/ discuss about evaluation of performance and others. This methodology exemplifies:

- design pathways for adaptive learning in mathematics, through the mappings between the phases of the DBR process and Simon's mathematical teaching cycle, and,
- design pathways for adaptive learning in general, through the mappings between the phases of the DBR process and Shulman's model

For example, in the analysis phase, the researcher had consulted the teacher's comprehension about the subject matter. This discussion informed and was informed by the problem statement, the research questions and the related literature, and so on for the next phases.

Phases of DBR process	**Topics/Elements**	**Phases of Simon's mathematical teaching cycle**	**Phases of Shulman's model of Pedagogical Reasoning and Action**
Analysis of practical problems by researchers and practitioners in collaboration	Problem statement		Consult teacher's comprehension
	Consultation with practitioners		
	Research questions		
	Literature review		
Development of solutions informed by existing design principles and technological innovations	Theoretical framework	Discuss about: -Assessment of student's prior knowledge -Identification of the learning goals -Hypothetical Learning Trajectory -Planning & design of proper learning activities	Discuss about and access content transformations, and alternative representations
	Development of draft principles to guide the design		
	Description of the proposed intervention		
Iterative cycles of testing & refinement of solutions in practice	Input for improvement of the intervention	-Observe teaching - Discuss about the assessment of students' understandings	- Observe instruction -Discuss about evaluation of performance
Reflection to produce "design principles" and enhance solution implementation	- Design principles - Designed artifacts - Professional development	-Discuss about next iteration	- Articulate reflections - Understand the new comprehensions

In the context of the Open Discovery Space project this methodology was investigated in tandem with the exploitation of resource-based learning [4] with encouraging results. Digital resources were incorporated on the ground that a roadmap from the mere use of data to meaning making can be fostered while focusing on the inherent difficulties of the topic, as described above. These inherent difficulties apply universally (see for example the "freshman's dream" error[1]), while: a) alignment of the curricula across Europe is incomplete and b) adaptive learning and remediation technologies are included among the challenges of the EC agenda. Consequently, this methodology can serve as a means of discussion and collaboration between school teachers, university tutors and researchers in a European-wide level, for example, through (online) communities of practice.

In this paper, we proposed a methodological framework that embraces close collaboration with the teacher, but we acknowledge that this supposition constitutes both a strength and a limitation, since although continuous and close collaboration would be ideal, oftentimes this is not possible and it certainly is not scalable. Also, it should be noted that the researcher in this case was also the developer of the adaptive e-course.

Acknowledgements. The adaptive e-course was created with the Recourse Learning Design Editor which was developed as part of the European-funded TENCompetence project.

This research is partially funded by the "Open Discovery Space: A socially-powered and multilingual open learning infrastructure to boost the adoption of eLearning resources" project, funded by CIP-ICT-PSP-2011-5, Theme 2: Digital Content, Objective 2.4: eLearning Objective 2.4

References

1. Dooren, W., Bock, D., Janssens, D., Verschaffel, L.: Pupils' over - reliance on linearity: A scholastic effect? British Journal of Educational Psychology 77(2), 307–321 (2007)
2. Fleming, N.D., Baume, D.: Learning Styles Again: VARKing up the right tree! Educational Developments 7(4), 4 (2006)
3. Herrington, J., McKenney, S., Reeves, T., Oliver, R.: Design-based research and doctoral students: Guidelines for preparing a dissertation proposal. Ed Media (2007), http://www.editlib.org/d/25967/proceeding_25967.pdf (retrieved)
4. Hill, J.R., Hannafin, M.J.: Teaching and learning in digital environments: The resurgence of resource-based learning. Educational Technology Research and Development 49(3), 37–52 (2001)
5. Lamon, S.J.: Ratio and proportion: Connecting content and children's thinking. Journal for Research in Mathematics Education 24(1), 41–61 (1993)
6. Mavroudi, A., Hadzilacos, T.: Broadening the use of E-learning standards for adaptive learning. In: Popescu, E., Li, Q., Klamma, R., Leung, H., Specht, M. (eds.) ICWL 2012. LNCS, vol. 7558, pp. 215–221. Springer, Heidelberg (2012)
7. Modestou, M., Gagatsis, A.: Students' improper proportional reasoning: A result of the epistemological obstacle of "linearity". Educational Psychology 27(1), 75–92 (2007)

[1] http://en.wikipedia.org/wiki/Freshman%27s_dream

8. Leite, W.L., Svinicki, M., Shi, Y.: Attempted validation of the scores of the VARK: Learning styles inventory with multitrait–multimethod confirmatory factor analysis models. Educational and Psychological Measurement 70(2), 323–339 (2010)
9. Noelting, G.: The development of proportional reasoning and the ratio concept: part II - Problem structure at successive stages; problems solving strategies and the mechanism of adaptive restructuring. Educational Studies in Mathematics 11, 331–363 (1980)
10. Popescu, E.: Adaptation provisioning with respect to learning styles in a Web - based educational system: an experimental study. Journal of Computer Assisted Learning 26(4), 243–257 (2010)
11. Shulman, L.: Those who understand: Knowledge growth in teaching. Educational Researcher 15(2), 4–14 (1986)
12. Shute, V.J.: Focus on formative feedback. Review of Educational Research 78(1), 153–189 (2008)
13. Siemens, G.: Learning analytics: envisioning a research discipline and a domain of practice. In: Proceedings of the 2nd International Conference on Learning Analytics and Knowledge, pp. 4–8. ACM (April 2012)
14. Simon, M.A.: Reconstructing mathematics pedagogy from a constructivist perspective. Journal for Research in Mathematics Education, 114–145 (1995)
15. Singh, P.: Understanding the concepts of proportion and ratio constructed by two grade six students. Educational Studies in Mathematics 43(3), 271–292 (2000)
16. Walker, D.: Toward productive design studies. In: Van den Akker, J., Gravemeijer, K., McKenney, S., Nieveen, N. (eds.), pp. 8–13 (2006)
17. Verschaffel, L., Greer, B., De Corte, E.: Making Sense of World problems. Swets & Zeitlinger, The Netherlands (2000)

Personalized Learning and Assessment

Ivana Simonova and Petra Poulova

University of Hradec Kralove, Rokitanskeho 62, Hradec Kralove, Czech Republic
{ivana.simonova,petra.poulova}@uhk.cz

Abstract. The paper deals with the research in the field of learning styles and assessment held on the Faculty of Informatics and Management (FIM), University of Hradec Kralove (UHK), Czech Republic. The main research objective was to discover whether tailoring the ICT-supported process of instruction to learner´s preferences results in the increase in learner´s knowledge. The method of pedagogical experiment was applied comparing learners´ performance before and after the process of instruction. The process of instruction was held in three versions of online course reflecting (1) individual student´s style of learning, (2) teacher´s style of instruction and (3) providing learners with all types of study materials allowing them to choose the most appropriate ones. The results did not prove statistically significant differences in learner´s knowledge. Then, the research focus shifted on the field of assessment. The theoretical background having been defined, a proposal of research design is provided.

Keywords: ICT-supported learning, e-learning, tertiary education, ICT, learning styles, assessment preferences.

1 Introduction

How can we pretend any longer that we are serious about creating a learning society if we have no satisfactory response to the questions how we ourselves learn, how the learning can be enhanced, whether learning difficulties could be better understood as the teaching problems, what learning model we operate with and how it should be used to improve our performance. These were the original questions asked by Coffield et al. [1] before they started research on the systematic and critical review of learning styles in post-16 pedagogy at the beginning of 2000s.

Within the last two decades the society has substantially changed. The information and communication technologies (ICT) have been implemented in all spheres, including education [2]. The core features of current society include world globalization and the call for new key competences, fast development of ICT and their influence on the educational process, open access to education and its impact on changes in the lifestyle and many others [3].

2 Theoretical Background

It is generally acknowledged that the instructor´s teaching style should match the students´ learning styles. Felder et al [4] say that mismatching can cause a wide range of further educational problems. It favors certain students and discriminates others,

E. Popescu et al. (Eds.): ICWL 2014, LNCS 8613, pp. 159–165, 2014.

especially if the mismatches are extreme. Gregorc [5] claims that only individuals with very strong preferences for one learning style do not study effectively, the others may be encouraged to develop new learning strategies. Only limited numbers of studies have demonstrated, e.g. Coffield [1] that students learn more effectively if their learning style is accommodated. The other ones have proved that there was no statistically significant difference in students´ knowledge built in the educational process supported by ICT and within the traditional, face-to-face instruction.

This research project the Learning Combination Inventory (LCI) designed by the Ch. A. Johnston was applied [6] which consists of 28 statements, responses to which are defined on the five-level Likert scale, and three open-answer questions. The responses to LCI describe the schema (pattern) that drives students´ will to learn. Respondents are categorized into four groups: (1) sequential processors, i.e. the seekers of clear directions, practiced planners, thoroughly neat workers; (2) precise processors, i.e. the information specialists, info-details researches, answer specialists and report writers; (3) technical processors, i.e. the hands-on builders, independent private thinkers and reality seekers; (4) confluent processors, i.e. those who march to a different drummer, creative imaginers and unique presenters.

3 Project Design

The project ran in several phases:

First, the Learning Combination Inventory was adapted to the conditions of the Czech university education, translated from English to Czech language, and piloted. Then, students´ preferences and learning style patterns were detected by LCI.

Second, an e-application was designed in order to match appropriate types of study materials and activities to individual student´s learning style pattern. The e-application re-organized the Course Content page of the online course described below. Single items of the Course Content, i.e. Study Materials, and exercises for fixing new knowledge were presented in such order which accommodated student´s preferences. Totally six types of study materials (i.e. fulltexts providing detailed information; short texts structured for the distance form of education, PowerPoint presentations; animations; video-recorded lectures; links to additional sources) and nine types of tests (multiple-choice with one correct answer, multiple-choice with more than one correct answer, matching, True/False, Yes/No, Junk sentences (word order), Fill-in the gap, Short open-answer and Paragraph (long) open- answer format) were implemented in the online course. The LCI data collected in phase 1 were provided in the form of four figures reflecting the individual combination of the sequential, precise, technical, confluent preferences which formed the individual pattern of each learner. Single types of study materials and exercises were classified by four figures of the value of -1, 0, 1 which corresponded to four types of processors preferences (Sequential, Precise, Technical and Confluent) as follows:

- minus one (-1) means this type is rejected, i.e. does not match the given learning style;
- zero (0) means the student neither appreciates, nor rejects, but accepts this type;
- one (1) means this type is appreciated and matches the given learning style.

Having evaluated the appropriateness of each type of study materials and exercises to single types of learning styles (Sequential, Precise, Technical and Confluent), and having detected the individual student´s learning style by LCI, all data were processed by the e-application and the Course Content page was re-structured for each student reflecting his/her individual learning preferences. Thus each student was provided by the online course tailored to the individual pattern. On the individualized page of Course Content the titles of preferred types of study materials are written in dark bold font while rejected ones are displayed in light color.

Third, the online course Library services – Information competence and education was designed. It was provided in three versions (1) reflecting the learner´s style (experimental group 1, online course LCI) where the e-application was used to tailor the course; (2) providing all types of study materials to the learner; the process of selection is the matter of individual decision, the choices were tracked and compared to the LCI group (experimental group 2, online course CG); (3) reflecting the teacher´s style (control group, online course K) where the course was designed according to the teacher´s style of instruction. The process of instruction in all groups was tracked by the LMS. Hardly any differences in the structure of all three research groups from the point of learning style pattern were detected, so the groups were considered equal. In case of LCI and CG group this result confirmed the role and process run by the e-application.

Fourth, the pedagogical experiment was run to find out whether using such methods of instruction which reflected individual learning styles resulted in statistically significant difference in the level of students´ knowledge in comparison to the situation when individual learning styles were not reflected. The experiment is based on the pre-test / instruction / post-test concept when the increase in knowledge in the experimental and control groups is calculated, statistically processed and assessed.

Fifth, students´ opinions on what format of assessment they prefer when showing the teacher what their knowledge is were collected by the multiple-choice questionnaire providing students with combinations of oral/written forms, individual/group exams, open-answer, multiple-, true/false-, yes/no-choice, matching and other formats. A place for adding any other ones, which would be appreciated by the students, was also provided; the hands-on approach was mentioned by several students (and many others voted for it when the analysis of results was introduced by the teacher, but they did not mentioned it in the questionnaire. It was intentional from teacher´s side not to include this format in the questionnaire but await quietly whether respondents will mention it, or not).

3.1 Sample Group for Pedagogical Experiment

The sample group consisted of students of University of Hradec Kralove who enrolled in the distance electronic course (e-course) on the Internet running in the LMS Blackboard. Nearly 400 respondents started the pedagogical experiment but only 324 finished it, from various reasons (K group – 113 respondents, CG group – 103, LCI group – 108).

3.2 Process of Verifying Hypotheses

The entrance knowledge in all groups was pre-tested before the process of instruction started; final knowledge was post-tested after the process of instruction was finished; the study results were statistically processed and analyzed.

Two hypotheses to be verified were defined as follows:

H_1: *Students reach higher increase in knowledge if the process of instruction is adjusted to their learning style (experimental group 1) in comparison to the process reflecting teacher´s style of instruction (group K).*

H_2: *Students reach higher increase in knowledge if they can study independently using all types of provided study materials (experimental group 2) in comparison to the process reflecting teacher´s style of instruction (group K).*

Table 1. Descriptive statistic

	Pre-test			Post-test		
	CG	K	LCI	CG	K	LCI
Mean	22.61	22.48	22.46	26.34	25.42	26.10
Min	6	13	6	14	12	14
Max	28	28	28	30	30	30
Range	22	15	22	16	18	16
SD	3.62	3.73	3.98	2.98	4.13	2.42
Modus	24	23	-	28	28	28
Median	24	23	23	27	27	27
t-test	-0.2506 (crit. 1.9706)		-	-1.8953 (crit. 1.9706)		-
	-	0.0366 (crit. 1.9704)		-	-1.4987 (crit. 1.9704)	
K-S test	0.16648 (crit.0.086)	0.16629 (crit. 0.08)	0.14513 (crit. 0.084)	0.18753 (crit. 0.086)	0.17832 (crit. 0.08)	0.16228 (crit. 0.084)
Z-value	0.3717=NR		-	1.5995 = NR		-
		0.1826=NR		-	0.1863 = NR	

NR: H_0 not rejected

3.3 Results of Pedagogical Experiment

Following statistic tests were applied to process the collected data [7]: the parametric equal variance t-test for the normal data distribution; the non-parametric Kolgomorov-Smirnov (K-S) test for different distribution; the Mann-Whitney test for difference in medians (Z-value) was applied. The results are displayed in table 1.

The results did not prove any statistically significant differences in students´ knowledge (test scores) whether their learning preferences were reflected within the process of instruction (exp1), whether they worked independently being provided all types of study materials and activities (exp2), or the process followed teacher´s style of instruction (group K).

3.4 Results of Assessment Preferences Evaluation

As the LCI structure in all three groups was nearly identical, learners´ preferences in the format of assessment were considered from the point of all respondents (324 students).

Four formats of oral and written formats were evaluated (table 2) on the 10-level scale (1 – I prefer this format; 10 – I reject this format). Results are presented in figure 1.

Table 2. Exam formats criteria

ORAL	I	individual	select question from the previously un/known list
	II	individual	teacher-student dialogue starting with ´What were you most interested in the subject?´question
	III	group	set question to a student1, student2,...
	IV	group	set question to the whole group, each student adds st. new + final critical analysis of the content
WRITTEN	V	individual	select question from the previously un/known list
	VI	individual	multiple-choice of 1 or 2+ correct answers
	VII	individual	true/false, yes/no
	VIII	group	present the project set before/at the beginning of the exam

While the preferred formats include Oral I, Oral II, Written II and Written III types, the least appreciated (rejected) ones are Oral IV and Written IV; both the appreciation and rejection were discovered with Oral I and Written I. Thus we can see the data do not show ´crystal clear´ results as we might expect, and further research will be required to define what assessment formats are really preferred and rejected by students of different learning patterns.

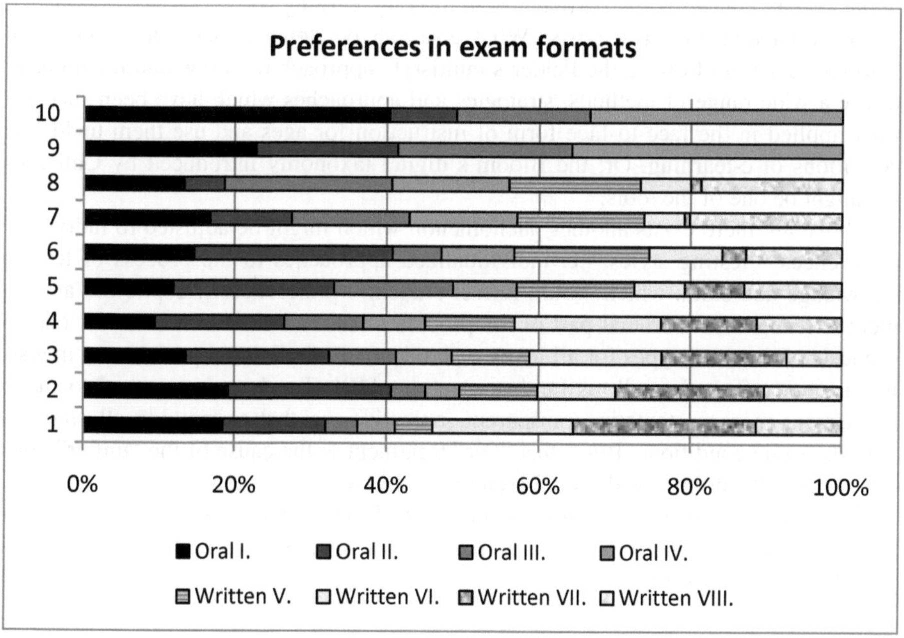

Fig. 1. Preferences in oral and written exam format

4 Discussions and Conclusions

The result we reached was surprising because the learning style reflection is widely understood to be a powerful factor providing strong impact on the process of learning, and statistically significant increase in knowledge of the LCI course participants was expected. There might be several reasons how to interpret the results.

First, we agree with e.g. [1], [4] or [5] saying that not tailoring the process of instruction to learners´ individual preferences results in increase the knowledge but they consider the developing new learning strategies to be more contributive to the learner. Thus the research question ´Is it really worth dealing with learning styles if the pedagogical experiment did not prove any increase in knowledge?´ is answered ´yes´. Above all, as stated in the theoretical part, there exist some researches (and researchers) that reject the theory of learning preferences resulting in the individually tailored process of instruction.

Second, there could be several other reasons why the expectations and hypotheses were not verified, both on the researchers´ and learners´ side (e.g. methodology, research sample, subject taught). In further research activities other approaches to running the process of instruction reflecting individual learning styles can be tested, i.e. tutor´s role as a facilitator could be strengthened and emphasized so that learners feel and study in a more friendly environment, being provided wider technical and didactic support; learner´s experience in online learning developed in this course could be extended etc. On the learners´ side the skill of independent work and study must be supported and gradually developed, as online learning has become standard not only in the tertiary education but particularly in lifelong learning.

The final question still exists: What else can be done to make the process of learning easier? Following the Felder´s multistyle approach [8] we would recommend to use a wide range of methods, strategies and approaches which have been successfully applied in the face-to-face form of instruction for ages and use them under the conditions of e-learning. Or, the Bloom´s digital taxonomy introduced by Churches [9] might be one of the tools.

Above all, there exists another phenomenon which might be adjusted to individual preferences – testing styles, i.e. individualized approaches to the process of testing knowledge and skills which would reflect student´s preferences. Despite the assessment is recognized a crucial part of the process of instruction, teachers often tend to use tests of the same types for all learners, i.e. learners ´individual preferences in testing are not reflected at all, as Leither mentions [10]. Teachers are pushed to make assessment more systematic, transparent, objective, so that to provide all students with the same conditions. But – this "fair" treatment is the cause of the "unfair" conditions from the point of individual preferences in styles of testing.

We would like to follow Leither´s pedagogical experiment [10, 417] and focus on sample group of bachelor and master IT students. Our partial results seem this approach might work well.

References

1. Coffield, F., et al.: Learning styles and pedagogy in post-16 learning. A Systematic and Critical Review. Newcatle University report on learning styles (2004), http://www.Isda.org.uk/files/PDF/1543.pdf
2. Šimonová, I., et al.: Klíčovékompetence a jejichreflexe v terciálním e-vzdělávání. E-learning v odbornéangličtině v komparaci s dalšímioblastmimanažerskéhovzdělávání. WAMAK, Hradec Kralove (2011)
3. Šimonová, I., et al.: Stylyučení v aplikacích e-learningu. M&V, Hradec Králové (2010)
4. Felder, R.M., Felder, G.N., Dietz, E.J.: The effects of personality type on engineering student performance and attitudes. Journal of Engineering Education 91(1) (2002)
5. Gregorc, A.F.: Learning/teaching styles: potent forces behind them. Educational Leadership 36 (1984)
6. Johnston, C.A.: Unlocking the will to learn. Corwin Press, Inc., Thousand Oaks (1996)
7. Hatch, E., Lazaraton, A.: The research manual. Design and statistics for applied linguistics. Heinle&Heinle Publishers, USA (1991)
8. Felder, R.M.: Are Learning Styles Invalid? (Hint: No!) (2010), http://www4.ncsu.edu/unity/lockers/users/f/felder/public/Papers/LS_Validity(On-Course)pdf
9. Churches, A.: Bloom´s Digital Taxonomy (2010), http://edorigami.wikispaces.com/Bloom%27s+Digital+Taxonomy
10. Leither, A.: Do student learning styles translate to different "testing styles? Journal of Political Science Education 7(4), 416–433 (2011)

Personalized Course Generation Based on Layered Recommendation Systems

Xiaohong Tan* and Ruimin Shen

E-Learning Lab, Shanghai Jiao Tong University, Shanghai, China
{xhtan,rmshen}@sjtu.edu.cn

Abstract. Personalized learning aims at providing services that fit the needs, goals, capabilities and interests of the learners. Recommender systems have recently begun to investigate into helping teachers to improve e-learning. In this paper, we propose a personalized course generation system based on a layered recommender system. The aim of this system is to recommend personalized leaning content for online learners based on the personal characteristics of learners, such as the prior knowledge level, learning abilities and learning goals. The recommender algorithm generates a knowledge domain and learning objects in three layers. The generated courses consider both the teaching plan of teachers and the learners' personal characteristics of the knowledge.

Keywords: personalized learning, course generation, recommender system, layered recommendation system.

1 Introduction

Personalized course generation is the process of assembling a sequence of learning objects that is adapted to an individual user's goals, preferences and capabilities. For formal online learning, the generation process includes the assembling of the knowledge domain and the learning resources. The knowledge domain consists of learning concepts and the structure of the knowledge. The learning resources consist of a set of learning objects.

A recommender system (RS) is an intelligent system that helps user to find their wanted items among a large collection of items. The increasing and successful use of RSs in e-commerce inspired researchers to design and develop specific RSs for e-learning environments [1,2,4,8],which consider the learners' various individual requirements and characteristics to achieve personalized learning.

There are several research motivations why to apply RSs for online learning. Recommender systems for adaptive hypermedia applications [10] recommend learning objects or concepts according to the learner's learning environment. These systems find suitable materials or resources based on a learner's preferences. The recommender agent for e-learning systems presented in [13] recommends actions to a learner, such as doing an exercise, reading messages, or running simulation, etc. The course

* Corresponding author.

E. Popescu et al. (Eds.): ICWL 2014, LNCS 8613, pp. 166–172, 2014.

recommendation system presented in [3] provides recommendations of learning objects in order to adapt the learners' progress towards particular learning goals. The recommendation mechanism Protus described in [8] adjusted learning content by a learner's learning style profile to accommodate to the variation. The system recommends online activities and resources from the current learning context for learner.

The employed algorithms differ. The research in [13] integrates web mining and web usage mining to discover user's actions, and then fed into the recommender system. While in [6], text mining is used to organize articles and documents based on topics and provide documents recommendation. In [3], the course recommendation process is an adaptive community-based hypermedia system which uses the explicit feedback from learners to recommend courses for them. Collaborative filtering is used by a recommender system [9] for online learners in learning network. It simulated rules for motivation and some disturbance factors in learning environment. A similar recommendation system is described in [7]. The adaptation and navigation system presented in [11] improves the performance of the developed courses by adding adaptive hypermedia courses. The ontology–based hybrid recommender system in e-learning [14] is driven by domain ontology model and the learner's interest-based and cluster-based. Ghauth and Abdullah [5] build an e-learning recommender system to recommender learning material using content-based filtering and good learner's rating.

In this paper, we present a personalized course generation based on a layered recommender system (PCG-LRS) for adapting individual online learners' different requirements on learning content, including knowledge domain of a subject and the learning objects. The recommendation of personalized learning concepts and learning objects are implemented in three layers. The article is structured as follows. We start by describing related work of the application RSs in e-learning environments. In the subsequent section, the framework of the PCG-LRS is described. Section 3 details the course generation process on the LRS. Then, section 4 reports the implementation and the evaluation results about teachers' and students' satisfaction of the PCG based on LRS. The last section gives a conclusion of this work.

2 Framework of the Layered Recommendation System

In order to construct a web-based course automatically, we first design a platform [12] for professional teachers, domain experts, and instructional designers. In this platform, the domain experts construct the knowledge domain structure including the knowledge concepts and the constraint relations between concepts. The instructional designers lay out various learning activities for different learning scenarios. The professional teachers provide learning objects for concept suitable for different learning activity. Through the above work, the knowledge base and the learning resource base are constructed. The framework of the LRS is presented as fig. 1. The recommendation procedure is implemented in three layers.

The first layer aims to generate the knowledge domain of a course based on the teaching outline from the knowledge base. The teaching outline is constructed by teachers before a semester.

The second layer is to generate personalized knowledge domain for individual learners from the knowledge domain of a course. It focuses on the leaning profile that collects learners' personal characteristics.

The third layer is to recommend learning objects based on the relation matrix between concepts and learning objects. The learning objects are extracted from the learning resource repository suitable for personalized knowledge domain.

The proposed LRS not only takes into account of both course outline and the personal characteristics of learners, but reduces the dimensions and the computation.

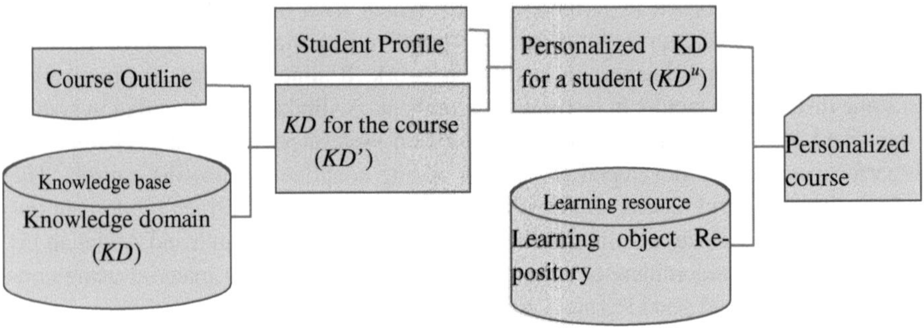

Fig. 1. Framework of the Layered Recommendation System

3 The Personalized Course Generation

3.1 Generation of the Knowledge Domain for a Course

Before generate a new web-based course, the teacher provides a teaching outline document in specified form given as a text document. Then a set of suitable learning concepts is generated. The knowledge domain is described as two-tuples like: $KD=\{C, R\}$. Here C is the set of all concepts, and R is the set of constraint relations. Suppose $\|C\|=N$, that means there are N different concepts in set C. they are described as N keywords as $C=(c_1,c_2,\ldots,c_N)$.

The teaching outline document D is separated into M independent records, as $D=(d_1,d_2,\ldots,d_M)$. The core of this algorithm is to extract sub space of the relevant feature keywords from the whole feature space C according to the set D.

First counting the feature vector of di using TF-IDF: $d_i=\{w_{i1},w_{i2},\ldots,w_{iN}\}$.

Then the feature concepts' weight in the teaching outline document is calculated:

$$\begin{array}{c} \\ d_1 \\ d_2 \\ \vdots \\ d_M \end{array} \begin{array}{c} \begin{array}{cccc} c_1 & c_2 & \cdots & c_N \end{array} \\ \begin{pmatrix} w_{11} & w_{12} & \cdots & w_{1n} \\ w_{21} & w_{22} & \cdots & w_{2N} \\ \vdots & \vdots & \vdots & \vdots \\ w_{M1} & w_{M2} & \cdots & w_{MN} \end{pmatrix} \end{array} = \Gamma \tag{1}$$

Counting the weight of each concept c_j in the document D

$$Dc_j = \sum_{k=1}^{M} w_{kj} \tag{2}$$

Set the threshold value d, select the subset C' based on the document D

$$C' = \{c_j \mid Dc_j \geq d, 1 \leq j \leq N, c_j \in C\} \tag{3}$$

Fine the solution of relationship R' from R based on the subset C'.

$$R' = \{r \mid r = < c_i, c_j >, c_i \in C', c_j \in C', 1 \leq i, j \leq N, r \in R\} \tag{4}$$

Construct the knowledge domain $KD' = \{C', R'\}$

3.2 The Personalized Knowledge Domain Generation

The algorithm in this section will construct the personalized knowledge domain from *KD'* for individual learners based on the learning profile.

The presentation of the student's learning profile is defined as table 1. It describes the learning attribution for each concept. For each concept, there are three different attributions, namely knowledge level, cognitive ability, and learning goal.

Table 1. The learning profile

Concept (C)	c_1	c_2	…	c_i	…	c_n
Knowledge level (S)	s_1	s_2	…	s_i	…	s_n
cognitive ability (B)	b_1	b_2	…	b_i	…	b_n
Learning goal (O)	o_1	o_2	…	o_i	…	o_n

According to the attribution of the relation, the set C' and the relation R' construct a directed acyclic graph. The personalized knowledge domain generation procedure is following.

Firstly, generate all the topological sort lists of the set C' according to the set R'. Set there are k-possible topological lists for C', namely $C_1, C_2, \ldots, C_k$. For each concept sequence C_i ($1 \leq i \leq k$), there are n concepts in it.

Then, for each sequence C_i, generate the possible leaning sequence, $C_1', C_2', \ldots, C_k'$, according to the knowledge character and objective character of learner u.

For each possible learning sequence C_i', select the appropriate sequence according to the ability character of learner u and the difficulties of the concepts in C_i'. Here using cosine distance to count the difference vector between learners' cognitive ability and the difficulty parameter of concepts.

Average the difference vector and select the closest concept set $C^u = \{ c_1^u, c_2^u, \ldots, c_p^u \}$. The relation set R^u is generated accordingly.

Finally, the personalized knowledge domain is generated, $KD^u = \{C^u, R^u\}$.

3.3 The Learning Objects Generation

The learning content is composed of learning objects. So this section describes the recommendation of learning content based on the personalized knowledge domain and the relation between concepts and learning objects. The set of learning objects are recommended to users adapted to the KD^u.

First, if the learning object r_i is related to any of the concepts in C^u, it also belongs to the learning resource of user u. From this way, the learning resource R^u for user u is created.

$$R^u = \{r_1^u, r_2^u, \ldots, r_{m'}^u\} \tag{5}$$

Then, create the relation matrix of R^u and C^u, RC^u.

$$RC^u = \begin{bmatrix} v_{11}^u & v_{12}^u & \cdots & v_{1p}^u \\ v_{21}^u & v_{22}^u & \cdots & v_{2p}^u \\ \cdots & \cdots & \cdots & \cdots \\ v_{m'1}^u & v_{m'2}^u & \cdots & v_{m'p}^u \end{bmatrix} \tag{6}$$

Comparing the difficult degree of r_i and the cognitive ability of the learner u for concept c_j, create a filtered resource R_u' for user u.

4 Implementation and Evaluation

In order to demonstrate the effectiveness of the PCG-LRS, we have carried out several experiments on the online learning system in the Continuous School of Shanghai Jiao Tong University.

There were 16 teachers construct 849 concepts in 105 topics in the knowledge base. The teachers and their assistant constructed 2441 learning objects for the concepts in the learning resource repository.

There were 16 different teaching outlines established by 16 teachers in different subjects. Accordingly, 16 courses generated from the PCG-LRS. The 16 teachers evaluated the generated courses. They evaluated each generated concept and learning object in the aspect of expertise. The Mean Error (ME) is calculated to determine the accuracy rating of the recommendation knowledge domain. The ME is the deviation between the concepts generated from PCG-LRS and the expected from expertise.

In the experiments, one teacher of the course Data Structure (DS) authored the teaching outline document A. There were 98 online learners majoring in DS evaluating the course generated from the system. They evaluated each generated concept and leaning object from the learning aspect. The Mean Difficulty-Easy Error (MDEE) was calculated to determine the accuracy rating of the recommendation of personalized concepts and the leaning objects.

The feedback from those 16 teachers shows that teachers are satisfied with the generation knowledge domain for their teaching outline. According to the average mean error value, the average satisfaction degree is 84.1%, which means that it successfully generates the knowledge domain for the teaching outline.

Out of 100 students who participant in the LRS learning system, 87 filled in the survey about the accuracy of the learning objects recommended from the system. The questionnaire includes the survey of the satisfaction to each learning object's and to the whole generated course. The results show that the average satisfaction degree of all the 87 students to their individual learning object is 85%. The average satisfaction degree to the whole courses is 76%. In their opinion, the system successfully recommends appropriate learning resource.

5 Conclusion

This paper describes a Personalized Course Generation (PCG) method based on a Layered Recommender System (LRS). It builds knowledge domain and learning objects of online courses for individual learners in three layers. From a technical perspective, the work advances the state of the art of course generation. It is the first system that separates the knowledge domain generation and the learning objects recommendation in three layers. This method solves the cold-start and the multi-dimensions problems of RSs. From a strategic point of view, the PCG fits the requirement of the normal setting education. The teaching outline from teachers is the basic of knowledge domain generation. The needs of individual learners are the personalized considering of the generation courses.

Acknowledgement. This paper is supported by National Key Technology R&D Program (No. 2012BAH55F01 & 2012BAH55F02) which conducted by the ministry of science and technology in China, is also one of the research results of Shanghai Science and Technology Development Fund (No. 13692106000).

References

1. Dikovic, L.J.: Applications GeoGebra into teaching some topics of mathematics at the college level. Computer Science and Information Systems, ComSIS 6(2), 191–203 (2009)
2. Dwivedi, P., Bharadwaj, K.K.: E-Learning Recommender System for Learners in Online Social Networks through Association Retrieval. In: Proceedings of the CUBE International Information Technology Conference, CUBE 2012, pp. 676–681 (2012)
3. Farzan, R., Brusilovsky, P.: Social navigation support in a course recommendation system. In: Wade, V.P., Ashman, H., Smyth, B. (eds.) AH 2006. LNCS, vol. 4018, pp. 91–100. Springer, Heidelberg (2006)
4. Fertalj, K., Hoic-Bozic, N., Jerkovic, H.: The integration of learning object repositories and learning management systems. Computer Science and Information Systems, ComSIS 7(3) (2010), doi:10.2298/CSIS081127001F.
5. Ghauth, K.I., Abdullah, N.A.: Learning material recommendation using good learners' ratings and content-based filtering. Educational Research and Development (2010), doi:10.1007/s11423-010-9155-4
6. Hammouda, K., Kamel, M.: Data Mining in e-Learning, pp. 1–28. Springer (2006)

7. Janssen, J., Van den Berg, B., Tattersall, C., Hummel, H., Koper, R.: Navigational support in lifelong learning: enhancing effectiveness through indirect social navigation. Interactive Learning Environments 15(2), 127–136 (2007)
8. Klasnja-Milicevic, A., Vesin, B., Ivanovic, M., Budimac, Z.: E-Learning personalized based on hybrid recommendation strategy and learning style identification. Computer & Education 56(2011), 885–899 (2011)
9. Koper, E.J.R.: Increasing learner retention in a simulated learning network using indirect social interaction. Journal of Artificial Societies and Social Simulation 8(2), 18–27 (2005)
10. Kristofic, A.: Recommender system for adaptive hypermedia Applications. In: Proceeding of Informatics and Information Technology Student Research Conference, Bratislava, pp. 229–234 (2005)
11. Romero, C., Ventura, S., De Bra, P.: Knowledge discovery with genetic programming for providing feedback to courseware. User Modeling and User-Adapted Interaction 14(5), 425–464 (2004)
12. Tan, X., Ullrich, C., Wang, Y., Shen, R.: The Design and Application of an Automatic Course Generation System for Large-Scale Education. In: Proceeding of IEEE International Conference on Advanced Learning Technologies, pp. 607–609 (2010)
13. Zaïane, O.R.: Building a recommender agent for e-learning systems. In: The International Conference on Computers in Education, ICCE 2002, pp. 55–59 (2002)
14. Zhuhadar, L.: Multi-model ontology–based hybrid recommender system in e-learning domain. In: ACM International Conference on Web Intelligence and Intelligent Agent Technology-Workshops, pp. 91–95 (2009)

Analysis of Sharable Learning Processes and Action Patterns for Adaptive Learning Support

Xiaokang Zhou and Qun Jin

Graduate School of Human Sciences,
Waseda University, Japan
xkzhou@ruri.waseda.jp, jin@waseda.jp

Abstract. In this study, we focus on the deep analysis of the learning behavior patterns in the task-oriented learning process, which aims to extract and describe the sharable learning processes for adaptive learning support. The LA-Patterns are extracted to represent an individual's learning behavior patterns. Three categories, named Regular Patterns, Successive Patterns, and Frequent Patterns, are classified to describe users' learning patterns with different features, which can be utilized to recommend users with the adaptive learning process as the learning guidance. The experiment and analysis results in a learning management system are discussed finally.

Keywords: Learning Pattern, Learning Analytics, Sharable Learning Process, Adaptive Learning.

1 Introduction

Learning analytics, which can be viewed as a multidisciplinary approach to integrating studies among technical, pedagogical, and social domains [1], has attracted wide attention from all walks of our lives. Meanwhile, with the high development of computing technologies, learning in a web-based learning system no longer means users can only learn following the pre-defined instructions in the pre-planned curriculums, but can learn from each other by observing the learning processes and behaviors of others and the outcomes of those behaviors. The learning activities generated by a variety of learners, including the information behaviors along with users' learning experience, should be viewed as an important learning recourse. Thus, it is essential to analyze the information generated in learning processes in and across the systems to improve teaching, learning and other related educational activities, in order to serve the needs of all stakeholders, such as teacher, learner and manager, by sharing the learning process information.

In our previous study, we have proposed a model to describe users' learning behaviors in both individual and collective way [2], and utilized the extracted learning action patterns for the recommendation of the next possible learning actions [3]. In this study, we concentrate on the deep analysis of the so-called LA-Patterns, which will be classified into three categories, named Regular Patterns, Successive Patterns, and Frequent Patterns, in order to discover the insights from the sharable learning processes for adaptive learning support.

E. Popescu et al. (Eds.): ICWL 2014, LNCS 8613, pp. 173–178, 2014.

2 Related Work

The concept of learning analytics has drawn a big body of researches in the web-based learning environment. Rahman et al. [4] presented the design of LASSIE (Learning Analytics for Social Systems in Institutional Education) as an open source analytics tool to analyze the students' behaviors on the Athabasca Landing site, to support learning and education in the social networking environment. Klamma [5] introduced two ongoing researches: ROLE (Responsive Open Learning Environments) and Learning Layers (Scaling up Technologies for Informal Learning in SME Clusters), which aimed to facilitate the learning processes through community learning analytics. Fournier et al. [6] discussed the possible usages of analytics tools for the facilitation of learning and education in the MOOC (Massive Open Online Course) environment. Clow [7] built a learning analytics cycle based on the five-step model (Capture, Report, Predict, Act, and Refine) of learning analytics, which showed several insights for the learning analytics practice. Kizilcec et al. [8] proposed a classification method to identify the trajectories of engagement among different course structures using the learning data generated from the MOOCs datasets. Renzel et al. [9] presented an application of learning analytics in a widget-based PLE (Personal Learning Environments) platform using the web logs data and discussed their benefits for learners.

3 Learning Behavior Pattern Analysis

3.1 Classifying of Learning Action Patterns

We focus on deep analysis of the so-called LA-Pattern (Learning Action Pattern) [2] to discover the insights hidden among them, which can benefit the analysis of the sharable learning processes to provide users with adaptive learning support. Three major types of the LA-Patterns are classified and defined as follows.

Regular Pattern: Regular Patterns are the learning patterns which have no repeated element in the learning action sequence. That is, given an LA-Pattern $< act_i >_u^w \rightarrow G$, where w denotes the frequency-based weight, and u denotes the user who has conducted this learning action sequence, if each learning action act_k in the whole learning action sequence $<act_i>$ is unique, it can be recognized as the Regular Pattern.

Successive Pattern: Successive Patterns are the learning patterns which contain a specific sub-sequence continuously occurring within the pattern. That is, given an LA-Pattern $< act_i >_u^w \rightarrow G$, if exists such a sub-sequence, $< act_1, act_2, \ldots, act_j >$, successively occurs in the whole learning action sequence $<act_i>$, it can be recognized as the Successive Pattern, and the sub-sequence, $< act_1, act_2, \ldots, act_j >^{w_s}$, is defined as the successive factor. Generally, the default values of j and w_s are 2, which stand for the successive factor should contain at least two actions occurring at least twice.

Frequent Pattern: Frequent Patterns are the learning patterns which contain a specific sub-sequence massively occurring in the patterns with the same learning purpose. That is, given an LA-Pattern $< act_i >_u^w \rightarrow G$, if exists such a sub-sequence, $< act_1, act_2, \ldots, act_j >$, massively occurs in the LA-Patterns with the same learning goal action G, it can be recognized as the Frequent Pattern, and the sub-sequence, $< act_1, act_2, \ldots, act_j >^{w_f}$, is defined as the frequent factor. Generally, the default value of j is 2, and the value of w_f is 1.

The Regular Pattern is identified based on the characteristics of the whole learning action sequence, while the other two patterns, the Successive Pattern and Frequent Pattern, are identified in accordance with the typical sub-sequences in each pattern. Note that we do not intend to make a partition under these three major patterns. That is, for instance, if a Regular Pattern contains a frequent factor, it can also be considered a Frequent Pattern. And if a successive factor massively occurs in other patterns with the same learning purpose, it may also be viewed as the frequent factor.

3.2 Toward Adaptive Learning Support

As for the learning guidance, the Regular Pattern can be viewed as the learning routine to provide the basic steps toward a certain learning purpose. Specifically, based on the calculation of similarities among a group of users, the target user will be provided with the most suitable Regular Patterns for the basic reference. On the other hand, the Successive Patterns and Frequent Patterns can be utilized to benefit the optimization of learning process. The Successive Patterns, especially the successive factors, can be viewed as a repeating means to pursue a better learning result, while the Frequent Patterns with the frequent factor, can be utilized to share users' learning experience for the same learning purpose. The procedure to analyze the LA-Patterns and provide the adaptive learning support is shown as follows.

Step 1: Divide the whole timeline into several learning periods (e.g., one week for a lesson). For each user u_i, extract all the learning action sequences in a selected learning period T to calculate and generate the LA-Patterns. Then, according to the pre-defined learning goal actions, divide all the LA-Patterns into several groups.

Step 2: According to the three categories of the LA-Patterns, in each group of patterns, assign the corresponding LA-Patterns into three sets: the Regular Pattern set, the Successive Pattern set, and the Frequent Pattern set.

Step 3.1: As for the Regular Pattern set, given a target user, calculate the similar user group based on the similarity of the LA-Patterns. Then, according to the target user's current learning purpose which is pre-defined by the learning goal action, provide him/her with the most relevant patterns generated from the similar user group as the reference of the basic learning steps.

Step 3.2: As for the Successive Pattern set, given a target user with his/her current learning purpose, calculate and extract all the successive factors with the same learning purpose. Then, provide the target user with the relevant Successive Patterns and the corresponding average repeating times to pursue a better learning result.

Step 3.3: As for the Frequent Pattern set, given a target user with his/her learning purpose, according to his/her current learning action, select the next possible learning action from those similar users based on the similarity of their learning behaviors. Then, provide the target user with the Frequent Patterns which contain the frequent factor beginning with the selected learning action as the learning guidance.

4 Experiment and Analysis

We conducted our experiment in a Moodle-based learning system, in which one course consists of 15 lessons. 18 kinds of learning actions have been pre-defined to represent users' learning actions within the system [3]. Totally, 57 students have used this system, and generated more than 12000 learning actions.

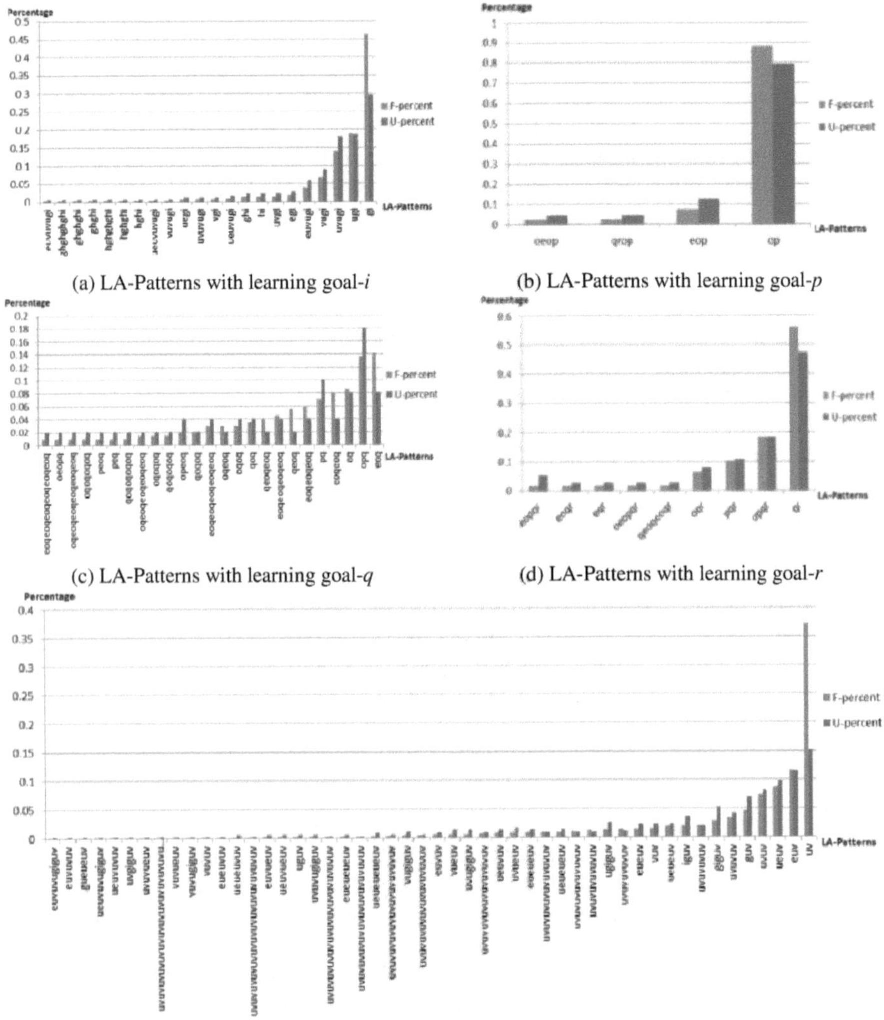

(a) LA-Patterns with learning goal-*i*

(b) LA-Patterns with learning goal-*p*

(c) LA-Patterns with learning goal-*q*

(d) LA-Patterns with learning goal-*r*

(e) LA-Patterns with learning goal-*v*

Fig. 1. Statistics for LA-Patterns with different learning goals

Finally, we have obtained totally 655 LA-Patterns. According to the pre-defined learning goal actions, these LA-Patterns are grouped into six types. Fig. 1 (a) - (e) show the statistics for each pattern based on two important factors: the frequency a certain pattern occurs in all users' learning action sequences, and the number of users who have conducted this pattern. The LA-Patterns with the learning goal-*j* has only one element *hj*, appearing three times, for which the graph is not created and showed.

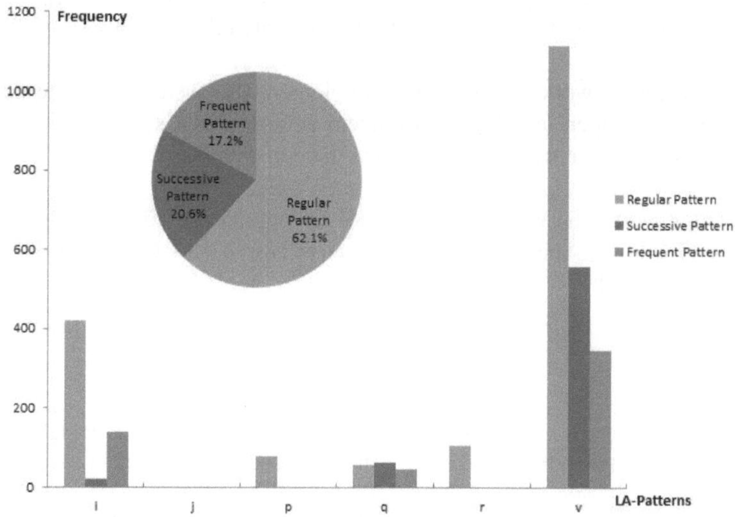

Fig. 2. Statistics based on the classification of LA-Patterns

After filtering the noise patterns which include the non-recommended or incorrect learning action sequences, we analyze the refined 634 LA-Patterns based on the classifications. Note that, in this case, we consider the learning patterns which discontinuously contain the frequent factor at least twice as the Frequent Patterns. As shown in Fig. 2, generally, the Regular Patterns occupy the most of the whole LA-Patterns, while the Successive Patterns and Frequent Patterns are 20.6% and 17.2% respectively. As we discussed above, different types of the learning patterns may contribute to different users in their different learning stages. The Regular Patterns, as the necessary steps for the basic learning process, can be provided to those users who are the first time to learn this course, or are not sure which should be done in the current stage. The Successive Patterns, especially with the average repeating times of the successive factor, can help the target user pursue a better learning result in an effective way. As for the learning action recommendation, the Frequent Patterns can not only provide the target user with the next possible learning action, but a series of learning actions based on other users' learning experience, to complete the learning task in a more reasonable way. Therefore, according to these learning patterns, we can share the suitable learning processes along with users' learning experience to the target users, in order to support their task-oriented learning.

5 Conclusion

In this paper, we have proposed an analysis approach to classifying users' learning behaviors which are characterized by the LA-Patterns, and analyzing the task-oriented learning processes, in order to extract the sharable learning processes along with users' learning experience for the adaptive learning support. Three major categories, Regular Patterns, Successive Patterns, and Frequent Patterns, were defined to classify and describe users' learning patterns with different features, which can be utilized to provide users with the adaptive learning support. Finally, the experimental analysis results in a Moodle-based learning system demonstrated the usability of our proposed method.

As for the future work, we will fully implement the system with the developed mechanisms in an open learning environment across MOOCs platforms. And more experiments should be conducted to evaluate the performance.

Acknowledgement. The work has been partly supported by 2013 and 2014 Waseda University Grants for Special Research Projects No. 2013A-6395, No. 2013B-207, and No. 2014K-6214.

References

1. Suthers, D., Verbert, K.: Learning analytics as a "middle space". In: Proc. LAK 2013 (3rd International Conference on Learning Analytics and Knowledge), Leuven, Belgium, pp. 1–4 (2013)
2. Zhou, X., Chen, J., Jin, Q.: Discovery of Action Patterns in Task-Oriented Learning Processes. In: Wang, J.-F., Lau, R. (eds.) ICWL 2013. LNCS, vol. 8167, pp. 121–130. Springer, Heidelberg (2013)
3. Zhou, X., Chen, J., Wu, B., Jin, Q.: Discovery of Action Patterns and User Correlations in Task-Oriented Processes for Goal-Driven Learning Recommendation. IEEE Transactions on Learning Technologies (2014), doi:10.1109/TLT.2013.2297701(2014)
4. Rahman, N., Dron, J.: Challenges and Opportunities for Learning Analytics When Formal Teaching Meets Social Spaces. In: Proc. LAK 2012, Vancouver, BC, Canada, pp. 54–58 (2012)
5. Klamma, R.: Community Learning Analytics – Challenges and Opportunities. In: Wang, J.-F., Lau, R. (eds.) ICWL 2013. LNCS, vol. 8167, pp. 284–293. Springer, Heidelberg (2013)
6. Fournier, H., Kop, R., Sitlia, H.: The Value of Learning Analytics to Networked Learning on aPersonal Learning Environment. In: Proc. 1st International Conference on Learning Analytics and Knowledge, Banff, Alberta, Canada (2011)
7. Clow, D.: The Learning Analytics Cycle: Closing the Loop Effectively. In: Proc. LAK 2012, Vancouver, BC, Canada, pp. 134–138 (2012)
8. Kizilcec, R.F., Piech, C., Schneider, E.: Deconstructing Disengagement: Analyzing Learner Subpopulations in Massive Open Online Courses. In: Proc. LAK 2013, Leuven, Belgium, pp. 170–179 (2013)
9. Renzel, D., Klamma, R.: From Micro to Macro: Analyzing Activity in the ROLE Sandbox. In: Proc. LAK 2013, Leuven, Belgium, pp. 250–254 (2013)

Towards Pedagogy-Driven Learning Design: A Case Study of Problem-Based Learning Design

Yongwu Miao[1], Mohamed Ally[2], Mohammed Samaka[3], and Avgoustos A. Tsinakos[4]

[1] Department of Computational and Cognitive Sciences, University of Duisburg-Essen, Duisburg, Germany
miao@collide.info
[2] Centre for Distance Education, Athabasca University, Athabasca, Canada
mohameda@athabascau.ca
[3] Computer Science and Engineering Department, Qatar University, Doha, Qatar
samaka.m@qu.edu.qa
[4] Eastern Macedonia and Thrace Institute of Technology Ag. Loukas 65404 Kavala, Greece
tsinakos@teikav.edu.gr

Abstract. Existing learning design languages are pedagogy-neutral. They provide insufficient support to explicitly represent pedagogy-specific approaches such as problem-based learning (PBL). As the first step towards pedagogy-driven learning design, we developed a PBL design language and an associated authoring tool by adopting a domain-specific language (DSL) approach. The language and the tool provide means for teachers to think and represent their own PBL designs in vocabularies that the teacher daily uses to describe their PBL approaches. This paper presents a case study to investigate whether the language and the tool can facilitate the design of a PBL course plan. Although participants had minimal knowledge of PBL and were not skilled in process modeling, after a short training they were able to prepare their own PBL course plans using the PBL authoring tool. They reported that the vocabularies in the PBL design language were easy to understand. Some thought that the tool provides flexibility and others did not think so. Nevertheless, some found the process somewhat difficult to represent the narrative into a course plan. In addition, most participants found that the tool is user-friendly and easy to learn.

Keywords: Learning design, IMS-LD, DSL, PBL, PBL design language, case study.

1 Introduction

Nowadays new pedagogies such as problem-based learning and inquiry-based learning and innovative use of technologies such as internet and virtual collaborative environment seem to offer much promise in terms of providing new educational experiences for learners. However in reality practitioners are overwhelmed by the plethora of choices and may lack the necessary skills to make informed design decisions about how to use these theories and technologies [7]. Designing high quality, technology-supported learning experiences is a significant challenge for educators [23]. Recently

E. Popescu et al. (Eds.): ICWL 2014, LNCS 8613, pp. 179–189, 2014.

learning design has emerged as a distinct field of research, which is concerned with the development of methods, tools, and resources for helping designers in their design process [4, 23]. Although learning design and instructional design are similar and both aim to maximize the benefit and impact of learning by using the right learning model and by designing the right conditions for learning, instructional design focuses more on designing learning content and assessment of outcomes for knowledge transmission from the perspectives of teachers. Whereas learning design focuses more on planning, structuring and sequencing learning activities and designing learning context and environment with technical support for knowledge construction from the perspectives of learners. Examples of such learning activities are: identifying and analyzing problems in a session, brainstorming learning issues using a digitalized whiteboard, gather information from internet with a search engine, proposing and discussing solutions in a discussion forum, and co-authoring a group report using wiki. In addition, the term of "learning design" also denotes the result or product of the design process, a computational description of a teaching-learning process that may happen in a lesson or a course. Learning design aims at providing a means to represent and communicate the designs of learning activities so that they can be shared among practitioners at design-time. Furthermore, the learning designs can serve as a means to orchestrate and scaffold teaching and learning practice at run-time [25].

Learning design was proposed by Rob Koper and his colleges at Open University of Netherlands [19, 20] when they developed an educational modelling language (EML) and initiated an international e-learning technical standard, called IMS-LD [17]. Since then many learning design languages and associated tools have been developed. Some learning design languages such as LDVS [1, 5], LDLite [28] and CompendiumLD [8] are intentionally developed for teachers to reflect on and exchange the pedagogic ideas and the rationale of the actual design through using semi-structured description as a tabular or a diagram. Such a learning design is to inspire teachers to implement them and hence improve practice [11]. Other learning design languages such as IMS-LD, LDL [24], MoCoLADe [15], and LAMS [9] emphasize more on the support of automation of teaching and learning processes through formally modelling a pedagogic strategy consisting of detailed activities with associated learning resources and services. This kind of learning design is mainly to enable machine to execute the process model and scaffold teaching and learning practice. No matter for teaching or for learning, these learning design languages are pedagogy-neutral and can be used to describe a wide range of pedagogical strategies. However, the practitioner has difficulties to represent complex learning activities using these languages like IMS-LD [14, 26, 27], because the vocabularies of these languages are pedagogy-irrelevant and technology-oriented terms such as "activity", "property", "learning object", and "data-type". They provide less or even no vocabularies and guidance to represent and implement specific pedagogic strategies such as problem-based learning and inquiry-based learning.

Some researchers have argued that it is almost impossible to develop a new generation of e-learning environments that are completely pedagogically neutral [22]. In comparison with a pedagogy-neutral learning design language like IMS-LD, a pedagogy-driven learning design language may be more useful and easy to use for practitioners. However, it is not realistic to define a high-level learning design language with a common set of vocabularies to explicitly describe various pedagogical approaches, because there are many different learning theories and pedagogies and they use different, sometimes incompatible concepts and terms to describe different teaching and learning approaches. Traditional classifications of learning activities (e.g., Bloom's taxonomy [6] and Gagne's nine instructional events [12]) are suitable for describing topic-centered instructional design, but they provide only limited view on task-centered instructional design [22]. In order to enable practitioners to represent, communicate, and share pedagogy-sound and technology-supported learning experience easily, we attempt to provide a set of pedagogy-specific learning design languages by adopting a model-driven architecture. All these pedagogy-specific learning design languages can be regarded as meta-models, which will be specified using the same meta-meta-model. A learning design represented in any pedagogy-specific learning design language can be transformed into a unit of learning (UoL) represented in IMS-LD. As a consequence, all high-level learning designs represented in a pedagogy-specific learning design language can be transformed and then executed in an IMS-LD compatible run-time environment. As the first step towards this goal, we developed a PBL design language and an associated PBL authoring tool by adopting a domain-specific language (DSL) approach. In order to investigate whether the PBL design language and the PBL authoring tool can facilitate the target user in designing a PBL course plan, we conducted a case study as a formative assessment. Our assumption is that after a short training session the teacher without comprehensive PBL knowledge and technical knowledge can create a PBL design by using the PBL design language and the PBL authoring tool. The remainder of the paper is organized in the following sections. Firstly it introduces the PBL design language and the PBL authoring tool. Then a case study is presented. Finally, the paper presents conclusive remarks and provides suggestions for future work.

2 A PBL Design Language

Dr. Howard Barrows, one of the developers of PBL, has defined PBL as a learning method based on the principle of using problems as a starting point for the acquisition and integration of new knowledge. According to [2], students think PBL is a more interesting, stimulating, and enjoyable learning method. It offers a more flexible and nurturing way to learn. The faculty also considers PBL a more nurturing and enjoyable curriculum. In comparison with traditional lecture-based learning, PBL is better with respect to creative thinking, self-directed learning, data gathering, problem-solving, evaluation techniques, and teamwork [3, 16]. However, PBL is not one commonly agreed upon concept, but rather encompasses a number of different interpretations and practices [18, 29]. Based on theoretical work, many PBL process models have been proposed such as Barrows model [3], the McMaster PBL model [32], the Maastricht model [30], and the Aalborg model [13]. Furthermore, each PBL process model can have different implementations. Many factors are influence on choosing a PBL process model and on arranging implementation details such as learning objectives, class and group size, students' characteristics (e.g., motivation, PBL skills, and prior knowledge), and exploited technologies. So far PBL researchers and practitioners usually describe a PBL strategy in natural language. There is no dedicated representation format to describe various PBL strategies.

As mentioned before, the term learning design refers to both the process to structure teaching-learning activities and the result of this process -- a description of a coordinated set of teaching-learning activities. The central concept of a learning design is activity. Our research work is based on activity theory [31] that provides "a philosophical framework for studying different forms of human praxis as developmental processes, both individual and social levels interlinked at the same time" [21]. Based on activity theory, we developed a meta-meta-model that provides basic building blocks for specifying a set of pedagogy-specific learning design languages as meta-models. In this paper we focus on describing the PBL design language – a domain-specific language (DSL). Domain-specific language (DSL) is usually a relatively small, declarative language that just expresses the logic of a computation without describing its control flow. Furthermore, a DSL offers expressive power through appropriate notations and abstractions focused on and usually restricted to a particular problem domain [10]. As van Deursen et. al [10] summarized, DSLs allow solutions to be expressed at the level of abstraction of the problem domain. As a consequence, domain experts themselves can understand, validate and often modify DSL models. The DSL models are concise and self-documenting to a large extent. They enhance productivity, reliability and maintainability.

When applying DSL paradigm in the domain of PBL, we developed the PBL design language by specifying the concepts of PBL that teachers usually use to describe a PBL approach. Using the PBL design language, a PBL design can be represented as a set of phases which can be executed in sequence (as the default structure), in parallel, in branch or in loop. When designing a phase, a teacher should choose one or more phase types from a list: *preparation, problem engagement, problem definition, idea generation, learning issue identification, plan, information sharing, investigation, reasoning, problem resolution, evaluation, application, reflection*, and *report.* In addition, associated phase types such as *facilitation, collaboration, basic cognition,* and *assessment* will be automatically associated with any phase. In a given phase, only certain types of activities are suggested to be completed and a type of activity may produce a certain type of artifact. For examples, in the phase *problem engagement* the following five types of activities are suggested: *describe case/situation, present scenario/phenomenon, introduce problem trigger, view,* and *clarify concept.* The artifact types of this phase are *case, scenario, situation, phenomenon,* and *observation.* A phase with a type of *learning issue identification* can contain the following activity types: *identify learning issue, formulate learning issue, organize learning issue,* and *identify knowledge need.* The artifact types of this phase type are *learning issue* and *learning need.* After the teacher defines a phase through choosing one or multiple phase types, the user can further specify the activity structure within the phase in details.

Each phase consists of one or several activities that may be performed in sequence (as the default structure as well), in parallel, in branch, or in loop. Various process structures can be specified using arrows. When designing an activity, one can only choose an activity type from the types specified by the chosen phase types. In addition, the constraints between the type of artifact and the type of activity are specified as well. For example, in a phase with a type of *learning issue identification*, one can arrange an activity by choosing an activity type *formulate learning issue* and define an artifact with a type of *learning issue* as an output. It also enables a detail design of an activity by defining the relations with actors, learning resources, and tools. For example, the teacher can assign the actor of activity with a type of *formulate learning issue* as *a learner, a facilitator, a group of learners, all groups in a class,* or *all learners in a class.* It is allowed to further define a learning setting for an activity with appropriate learning resources and tools.

3 PLATE Workbench: An PBL Authoring Tool

In order to facilitate PBL practitioners to design their own PBL strategies, we develop a web-based graphical PBL authoring tool, called PLATE Workbench. Rather than using pedagogy-irrelevant constructs provided by IMS-LD authoring tools such as Re-Course [14] and Prolix OpenGLM [27], the teacher can use the vocabularies and rules specified by the PBL design language. Fig. 1 and Fig. 2 show two screenshots of the tool to edit a PBL design at a high-level and a low-level, respectively. The user interface of the tool consists of five parts. The menu bar on the top lists basic function and the state bar on the bottom indicates the current edit state. The central area contains the file manager (on the left), the graphic edit space (in the middle), and the property edit panel (on the right).

As illustrated in Fig. 1, a PBL design is defined as a set of phases at a high-level. The meta-information about this PBL design can be specified and viewed in the property edit panel. This example PBL design was created by a student in the case study. The participants and their organization were specified as well. The tool enables to edit a PBL design by manipulating diagrams with nodes and links. A phase is created through dragging a phase node and dropping it in the graphic edit space. A dialog window will pop up and the user can choose one or more phase types for specifying this phase. For example, the user can choose a phase type "*problem engagement*". The user can design a title for a phase, but this user simply used the phase type as its title. The user can also type information as the values of attributes of the phase in the property edit panel. The user can define process structure by creating links between phases and specify the start and termination conditions.

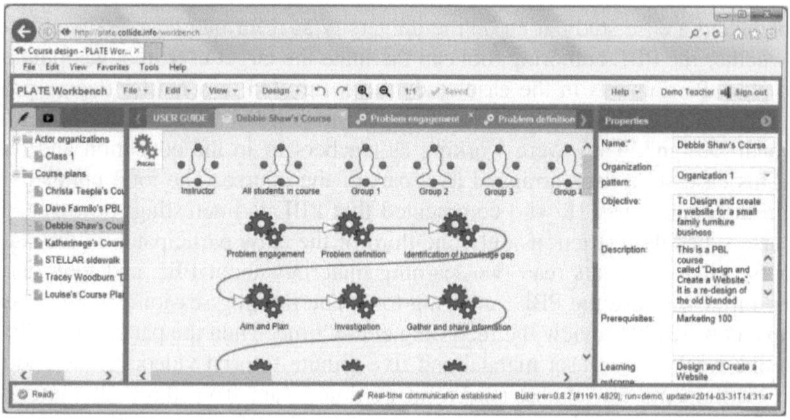

Fig. 1. A high-level PBL design and the associated user interface of the tool

The teacher can define the internal activity structure of a phase by clicking the corresponding phase node (the first phase node *problem engagement* in this case) in the high-level diagram. The tool will enable the teacher to define activities by dragging and dropping an activity node in a similar way to create a phase node as shown in Fig. 2. The type of the activity can be defined by choosing one from a list of activity types (shown in the combo-box) that are specified in the selected phase types (the type of problem engagement in this case) and the associated phase types (facilitation, collaboration, and assessment). The activity can be further defined by assigning values of attributes and by connecting with actor nodes, resource nodes, tool nodes, and artifact nodes. The specified relations between concepts (e.g., which type of activity can produce which type of artifact using which kind of tool) within the PBL design language will be used as constraints to guide and restrict the construction of the diagram.

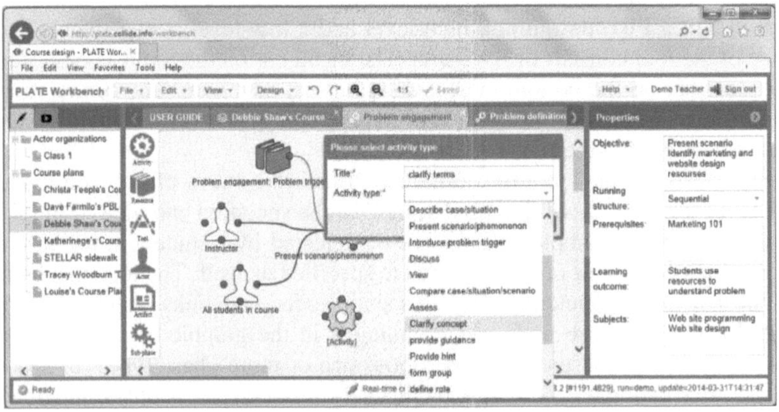

Fig. 2. A part of low-level PBL design and the associated user interface of the tool

4 Method

We conducted a case study at an online university as a formative assessment to determine whether the PBL authoring tool can facilitate the target user in developing a PBL course plan. Participants in the case study were enrolled in a master degree program completing an advanced instructional design course titled "Trends and Issues in Instructional Design". They were working as teachers or in the education and training field. This case study was arranged as a part of the course. The total number of students in the course was 18 who commented that PBL is interesting; however, due to the course schedule restrictions only one-third of the class participated in the study. In the course all participants read two learning materials about PBL and took one hour training on how to use the PBL authoring tool. The training session was recorded and participants were able review the recording at any time. Then the participants did practice in one week with a user manual and five-minute tutorial video. At the end of the course, participants can choose one form of final exam from three alternate assignments. One option is to design and create a blended PBL course called "Design and Create a Website" with the PBL authoring tool. Six participants chose this assignment.

Among them five participants completely and successfully created their own PBL designs using the tool in the exam. After the exam all participants responded to a questionnaire. The questionnaire includes questions on the aspects of background information, the PBL scripting language, the PBL authoring tool, and the general PBL design approach.

5 Results and Discussion

The data show that the case study participants had minimal knowledge of PBL. They had computer experience in terms of using generic computer software such as WinWord and PowerPoint. They also had experience using generic communication tools such as chat rooms, forums, etc. Some had experience using education-specific tools such as digitalized whiteboards or online questionnaire authoring and responding tools. Others had less and even no such experience. However, almost all participants had more or less experience in using learning management systems (LMSs) such as Moodle or Blackboard. The participants reported that they were not skilled at process modelling with UML or computer programming.

When answering the questions about the PBL design language, most participants reported that the two-layer structure of the PBL design is easy to understand and use; the vocabulary used to define the phase or activity in the course plan is understandable and the activity structure that includes actors, resources, output artefacts and their relations is easy to understand; and it is easy to find an appropriate term or vocabulary to represent their design ideas. Some participants provided the following comments:

"*I liked how there were many choices of phases from the drop down menu. This allows for flexibility and customization of the PBL scenario. Linking the phases also allows for different learning outcomes from the PBL format.*"

"*I believe the tool has huge potential for designers to develop a PBL course. It provides a template that even a novice PBL instructor like me can use effectively to produce quality instructional material.*"

However, one participant had opposite thought: "*My greatest difficulty was translating my pen and paper version to the online work area. ... I had a hard time figuring out the difference between phases and activities. I was not sure how to construct a phase. I tried to include some activities within phases, but I was not sure how much detail to get into. ... I found the phase definition vocabulary very straight forward but the activity definition was not as intuitive.*"

Almost all answers to the questions about the tool are positive. They reported that it is easy to create a phase, an activity, and an artefact by dragging and dropping and to specify their relations by creating a link between two nodes intuitively. It is also easy to learn. The comments from participants include the following.

"Overall I found the functions of the tool easy to use with the drop and drag features, drop down selections and linking of actors to activities and artefacts."

"The PLATE workbench is an excellent tool to create a PBL environment that encourages learner's self-direction and collaborative learning through the use of instructor created and customized PBL learning plans."

"Navigating within the PBL authoring tool was easy."

"The visual representation of the PBL that the PLATE workbench creates really helps the instructor figure out all the steps required for the students to work through the presented problem. The breakdown of all the steps necessary to work through PBL is clearly outlined through the use of the PLATE workbench."

Only one participant commented negatively: "*I did not fully understand why I needed to define Work Mode* and *Complete Condition.*"

Participants were asked to provide suggestions to improve the tool. The suggestions are listed below.

"It would be very beneficial to add a copy and paste function that can allow an instructor to copy a whole phase (including actors, activities, tools, resources, and artifacts) into another phase."

"Improve interface of the three areas to integrate functions of these areas better. One solution is to have the window enlarge when you are typing information so that you can see the whole screen in one view." "More examples would be excellent for novices."

Participants were asked to describe their evaluations of the general approach. The comments were collected and listed below.

"Because the tool is built based on the PBL model and uses the PBL terminology, it is useful in supporting the PBL practice, and provides support for users less familiar with the PBL. However, given that the tool comes with a particular structure, it may not be flexible enough for more experienced PBL users."

"... The tool is also rigid and restrictive and doesn't give much flexibility in the hands of the teacher. However if the aim is to have a novice like myself create a PBL course easily, it does accomplish that goal."

"The PLATE workbench was fairly flexible in allowing the author to create the learning plan. The ability to move the elements around within the phase was very beneficial and incorporating the grid to line up the elements was helpful."

"The potential is definitely there. I think anything that can help a teacher improve learning for students is a step in the right direction."

In summary, the feedback on the tool and the underlying language are quite positive and encouraging. Although one participant did not complete the assignment and had negative feedback, five participants created their own PBL designs. The quality of the created PBL designs was acceptable for the participants who had minimal knowledge of PBL. The participant who did not finish the assignment had less PBL knowledge and less experience in using LMS, and asked for more training. Through analysis, we can have a preliminary conclude that it is not difficult for the target users to develop a PBL design using the tool if they have certain experience in using LMSs and education-specific tools or get enough training. In addition, it seems that participants had opposite opinions about whether the tool is flexible or rigid. Our interpretation is that the guidance and restrictions provided by the PBL design language are useful for the novice. As the user becomes skilled at designing PBL, she or he may need more flexibility and freedom.

6 Conclusions and Future Work

Feedback received from the case study participants indicated that most agreed that the PBL authoring tool is easy to use the function to define groups, create or delete a phase, an activity, an actor, and an artefact, and specify their relations. Participants also reported that it is easy to specify a PBL design using the vocabularies and rules. These results are encouraging since the participants in the case study had minimal knowledge of PBL and this was the first time they were using the PBL authoring tool.

Based on the feedback from the participants, it is important to train potential users on the theory of PBL so that they know what PBL is and what are informed decisions and possible choices. Also, it is important to provide training on how to use the PBL authoring tool and to provide support to users as they develop the PBL course plans. The feedback from participants in this case study indicates that the PBL authoring tool will be useful for teachers and trainers to develop PBL course plans.

As mentioned before, this case study was conducted as a formative assessment. According to the feedback, we have improved the PBL design language and the tool. Since this study involved a small number of participants, we plan to conduct large-scale evaluations to investigate the expressiveness of the PBL scripting language and to which extent the language and the associated tool can facilitate the representation and communication of PBL designs. We are also developing transformation module to map a PBL design into a unit of learning represented in IMS-LD. Then we will apply this approach in other pedagogies and developing an integrated, pedagogy-driven, new generation of learning design environment.

Acknowledgement. This paper was made possible by NPRP grant # NPRP 5 - 051 - 1 – 015 from the Qatar National Research Fund (a member of Qatar Foundation). The statements made herein are solely the responsibility of the authors. Many thanks to Disi Wang, Zeyad Ali, and John Impagliazzo for their valuable contributions to the implementation of the PBL authoring tool and the conduct of the case study.

References

1. Agostinho, S., Harper, B., Oliver, R., Hedberg, J., Wills, S.: A visual learning design representation to facilitate dissemination and reuse of innovative pedagogical strategies in university teaching. In: Botturi, L., Stubbs, T. (eds.) Handbook of Visual Languages for Instructional Design: Theories and Practices. Information Science Reference (2008)
2. Albanese, M.A., Mitchell, S.: Problem-based learning: A review of literature on its outcomes and implementation issues. Academic Medicine 68, 52–81 (1993)
3. Barrows, H.: The Tutorial Process. Springfield Illinois: Southern Illinois University School of Medicin (1989)
4. Beetham, H., Sharpe, R. (eds.): Rethinking pedagogy for a digital age. Routledge Falmer, London (2007)
5. Bennett, S., Agostinho, S., Lockyer, L., Harper, B., Lukasiak, J.: Supporting university teachers create pedagogically sound learning environments using learning designs and learning objects. International Journal on WWW/Internet 4(1), 16–26 (2006)

6. Bloom, B.S. (ed.): Taxonomy of Educational Objectives, the classification of educational goals – Handbook I: Cognitive Domain. McKay, New York (1956)
7. Conole, G., Oliver, M., Falconer, I., Littlejohn, A., Harvey, J.: Designing for learning. In: Conole, G., Oliver, M. (eds.) Contemporary Perspectives in e-Learning Research: Themes, Methods and Impact on Practice. Routledge Falmer (2007)
8. Conole, G., Brasher, A., Cross, S., Weller, M., Clark, P., White, J.: Visualising learning design to foster and support good practice and creativity. Educational Media International 54(3), 177–194 (2008)
9. Dalziel, J.: Implementing learning design: The Learning Activity Management system (LAMS). In: Proc. Ascilite Conference, pp. 593–596. Ascilite, Figtree (2003)
10. van Deursen, A., Klint, P., Visser, J.: Domain-specific languages: an annotatedbibliography. SIGPLAN Notices 35(6), 26–36 (2000)
11. Falconer, I., Littlejohn, A.: Representing Models of Practice. In: Lockyer, L., Bennet, S., Agostinho, S., Harper, B. (eds.) Handbook of Research on Learning Design and Learning Objects: Issues, Applications and Technologies, pp. 20–40. IDEA group (2008)
12. Gagné, R.: The Conditions of Learning and the Theory of Instruction, 4th edn. Holt, Rinehart, and Winston, New York (1985)
13. de Graaff, E., Kolmos, A.: History of problem-based and project-based learning. In: de Graaff, E., Kolmos, A. (eds.) Management of Change: Implementation of Problem-Based and Project-Based Learning in Engineering, pp. 1–8. Sense Publishers, Rotterdam (2007)
14. Griffithsa, D., Beauvoira, P., Libera, O., Barrett-Baxendaleb, M.: From Reload to ReCourse: learning from IMS Learning Design implementations. Distance Education 30(2), 201–222 (2009)
15. Harrer, A., Hoppe, U.: Visual Modelling of Collaborative Learning Processes – Uses, Desired Properties, and Approaches. In: Botturi, L., Stubbs, S.T. (eds.) Handbook of Visual Languages for Instructional Design: Theory and Practices, pp. 281–298. Information Science Reference, Hershey (2008)
16. Hmelo-Silver, C.E., Eberbach, C.: Learning theories and problem-based learning. In: Bridges, S., et al. (eds.) Researching Problem-Based Learning in Clinical Education: The Next Generation, pp. 3–17. Springer, New York (2012)
17. IMS Learning Design Specification (2003), `http://www.imsglobal.org`
18. Kolmos, A., Graaff, E.D.: Characteristics of problem-based learning. International Journal of Engineering Education 19(5), 657–662 (2003)
19. Koper, E.J.R.: Modeling Units of Study from a Pedagogical Perspective: The Pedagogical Meta-Model Behind EML. Open University of the Netherlands (2001)
20. Koper, R., Tattersall, C. (eds.): Learning design: A handbook on modelling and delivering networked education and training. Springer, Berlin (2005)
21. Kuutti, K.: Activity theory as a potential framework for human-computer interaction research. In: Nardi, B.A. (ed.) Context and Consciousness: Activity Theory and Human-Computer Interaction. MIT Press, Cambridge (1996)
22. Laanpere, M., Pata, K., Normak, P., Põldoja, H.: Pedagogy-driven Design of Digital Learning Ecosystems. Computer Science and Information Systems 11(1), 419–442 (2012)
23. Lockyer, L., Bennett, S., Agostinho, S., Harper, B.: Handbook of Research on Learning Design and Learning Objects: Issues, Applications and Technologies. Information Science Reference, Hershey (2008)
24. Martel, C., Vignollet, L., Ferraris, C., David, J., Lejeune, A.: Modelling collaborative learning activities in e-learning platforms. In: Proc. of ICALT 2006, pp. 707–709. IEEE Computer Society, Los Alamitos (2006)

25. Miao, Y., Hoeksema, K., Hoppe, U., Harrer, A.: CSCL Scripts: Modeling Features and Potential Use. In: Proceedings of CSCL 2005, Taipei, Taiwan, pp. 423–432 (2005)
26. Miao, Y., Koper, R.: An Efficient and Flexible Technical Approach to Develop and Deliver Online Peer Assessment. In: Proceedings of the 7th Computer Supported Collaborative Learning Conference, New Jersey, USA, July 16-21, pp. 502–511 (2007)
27. Neumann, S., Oberhuemer, P.: User Evaluation of a Graphical Modeling Tool for IMS Learning Design. In: Spaniol, M., Li, Q., Klamma, R., Lau, R.W.H. (eds.) ICWL 2009. LNCS, vol. 5686, pp. 287–296. Springer, Heidelberg (2009)
28. Oliver, R., Littlejohn, A.: Discovering and describing accessible and reusable practitioner-focused learning. In: Minshull, G., Mole, J. (eds.) Proceedings of Theme 1 of the JISC Online Conference: Innovating e-Learning, pp. 30–33 (2006)
29. Ryberg, T., Glud, L.N., Buus, L., Georgsen, M.: Identifying differences in understandings of PBL, theory and Interactional interdependencies. In: Proc. 7th International Conference on Networked Learning, pp. 943–951 (2010)
30. Wilkerson, L., Gijselaers, W.H. (eds.): Bringing Problem-Based Learning to Higher Education: Theory and Practice. New Directions for Teaching and Learning, vol. 68. Jossey-Bass Publishers, San Francisco (1996)
31. Vygotsky, L.S.: Mind in society: The development of higher psychological processes. Harvard University Press, Cambridge (1978)
32. Woods, D.R.: Problem Based Learning: How to Get the Most from PBL, 3rd edn., vol. 20(6), pp. 481–486. McMaster University (1996)

The Load-Based Learner Profile for Incidental Word Learning Task Generation

Di Zou[1], Haoran Xie[2], Qing Li[2,3], Fu Lee Wang[4], and Wei Chen[5,6,*]

[1] Department of English, City University of Hong Kong, Hong Kong SAR
[2] Department of Computer Science, City University of Hong Kong, Hong Kong SAR
[3] Multimedia Software Engineering Research Centre, City University of Hong Kong, Hong Kong SAR
[4] Caritas Institute of Higher Education, Hong Kong, Hong Kong SAR
[5] Agricultural Information Institute, Chinese Academy of Agricultural Sciences, China
[6] Key Laboratory of Agri-information Service Technology, Ministry of Agriculture, China

{dizoudaisy,hrxie2}@gmail.com, itqli@cityu.edu.hk,
pwang@cihe.edu.hk, chenwei@caas.cn

Abstract. In recent years, the popularity and prosperity of mobile technologies and e-learning applications offer brand-new learning ways for people. English, as the most widely used language and the essential communication skill for people in the 'earth village' nowadays, has been widely learned by speakers of other languages. The importance of word knowledge in learning a second language is broadly acknowledged in the second language research literature. However, comparing with incidental word learning, the intentional learning method has the shortages of motivating reduction, simple acquisition and contextual deficiency. To address these problems, in this paper, we therefore proposed an incidental word learning model for e-learning. In particular, we measure the load of various incidental word learning tasks from the perspective of involvement load hypothesis so as to construct load-based learner profiles. To increase the effectiveness of various word learning activities and motivate learners better, a task generation method is developed based on the load-based learner profile. Moreover, we conduct experiments on real participants, and empirical results of which have further verified the effectiveness of the task generation method and the enjoyment of word learning.

Keywords: learner profile, involvement load, incidental word learning.

1 Introduction

Brand-new learning ways for people continue to proliferate in recent years with the popularity and prosperity of mobile technologies and e-learning applications. E-learning systems through mobile devices enable learners to gain new knowledge and learn skills without being constrained neither spatially nor temporally. The

* Corresponding author.

E. Popescu et al. (Eds.): ICWL 2014, LNCS 8613, pp. 190–200, 2014.

significance of English as a lingua franca and an essential communication skill for people in the 'earth village' has been widely acknowledged. The essentiality of word knowledge in second language acquisition has been noted by many studies in this field [17,15,14].

Rather than acquiring words while intending to do so, which is a typical feature of intentional word learning, incidental word learning refers to learners acquiring new words from contexts without deliberately attempting to do so, such as picking up new words during free reading [1]. For example, when a language learner encounters an unknown word while watching a movie, he/she will infer its meaning according to the context. Specifically, comparing with incidental word learning, the intentional learning approach has the following weaknesses:

- **Motivating Reduction.** Different from natural learning process, intentional word learning explicitly forces learners to concentrate on certain aspects of word knowledge. This not only makes the whole learning process more boring and tiring, but also reduces learner motivation.
- **Simple Acquisition.** As incidental word learning does not focus only specifically on the learning of various aspects of word knowledge, it plays also a facilitative role in promoting the development of learners other language skills like listening, speaking, reading and writing. However, intentional word learning concentrates solely on the learning of word knowledge, thus it has quite limited help for the improvement of learners other language skills.
- **Contextual Deficiency.** Rather than having rich contexts of target words, which is one main merit of incidental word learning, intentional word learning provides learners with very restricted contexts of target words. Sometimes learners are even asked to learn words without contexts. Therefore, learners may only grasp a single aspect of word knowledge through intentional word learning.

To address the above problems, an incidental word learning model for e-learning, which has more natural learning environment, richer contexts, better facilitativeness on the development of other language skills, is indispensable and primary. However, existing e-learning systems for vocabulary acquisition mainly follow the intentional word learning method [3,4]. Thus, in this paper, we propose the personalized incidental word learning model for e-learning systems. There are mainly three research questions to be discussed and addressed:

- How to measure the loads of various incidental word learning tasks?
- How to construct a load-based learner profiles if we can measure the loads of various word learning tasks?
- How to generate (or recommend) a new incidental learning task to facilitate word learning and motivate learners based on the obtained load-based learner profiles?

The remaining parts of this paper are organized as follows. In Section 2, related work in areas of vocabulary acquisition and e-learning systems are reviewed. In Section 3, we present a load-based learner profile in light of the involvement load hypothesis (ILH) [10]. We further propose the task generation approach based on the constructed learner profile in Section 4. In Section 5, the experimental settings, processes and results are introduced and discussed. Finally, in Section 6, we summarize this work and outline the potential research plans.

2 Related Works

In this section, we review some related works in areas of vocabulary acquisition and the relevant e-learning systems.

Vocabulary Acquisition. Generally, research on vocabulary acquisition can be categorized into two classes. One of which focuses on the word knowledge. In this field, it is commonly agreed that word knowledge is a continuum of one unique system including receptive and productive knowledge [17]. To measure word knowledge, some researchers [15,14] believe that there is a distinction to be made between the dimensions of breadth and depth of word knowledge. The breadth dimension (also known as vocabulary size) is the quantity of words learners know at a particular level of language proficiency [7]. On the other hand, the depth dimension denotes the quality of words known by a learner [16]. The other class is exploring the word learning process and facilitating word learning. In [5], Fraser believes that word learning essentially is a cumulative process with incremental nature. A theory, called involvement load hypothesis (ILH) proposed by Laufer and Hulstijn [10], is used to examine and evaluate the involvement load of various tasks in incidental word learning. Some further empirical studies [9,16] verify and support the correctness of this theory, enabling us to quantify the involvement loads for learners during their learning processes.

E-learning Systems for Word Learning. The development of e-learning systems is quite rapid [11]. However, conventional systems mainly base on intentional word learning. In [13], Loucky designed a task-based distance learning system to maximize vocabulary development. To facilitate the vocabulary learning of Arab students, Hassan [6] developed a computer-aided learning software 'ArabCAVL' via a blended learning environment. Moreover, by integrating online reading materials, Computer-Assisted Language Learning was developed and established by Loucky [12]. Chen and Chung [3] presented a personalized mobile English vocabulary learning system based on the item response theory through tracking the user learning history. Moreover, the context-aware techniques were incorporated in the above system so that ubiquitous learning is supported in mobile devices [4]. In [8], Huang et al. investigated both the usefulness and ease-of-use of ubiquitous vocabulary learning system, and then found that active learners care more about the former feature while inactive ones consider more on the latter one. Başoğlu and Akdemır [2] compared the vocabulary learning of two group of undergraduate students who use two learning systems based on the mobile phones and flash cards respectively.

3 Load-Based Learner Profiling

In this section, we will discuss and address the first two research questions as mentioned in Section 1. In particular, we firstly introduce the theoretical foundation, the involvement load hypothesis (ILH), which is commonly used to estimate load of the incidental word learning; secondly, we apply the ILH to measure the various e-learning tasks of incidental word learning so that the learner profiles can be constructed.

Table 1. The dimensions, components and degrees in the ILH

	Cognitive Dimension		Motivational Dimension
	Search	Evaluation	Need
None	✓	✓	✓
Moderate	✓	✓	✓
Strong	–	✓	✓
No. of Levels	2	3	3

3.1 Involvement Load Hypothesis

As shown in Table 1, the involvement load hypothesis evaluates the effectiveness of incidental word learning tasks from the motivational and cognitive dimensions, based on which, its three components of need, search and evaluation[1] were proposed [10]. Need, which is from the motivational dimension, has three different levels (two degrees of prominence and none). It is moderate when it is externally imposed yet strong if intrinsically motivated. Search, which refers to the attempt to figure out the meaning of an unknown word or form of an unfamiliar word, has two different levels (one degree of prominence and none). Evaluation, the other cognitive component, has three levels (two degrees of prominence and none). Moderate evaluation involves comparing different meanings of one word or different words with similar meaning, yet strong evaluation involves combining other words with the target words to create original contexts. The involvement load of a certain task is the combination of the degrees of prominence of the three components. Other factors being equal, tasks with higher involvement loads are more effective than those with lower loads, and words being processed with higher involvement loads will be learnt better than those with lower loads [9]. For example, if a reading comprehension task requires learners to infer the meanings of target words from the contexts, then its involvement load consists of moderate need, search and no evaluation. Because learners are imposed by the task to learn these words, moderate need is involved. Search is present as the attempt to find meanings of words is entailed, yet evaluation is absent since neither comparisons of meanings or forms nor generation of original contexts

[1] Note that here the terminology 'search' and 'evaluation' are inequivalent with their meanings in the computer science area.

is involved. If a task asks learners to write a composition using target words, the meanings of which are provided by marginal glosses, its involvement load is moderate need, no search and strong evaluation.

Thus, we can estimate the involvement load of an incidental learning task according to the ILH. In other words, the load for each incidental word task can be mapped to involvement load in search, evaluation and need components. Moreover, the task type and target learning words are considered in the task profiling. Therefore, we formally define the **task profile** for a learning task T_i as follows.

Definition 1. *The **task profile** of the learning task t_i, which is denoted by a tuple of three elements:*

$$t_i = (f_i, L_i, W_i)$$

- *f_i is the type of incidental word learning task, which is an element of the set of all available kinds of tasks ($f_i \in F$).*
- *L_i is the involvement load of t_i, which is the tuple of load in search, evaluation and need components: $L_i = (s_i, e_i, n_i)$, where $s_i \in \{0, 1\}$, $e_i \in \{0, 1, 2\}$, $n_i \in \{0, 1, 2\}$ (0 is none, 1 is moderate and 2 is strong).*
- *W_i is a word set, which consists of all learning target words in t_i.*

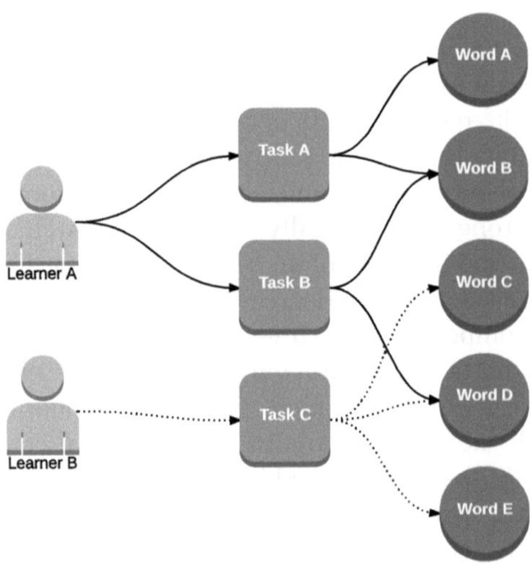

Fig. 1. The tripartite graph of learners, tasks and words

As the number of task types $|F|$ is quite limited [9], it is easy to specify the involvement load for each task type via a set of rules according to the ILH. So far, we have proposed a method to address the first research question, which is 'how to measure the loads of various incidental word learning tasks'. Then we move to discuss the second research question, which is 'how to construct load-based learner profiles'. The main purpose of constructing learner profiles is to figure out the involvement loads for target words by a particular learner. As shown in Fig. 1, the relationships among learners, tasks and words can be viewed as a tripartite graph. Since we have already obtained the involvement load for each task as given in Definition 1, the load-based learner profile can be considered as an aggregation of the loads of his/her past tasks. Consequently, we formally define the **learner profile** for a learner u_j as follows.

Definition 2. *The* ***learner profile*** *of the learner u_j, which is denoted by a tuple of three elements:*

$$u_j = (H_j, P_j, R_j)$$

- *H_j is the set of all historical learning tasks by u_j, and $H_j = \{(t, c_t))|t \in T_j\}$, where T_j is the set of all historical tasks by u_j, c_t is the time stamp of achieving task t.*
- *P_j is a set of the task types and preferences pairs, which is in the form of $P_j = \{(f, p_f))|f \in F_j\}$, where F_j is the set of task types of T_j and p_f is a relevance function on the type f. The preference measurement for task type is introduced later in Section 4.*
- *R_j is a set of the words and degrees of load pairs, $R_j = \{(w, d_{wj})|w \in W_j'\}$, where W_j' is the set of w and d_{wj} is the degree of load for word w. The degree of load d_{wj} for each word w is an aggregation of the involvement load of those learning tasks by u_j involving word w, which is calculated by:*

$$d_{wj} = \sum_{\forall d_{wj} \in W_j', t_j \in T_j} \theta(c_{t_j}, \eta(L_{t_j})) \tag{1}$$

$$\eta(L_{t_j}) = \alpha_1 \cdot s_{t_j} + \alpha_2 \cdot e_{t_j} + \alpha_3 \cdot n_{t_j} \tag{2}$$

$$\theta(c_{t_j}, \eta(L_j)) = e^{-|c-c_{t_j}|/\Delta t \cdot \eta(L_{t_j})} \tag{3}$$

where $\eta(L_{t_j})$ is to calculate the unified involvement load by adding the parameters α_1, α_2 and α_3 (they are equally set as 1/3 as default setting), s_{t_j}, e_{t_j} and n_{t_j} are the load in search, evaluation and need as given in Definition 1, $\theta(c_{t_j}, \eta(L_{t_j}))$ is to re-calculate the load through adding a time-decay damping factor according to the Ebbinghaus Forgetting Curve [18], $|c - c_{t_j}|$ is the time frame between the current time and the time when the task is finished, Δt is the time unit. The aggregating involvement load is calculated based on the load of those tasks involving the target word w and how long these tasks have been taken so far. If d_{wj} is lower than a threshold, it will be set to '0' as there is a long time since the word been learnt.

4 Learning Task Generation

In this section, we mainly tackle the last research question, which is 'how to generate (or recommend) a new incidental learning task to facilitate word learning and motivate learners based on the obtained load-based learner profiles'.

The question can be further divided into two-sub questions, which are 'how to determine the task type' and 'how to determine what target words should be included' in a task that is specifically generated for a learner. To address these two sub-questions, we mainly consider the following two criteria during the task generation process so as to address them separately:

- **Task Diversity.** The notion of task diversity can be interpreted as the total dissimilarity between the task to be generated and recent learning tasks taken by a learner. Moreover, we assume that the task types which are taken more recently and more frequently are less likely to be preferred by the learner. According to this assumption, the task preference degree p_f (as discussed in Definition 2) can be similarly measured by the sum of weighted frequency for the task type f.

$$p_f = \frac{1}{N_j} \times \left(\sum_{\forall f \in F_j, t_j \in T_j} e^{-|c - c_{t_j}|/\Delta t} \right) \tag{4}$$

where $|c - c_{t_j}|$ is the time frame between the current time c and the time moment (c_{t_j}) that the task completion, Δt is the time unit, and N is learning frequency of this task type by learner l_j. The diversity is thus calculated by:

$$div(f_*) = \sum_{\forall f \in F_j} p_f \cdot (1 - Sim(f_*, f)) \tag{5}$$

where f_* is the candidate task type to be generated, $Sim(f_*, f)$ is the similarity between any two incidental learning tasks, which is assumed to be specified by domain expert.
- **Word Coverage.** The word coverage means that the task to be generated should cover those words with less involvement loads so that unknown (or unfamiliar) target words can be reviewed in the learning tasks. To this end, the target words could be ranked by their current involvement loads, and then the words with least involvement loads will be included in the task.

$$w_* = \arg\min_{(w_j)} \{d_{wj} | d_{wj} \in W_j'\} \tag{6}$$

where d_{wj} is the degree of involvement load , and R_j is a set of the target words and degrees of load pairs for learner u_j as given in Definition 2. To achieve a high word coverage by a giving learning size N (the number of words to be learned in a task), top-N words with least involvement loads could be selected.

Therefore, the task to be generated for the learner is based on task diversity and word coverage. The detailed steps are shown in Algorithm 1. Firstly, the task type with maximal diversity by Eq (5) will be selected. Then, the words with zero involvement loads will be examined and added to set W^*. If the specified learning size N is less than (or equal to) $|W^*|$, we can directly select N words from set W^* since all words are with zero-involvement load. Conversely, if the learning size is greater than $|W^*|$, we can select all words from $|W^*|$ and then pick the remaining top-m words ($m = N - |W^*|$) with minimal involvement loads from $W'_j - W^*$, and form the set of target words for the task to be generated to the learner.

```
Data: Learner profile u_j; Learning size N; Target word corpus W;
Result: Task t_g (specifying task type f_g and target word set W_g).
for each f_x ∈ F do
 | Find div(f_*) with maximal diversity by Eq (5);
end
f_g ← f_*;
W* ← W − W'_j;
for each w ∈ W'_j do
 | if d_wj ≤ ε then
 |  | W* ← W* ∪ w;
 | end
end
if N ≤ |W*| then
 | Randomly select a subset W*_N with N words from W*;
 | W_g ← W*_N;
end
else
 | m ← N − |W*|;
 | Select a subset W*_m with top-m words by Eq (6) from W'_j − W*;
 | W_g ← W* ∪ W*_m;
end
```

Algorithm 1. The learning task generation (LTG) algorithm

5 Experiments

In this section, we conduct the experiment on the real participants to verify the effectiveness of the proposed model. Rather than simply making use of the metric of *word retention rate*, we also compare the metrics *learning completion rate* and *learning enjoyment score* via learning logs and questionnaires.

- **Word Retention Rate (WRR)**: The ratio of words remembered in the test by the subjects, which are examined in both pre-test and post-test.
- **Learning Completion Rate (LCR)**: The ratio of learners who have achieved 50% of the learning tasks, which can be identified from the learner profiles.
- **Learning Enjoyment Score (LES)**: The score of scale 1 (Very Boring) to 5 (Very Interesting) given by learners to score the degree of enjoyment of different approaches in the questionnaires.

As shown in Table 2, we conduct the experiment on three independent groups, which contain 20, 23 and 22 students who are fresh undergraduates from universities in L2 countries. Through the pilot studies, we have selected 40 target

Table 2. The learner groups for comparison

	#Learners	WRR (pre-test)	Approaches for word learning
Group 1	20	56.50%	Intentional word learning
Group 2	23	56.74%	Incidental word learning
Group 3	22	54.55%	Personalized incidental word learning

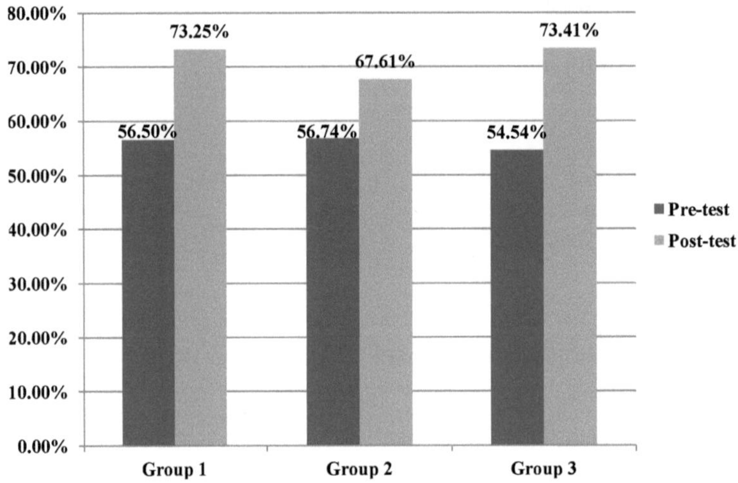

Fig. 2. WRR of pre-test and post-test by three groups

words for the experiment. We use 20 words for the pre-test and the differences of the WRR among groups are quite low of the WRR in pre-tests. Then, we pick the remaining 20 target words for learning purposes and evaluated the learning of them in the post-tests. For Group 1, we have employed the intentional word learning method, which repeats a single task 7 times at different time intervals (mainly follow the forgetting curve). The only difference between Group 2 and 3 is whether learner profiles have been made use of or not. For Group 2, we randomly generate a sequence of 7 tasks with different types (may contain duplication) and each task with 10 learning target words, while the load-based learner profiles and LTG algorithm are adopted in Group 3.

The results of post-tests are shown in Fig. 2. There is no significant difference of WRR performance between Group 1 and Group 3 (73.25% v.s. 73.41%, $p > 0.1$)[2]. However, their improvements on WRR between pre-test and post-test have the significant differences (16.75% v.s. 18.87%, $p < 0.05$), indicating that Group 3 has the greatest improvements on the metric WRR. Also, we can observe that Group 2 has the worst performance (67.61%) without personalization. Furthermore, the performance on metrics LCR and LES can be found in Fig. 3, which plots all three metrics by three groups. Specifically, Group 1 achieves the worst in both LCR (65%) and LES (2.7 out of 5 (54%)), which can be

[2] The p value is calculated through Student t-Test analysis.

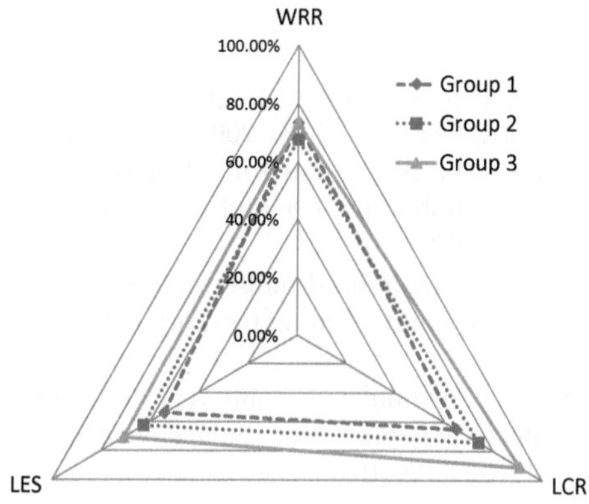

Fig. 3. Overall WRR, LCR and LES by three groups

interpreted as that intentional word learning is quite boring and some learners are reluctant to finish all tasks during the learning process. Meanwhile, Group 3, which outperforms both Group 1 and 2, achieves 90.91% on LCR and 3.55 out of 5 (71%) on LES. We find that the task diversity and word coverage can increase the system enjoyment and improve the word retention performance of the learners.

6 Conclusion

In this paper, we present a model of incidental word learning to overcome the problems in the existing e-learning systems which are based on intentional word learning. Moreover, we introduce the learner profile construction according to the theory of the ILH. Furthermore, the task generation approach is proposed by considering the task diversity and word coverage. Through the experiments on real learners, the effectiveness of our proposed method has been verified. In future research, we plan to conduct the experiment on a larger scale and figure out how to automatically identify the similarity between different task types.

Acknowledgement. The research presented in this paper has been supported by National Natural Science Foundation of China (Project no. 61003263), Key Projects of National Key Technology R&D Program during the Twelfth Five-Year Plan Period (No. 2012BAH20B04), Key Projects of National Key Technology R&D Program during the Twelfth Five-Year Plan Period (No. 2012BAH20B04), and the "948" project of Ministry of Agriculture of China (No. 2013-S2), and Agricultural Science and Technology Achievements Transformation Funds of Ministry of Science and Technology of China (No. 2013GB23260570).

References

1. Barcroft, J.: Second language vocabulary acquisition: A lexical input processing approach. Foreign Language Annals 37(2), 200–208 (2004)
2. Başoğlu, E.B., Akdemır, Ö.: A comparison of undergraduate students'english vocabulary learning: Using mobile phones and flash cards. Turkish Online Journal of Educational Technology 9(3) (2010)
3. Chen, C.-M., Chung, C.-J.: Personalized mobile english vocabulary learning system based on item response theory and learning memory cycle. Computers & Education 51(2), 624–645 (2008)
4. Chen, C.-M., Li, Y.-L.: Personalised context-aware ubiquitous learning system for supporting effective english vocabulary learning. Interactive Learning Environments 18(4), 341–364 (2010)
5. Fraser, C.A.: Lexical processing strategy use and vocabulary learning through reading. Studies in Second Language Acquisition 21(2), 225–241 (1999)
6. Hassan, R.E.H.: Software application for computer aided vocabulary learning in a blended learning environment. Master's thesis, American University in Cairo, Cairo, Egypt (2006)
7. Horwitz, E.K.: The beliefs about language learning of beginning university foreign language students. The Modern Language Journal 72(3), 283–294 (1988)
8. Huang, Y.-M., Huang, Y.-M., Huang, S.-H., Lin, Y.-T.: A ubiquitous english vocabulary learning system. Computers & Education 58(1), 273–282 (2012)
9. Hulstijn, J.H., Laufer, B.: Some empirical evidence for the involvement load hypothesis in vocabulary acquisition. Language Learning 51(3), 539–558 (2001)
10. Laufer, B., Hulstijn, J.H.: Incidental vocabulary acquisition in a second language: The construct of task-induced involvement. Applied Linguistics 22(1), 1–26 (2001)
11. Li, Q., Lau, R.W.H., Wah, B., Ashman, H., Leung, E.W.C., Li, F., Lee, V.: Emerging internet technologies for e-learning. IEEE Internet Computing 13(4), 11–17 (2009)
12. Loucky, J.P.: Constructing a roadmap to more systematic and successful online reading and vocabulary acquisition. Literary & Linguistic Computing 25(2), 225–241 (2010)
13. Loucky, J.P.: Designing distance learning tasks to help maximize vocabulary development. International Journal of Virtual & Personal Learning Environments 3(2), 35–58 (2012)
14. Nassaji, H.: The relationship between depth of vocabulary knowledge and L2 learners' lexical inferencing strategy use and success. Canadian Modern Language Review/La Revue Canadienne des Langues Vivantes 61(1), 107–135 (2004)
15. Read, J., Chapelle, C.A.: A framework for second language vocabulary assessment. Language Testing 18(1), 1–32 (2001)
16. Schmitt, N.: Review article: Instructed second language vocabulary learning. Language Teaching Research 12(3), 329–363 (2008)
17. Webb, S.: Receptive and productive vocabulary learning. Studies in Second Language Acquisition 27(1), 33–52 (2005)
18. Wixted, J.T., Ebbesen, E.B.: Genuine power curves in forgetting: A quantitative analysis of individual subject forgetting functions. Memory & Cognition 25(5), 731–739 (1997)

Multilingual E-learning System for Information Security Education with Users' Consciousness

Yutaka Kigawa[1], Kiyoshi Nagata[2], and Tomoko Aoki[3]

[1] Faculty of International Communication,
Musashino Gakuin University, Saitama, Japan
y.kigawa@musa.ac.jp
[2] Faculty of Business Management,
Daito Bunka University, Tokyo, Japan
nagata@ic.daito.ac.jp
[3] Faculty of Law,
Heisei International University, Saitama, Japan
aoki@hiu.ac.jp

Abstract. In an advance information society, the information security related issues are very important subject to be handled in any types of companies or organizations. Some companies introduce a technology based security system in order to solve these problems, however most of information related problems many organization have been facing are caused by humans. There are many risks of becoming perpetrators as well as victims. Therefore the education on information security is very important not only for business person but also for ordinary people live in the highly information oriented society. Some Universities or Colleges have lectures on information security or ethics. However, these lectures are tend to uniform and do not address characteristics of individuals, and seemed not to be effective especially if he/she grew up in legal and social environment different from Japan. We try to construct a multilingual e-learning system for complementing such problems by reflecting individual's consciousness cultivated in their countries' environment.

Keywords: Information security, Multilingual e-learning system, Consciousness factors, Asian students.

1 Introduction

With development of the information society, companies have been exposed to various types of information related risks high percentages of which are caused by human factors. Thus the enhancement of the information security educations are essential.

The study course of information have been compulsory from 2003 in high schools in Japan, and topics on information security or ethic are taught at Universities or colleges these days. In these courses, problems caused by several types of threats are stated and feasible measures or methods are shown by quoting some practical cases.

E. Popescu et al. (Eds.): ICWL 2014, LNCS 8613, pp. 201–206, 2014.

On the other hand, Japan have accepted students from many countries, especially from Asian countries, such as China, Republic of Korea, Taiwan, etc. In 2012, percentages of students from each country are 67.9%(China), 13.1%(Republic of Korea), 3.6%(Taiwan), 3.4%(Vietnam), and so on[1]. Although Chinese students are majority, we have certain number of students from several countries whose political, cultural, legal situations are different from each other. We could not offer any particular lectures for them caring their characteristics, and usually give them uniform learning contents suitable only for Japanese students. So we consider e-learning system is effective as a subsidiary educational system.

2 Consciousness Factors

In order to construct a user's consciousness oriented e-learning system for information security education, we have started to research on several Asian countries' situation and University students' consciousness by making questionnaire since 2008. The number of respondents are 117 Japanese, 277 Koreans, 82 Filipinos, 277 Singaporean, 302 Chinese, 187 Taiwanese, and questionnaires are written in Japanese for Japanese students, in English for Filipino and Singaporean students, in Hangul for Korean students, and in Mandarin Chinese for Chinese students, [2], [3].

2.1 Questionnaire Form

The questionnaire sheet is composed of two parts, the first part is the attribute part where student's educational experiments and their legal recognition and knowledge are inquired. The second part is for consciousness factor extraction with 20 questions about information security related issues. The answers should be given in Ricardo scale from 0 to 5, and extract factors by factor analysis using an numerical analysis application software, SPSS.

2.2 Result of Attribute Data Analysis

Figure 1 describes the average value of answers in each attribute item, from which we can see critical differences in countries. The first item is on students' educational experiment and if the answer is "Yes" it is transformed to the value 0 and if the answer is "No" it is transformed to the value 1. In the second item row, the values represent the approximated age they have got such classes, the values 1, 2, 3, and 4 are corresponding to primary school, junior high school, high school, and University respectively.

We asked students' knowledge or recognition on their own countries' legal conditions for four subjects such as "Copyright", "Intellectual Property Right", "Personal Information", and "Unlawful Access". If they know or consider that a kind of law exits the answer must be 0, else if there are no such law the answer is 1, and 2 for otherwise.

[1] `http://www.jasso.go.jp/statistics/index_e.html`, available 01/04/2014

The second row from the last is on the tolerance degree for pirate edition selling, where the higher value the higher tolerance degree, that is the value 2 represents one thinks that pirate edition should be controlled but not so severely and 3 represents that only the malicious or large-scale marketing should be controlled.

The last item is related to the network anonymities, asking students whether they believes anonymity of their data exchanges through digital network communications. If he/she believes the anonymity "Yes" is marked and transformed the value 0, if "Not at all", the value is 4, and 1, 2, 3 are corresponding intermediate values.

All the differences of figures are statistically verified by t-test and investigated considering educational, social, and even political conditions of each county's students. We also asked what subjects are important or necessary to be taught in their college ages. Especially in China, percentage of students who are interested in or care about their personal information is relatively high. We could guess reasons for their sensitivity by referring the report paper [5], where authors have cited several reasons for caring about personal informations, such as "Peaceful life is disturbed", "Feel the mental stress", "Threats to life and property", and so on. They also pointed out some problems on the state of personal information related laws and regulations in China.

		Countries						
		CH	J	K	PH	SG	TW	Total
Educational Situation on Information Security	Yes/No	1.64	1.46	1.71	1.82	1.69	1.43	1.62
	When?	3.21	1.52	3.03	2.88	4.57	2.76	3.15
Necessity of Education	Yes/No	1.10	1.49	1.09	1.11	1.32	1.42	1.22
Necessity Subjects								
	Copyright	.69	.73	.61	.70	.81	.73	.71
	Personal Information	.81	.51	.53	.55	.74	.57	.66
	Lawless Access	.58	.54	.22	.09	.76	.58	.52
	Computer Virus	.66	.67	.40	.20	.82	.52	.60
	Netiqeutte	.55	.55	.60	.63	.53	.51	.55
	Rule about e-mail	.47	.35	.10	.12	.48	.32	.35
	Harmful Site	.58	.56	.22	.20	.64	.39	.47
Legal Situation:								
	Copyright	.04	.00	.07	.26	.05	.08	.49
	Intellectual Property Right	.06	.16	.12	.28	.13	.31	.57
	Personal Information	.73	.03	.18	.74	.40	.58	.87
	Unlawful Access	.94	.55	.76	.87	.27	.26	.99
Tolerance of Pirate Edition		2.62	.96	1.50	1.57	1.38	2.60	1.90
Network Anonymity		1.07	.53	.51	.78	.83	1.08	.85

Fig. 1. Averages of Attribute Data

2.3 Result of Consciousness Data Analysis

We extracted consciousness factors and each student's factors points by processing factor analysis of the responses of second parts. We have been in a continuous series of research on information security or ethic consciousness of Japanese college students for more than 10 years, and we have a definite structure of factors. Items for the second part of the questionnaire are those of our previous researches, and the extracted factors are almost coincides with factors for Japanese college students. We extracted three factors of eigenvalues greater than

1 with cumulative contribution rates 48.7%, and they are interpreted as "curiosity", "easiness", and "unguardedness" from first to third factors respectively.

Taking the averages of students' factor scores over each country, we could see the difference among them just from the factor scores SPSS outputs. Since we try to construct an e-leaning system reflecting individual's consciousness through the factors, transformation of his/her raw values from consciousness questionnaire are required. In order to do this process, we try to use the transformation matrix being output while performing the factor analysis by SPSS.

Although there are some differences for some countries, calculated values also represents the students' consciousness property of each country. Then we use this transformation formula to calculate the individual factor scores.

3 Proposed E-learning System

Our proposed system consists of two major parts, one is the data part such as database of stories categorized according to information security related issues, the other is user's interface representing stories, explanations, and so on.

3.1 Process Outline of the System

The flow of the system is as follows,

1. Login the system using the user's ID and password
   - If it's first time to login, then ID is issued and a password is set,
   - Choose the country or language from the selection box.
2. Show the initial page of the e-learning system with selected language.
   - Three buttons are disposed in the "Menu Area" on the left,
   - The white box on the right, called "Presentation Area", is used for presenting user's characteristics and learning materials.
3. Choose one of three buttons
   - If the "Attribute Q." button is selected, the attribute questionnaire sheet is displayed, and the attribute file of the user is created or recreated,
   - If the "Consciousness Q." button is selected, the Consciousness questionnaire sheet is displayed, and the consciousness file of the user is created or recreated,
   - If the "Recommended Study Stories" button is selected, user's consciousness scores along with rating comments by comparing each score value to the average value of students in the same country, and some buttons for recommended stories appear in the "Presentation Area" shown in figure 2.
4. Learning proceeds repeatedly by showing each story and by reading the explanation of the story
   - At first select the "Best Story" button, and the first story which seems to be best for the current user appears in the box just below the buttons, and the "Best Story" button disappear as shown in figure 2,
   - The next best story appears in the area by selecting "Next Story" button,
   - When the "Show Explanations" button is selected, explanations related to the story in a part of "Presentation Area".

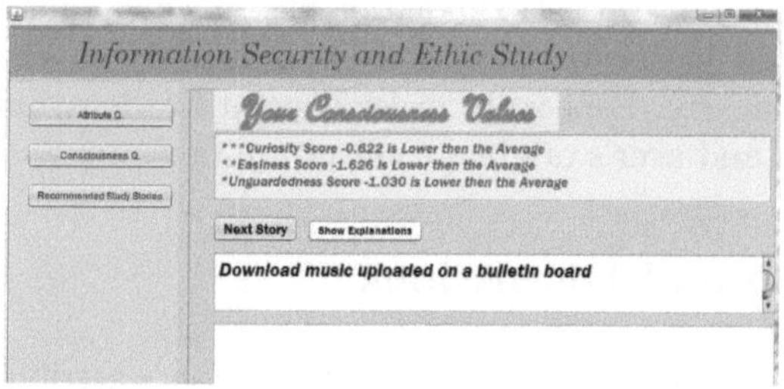

Fig. 2. Presentation of Consciousness Score and Story

3.2 Details of Inner Process

One of unique points of our proposed system is reflecting user's individual and educationally experienced characters when choosing learning subjects. This is performed by comparing user's consciousness factor scores and value vectors preassigned to each story. We assume the "harmonize priority policy", which means that studying story related subjects whose value vector is harmonizing to the user's one is better for obtaining educational effects. Here we define the harmonizing index $h(\boldsymbol{s}, \boldsymbol{u})$ of story's vector $\boldsymbol{s} = (s_1, s_2, s_3)$ and user's vector $\boldsymbol{u} = (u_1, u_2, u_3)$ with $h(\boldsymbol{s}, \boldsymbol{u}) = 1/\sqrt{\sum_{i=1}^{3} w_i(s_i - u_i)^2}$ if $\boldsymbol{s} \neq \boldsymbol{u}$, and ∞ if $\boldsymbol{s} = \boldsymbol{u}$, where w_i $(i = 1, 2, 3)$ are normalized weights corresponding to three factors. From the definition, the bigger the value the more harmonizing.

In order to give an order to each story, we recommend to apply the fuzzy outranking method. Because the fuzzy outranking method reflects the uncertainty of numerical values by introducing a fuzzy set for concordance and discordance degrees, [1], [4].

3.3 Data Part

The data part consists of several data files, such as ID file, user's attribute file, user's consciousness factor files, story files, and explanation files.

- ID file stores user ID with corresponding hash value
- Attribute file is created when the attribute questionnaire is completed, and used to determine the preferable degrees of story categories such as "Personal Information", "Copyright", and so on.
- Consciousness factors' score file is created when the consciousness questionnaire is completed. The calculation is done based on the factor transformation briefly mentioned in the section 2.3.
- Story file involves several stories in each category, and a vector with three value components corresponding to consciousness factors is assigned to each story. These values should have been given carefully considering the meaning of story.

- There are number of stories' explanation files in which each story is explained and commented in several perspectives such as legal, ethical, Netiquette, safety, financial, etc. Especially in legal point of view, differences between laws in Japan and user's original country are taken up and explained.

4 Conclusion and Discussions

We proposed an e-learning system which reflects user's attribute and consciousness characteristics to learning information related subject based on the research and analysis we have done in several Asian countries and Japan. We actually made a program using JAVA which is still stand alone version. Web site version is expected in order to confirm the effect of our system, and collecting more data is needed for improvement. In our currently implemented program, the attribute part is not fully reflected.

Another important discussing point is about the content of material. We need many stories from several categories, and explanations should be carefully considered from information quality point of view such as timeliness, relevance, appropriate amount, consistent representation, etc. It is also necessary to continue investigation on regal conditions of Asian countries.

Acknowledgments. This work is supported by JSPS(Japan Society for the Promotion of Science) Grants-in-Aid for Scientific Research(C) Number 25350350.

References

1. Hirose, H.: Prediction of Learning Effects though Fuzzy Outranking and Proposal for Instruction Model. In: Proceedings of ED-MEDIA 2009 Association for the Advancement of Computing in Education, Honolulu, USA, pp. 2828–2837 (2009)
2. Kigawa, Y., Nagata, K., Ogiwara, H., Aoki, T.: Consciousness on Information Ethic of Asian College Students and Information Law. In: Proceedings of 22nd Symposium on Information Processing Education, Tohoku University, Japan, pp. 203–206 (2009) (Japanese)
3. Kigawa, Y., Nagata, K., Ogiwara, H., Aoki, T.: On Educational Conditions for Information Ethic in Asian Countries. In: Proceedings of 23rd Symposium on Information Processing Education, Kyoto University, Japan, pp. 171–174 (2010) (Japanese)
4. Nagata, K., Amagasa, M., Hirose, H.: Multi-attribute Decision Making Based on Fuzzy Outranking. In: Proceedings of 13th IEEE International Symposium on Computational Intelligence and Informatics, Budapest, Hungary, pp. 169–174 (2012)
5. Research Team on Status Quo and Public Awareness on Personal Information Protection in China: Report on Current Situation of Personal Information Protection in China. Annual Report on China's Rule of Law (7), 355–371 (2009) (Chinese)

Visual Analysis Based on Dominator Trees with Application to Personalized eLearning

Luigi Laura[1,2], Umberto Nanni[1,2], and Marco Temperini[1]

[1] Dept. of Computer, Control, and Management Engineering "Antonio Ruberti", "Sapienza" University of Rome, Via Ariosto 25, 00185, Roma, Italy
{laura,nanni,marte}@dis.uniroma1.it
[2] Research Centre for Transport and Logistics (CTL), "Sapienza" Università di Roma, Italy

Abstract. The visualization of large graphs in interactive applications, specifically on small devices, can make harder to understand and analyze the displayed information. We show as simple topological properties of the graph can provide an efficient automatic computation of properties which improves the "readability" of a large graph by a proper selection of the displayed information. We show an approach to the visualization of a learning activity based on connectivity and related concepts as effective tools for visual analysis by learners, and by administrator of a repository.

1 Introduction

Many interactive applications require the visualization of a graph. If the quantity of the displayed information is excessive, the visualized network may become hard to understand and/or to analyze and the effectiveness of the interaction becomes disputable. The sensitivity to a loss of "understanding" of a large graph can be particularly relevant in case of small devices such as smartphones. Actually, in application where a potentially large network has to be displayed, such as in a navigator, the arcs of the graph are stratified in layers, by a manual process or based on individual properties of the arcs stored in a database. In a visualization with a low zoom factor, the arcs are displayed up to a given layer, in order to avoid an information overload.

Given a network and a distinguished vertex r, called root, one of the most natural question is whether or not the root is able to reach all the other vertices in the network. In both the cases, a basic and related question is the following: given the root r and the set of all the vertices reachable from r, do we have freedom in the choice of the path from r to a vertex target t, or are we forced, if we want to reach t, to pass through a mandatory sequence of vertices?

In graph theory, the above questions can be restated simply in the following: *does the graph have dominators*? More formally, given a *flow graph*, i.e. a directed graph with a distinguished *root* vertex r such that every vertex is reachable from r, a vertex u is a *dominator* of a vertex v (u *dominates* v) if every path from r to v contains u; u is a *proper dominator* of v if u dominates v and $u \neq v$.

E. Popescu et al. (Eds.): ICWL 2014, LNCS 8613, pp. 207–212, 2014.

Most notably, the dominance relation is reflexive and transitive, and its transitive closure is a tree, called the *dominator tree*. The dominator tree is a central tool in program optimization and code generation. Dominators have applications in several other areas, including theoretical biology, constraint programming, memory profiling, circuit testing, and connectivity. We refer the interested reader to the recent survey of Parotsidis and Georgiadis [10].

However, so far, to the best of our knowledge, the dominators have not been considered in the visual analysis of a network, despite the richness of the information depicted by the dominator tree, whose edges may not correspond to edges of the original graph.

An Application to Personalized eLearning. Personalized e-learning aims to provide the learner with a course specially fitted to her/his relevant individual characteristics; a course is adaptive when its content can change during course taking, according to the evolution of the individual characteristics of the learner [5,12]. A personalized course can be, by constitution, composed by a set of learning activities fostering the increase of knowledge/skills in the individual learner. On the other hand attempts are known to integrate such individual activities with social-collaborative e-learning activities [6,11,2,8] for the enrichment in motivation and involvement a social dimension can add.

Visualization tools can play a crucial role in the delivery of a network based course: they are important when it comes to delivering a single learning activity, yet in this paper we are interested in the role of visualization at the whole course level. In particular we apply the approach to graph drawing and transformation mentioned above to the visualization of the e-learning course prepared for an individual learner.

By exploiting the concepts originated in the educational theory of Lev Vygotskij [3] we aim to provide the learner with a visual tool allowing her/him to select, significantly and freely one of the course's learning activities and have it as next activity in the course. Namely, the learning activities that are affordable with respect to the present state of knowledge of the learner are clearly collected in a set (the *Zone of Proximal Development*), in which the choice for the next activity can be for the learner to do, according to informal personal preferences, such as the available time, the attraction for a topic (rather than for another) or the possibility to presently collaborate with a fellow learner on an activity. In our view this allows to leverage a minimally guided self-determination of the learner, increasing her/his motivation and engagement in study.

Our Contribution and Organization of the Paper. In this paper, motivated by an eLearning application for dynamic configuration of paths of learning activities, we developed a visualization that uses (the informative subtree of) the dominator tree, in order to show whether dominators are existing in the paths towards a given target knowledge (i.e., there are learning activities that are anyway mandatory in order to reach the target). The paper is organized as follows:

in the next section we recall the necessary background from graph theory whilst our main contribution, i.e. the visualization of Personalized Learning Pathways, is detailed in Section 3.

2 Preliminaries

As mentioned in the introduction, a *flow graph* is a directed graph with a distinguished *root* vertex r such that every vertex is reachable from r. If the graph contains vertices not reachable from the root, they can be simply either removed or marked as unreachable in the visualization; thus, in order to simplify the discussion, in this paper we will assume, without loss of generality, that we are dealing with flowgraphs. A vertex u is a *dominator* of a vertex v (*u dominates v*) if every path from r to v contains u; u is a *proper dominator* of v if u dominates v and $u \neq v$. The dominator relation is reflexive and transitive. Its transitive reduction (i.e., a graph with as few edges as possible that has the same reachability relation as the given graph) is a rooted tree, the *dominator tree D*: v dominates w if and only if v is an ancestor of w in D. If $v \neq s$, $d(v)$, the parent of v in D, is the *immediate dominator* of v: it is the unique proper dominator of v that is dominated by all proper dominators of v.

In Figure 1 we can see a flowgraph G (left-hand side) and a corresponding dominator tree (right-hand side). What can we see from this tree? By a visual inspection of the original graph, on the left, vertices 1, 6 and 5 are "above" vertex 2. The dominator tree, on the right, shows vertex 2 to be "appended" under vertices 6 and 5 (its *dominators*), but not under vertex 1. This means that *in the original graph* in order to reach vertex 2 from the root, it is mandatory to pass through both vertices 6 and 5 (in this order), but one can skip vertex 1.

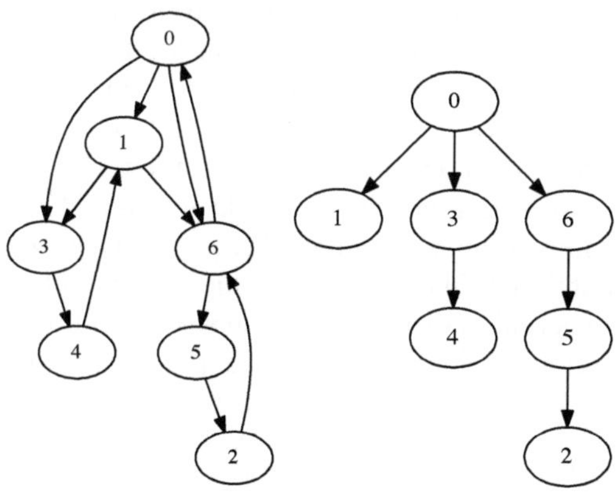

Fig. 1. (left) A directed graph G: the root is vertex 0, that can reach all the vertices of the graph. (right) The dominator tree of G.

3 Visualization of Personalized Learning Pathways

Our work was motivated by the idea of improving the visualization capabilities to the e-learning framework presented in [9]. In this framework, one main issue is in the personalization of the learning pathways according to the learning characteristics of an individual students or of a group of learners, and in the automatic adaptation of such pathways to the changing assessment of the above mentioned characteristics. The framework allows to define a course as a *Learning Path* (*LP*), i.e. a sets of *learning activities* (*la*), and to maintain a *Student Model* (*SM*), i.e. a model of the learner's characteristics relevant to learning.

Learning activities can be defined in such a way that collections of *las* can be stored in repositories and appropriately selected to build a course. Once *Target Knowledge* (*TK*), i.e. the goals, are established for a given learner, a course can be created by selecting from the repository only the relevant learning activities, in accord with the learner's *SM* and the course's goals.

In particular the definition of a learning activity *la* points formally out:

- the *Required Knowledge* (*RK*, or *la.RK*), i.e. the specification of the skills required in order to fruitfully take the *la*,
- the *Acquired Knowledge* (*AK*, or *la.AK*), i.e. the skills that can be acquired by taking the *la*.

In the framework, a skill is the specification of an item of knowledge, defined in terms of the concepts it involves and the cognitive level [1] of its possession by the learner.

It is very likely that the skills acquired through an *la* may be required by another *la*'. This introduces a straightforward relation of derivation among the *las* in the repository, that allows to draw the repository as a graph. So, in the framework, the *LP* of a course is in fact a subgraph/subset of the repository.

The learner can be presented with a linearized version of such subgraph: a sequence of the *las* in *LP* not violating the relation of derivation seen above - i.e. an *la* never precedes an *la*' such that skills in *la*'.*AK* are in *la.RK*. We think, though, that such a presentation would hinder the learner's self-conscience and motivations, and could have bad effects on her/his general engagement in the course. Moreover, we aim to let the framework allow the learner to work in a social-collaborative e-learning environment, so we should allow the learner to select the next learning activity to undertake: in this view the student is as free as possible, so to match her/his motivations and opportunities: the only limit in such choice is in the actual affordability of the selected *la* by the student (which may also guard against disappointment by the part of the student).

So in the framework the course is to be presented in such a way that only those *las* in *LP* are shown that are affordable by the learner, according to the present state of her/his *SM*. While the *SM* grows (for hopefully it does during the study activity) also the portion of course available to the learner for further learning activities is to be updated and shown. The theory developed by Vygotskij on child mind evolution and learning [13,3] is a great source to support the learning framework we are discussing, and its bend towards the development of a social-collaborative approach to undertaking learning paths [8,4].

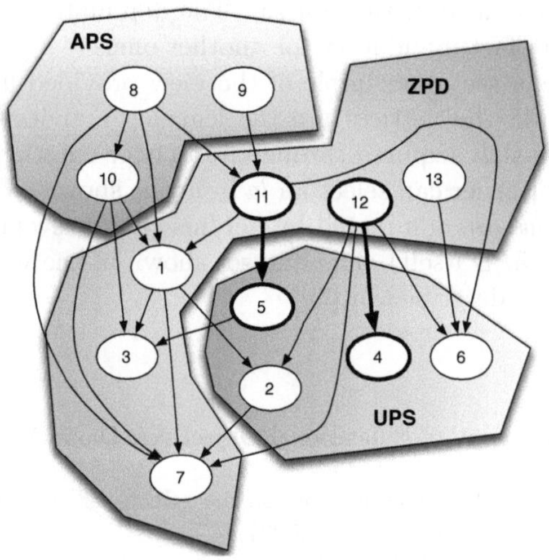

Fig. 2. Example of visualizations in the personalized eLearning application. The *las* are partitioned in the *APS*, *ZPD*, *UPS* sets; the dominators are the activities in bold: vertex 11 is the only vertex that can reach vertex 5, and, similarly, vertex 12 dominates vertex 4. Vertices 8, 9, 12 and 13 have no entering edges: these *las* have no prerequisites.

One main issue we have tried and implemented in the framework is Vygotskij's partition of the learning domain associated to a course, in three "zones": the area of *Autonomous Problem Solving* (*APS*), where the learner has succeeded in previous learning activities, so that the knowledge is (the skills are) firm; the area of *Unreachable Problem Solving* (*UPS*), where, according to the evidence of the student model, the learning activities couldn't be feasibly attacked; and the *Zone of Proximal Development* (*ZPD*) where skills/learning activities of the course are located, that can be fruitfully undertaken (these are the activities affordable basing on the skills already possessed, with the help of a peer or of the teacher, and likely to bring new acquired skills).

In an educational perspective the *ZPD* of a learner is the area where real growth can more likely occur; so a main issue, while an e-learning system is delivering a course, is to make the *ZPD* boundaries clear to the learner, in order to allow for a sensible choice of the next learning activity to take, while according maximal freedom of choice. On the other side, a course designer can get a relevant advantage based on visual analysis techniques, especially in case of a large repository of learning contents. In this scenario, the designer can investigate the "best" learning paths which start from a Required Knowledge matching the profiles of the learners, and end up with a Target Knowledge matching the educational goals. In particular, the approach proposed in this paper allow this user to spot the mandatory *las* and visualize alternative learning patways.

By exploiting the graph visualization technique discussed in the previous section, we are equipping the e-learning framework with a graphic tool that allowed students to see the *ZPD* and so, to some extent, to appreciate the possible routes to their goals (i.e. to an *la* in the course). The dominator tree can be used to show what *las* are in fact mandatory for another one.

In Figure 2 we can see an example of the view provided in the personalized e-learning framework: the vertices are the learning activities; an edge exiting from an *la* denotes a skill acquired through it; an edge entering a vertex is a skill required by it. The learner can select an *la* from the shown *ZPD*, being aware of what, of the other *las* are dominated by her/his choice (eventually in the *UPS*, and possibly in the *ZPD* itself). The dataset shown in the visualization is from the eLearning system described in [7].

References

1. Bloom, B.E.: Taxonomy of Educational Objectives. David McKay Company Inc., New York (1964)
2. Cheng, Y., Ku, H.: An investigation of the effects of reciprocal peer tutoring. Computers in Human Behavior 25 (2009)
3. Daniels, H., Cole, M., Wertsch, J.: The Cambridge Companion to Vygotsky. Cambridge University Press (2007)
4. De Marsico, M., Sterbini, A., Temperini, M.: A strategy to join adaptive and reputation-based social-collaborative e-learning, through the zone of proximal development. International Journal of Distance Education Technologies (IJDET) 11(3), 12–31 (2013)
5. Graf, S., Kinshuk: Providing adaptive courses in learning management systems with respect to learning styles. In: Proc. World Conf. on E-Learning in Corporate, Government, Healthcare, and Higher Education, pp. 2576–2583 (2007)
6. Kreijns, K., Kirschner, P., Jochems, W.: Identifying the pitfalls for social interaction in computer supported collaborative learning environments: a review of the research. Computers in Human Behavior 19, 335–353 (2003)
7. Limongelli, C., Sciarrone, F., Temperini, M., Vaste, G.: Virtual cultural tour personalization by means of an adaptive e-learning system: A case study. In: Lytras, M.D., et al. (eds.) WSKS 2009. LNCS, vol. 5736, pp. 40–49. Springer, Heidelberg (2009)
8. De Marsico, M., Sterbini, A., Temperini, M.: The definition of a tunneling strategy between adaptive learning and reputation-based group activities. In: Proc. 11th IEEE Int. Conf. on Adv. Learning Technologies, ICALT, pp. 498–500 (2011)
9. De Marsico, M., Sterbini, A., Temperini, M.: A framework to support social-collaborative personalized e-learning. In: Kurosu, M. (ed.) HCII/HCI 2013, Part II. LNCS, vol. 8005, pp. 351–360. Springer, Heidelberg (2013)
10. Parotsidis, N., Georgiadis, L.: Dominators in Directed Graphs: A Survey of Recent Results, Applications, and Open Problems. In: Capuni, I., Georgiadis, L., Altun, O. (eds.) 2nd International Symposium on Computing In Informatics And Mathematics (ISCIM 2013), Rinas–Tirana, Albania, vol. 1, pp. 15–20. Epoka University (2013)
11. Popescu, E.: Providing collaborative learning support with social media in an integrated environment. World Wide Web (2012)
12. Sterbini, A., Temperini, M.: Selection and sequencing constraints for personalized courses. In: Proc. 40th IEEE Frontiers in Education (2010)
13. Vygotskij, L.S.: Mind in society: The development of higher psychological processes. Harvard Univ. Press (1978)

MaVeriC – A Constraint-Based System for Web-Based Learning

Claus Zinn

Department of Computer Science, University of Konstanz
claus.zinn@uni-konstanz.de

Abstract. We present a constraint-based system for web-based learning. Its constraint engine has a concise and elegant embedding in the Prolog programming language, and it offers an easy-to-read and easy-to-write constraint language. We use its glass-box design as a formal playground to investigate the nature of constraint-based tutoring.

Keywords: Constraint-based tutoring, cognitive diagnosis, Prolog.

1 Introduction

Constraint-based tutoring diagnoses the correctness of learner input in terms of a *problem state*, given a set of constraints that test whether relevant aspects of the state are satisfied or not. Following [8], a constraint is a pair $< C_r, C_s >$, where C_r is the *relevance condition*, identifying "the class of problem states for which the constraint is relevant", and C_s the *satisfaction condition*, identifying "the class of (relevant) states in which the constraint is satisfied". The following constraint encodes, for instance, the domain principle that only fractions with equal denominators can be added: *If the problem is* $\frac{n_1}{d_1} + \frac{n_2}{d_2}$ *and if* $n = n_1 + n_2$, *then it had better be the case that* $d_1 = d_2$ *(or else something is wrong).*

Constraint-based tutoring has gained traction [6]. It now competes with the most prominent programming paradigm for building intelligent tutors, the model-tracing tutors that are based on production rule systems [2]. But which approach is better suited to capture, monitor and address learners' (potentially erroneous) problem solving? Does it depend on the domain of instruction to be modeled? How about the costs of authoring and running task models?

In this paper, we aim at contributing to the pending controversy about the nature and potential of constraint-based tutoring [4,3,7]. For this, we have implemented a constraint-based system for basic mathematics. While its outer loop is very simple – learners can define arbitrary fraction addition tasks – it offers a fully-fledged inner loop to diagnose whether a learner action is correct or not, to give error-specific feedback on an incorrect step, and to generate hints on the next step. The system architecture follows the model-view-controller design pattern to enforce a separation of concerns between components. The paper focuses on the model, which offers a simple, concise but powerful constraint engine that is re-usable and runs independently from the other system components.

E. Popescu et al. (Eds.): ICWL 2014, LNCS 8613, pp. 213–218, 2014.

We use the constraint engine as a playground for complementing *state constraints* with three other types of constraints, which helps clarifying some of the pending issues in constraint-based tutoring.

2 A Constraint System

2.1 Domain of Instruction: Adding Fractions

Given two fractions n_1/d_1 and n_2/d_2, compute their sum. When the two input fractions do not share a common denominator, it must be computed. Once the lowest common denominator d for d_1 and d_2 is determined, the numerators must be rewritten in terms of d_1, n_1 and d, and d_2, n_2 and d (yielding d_{11}, d_{22}, n_{11} and n_{22}, with $d_{11} = d_{22} = d$). The converted fractions are then added by adding their numerators. When the resulting fraction n/d is improper, it must be reduced to a proper one: the greatest common divisor g of n and d is computed, and a reduced fraction returned where n and d are both divided by g (yielding n_r and d_r). The problem state can be captured as

$$\frac{n_1}{d_1} + \frac{n_2}{d_2} =^c \frac{n_{11}}{d_{11}} + \frac{n_{22}}{d_{22}} = \frac{n}{d} =^r \frac{n_r}{d_r}.$$

2.2 The Constraint Engine

Our system to define and process constraints is embedded in Prolog. The problem solving state is defined as a Prolog fact `current_state/2` with two argument terms: `given/1` encodes the givens as a list of values; `sought/1` encodes a list of values for learners to determine to solve a given problem, for instance,

current_state(**given**($[5, 7, 4, 9]$), **sought**($[45, 63, 28, 63, N, D, NR, DR]$)).

The fact `problem_context(_N1/_D1+_N2/_D2)` encodes the general task to be solved, here the addition of two arbitrarily given fractions.

Constraints are represented by 5-ary Prolog facts

constraint(*Name*, *State*, *Relevance*, *Satisfaction*, *Feedback*).

The first argument identifies the constraint with a name, for convenience, testing and debugging. Its second parameter is used for passing on the current problem state to the constraint. A constraint's third and fourth argument encode the relevance and satisfaction conditions as a Prolog goal structure. The last argument associates feedback with the constraint. It consists of a feedback string and a list of state variables affected by the constraint.

A constraint engine examines all constraints, filters out those that are relevant for a given state, and then checks whether the relevant ones are satisfiable or not. Fig. 1 depicts the full implementation of our constraint engine. It fits in 20 lines of Prolog code. The main clause `constraint_engine/2` returns as result all satisfiable relevant clauses and all non-satisfiable relevant clauses. First, the

```
constraint_engine(Satisfied, UnSatisfied) ←current_state(Given, Sought),
  findall( constraint(Name, Sat, Fb),
           ( constraint(Name, state(Given, Sought),
                 relevance_cond(Rel), satisfaction_cond(Sat), Fb),
             call(Rel)), RelConstraints),
  test_constraints(RelConstraints, Satisfied, UnSatisfied).

test_constraints([], [], []).
test_constraints([ constraint(Name, Sat, _Fb)|OtherC], [Name|SatisC], UnSatisC) ←
  call(Sat), !, test_constraints(OtherC, SatisC, UnSatisC).
test_constraints([ constraint(Name, _Sat, Fb)|OtherC], SatisC, [(Name, Fb)|UnSatisC]) ←
  test_constraints(OtherC, SatisC, OtherUnSatisC).
```

Fig. 1. A Constraint Engine in Prolog

current problem state – as represented in the Prolog system – is retrieved. Then, the all-solutions predicate `findall/3` identifies all constraints that are relevant in the given state. Here, note the passing on of the values `Given` and `Sought` to `constraint/5`, and the use of `call/1` to execute the goal structure `Rel`. The relevant constraints are collected with their names, their satisfaction conditions, and their feedback terms. Then, `test_constraints/3` processes relevant constraints. Its first clause tests for termination, and the subsequent definitions deal with the two cases of a constraint being satisfied (`call/1` succeeds) or not satisfied.

The following predicate drives constraint-based diagnosis:

```
get_diagnosis(Task, Solution, Diagnosis) ← set_current_state(Task, Solution),
      constraint_engine(Satisfied, UnSatisfied),
      construct_remedial_feedback(UnSatisfied, Diagnosis).
```

With the problem state set, the engine is called to determine all relevant constraints; the unsatisfied constraints are aggregated to construct the feedback.

2.3 State Constraints for Adding Fractions

Each state constraint specifies certain conditions that must be satisfied by all correct solutions. Only all constraints taken together test the learner solution for correctness in all relevant aspects. Fig. 2 depicts Ohlsson's aforementioned example constraint. Its second argument is used to establish bindings for the

```
constraint(check_denom_when_n_equals_n11_and_n22,
   state(given([N1, D1, N2, D2]),
         sought([N11, D11, N22, D22, N, _D, _NR, _DR])),
   relevance_cond((problem_context(N1/D1 + N2/D2),
                   integers([N, N11, N22, D11, D22]), N is N11 + N22)),
   satisfaction_cond((D11 == D22)),
   (['Only add the numerators', N11, 'and', N22,
     'when they share a common denominator'], [n, d11, d22])).
```

Fig. 2. A State Constraint for Adding Fractions

Prolog input variables `N1`, `D1`, `N2` and `D2`, and the Prolog output variables `N11`, `D11`, `N22`, `D22`, and `N`. Its relevancy condition specifies that (i) we are in a task context where fractions are being added; (ii) the relevant cells all have been given integer values (the content of the other cells is ignored); and (iii) the value of the n cell equals the sum of adding n_{11} and n_{22}. The constraint's satisfaction condition then checks whether the converted fractions share a common denominator, *i.e.*, whether d_{11} equals d_{22}. The fifth argument is used for constructing a feedback string, and for supporting the GUI to highlight the corresponding cells.

2.4 Other Types of Constraints

An ITS must cope with and support learners that fail to advance a problem state, perform steps in the wrong order, or exhibit errors common to a domain of instruction. For these cases other types of constraints are necessary, see Fig. 3.

```
constraint(hint_find_lcd,
    state(given([N1, D1, N2, D2]), sought([N11, D11, N22, D22, N, D, NR, DR])),
    relevance_cond((problem_context(N1/D1 + N2/D2),
                    vars([N11, D11, N22, D22, N, D, NR, DR])),
    satisfaction_cond((fail)),
    (['Seek␣common␣denominator␣of', D1, 'and', D2], [])).

constraint(path_missing_intermediate,
    state(given([N1, D1, N2, D2]), sought([N11, D11, N22, D22, N, D, _NR, _DR])),
    relevance_cond((problem_context(N1/D1 + N2/D2),
                    vars([N11, D11, N22, D22]), integer(N), integer(D),
                    lcd(D1, D2, D), rewrite_numerator(N1, D1, D, N11),
                    rewrite_numerator(N2, D2, D, N22), N is N11 + N22)),
    satisfaction_cond((fail)),
    (['Correct␣result,␣but␣missing␣steps'], [N11, D11, N22, D22])).

constraint(remedial_sum_reduced_partially_nr,
    state(given([N1, D1, N2, D2]), sought([N11, D11, N22, D22, N, D, NR, _DR])),
    relevance_cond((problem_context(N1/D1 + N2/D2),
                    integers([N11, D11, N22, D22, N, D, NR]),
                    gcd(N, D, G), ( ⊬ NR is N / G), get_multiple(NR, N),
                    Fact is N / NR, Fact > 1)),
    satisfaction_cond((fail)),
    (['Answer numerator␣only␣partially␣reduced.', 'The␣GCD␣of', N, 'and', D,
      , 'is', G, '.', 'Divide', N, 'by', G, 'rather␣than', Fact, '.'], [nr])).
```

Fig. 3. Three Other Types of Constraints

Next-Step Help Constraints help learners that are stuck. All the learner's problem state advances are correct, but some values are missing. For learners stuck in the initial state, we add the constraint `hint_find_lcd`. It is only relevant if none of the fields has a value, *i.e.*, when all the terms in the `sought` list are variables. The constraint's feedback component gives-away process-related information. Feedback may include the elicitation of the task's goal structure, *e.g.*, by mentioning the next goal to be tackled, or by decomposing a goal into subgoals. The definition of help constraints follows a pattern: their relevancy conditions test whether some `sought` cells are variable; also, they have a single satisfaction condition `fail`, which is bound to fail.

Path Constraints check whether learners perform steps in the correct order. They are related to next-step help constraints because they also check for gaps. Consider the following world state, where the answer is correct but lacks the intermediate conversion steps: $5/7 + 4/9 =^c \square/_{\square} + \square/_{\square} = 73/63 =^r \square/_{\square}$.

The constraint `path_missing_intermediate` captures this behaviour. Here, relevancy conditions not only check for empty cells, but also ensure that all given values are correct. Again, there is the single satisfaction condition `fail`.

Buggy Constraints address the wrongness of the situation. While the satisfaction conditions for state constraints enforce the correctness of values in the problem space (if a relevant state constraint is unsatisfiable, then *something* in the problem space is incorrect), the relevancy conditions of buggy constraints test whether a problem state is incorrect *in a certain way*; their feedback component provides remediation that is specific to the nature of the error. Consider a problem state where the learner is only partially reducing a fraction (*e.g.*, the fraction $\frac{16}{24}$ is only reduced to $\frac{8}{12}$ rather than $\frac{2}{3}$). The buggy constraint `remedial_sum_reduced_partially_nr` captures this situation. Its relevancy conditions `gcd(N,D,G), (\+ NR is N/G)` check whether `NR` is *not* the result of dividing `N` by `G`. If `N` is a multiple of `NR`, and if `N` divided by `NR` is greater than 1, then the learner only partially reduced the non-proper fraction.

When learners commit multiple errors, more than a single relevant constraint will be unsatisfied. Moreover, when learners commit an erroneous partial solution, unsatisfied relevant state constraints will be joined by relevant unsatisfied next-step help constraints and buggy constraints. Here, the tutoring system must attack erroneous behaviour in a step-wise manner. Rather than presenting learners with the direct output of the constraint engine, the system selects the next best issue, following this heuristics: if a buggy constraint "fired", then address the captured learner's misconception first, before addressing next-step help, path, and state constraints; if a state constraint "fired", then omit hints resulting from next-step help and path constraints; otherwise give feedback from next-step help and path constraints. – We extend our constraint language by a sixth argument to specify the type of the constraint: *state*, *hint*, *path*, and *buggy*.

3 Discussion

The ASPIRE system is a constraint-based system that also offers an authoring environment for instructional designers [5]. Its architectural design is rather monolithic: its constraint engine, which is not available independently, seems to be tightly interwoven with the user interface as many of the ASPIRE constraints for fractions suggest. As there is no clear separation between the different components, the constraint model cannot be developed and debugged independently from the overall system, which in turn, raises development costs. In contrast, MaVeriC follows a modular design philosophy. Its constraint-based model can be designed, implemented and tested independently from the other system components, using an easy-to-use constraint language, and a standard Prolog shell with its built-in debugging capabilities. Only little Prolog expertise is required. With regard to modularization, we would like to see our constraint engine on par with the JESS production rule engine (see `http://herzberg.ca.sandia.gov`), which is used in the cognitive tutor authoring tools [1].

With regard to the nature of constraint-based tutoring, we propose four different types of constraints for modeling. *State constraints* check whether the learner's solution is correct and whether its parts are in a correct relation with one another. *Next-step constraints* check for an incomplete solution. They identify the missing parts and have feedback that hint learners toward filling the gaps. *Path constraints* capture "jumping to the conclusion" situations with intermediate steps missing; their feedback instructs learners to perform steps in a proper order. *Buggy constraints* check whether a given solution is incorrect in a certain way. They encode typical errors in a domain and give error-specific remediation to learners to correct the errors. – We invite researchers to use our glass-box and highly re-usable constraint engine as a formal playground to make their case and to further investigate the nature of constraint-based tutoring.

References

1. Aleven, V., McLaren, B., Koedinger, K.: Rapid development of computer-based tutors with the cognitive tutor authoring tools (CTAT). In: Proc. of the Int'l Conf. on Artificial Intelligence in Education, pp. 990–990. IOS Press (2005)
2. Anderson, J.R., Corbett, A.T., Koedinger, K.R., Pelletier, R.: Cognitive tutors: Lessons learned. Journal of the Learning Sciences 4(2), 167–207 (1995)
3. Kodaganallur, V., Weitz, R., Rosenthal, D.: A comparison of model-tracing and constraint-based intelligent tutoring paradigms. Int. J. of Artif. Intell. in Educ. 15, 117–144 (2005)
4. Mitrovic, A., Koedinger, K.R., Martin, B.: A comparative analysis of cognitive tutoring and constraint-based modeling. In: Brusilovsky, P., Corbett, A.T., de Rosis, F. (eds.) UM 2003. LNCS, vol. 2702, pp. 313–322. Springer, Heidelberg (2003)
5. Mitrovic, A., Martin, B., Suraweera, P., Zakharov, K., Milik, N., Holland, J., McGuigan, N.: Aspire: An authoring system and deployment environment for constraint-based tutors. Int. J. of Artif. Intell. in Educ. 19(2), 155–188 (2009)
6. Mitrović, A., Mayo, M., Suraweera, P., Martin, B.: Constraint-based tutors: A success story. In: Monostori, L., Váncza, J., Ali, M. (eds.) IEA/AIE 2001. LNCS (LNAI), vol. 2070, pp. 931–940. Springer, Heidelberg (2001)
7. Mitrovic, A., Ohlsson, S.: A critique of Kodaganallur, Weitz and Rosenthal, "A comparison of model-tracing and constraint-based intelligent tutoring paradigms". Int. J. of Artif. Intell. in Educ. 16(3), 277–289 (2006)
8. Ohlsson, S.: Constraint-based student modeling. Int J. of Artif. Intell. in Educ. 3(4), 429–447 (1992)

How a Flipped Learning Environment Affects Learning in a Course on Theoretical Computer Science

Dorina Gnaur[1] and Hans Hüttel[2]

[1] Department of Learning and Philosophy, Aalborg University, Denmark
[2] Department of Computer Science, Aalborg University, Denmark

Abstract. This paper reports initial experiences with flipping the classroom in an undergraduate computer science course as part of an overall attempt to enhance the pedagogical support for student learning. Our findings indicate that, just as the flipped classroom implies, a shift of focus in the learning context influences the way students engage with the course and their learning strategies.

1 Introduction

The notion of a flipped classroom has emerged in recent years [6] in the context of education in the United States. The idea is to use technology to move traditional 'in-class' activities out of the actual classroom, often in the form of audio or video podcasts. Practical sessions now become the central in-class activities. A common argument is that this will re-focus teaching on student-centered learning.

In this paper we assess experiences with a web-based notion of a flipped classroom in the setting of the course *Computability and Complexity*. The course has been taught by the second author since 2011. The course is followed by students in the third year of the undergraduate programmes in computer science and software technology. The decision to flip the classroom stems from two observations made by the second author in previous courses: firstly, attendance at lectures appeared to be notably higher than the attendance at the student-focused part of teaching in the course, e.g. practical sessions; and secondly, that many students appeared not to have read the texts associated with these teaching activities that depended on this. The hope was that a flipped classroom, through which the focus is purposely directed towards the active part of teaching, would induce students to embrace active learning, which is known to enhance deep learning.

Since a flipped classroom redefines teaching practice, it is important to understand its relation to the general teaching practice within the subject area. Every teaching activity within an academic subject can be seen in relation to its adherence to the underlying signature pedagogy, a notion due by Shulman who defines it as follows [11]:

> These are types of teaching that organize the fundamental ways in which future practitioners are educated for their new professions. In these signature pedagogies, the novices are instructed in critical aspects of the three fundamental aspects of professional work to think, to perform, and to act with integrity.

Computer science spans diverse scientific paradigms; in some areas, the signature pedagogy is related to that of pure mathematics with a focus on mastering formal definitions, theorems and proofs and on solving well-defined mathematical problems. Very

E. Popescu et al. (Eds.): ICWL 2014, LNCS 8613, pp. 219–228, 2014.

often the focus is on lectures that expound the material on the blackboard. This signature pedagogy is also characteristic of the course Computability and Complexity. The course, found in most computer science degree programmes today, covers topics in the mathematical theory of computation that are central to computer science and arose in the context of mathematical logic.

Signature pedagogies represent the distinct ways of thinking and practicing which are characteristic of a discipline [11]. The process of gradual initiation into the disciplinary field is marked by narrow passages into areas of increased insight, also called *threshold concepts*. One of the threshold concepts of the course is the integration of basic, declarative knowledge (in particular definitions and theorems), another that of being able to master the mathematical reasoning strategies associated with the course (that is, the proofs of theorems). The two concepts are closely linked, as mathematical proof strategies depend on the learner being able to integrate declarative knowledge that is, being able to 'speak the language' of the subject.

2 Theoretical Framing

Research in higher education pedagogy stresses learning rather than teaching and the importance of student centred activities to enhance learning [7,1]. The research indicates furthermore that students make decisions on learning approaches based on their perception of the learning objectives of a program component. In more general terms, they may decide on relatively superficial or on more in-depth approaches, and adopt corresponding strategies. Unless the subject matter is of inherent interest to them or elicits specific types of engagement or assessment requirements, students tend toward surface approaches to reduce workload and concentrate on what they perceive as more demanding components. It follows that the teaching and learning context has to be explicitly aligned with the intended learning outcomes of a course. As suggested by the theory of constructive alignment [1], the teaching system must align teaching methods and assessments to the learning activities stated in the objectives, the purpose of teaching being to support student learning towards higher complexity levels.

Students' perception of the course context manifests itself as a combination of intention and strategy: the level of knowledge they choose to pursue and the associated strategies they will apply to reach that level. Meanwhile, students encounter obstacles on the learning path; if they are unable to achieve set objectives, they may resort to 'mimicry' or other simulation strategies. This is another reason for students being stuck within surface approaches. Advancement within a field requires basic building blocks that integrate lower level concepts and continuously expand through new entries into the discipline as well as a gradual initiation into the ways of thinking and practicing that are specific to the discipline. [4].

If we want to understand how students get initiated into a discipline, a crucial notion is that of its *threshold concepts*. A threshold concept brings forth the idea of a portal that opens up

> ...new and previously inaccessible way[s] of thinking about something. It represents a transformed way of understanding, or interpreting, or viewing something without which the learner cannot progress [8]

In other words, threshold concepts are troublesome – but once a student has mastered them, the concepts are revelatory and irreversible, for they transform the disciplinary identity of the student and how he/she thinks about and practices the subject.

In this perspective, the task for teachers is to capitalize on key components of understanding as well as to locate 'stuck places' or inadequate approaches that may hinder students' progress, in order to align teaching methods in ways that facilitate learning. The learning context is meant to act as a 'holding environment' that will convince students to step outside their comfort zones and enter zones of uncertainty, while supporting their endeavours through the provision of adequate learning resources and technologies as well as access to enhanced student-teacher interaction [10]. Teaching is thus an expression of discipline-based pedagogy, i.e. 'the ways of representing and formulating the subject that make it comprehensible to others' including 'an understanding of what makes the learning of specific topics easy or difficult' [11, p. 9-10]. Technology serves intentional presentation purposes as well as enhanced access to disciplinary knowledge.

3 The Main Teaching Activities

In this section we describe the main teaching activities that took place in the course Computability and Complexity, henceforth abbreviated CC.

3.1 Pencasts and Text-Related Questions

The CC course used the Moodle e-learning platform [9] and was organized as 15 sessions. Each session (apart from one extended problem solving session) dealt with a specific topic, supported by textbook. A central goal of the teaching activities was to support the aspect of a thorough reading of the text related to the session. Previous anecdotal experience suggests that students are often not used to reading mathematically-oriented texts with an emphasis on precise definitions and on applying these. Therefore, the text-related questions focused on the declarative aspects of the learning goals with a set of text-related questions for each session. The answers to these constituted a personal portfolio, i.e. a collection of personal documents that were allowed at the final exam as the only aid. Students were supposed to submit their answers according to the deadlines indicated on the course Moodle platform. The answers must be written in LaTeXand were subjected to a peer review by a fellow student.

At the same time, the lectures dealing with declarative knowledge were replaced by a collection of pencasts. These were produced on an iPad using the Doceri app [2], a rubber-tipped stylus and an iPhone headset and later edited under Mac OS X using iMovie. Every session, apart from an extended problem-solving session half way through the course that recapitulated the material of the first 7 sessions, had an associated pencast consisting of 3 to 5 video segments each having a duration of 8 to 15 minutes. Each such segment addressed a part of the text associated with the session. The presentation style of the videos involved a combination of handwritten text and recorded sound; the intention was to stay close to the signature pedagogy of the subject and approach the exposition in the style of a chalk-and-blackboard only lecture, a mode of lecturing that the second author had used previously with good results. Fig. 1 shows a screen capture from a pencast segment.

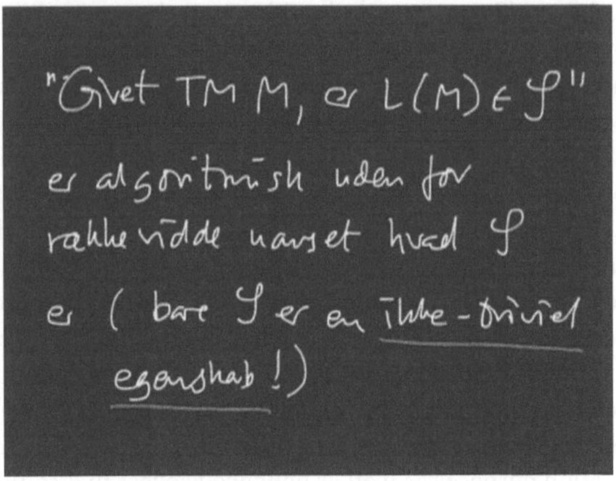

Fig. 1. Screen capture of pencast (in Danish)

As part of the pencast associated with each session, the exposition ended with a 'horror story' intended to highlight typical pitfalls and misconceptions within the topic of the session; this was an extension of the practice within the earlier lecture-based teaching by the second author. Students were expected to have watched the relevant pencasts and read the corresponding material in the textbook before the practical sessions. Each set of pencasts could be downloaded as a zip archive of Quicktime files released under the Creative Commons licence 3.0. All pencasts can be played on computers, tablets and smart phones. Initially, each pencast-based session was supported by a discussion forum on Moodle. However, the fora saw very little activity (only two questions were asked), so this idea was eventually scrapped.

3.2 Practical Sessions

Each pencast session had an associated practical session. Due to constraints on rooms, the students were distributed over three large seminar rooms for these practical sessions. Each practical session involved solving a problem set that would focus on central notions (definitions, theorems and their proofs and associated proof techniques). The problems in each set were deliberately chosen to be similar in form and content to ones that students would encounter at the final exam – as part of the alignment strategy.

4 Evaluating the Experience

The authors together prepared a questionnaire, which was followed up by 4 qualitative interviews with a total of four groups of students by the first author, who was unknown to the students and so less biased.

4.1 Analysis of the Questionnaire

At the end of the course, the students were given a questionnaire focusing on evaluating student learning. 40 out of 101 students answered these questions, which aimed at determining the perceived effects of pencasts on their learning experience. The following is a summary of the replies to two crucial questions. Fig. 2 summarizes the replies to the question of how students perceived that pencasts supported their learning. The vast majority felt that the pencasts indeed supported their learning. Note that the question about the usefulness in an exam setting may appear partly misleading as the answers were collected well in advance of the exam and can only represent a statement of intent on the part of the students.

	No. of students	Percent
They constituted an important means of having access to the contents of the course	22	55
They made it possible for me to plan my learning in the way that I preferred	24	60
They helped me catch up on topics if I had been away	20	50
They were a better way of approaching topics than a lecture would have been	15	37.5
They made it easier for me to prepare for the problem-solving sessions	22	55
They made it easier for me to prepare for the exam	17	42.5
None of the above	1	2.5
Other	4	10

Fig. 2. Students' answers to the question *To which extent did you experience that the pencasts of Computability and Complexity supported your learning?*

The students were also asked, which of the activities of the course that, in their opinion, were most helpful for learning. Fig. 3 summarizes the answers. The answers indicate that the intent of the teaching design, namely to emphasize the importance of problem solving, was fulfilled. Pencasts as such are not producing learning; yet they are valued in combination with an active learning element such as problem solving.

	No. of students	Percent
Text-related questions	0	0
Pencasts	1	3
Problem-solving sessions	5	13
Text-related questions together with pencasts	5	13
Text-related questions together with problem-solving sessions	8	20
Pencasts together with problem-solving sessions	13	33
The combination of all three activities	8	20

Fig. 3. Students' answers to the question *Which combination of activities was the most helpful for your learning?*

4.2 Analysis of the Interviews

The first author carried out group interviews with 2 groups of computer science students, and 2 groups of software students, that all followed the course. The students were offered anonymity in the sense of referring to the output as a common voice, with neither individual nor the particular group reference. The interviews were transcribed and analysed using an interpretivist methodology, where the emphasis lies on the ways a phenomenon appear to make sense to the involved parties in the specific situation (Erickson, 1998), and were codified as per the strong points within each group as well as the per the salient issues across the groups. The discussions were guided along various themes such as: study habits in traditional lecture-based courses and in a flipped setting; perceived benefits and disadvantages of pencasts; and student-teacher roles in the flipped setting. The quotes were selected across the groups, respective to how representative they were for the salient points.

Study Habits Regarding Lectures. Just as the second author had assumed, the interviews show that in all four groups students attend lectures without much preparation, just to orient themselves in the content knowledge so that they can make decisions for what is needed to solve practical exercises or to improve their current grasp of the subject. Lectures are mainly associated with declarative knowledge and a rather superficial view of learning oriented towards satisfying perceived exam requirements:

> What we need [from lectures] is an overview of the content to decide what we need for resolving the exercises. You rarely learn more than what is needed.

> Exams are based on resolving exercises and memorization (...) The exam tasks don't test whether you understand, but whether you can answer in a precise, specific way.

Meanwhile, the groups all agree that learning only occurs as the result of their active involvement with tasks and problems, or in other ways actively processing the specific field of knowledge.

> You don't learn by watching and listening, only by being active yourself, and here, the exercises and problems we have to solve ourselves, it's what you learn from.

> Pencasts make really good sense, when you just watch. Yet, we don't learn from watching. We only learn by being active ourselves, and therefore the practical sessions and whenever we sit together and solve problems, it's what we learn from!

Perceived Benefits of Pencast-Based Lectures. The pencasts are perceived as offering major advantages in enhancing study strategies, i.e. deriving concise theoretical explanations needed in order to solving problems in the practical sessions. They are valued for the possibility of revisiting difficult issues and rehearse for exams:

> I like the concept [of pencasts], because if I miss something or don't quite get it, than I can go back to it, as many times as I need, and whenever it suits me.. I don't function very well at 8 o'clock in the morning. A lecture is a one-take

> event. And especially when studying for the exam, it is really valuable to go back to the topics explained rather than pondering on what was meant on some topic at the beginning of the term. You just pick up the video clip and watch it afresh.

Furthermore, students appreciate the delivery efficiency in terms of the lesser time it takes to convey the actual content knowledge without the frequent deviations during normal lectures. Students indicate further presentational advantages such as delimiting theory from examples.

> I get the same out of it [pencasts] as from the lectures, and we skip a lot of superfluities. With pencasts, you get the same content, effectively explained in only half the time.

> I wish that the pencasts were divided in theory-only with reference to 1-10 examples separately (...) we don't dare skip any of them out of fear for missing some important theoretical point.

Perceived Drawbacks of Pencast-Based Lectures. Students are generally enthusiastic about pencasts and argue for their usefulness as a learning resource. When asked about the possible drawbacks, they point to the lack of possibility of spontaneously asking questions and suggest compensatory strategies in the form of quality time', i.e. enhanced interaction with the teacher:

> It would be nice to meet in class once in a while, say after the first part of the course, for a summing up and discussion of the main points and the possibility of asking questions ...

> ...that little thing that you could always interrupt and ask a question to understand how he got from this step to that step ... it's difficult with pencasts.

> There should preferably more time with the teacher to focus on individual questions, now that he doesn't use his time lecturing anymore, going in depth with issues that give us problems.

Paradoxically, this also makes students value and attend to the interactive part of the teaching, as was the intention:

> We would prefer a 50-50 % distribution between digital presentation material and face-to-face interaction at university – mainly for the practical or active sessions including some lectures, especially in subjects that require discussion.

Students distinguish between courses that may benefit from digital mediation, i.e. those containing theoretical, factual knowledge; and ones that may not fit this format, including ones where interactivity and discussions are seen as instrumental to learning. Nevertheless, the interactive aspect of learning is valued also in the context of theoretical courses.

> Pencasts are better for the more theoretical courses, like CC, it's here that you need to watch again and again. While courses like 'Design of user interfaces', well here it wouldn't be just as relevant because it doesn't matter if you miss something (...) because it's a much more fluid course: in design, there is not much right or wrong, it's more like: this is right in this context and the opposite may also be right.. It's the discussion, some course types or some teachers insist more on the discussion, and if you engage actively, then you really learn a lot! It's not possible with podcasts, therefore it's mainly the theory and some standard demonstration that you can store like that. But I really don't think that we should just give up the discussions in the theoretical courses either, therefore I'm happy that we have kept the practical sessions intact, so we can discuss the things with him.

Furthermore, students favour technologies that support elements of signature pedagogies, such as processual explanations using the blackboard:

> Power Point slides with voiceover would perhaps be more suitable for software courses, with the many models, but here, where we have so much theory and definitions, it's better to use technologies that remind of the blackboard.

4.3 Conflicting Learning Strategies: Flexibility and Control

Students had to comply with a scheduled plan for submitting answers to text-related questions and for peer reviews of answers; in the interviews students expressed dissatisfaction with these deadlines and what they saw as a contrast to the flexibility paradigm introduced by pencasts.

> It is problematic because we are forced to keep some deadlines that don't make sense (...) because you don't have the time to work seriously with the theory. Yet, if we don't deliver in time, we can't take it in at the exam. I don't understand why we can't just have one final deadline, sometime before exam, so we can still make it, only not so tight. The idea of peer feedback is fine as such, we do it all the time, in group work. The problem is when it is forced, because then we have to do it in a more superficial way than if it fit our study plans.

Similarly, in order to support students in viewing the pencasts on an ongoing basis, and preferably in the company of peers, these were scheduled for viewing in class, as in-between sessions, i.e. between two on-campus activities, with the possibility of asking questions in a virtual forum, with synchronous teacher assistance. However, few students actually watched the pencasts at the times scheduled and perhaps therefor, the virtual fora saw very little activity.

Generally, all groups agree that pencasts are a very good alternative and/or a supplement to the ordinary classes, particularly in more theoretical courses. Yet, they would far from having all courses digital as they would miss the human contact and possibility of interaction. Similarly, it might alter the very act of studying, making it difficult to navigate the learning process:

Pencasts, and so on, means flexibility, so they are welcome. Yet we wouldn't like all courses to be that way, it would feel whirred... then you just sat there with a pile of pencasts that you had to go through every week, having to find the time to just watch through the whole lot.

5 Conclusions and Further Work

We have studied the pedagogical aspects of a web-based flipped classroom setting in a 5th semester computer science course. Essential to the setting was that it should emphasize teaching activities that encourage deep learning and emphasize the threshold concepts of the subject area.

The CC course has two central threshold concepts that interact, one being the integration of declarative knowledge of definitions and theorems, the other being the procedural knowledge associated with mathematical reasoning strategies for understanding and proving theorems. Pencasts and text-related questions were intended to emphasize both of these, while practical sessions mostly focused on the latter.

The survey conducted indicates that the experience was in many ways positive. Interviews showed that students approved of the emphasis being explicitly moved towards active learning in the form of using pencasts to prepare for the practical sessions, which were appreciated as an opportunity for learning through interaction with teacher and peers. Students also seemed to agree that the pencasts would be particularly useful in preparing for exams as they support the retrieval of learning cues from the original context. In further work, we plan to investige if and how the pencasts and similar material can be used by students when preparing for exams and other forms of summative assessment.

Students' learning intention for the CC course was the acquisition of declarative knowledge through a postponement strategy of studying for the test. The pencast delivery option matched their learning intention and was highly appreciated for the inherent flexibility, time efficiency and rehearsability option in view of the exam. However, this rather superficial approach to learning was challenged by the teaching design that aligned the intended learning outcomes [1] with the ongoing processing of the subject content through text-related questions and peer feedback to support the continual integration of declarative knowledge, as well as through the development of performative competence through problem solving sessions.

This is in agreement with students' very own perceptions of learning as the result of active engagement and problem solving, yet not to their first choice of strategy. This shows how a minor shift in the learning context induces students to reassess the role of active learning, and to value the teacher-learner interaction in this context.

It is important to note that just as the flipped environment was inspired by the unflipped one, the students also saw the new learning experience through the lens of their normal lecture experience. Thus, their concerns about the lack of interaction with the teacher may be a consequence of this. The web-based fora for discussion certainly turned out *not* to be a relevant means of student-teacher interaction. As intimated by their testimonies, the student-teacher interaction might see new qualitative heights when re-directed towards the active dimension of teaching and learning. Another direction for further work is to investigate how teacher-student interaction can be strengthened in this particular flipped setting.

It is unclear how convinced the students may have been while working with the text-related questions, as it appears that they may have been subject to the double-bind of resistance to fixed deadlines, and the interest in producing exam support material. Arguably, the teaching strategies to support learning goals should not overrule student learning strategies, but seek to meet them by agreeing on the actual rather than perceived intended learning outcomes for the course and negotiate appropriate teaching and learning strategies together with the students.

This would be an adequate opportunity to render explicit the aims of the course in terms of the threshold concepts, which might otherwise be elusive to them. It might shed light on the necessary constituents of a holding learning environment, meant to support students in withstanding states of uncertainty and provide a good training ground. In other words, making the implicit design explicit might benefit student engagement. The study of how to best achieve this is also a topic for further work.

In conclusion, flipping the classroom is not a universal formula for effective teaching but an opportunity for rethinking the teaching design and aligning it with intended learning outcomes. It helps in reorganising the learning context with due regard to what is essential to learning, i.e. students' active engagement and a qualitatively enhanced interaction with the teacher. It points at the need to employ learning technologies to support and if necessary alter signature pedagogies in according with the overall learning and teaching strategy.

References

1. Biggs, J.: Teaching for quality learning at university. Society for Research into Higher Education and Open University Press, Buckingham
2. Doceri - the Interactive Whiteboard App, `https://doceri.com`
3. Erickson, F.: Qualitative research methods for science education. In: Fraser, B.J., Tobin, K.G. (eds.) International Handbook of Science Education, pp. 1155–1173. Kluwer Academic Publishing, Dordrecht (1998)
4. Entwistle, N.: Teaching for understanding at university. Deep approaches and distinctive ways of thinking. Palgrave Macmillan, Basingtoke (2009)
5. Entwistle, N.: Understanding classroom learning. Hodder and Stoughton, London (1987)
6. Hoffman, E.S.: Beyond the Flipped Classroom: Redesigning A Research Methods. Course For e3 Instruction, Contemporary Issues In Education Research 7(1) (2014)
7. Marton, F., Hounsell, D., Entwistle, N. (eds.): The experience of learning. Scottish Academic Press, Edinburgh (1997)
8. Meyer, J.H.F., Land, R.: Threshold concepts and troublesome knowledge: linkages to ways of thinking and practising. In: Rust, C. (ed.) Improving Student Learning - Theory and Practice Ten Years On, pp. 412–424. Oxford Centre for Staff and Learning Development (OCSLD), Oxford (2003)
9. Moodle, `http://moodle.org`
10. Savin-Baden, M.: Learning Spaces: Creating Opportunities for Knowledge Creation in Academic Life, pp. 25–26. McGraw Hill, Maidenhead (2008)
11. Shulman, L.: Signature pedagogies in the professions. Daedalus 134(3), 52–59 (2005)
12. Shulman, L.: Those who understand: knowledge growth in teaching. Educational Researcher 15(2), 4–14 (1986)

Bringing a New Culture of Learning into Higher Education

Terje Väljataga and Sebastian H.D. Fiedler

Centre for Educational Technology, Tallinn University, Tallinn, Estonia
{terje.valjataga,fiedler}@tlu.ee

Abstract. Accelerated social, economical, technological and cultural change largely driven by global digitalisation and networking invites us to scrutinise and reconsider the theoretical assumptions underpinning our contemporary teaching approaches in higher education. This paper explicates the authors' rationale and its underlying assumptions for designing and implementing interventions into current teaching and studying practices to foster the emergence of a "new culture of learning" in formal higher education. It discusses the role of conversational tools and procedures for coaching students in this context and the personal barriers the authors' have experienced in a series of intervention studies in the field.

Keywords: higher education, new culture of learning, intervention, teaching practice, personal learning contract procedure.

1 Introduction

We live in a fast-changing, irrevocably "technologically textured" world [16] in which domains of human knowledge and activity change considerably over the average lifetime of an individual. Gradually a wide range of activities are presently augmented and transformed through the expansive growth of digitalisation and networking. New ways for accessing, producing, sharing, and exchanging knowledge are emerging in rather rapid succession [20]. Because of this swift technological development "we can no longer count on being taught or trained to handle each new change in our tools, the media, or the ways we communicate on a case-by-case basis" [24, p. 43]. The ongoing developments seem to support the emergence of a fundamentally "new culture of learning" [24] within our increasingly networked society. In response it seems paramount to re-conceptualise and re-design our educational models and practices. However, the way higher education has responded so far to the rapidly changing demands from society and the transformative power of global digitalisation and networking is rather questionable. The transmission view of education is still very much alive. This mainstream approach focuses almost exclusively on specific deficits in particular domains of knowledge and practise. It rarely allows for any systematic attempt to advance a wider set of dispositions for coping with change and (self-)development. By and large the prevalent use of technology in education appears to be a mere re-instantiation and repetition of old patterns of control and responsibility, where traditional values, beliefs and practices prevail.

E. Popescu et al. (Eds.): ICWL 2014, LNCS 8613, pp. 229–238, 2014.

In response to our changing technological and social landscapes, teaching and studying in formal higher education settings need to be (re-)built upon rather different assumptions. The authors of this paper believe in the necessity for changing our focus from what is learned to how is learned, from an exclusive fixation on domain knowledge and skills to the advancement of dispositions for self-directing one's intentional learning and change projects within and beyond the confines of higher education. In the following paragraphs we outline our understanding of the changes our current "culture of learning" in higher education requires in the midst of unrelenting, continuous societal, economical and technological development. We briefly describe our own humble attempts to intervene into current practice with the purpose to create conditions for a new culture to emerge and new dispositions to be developed. We also discuss our experiences with and reflections on the recurrent challenges and contradictions that we encountered in the field.

2 Theoretical Assumptions for Intervention Designs

We hold the view that the digital transformation can be characterised as fundamentally co-evolutionary: while human needs, imagination, and activity drive the ongoing expansion of digital instruments for mediation, the technological development in turn shapes the emergence of new human dispositions and abilities [10]. We acknowledge that the choice of technology mirrors our attitudes, values and beliefs, but also our flaws and limitations. Bringing digital and networked instruments into teaching, we have to be careful not to merely support and extend the activity of teaching and instruction as we know it [15]. Instead, we should allow for the systematic experimentation with the values and practices that these very instruments promote or simply carry along. As pointed out by Feenberg [5], when one chooses to use a particular technology one doesn't simply render an existing way of life more efficient. One often chooses a different way of life. This different way of life brings about changes in our behavior, our beliefs and practices, and our wider social norms and structures. To sum it up with the words of Tripathi [25]: "Technology transfer without appropriate cultural transfer is not sufficient" (p. 7). Therefore, we should reconsider key principles of designing educational experiences, changes in the process of knowledge construction, our role-based control and responsibility structures, and the composition of learning environments.

To establish a new culture of learning, participants have to become immersed in new experiences. Thus, we need to intervene into existing teaching and studying practices in a way that mirrors, accommodates and reconciles the values, beliefs and assumptions that currently dominate our understanding of teaching and learning in a formal higher education. Our own re-design and intervention efforts for adopting and facilitating the emergence of new culture have been driven by the following set of assumptions:

Our first assumption is that higher education needs to emphasise the increasingly dynamic and social nature of knowledge-construction in networked societies. Knowledge is progressively more constructed and co-developed with peers and facilitators through conversations and (inter-)actions. Through reflection, productive action and interaction with significant others, people construct knowledge [4]. Learning-to-be a competent practitioner in a particular field of activity thus becomes a more prominent point of orientation than just learning about a particular content area.

Our second assumption is that successful co-construction of knowledge presupposes the open sharing of information and the systematic support of that sharing [4]. It is hard to support the acquisition and advancement of dispositions that are necessary to be a competent practitioner if everybody is working individually in a hidden corner. Educational episodes should be increasingly designed for openness. We have to consider moving beyond our institutional boundaries, making the processes of teaching and learning visible, and more apparent as work in progress [2]. This allows (networked) individuals to carry out various conversations on regulative, coordinative and productive actions that are necessary for the co-construction of knowledge.

Our third assumption is that networks and communities support participants to learn in order to belong, while they invite them to belong in order to learn. This allows participants to negotiate, work around, or redraw the boundaries of their communicative practices and means of mediation [19]. Conversational and knowledge sharing practices and "spaces" create potential triggers for the formation of networks and communities. Practising being part of these conversational networks and communities helps participants to form and develop their own personal and interpersonal learning environments over time.

Our fourth assumption is that a culture of sharing and networked co-construction of knowledge requires a re-configuration of patterns of control and a redistribution of responsibility over instructional functions (such as setting objectives; selecting and executing appropriate actions and activities; selecting, combining, and integrating resources and technological tools and services; and defining criteria and procedures of evaluation) [27]. This means creating more egalitarian participation structures, in which facilitators and students collaborate to co-design their collective educational experience and to refine the co-construction of knowledge. Individuals should progressively gain awareness and execute control over significant elements of their learning activity and its specific personal environment and instrumentation.

Our fifth assumption is that digital media and networked technologies need to be considered as essential instruments for the (re-)mediation of individual and collective learning activity in higher education. We have to encourage the exploration of a wide range of digital and networked instrumentation options for complementing individuals' personal learning environments. As much as possible we should give preference to open access and open source tools and services (wikis, weblogs, and so forth) that can be fully appropriated and adapted to serve as instruments in one's environment within an extensive variety of activities. Analysing what kind of tool or service appears to be suitable for reaching a particular action goal under specific conditions presumes participants reflect upon perceived affordances, expectations, orientations and so forth. This often requires an explorative approach to find out how the potential of existing instruments can be unlocked and utilised [17].

Our sixth assumption is that higher education needs to re-focus its conception of intended change and individual development. The purpose of our educational efforts should not be measured exclusively in terms of immediate performance gains or the acceleration of content acquisition [21]. Individual development within the unfolding digital transformation of society requires room for personal experimentation, failure, and changes of direction. It cannot be measured comprehensively against pre-defined standards and expectations of outcome and process. Developing and refining new forms of (digitally mediated) individual and collective learning activity becomes equally important as the mastery of a body of public knowledge and skills within a given area of human practise.

3 Procedural Support for Facilitating the Adoption of New Culture of Learning

To successfully intervene into existing teaching and studying practices with the aforementioned assumptions for bringing in new culture of learning, individuals first need to understand how they go about their own learning and self-development. The conversational use of a *learning contract procedure* provides a conceptual framework and guidance for explicating and structuring the crucial components of a particular learning project and its (personal) environment (see for example [1,3,12,23]. In general, a learning contract is understood as a negotiated and explicated agreement about what and how an individual (or collective) will "learn" and how possible outcomes and products will be measured [3]. It can be used as a systematic, conceptual vehicle for externalising, guiding, monitoring, and managing learning activity [1] and its environment; and can be an effective tool to help adult learners become (self-determining) subjects of their own learning and self-development.

Harri-Augstein & Thomas [13] have embedded the use of such instrument in an elaborate, conversational, reflective, coaching framework that emphasises the need for refining the initial, structured description of a project in the light of its ongoing execution effort. They promoted the integration of records of actions and items of experience (and reflection) to support the necessary reflective and evaluative processes. As the term "learning contract" carries some rather unfortunate, legalistic and bureaucratic connotations that create unnecessary barriers for communicating its conceptual and procedural aspects [18], we have thus started to rather talk about Personal Learning Project (PLP) outlines, and their revisions, and an overall process of "bootstrapping" such projects through ongoing recording, reviewing, and revising practices.

In the context of our intervention studies (see for example [27,28] we used a version of the structured personal learning project outline that was adapted from several proposals [1,3,23,12]. The minimal structural components of our personal learning project outline consisted of: a topic or a task; specific purposes in relation to the topic or the task that drives one's project and describes what one wants to achieve; a statement on "strategies" explicating what actions one intends to carry out and what resources might be used for achieving the intended purposes; the anticipated and actual "outcome" together with criteria for allowing to evaluate if or how successful a project was (see Figure 1).

While the conversational use of PLP outlines and the overall bootstrapping process in (adult) education had originally been implemented on paper or with the help of stand-alone software packages (see for example [27]), we are now in the comfortable position to be able to choose from a wide range of digital, networked tools and services to mediate the overall procedure. In our intervention studies, for example, we made extensive use of personal web-publishing applications such as weblogs. Students drafted and published their PLP outlines (including their revisions), documented records of actions they undertook, and provided their reflections as addressable items of (micro-)content on the Web.

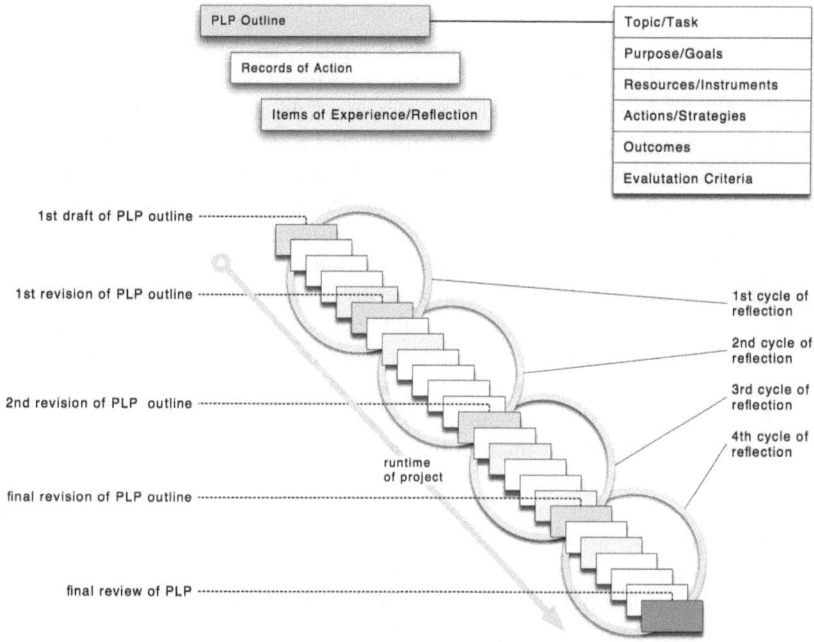

Fig. 1. Visualisation of the elements of the PLP externalisation and "bootstrapping" procedure [10]

By (re-)mediating this overall, conceptual procedure with open, generic, web-publishing instruments, we gain a whole set of new, interesting affordances (in the sense of perceived potentials for action) that influence the qualities of the type of material that participants elicit and externalise in such a setting [10]. The open nature of web-publishing instruments broadens the scope of learning, widens individual's participation in learning experiences and opens up the boundaries of knowledge and resources, thus, enabling continuous reviewing, cross-referencing, and commenting among the networked peers and facilitators through the majority of the overall run-time of the project. The realisation of the externalisation of PLP outlines and their revisions, records of action, and items of experience and reflection, in an open, net-workable format affords the mediation of numerous conversational, reflective exchanges [10]. Individual items are universally addressable, can be commented on, (hyper-)linked to, and drawn into a wide range of additional tools and services that eventually make up a personal or distributed learning environment [6]. In our experience the result of these combined practices is very often the emergence of rich networked descriptions of personal learning. This type of material is a rich source for facilitators who are trying to monitor, understand, and support a particular individual's (developmental) progress and its dynamics. On the other hand it offers unique opportunities for learners to understand changes in their own learning. That way Personal Learning Project (PLP) outlines, their revisions, and an overall process of "bootstrapping" offers individual's perspective on new learning culture and provides means to organise and assess the appropriation of this culture.

4 Reflecting on Intervention

The omnipresent and continuously expanding digital transformation requires -and at the same time- enables fundamental shifts and significant changes from old models to new approaches of learning [10]. The attempt to establish a new culture of learning within the boundaries of contemporary formal higher education is a rather complicated endeavor challenging the comfort zone of participants and existing organisational structures. Becoming immersed in the new culture, participants undergo a process of transformation in which they either adapt to the customs and conventions of the new culture and become integrated into it or find they cannot adapt and elect to leave [24].

Since 2007 we have been engaged in a series of intervention studies that tried to promote a shift towards a different culture of learning at author institution [8,26,28,29]. The vehicle for our educational work has mainly been two courses that are offered to students of different master programs administered by the Institute of Informatics. We have used these courses as an evolving test-bed for the iterative implementation and evaluation of intervention ideas and concepts. Throughout the intervention studies we have experienced that translating the aforementioned assumptions into our intervention designs bring about considerable implications and some unpredictable consequences.

Throughout our intervention studies we constantly found ourselves bumping against internal, personal beliefs and values of our participants. We noticed that some of the students tended to "assimilate" new practices and technologies during the early stages of adoption and attempted to replicate existing practices and trusted patterns of action [7]. They demonstrated how imprisoned they were by their rather rigid and deeply engrained (rather self-limiting) beliefs and understandings, which Harri-Augstein and Thomas [13] quite appropriately call "learning myths".

If for most of the twentieth century our educational system has been built on the assumption that teaching is necessary for learning to occur [24], it is no wonder that this has produced pervasive beliefs of how education in general and learning experiences in particular should be designed, structured and organised. The continued exposure to teacher-dependent learning activity throughout formal schooling leads many people to develop a set of potentially disabling beliefs and convictions. These convictions have become a dominating, deep-seated pattern in our culture and for many adults started to function as a personal "commentary" on their own capability for learning [12].

Our observations continuously indicated that the reconfiguration of typical patterns of control and responsibility, the emphasis on the exploration of personal digital instrumentation options, and the promotion of open, networked learning seemingly clashed with the learning myths of a good number of our students. These students expressed very strong beliefs on how formal educational environments should be structured and organised and what conditions need to be met to make "learning" in such settings possible for them. Various personal learning myths played a key role for the individual acceptance of structural and procedural changes to existing teaching and studying practices among our student body. Interested readers can find an extended, systematic review of data in [9] that can be interpreted as the expression of personal learning myths running counter to the intentional change goals promoted through our interventions. Harri-Augstein and Thomas [13] were able to show in their empirical work that such myths were regularly invoked in educational settings and influenced the capacity to learn of many adults. Thus, students who are unable to revise their personal myths run the risk of remaining victims of their own, strongly rooted constructions. This often may result in low levels of motivation, performance, and commitment, if not an overall drop out from their educational undertaking.

However, we were able to observe a reoccurring developmental trajectory among a number of students whose initial rejection of all concepts and practices that ran against their myths slowly gave way to personal experimentation and exploration, and finally resulted in the adaptation and reconstruction of their own systems of meaning. Nevertheless, even if students embrace new practices by the end of a course, it is often not enough to achieve a sustainable and lasting effect on students if this is their only experience of that kind. The new practices need to continue in the context of other course environments or educational episodes to encourage students to refine, elaborate, deconstruct and re-build personal learning myths that can be actually experienced as enabling within an increasingly networked culture of learning. This can be a time consuming process as personal myths do not tend to be changed overnight, however, they can be purposefully and self-critically brought into awareness [14] by consciously and systematically exploring, analysing and discussing them.

Changing the pattern of responsibility and control, recognising knowledge as co-constructed and co-developed with peers and facilitators through conversations, making learning activity open and visible through the use of personally chosen digital and networked instruments, and emphasising "learning to be" over "learning about", indicates a rather thorough and fundamental shift of teaching and studying. These type of changes invite a fundamental shift in the balance of power, thus altering significantly the role of teachers and students in higher education and the foundations underpinning their relationship. Adopting a new culture of learning involves a significant shift in teachers' tasks and a radical change from being a transmitter and controller of instruction to that of a facilitator, supporter and conversational partner. In such a setting it is not an option anymore to insist on a rigid, pre-planned design and declare ownership of the educational experience. Instead, it becomes more important to understand the dynamics of students' trajectories of development and adaptation, reasons for their decisions, the different level of dissonance and conflicts they experience, their interests regarding the area of study and personal change, and their particular objectives. Thus, in the midst of an emerging new culture of learning finding the most appropriate conversational instruments and strategies is a continuous search process, acting between one's myths and ideas of intervention, intentional change, and improvement.

5 Concluding Remarks

We have experienced that establishing a new culture of learning can only be embraced if one understands the conflicts and barriers entailed by students. The process of bringing about considerable changes within formal educational settings is fundamentally restricted by the participants' values, myths and beliefs about education and studying. Innovative approaches that are conflicting with the current traditional views and principles of formal education require much more than just the implementation of new technological instrumentation. It needs to be based on rather different mindsets, values and beliefs. These need to be gradually established and carefully supported to achieve sustainable, new patterns of action.

Referring to our reflections, the conversational use of open, web-published, universally addressable outlines of personal learning projects (PLPs) (consisting of records of action, and items of experience and reflection) turned out to be a very useful instrument to facilitate the adoption of previously described six assumptions and the occurring challenges the facilitators experienced. We realised that the chosen conceptual procedure with open, generic, web-publishing instruments serves not only learners as a procedural support tool while outlining and executing their projects and expressing their personal beliefs and perceived obstacles. It gives us also indications of how we can better support students to overcome their difficulties while they are getting gradually immersed into a new culture of learning. Many students need to be supported while they are undergoing (an often under-estimated) process of personal transformation in which they need to adapt to the practices and conventions of open and networked learning, re-construct their learning myths accordingly, and become integrated into the new culture.

To conclude our reflection we learned that one should never underestimate the impact of previous experiences of all the actors and the powerful drivers within the formal education system. We should focus more on the interplay between mutual observations and expectations of all actors. We need to monitor, interpret, and negotiate each other's actions and underlying objectives, to improvise accordingly. As teachers in higher education we are presently facing a cultural transition phase that can be characterized by a wide variety and considerable disparity of individual developmental stages and trajectories in relation to the unfolding digital transformation of society and its systems of activity. Currently, we are mainly trying to target first-order change in our educational systems, focusing on incremental improvements within existing modes of practice. However, achieving second-order change [11] that intends to fundamentally alter how things are done within a specific human activity system is a long and slow process. Finding meaning and coherence in our teaching in the midst of the present social, economical, technological and cultural transformation will remain a constant work in progress for the foreseeable future.

References

1. Anderson, G., Boud, D.: Introducing Learning Contracts: A Flexible Way to Learn. Innovations in Education and Teaching International 33 (1996)
2. Batson, T., Paharia, N., Kumar, M.S.V.: A Harvest Too Large? A Framework for Educational Abundance. In: Iiyoshi, T., Kumar, M.S.V. (eds.) Opening Up Education. The Collective Advancement of Education Through Open Technology, Open Content, and Open Knowledge, pp. 89–104. The MIT Press, London (2008)
3. Boak, G.: A Complete Guide to Learning Contracts. Gower Publishing Ltd., Hampshire (1998)
4. Cambridge, B.: Scaffolding for Systemic Change. In: Iiyoshi, T., Kumar, M.S.V. (eds.) Opening Up Education. The Collective Advancement of Education Through Open Technology, Open Content, and Open Knowledge, pp. 357–374. The MIT Press, London (2008)
5. Feenberg, A.: Ten Paradoxes of Technology. Techné 14 (2010)

6. Fiedler, S., Pata, K.: Distributed Learning Environments and Social Software: In Search for a Framework of Design. In: Hatzipanagos, S., Warburton, S. (eds.) Handbook of Research on Social Software and Developing Community Ontologies, pp. 145–158. IGI Global, Hershey (2009)
7. Fiedler, S., Väljataga, T.: Interventions for Second-Order Change in Higher Education: Challenges and Barriers. Electronic Journal of e-Learning 8, 85–92 (2010)
8. Fiedler, S., Väljataga, T.: Expanding the Concept of Learner Control in Higher Education: Consequences for Intervention Design. In: Aedo, I., Chen, N.-S., Sampson, D.G., Spector, J.M., Kinshuk (eds.) Proceedings of the 2011 11th IEEE International Conference on Advanced Learning Technologies, pp. 262–264. IEEE Computer Society, Athens (2011)
9. Fiedler, S.H.D., Väljataga, T.: Challenging Learning Myths Through Intervention Studies in Formal Higher Education. In: Ley, T., Ruohonen, M., Laanpere, M., Tatnall, A. (eds.) OST 2012. IFIP AICT, vol. 395, pp. 141–146. Springer, Heidelberg (2013a)
10. Fiedler, S.H.D., Väljataga, T.: Networked Narrative Accounts of Personal Learning Projects: An Instrument for Systemic Intervention Research in Higher Education. In: Reynolds, N., Webb, M. (eds.) Proceeding of 10th World Conference on Computers in Education. Learning While We Are Connected, pp. 29–37. Nicoloaus Copernicus University Press, Torun (2013b)
11. Foster-Fishman, P.G., Nowell, B., Yang, H.: Putting the System Back Into Systems Change: A Framework for Understanding and Changing Organizational and Community Systems. American Journal of Community Psychology 39, 197–215 (2007)
12. Harri-Augstein, S., Cameron-Webb, I.M.: Learning to Change. A Resource for Trainers, Managers and Learners Based on Self-organised Learning. McGraw-Hill, London (1996)
13. Harri-Augstein, S., Thomas, L.: Learning Conversations: The Self-organised Way to Personal and Organisational Growth. Routledge, London (1991)
14. Harri-Augstein, S., Thomas, L.: Learning Conversations: A Person-centered Approach to Self-organised Learning. British Journal of Guidance & Counselling 7, 80–91 (1979)
15. Holton, D.: Teaching is Technology: A Little Philosophy of Technology & Media Theory, `http://edtechdev.wordpress.com/2010/01/21/teaching-is-technology-a-little-philosophy-of-technology-media-theory/`
16. Ihde, D.: Technology and the Lifeworld. Indiana University Press, Bloomington (1990)
17. Johnson, M., Liber, O.: The Personal Learning Environment and the Human Condition: from Theory to Teaching Practice. Interactive Learning Environments 16, 3–15 (2008)
18. Knowles, M.S.: Self-directed Learning. A Guide for Learners and Teachers. Prentice Hall, Englewood Cliffs (1975)
19. Lievrouw, L.A.: The Uses of Disenchantment in New Media Pedagogy. Teaching for Remediation and Reconfiguration. In: Hammer, R., Kellner, D. (eds.) Media/cultural Studies: Critical Approaches, pp. 560–575. Peter Lang Publishing, New York (2009)
20. Richardson, C.R.: Open Educational Knowledge: More Than Opening the Classroom Door. In: Iiyoshi, T., Kumar, M.S.V. (eds.) Opening Up Education. The Collective Advancement of Education Through Open Technology, Open Content, and Open Knowledge, pp. 279–288. The MIT Press, London (2008)
21. Schejbal, D.: In Search of a New Paradigm for Higher Education, `http://www.springerlink.com/content/f6737477774135w2/`
22. Slusarski, S.B.: Enhancing Self-direction in the Adult Learner: Instructional Techniques for Teachers and Trainers. In: Hiemstra, R., Brockett, R.G. (eds.) Overcoming Resistance to Self-direction in Adult Learning. Jossey-Bass Publishers, San Francisco (1994)
23. Stephenson, J., Laycock, M.: Using Learning Contracts in Higher Education. Kogan Page, London (1993)

24. Thomas, D., Seely Brown, J.: A New Culture of Learning: Cultivating the Imagination for a World of Constant Change. Createspace (2011)
25. Tripathi, A.K.: Reflections on the Philosophy of Technology. Culture of Technological Reflection, http://ebookbrowse.com/v7i29-tripathi-pdf-d185134342
26. Väljataga, T.: If a Student Takes Control: A Facilitator's Tasks and Responsibilities. In: Spaniol, M., Li, Q., Klamma, R., Lau, R.W.H. (eds.) ICWL 2009. LNCS, vol. 5686, pp. 390–399. Springer, Heidelberg (2009)
27. Väljataga, T.: Learner Control and Responsibility: Expanding the Concept of Self-directionin Higher Education. Tampere University of Technology, Tampere (2010)
28. Väljataga, T., Fiedler, S.: Supporting Students to Self-direct Intentional Learning Projects with Social Media. Journal of Educational Technology & Society 12, 58–69 (2009)
29. Väljataga, T., Laanpere, M.: Learner Control and Personal Learning Environment: A Challenge for Instructional Design. Interactive Learning Environments 18, 277–291 (2010)

Didactic Support of Diversity of Learning Styles? Potential Analysis of Three Collaborative Learning Methods within e-Business Education

Elisabeth Katzlinger and Michael A. Herzog

Johannes Kepler University Linz, Austria
Magdeburg-Stendal University of Applied Sciences, Germany

Abstract. Media-supported learning scenarios achieve varying successful learning results and consequently students evaluate them differently. The impact on learning success that gender, occupation, graduation level and especially learning styles of students may have is subject to this study. 555 students participated in a transnational cooperation between two universities by applying collaborative media in different e-business-courses since 2010. Thereby three different media-supported learning scenarios were compared: virtual case study, game-based simulation (Beer Game) and online peer review. The results of the accompanying study made clear that different learning settings benefit different learning types. Thus the major goal of the long-term study is to evaluate how specific learning patterns or the different learning types can be supported more specifically by the use of different learning methods. Such approach includes the potential of a better didactic support regarding the diversity of students.

Keywords: Virtual collaborative learning, e-business education, media-supported learning, cross teaching.

1 Introduction

Media-supported learning scenarios are evaluated differently by students and achieve varying successful results, for example concerning handling the media when communicating within the learning group or learning success. The influence of different prerequisites on the part of the students, such as learning style, gender or graduation level is the object of the present study within business education. Initially it should be investigated, which media didactic adaptation should be considered in order to achieve better learning success and higher study satisfaction.

For the study a game-based learning scenario, a peer review process and a virtual case-study work were accompanied by an empirical study with 555 participants (basic population approx. 900 students), who attended several courses. The concept of the courses - which provides the basis of this study - is grounded on a variety of learning media as well as teaching and learning methods in order to address the different learning types and to provide high-quality and diversified courses.

E. Popescu et al. (Eds.): ICWL 2014, LNCS 8613, pp. 239–244, 2014.

2 Crossteaching Learning Setting

With the aid of ERASMUS lecturer mobility programme a cooperation between Magdeburg-Stendal University, Germany and Johannes Kepler University Linz, Austria was established. At the inception of the programme several course units were recorded and provided to the other university. Furthermore a direct exchange of lecturers was organised to benefit from individual expertise of such teachers. Additionally students formed interregional groups, which were partly supported by tutors. For collaboration within these learning groups different communication media were used, which were either provided by the lecturers or chosen by the students (Fig. 1).

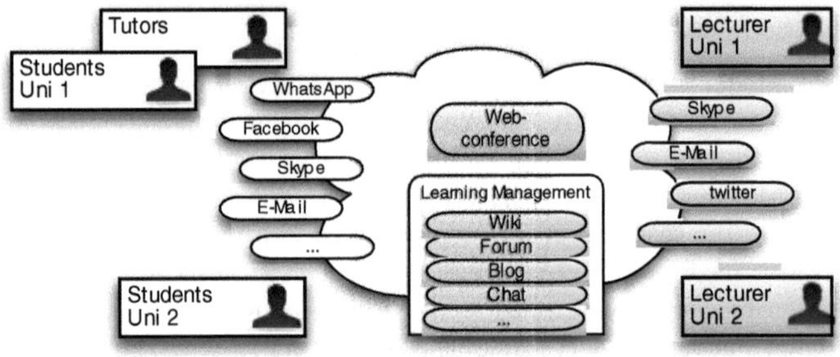

Fig. 1. Crossteaching scenario

Teaching and Learning Methods

(1) For the *virtual case study* learning situations were created that resembled the virtual collaboration in globalised companies and achieve developing media competency at academic level. In this learning setting, which was mainly supported by asynchronous media, students worked in interregional learning groups of 5-6 on different case studies regarding e-business topics, which were documented in a WIKI and presented at the respective university. The case study method (Harvard Method) is a renowned learning concept within business courses [1]. It supports learning by use of realistic problems and tasks as well as though co-operative learning, which fits the approach of moderate constructivism [2, p. 876]. Students could either choose from a range of given cases studies (e.g. from Harvard Business Manager) or develop their own business case with reference to e-business. For this interregional cooperation a course in the learning management system Moodle was implemented, which was accessible at both universities. The group members used forum and chat for verbal communication, for the written report the WIKI module. In addition students opted for a variety of other communication media beside the opportunities in Moodle.

(2) For the *game-based learning scenario* an online simulation game on Supply Chain Management was applied, namely the Beer Distribution Game. On the basis of a four-part supply chain – from brewery to consumer – complexity and dynamics of the system are simulated. The Beer Distribution Game was developed in the mid-sixties at the MIT (Massachusetts Institute of Technology) in order to give students an understanding of the concepts of complex and dynamic systems [11]. During the

game students receive immediate feedback on their decisions and are thus able to connect their subjective experience with objective results [7].

(3) Within the *online peer review process* students assess and comment the work of their fellow students. Peer review is known as a cornerstone concerning self-organisation and academic quality management [8, 9] as well as an evaluation method in social media [4]. Trautmann [12] documented that students gain from new perspectives through seeing both good and bad examples. After the anonymous submission of the own paper students get a number of papers of fellow students for reviewing. When used as a learning method, peer review is well scalable concerning the size of the group – many submissions lead to many reviewers [10 p. 32]. The peer review process was realised with the workshop-activity in Moodle.

3 Research Method

Learners have different preferences concerning the aquirement and processing of learning contents. Various authors follow different typologies. For example Honey & Mumford [3] regard learning as a cyclic process that consists of successive steps. Depending on the steps the learner prefers, they distinguish activist, theorist, reflector and pragmatist concerning the different learning styles. However, in the present study Kolb's [5, 6] LSI (Learning Style Inventory) was applied. Kolb considers learning as a continuous process, which is based on different elements and activities: taking up information via experience vs. thinking (conceptualisation) and processing information via experimentation vs. observation and reflection. From these opposing activities Kolb derived a learning cycle. Each learner passes through the whole cycle but develops preferences. Therefrom Kolb deduced four learning styles: accommodators prefer active experimentation and concrete experience; divergers prefer reflective observation and concrete experimentation; the opposite are convergers and finally assimilators who favour a learning style opposite to the accommodators' preference.

Due to the widespread use of the LSI and the resulting possibility of using other studies as references, a learning style investigation according to Kolb [6] was conducted for this study and related to the three learning scenarios described above. The major goal of the long-term study is to realize how specific learning patterns or the different learning types can be supported more specifically by the use of different learning methods. This includes the potential of a better didactic support regarding the diversity of students. The discussion of results in this paper will reflect the advantages and benefits of these learning concepts for students as well as for lecturers. Apart from the analysis of learning styles other features of diversity, such as gender, occupation, graduation level or interculturalism were investigated too.

Table 1 demographically describes the basic population of the study. On average students from Linz are older than students from Magdeburg, which can be partly explained by the different position of the course within the curricula, partly by the different education systems of the two countries and partly by the two different types of tertiary institutions. Occupation has to be taken into consideration too. 28% of the students from Linz and 10% from Magdeburg work full-time.

Table 1. Average age and gender ratio (N=551)

	Number of men	No. of women	Total number	Age
Linz (AUT)	117	67	184	26,8
Magdeburg (GER)	204	163	367	24,2
Total	321	230	551	25,0

The gender ratio in this study is 64:36 in Linz, and – more balanced – 56:44 concerning the students from Magdeburg. Results reveal several gender distinctions, as for example a difference regarding weekly Internet usage time; only 26% of female students and 43 of male students use the Internet more than 20 hours weekly.

4 Results

The learners assessed the three learning scenarios on the basis of a four-part Likert scale: not useful [1] – to - very useful [4]. These evaluations were correlated with the learning styles according to Kolb (Fig. 2).

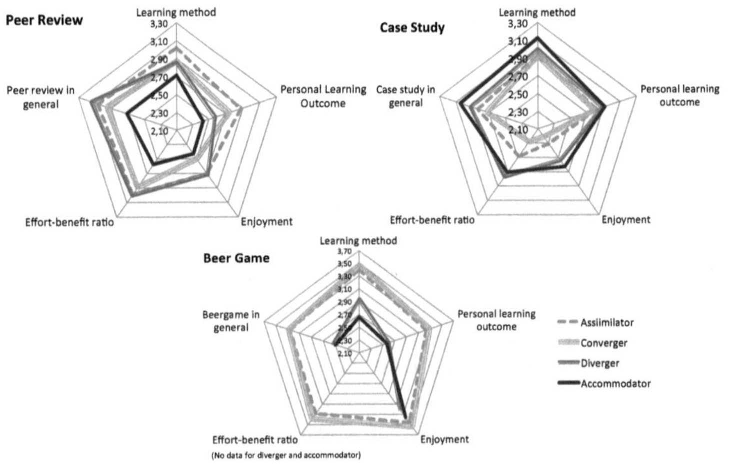

Fig. 2. Comparison of the learning scenarios case study, Beer Game and Peer Review regarding learning styles (N=265/274/310)

Even though all three methods were overall rated as positive (Case Study ø 2,82; Beer Game ø 3,19; Peer Review ø 3,01), the three scenarios clearly differ for the different learning style groups. While the accommodators and divergers rate the open and constructivist learning situation of the case study better, they evaluate the rather closed learning environment of the Beer Game less positive as compared to convergers and assimilators. Although all groups rate the enjoyment of the game-based simulation as high, the different groups of learners rate all other criteria – and thereby especially the learning effect – quite differently. In the learning situation of the Beer Distribution Game the theoretical background was explained in detail at the beginning of the course (briefing) and reflected after each round of the game (debriefing), which obviously benefits the theory-oriented learners convergers and assimilators (abstract conceptualisation) well. However, the method seems less suitable for the learning types accommodators and divergers, who prefer concrete experiences. The learning situation peer review is rated as rather negative by accommodators regarding all criteria, whereas it is rated better by the divergers and even much better by convergers and assimilators. Assimilators, who prefer abstract concepts and reflective observation according to Kolb's classification, rate the personal learning effect through the peer review best.

Apart from an analysis of learning styles, also learning success was compared, if data were available (Fig. 3). For the measurement of the learning success, the assessment of the individual tasks (scores for the case study and for the examination on the Supply Chain Management, SCM) and the overall grade for the course were used. Accommodators and divergers scored highest in the case study and both groups rated it as a useful method. Convergers and assimilators scored highest in the Beer Game and both groups rated it as best of the three learning methods. Thus the data show that learners learn best with the method they personally prefer and which they rate as best.

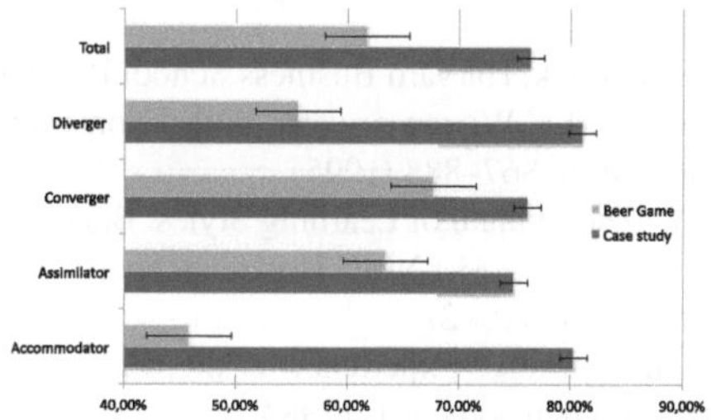

Fig. 3. Learning success and learning style (n=152)

The further evaluation of the learning success was striking, too, as the group of full-time working students achieved better than average results. Nearly half of the full-time working students were graded excellent (47%), while the group of part-time working students did worst (27% graded excellent). The reason for that probably is that full-time working persons, who decide to commence studies have to bring along extraordinary commitment and high motivation.

5 Conclusion and Prospects

The study clearly revealed that learning success as well as the students' reflection on the learning methods can be distinguished not only by classical features of diversity but also on the basis of different learning styles. In order to increase learning success of the less successful groups, further strategies have to be considered and studied in connection with the scenarios investigated. Whether a division into groups according to learning styles (homogenisation) or a mixing of learning styles (diversification) is more advantageous depends on the learning goals as the following examples show.

The learning scenario virtual case study seems to be best suitable for the development of media competency, as here an international collaboration between students and active Internet usage in terms of content creation in the WIKI is encouraged and trained. In game-based simulations the formation of groups according to learning styles could be advantageous, if the didactic dramaturgy is organised in such way that accommodators and divergers get space for experimentation in the beginning, whereas convergers and assimilators benefit from a theoretical introduction at the beginning. However, in relation to the case study, a mixing of learning styles could lead to a better group success, as different abilities of group members complement each other. On the other hand in such mixed groups communication problems between different learning styles might occur, which could impede the teamwork process, an aspect that has to be further analysed. Further investigations will also have to consider the effort-benefit-balance as a criterion within the framework of development of learning style adaptive approaches for improvement of technical and media competency.

References

1. Ellet, W.: Case Study Handbook. Harvard Business School Press, Boston (2007)
2. Gerstenmaier, J., Mandl, H.: Wissenserwerb unter konstruktivistischer Perspektive. Zeitschrift für Pädagogik Nr. 6, 867–888 (1995)
3. Honey, P., Mumford, A.: The Manual of Learning Styles. Berkshire, Maidenhead (1992)
4. Johnson, L., Adams, S., Cummins, M.: NMC Horizon Report: 2012 Higher Education. The New Media Consortium, Austin (2012)
5. Kolb, D.A.: Experiential Learning: Experience as the Source of Learning and Development. Prentice-Hall, Inc., Englewood Cliffs (1984)
6. Kolb, D.A., Oslond, J.S., Rubin, M.: Organizational Behavior. An experiental approach. Prentice Hall, Englewood Cliffs (1995)
7. Noy, A., Raban, D.R., Ravid, G.: Testing social theories in computer-mediated communication through gaming and simulation. Simulation & Gaming 32(2), 174–194 (2006)
8. Pöschl, U., Koop, T.: Interactive open access publishing and collaborative peer review for improved scientific communication and quality assurance. Information Services and Use 28(2), 105–107 (2008)
9. Reinmann, G., Sippel, S., Spannagel, C.: Peer Review für Forschen und Lernen. Funktionen, Formen, Entwicklungschancen und die Rolle der digitalen Medien. In: Mandel, S., Rutishauser, M., Seiler-Schiedt, E. (Hrsg.) Digitale Medien für Lehre und Forschung, pp. 218–229. Waxmann Verlag, Münster (2010)
10. Sharples, M., McAndrew, P., Weller, M., Ferguson, R., FitzGerald, E., Hirst, T., Mor, Y., Gaved, M., Whitelock, D.: Innovating Pedagogy 2012: Open University Innovation Report 1. The Open University, Milton Keynes (2012)
11. Sterman, J.D.: Teaching Takes Off: Flight Simulators for Management Education. OR/MS Today, pp. 40–44 (October 1992)
12. Trautmann, N.M.: Interactive learning through web-mediated peer review of student science reports. Educational Technology Research and Development 57(5), 685–704 (2009)

Author Index

Author Index

MIX
Papier aus verantwortungsvollen Quellen
Paper from responsible sources
FSC® C105338

If you have any concerns about our products,
you can contact us on
ProductSafety@springernature.com

In case Publisher is established outside the EU,
the EU authorized representative is:
Springer Nature Customer Service Center GmbH
Europaplatz 3, 69115 Heidelberg, Germany

Printed by Libri Plureos GmbH
in Hamburg, Germany